Rasch Measurement

Myint Swe Khine
Editor

Rasch Measurement

Applications in Quantitative Educational Research

Springer

Editor
Myint Swe Khine
Emirates College for Advanced Education
Abu Dhabi, United Arab Emirates

Curtin University
Perth, Australia

ISBN 978-981-15-1799-0 ISBN 978-981-15-1800-3 (eBook)
https://doi.org/10.1007/978-981-15-1800-3

This Springer imprint is published by the registered company Springer Nature Singapore Pte Ltd.
The registered company address is: 152 Beach Road, #21-01/04 Gateway East, Singapore 189721, Singapore

Contents

Editor and Contributors

About the Editor

Myint Swe Khine is a Professor at the Emirates College for Advanced Education, United Arab Emirates. He is also an Adjunct Professor at Curtin University, Australia. He has taught at leading universities throughout Asia including Nanyang Technological University in Singapore. He holds master's degrees from the University of Southern California, USA, and the University of Surrey, UK and a Doctorate in Education from Curtin University in Australia. His research interests are in learning sciences, and educational measurement and assessment. He has published widely in international refereed journals and edited several books. One of his recent books, *International Trends in Educational Assessment: Emerging Issues and Practices* is published by Brill in the Netherlands in 2019.

Contributors

Francisco Ben is currently Senior Lecturer and Head of Postgraduate and Research at Tabor Faculty of Education—a private tertiary education provider in South Australia. His research areas include Science and Mathematics Education, and ICT in Education. His research also covers measurement and evaluation in Education. He mainly employs in his data analysis newer psychometric techniques including the Rasch Model and multilevel modeling. Francis continues to publish in the following areas: The use of ICT in teaching; Examination of the utility of survey scales; and Physics/Science Education. He is a co-founder of the Transdisciplinary Measurement and Evaluation Research Group (TMERG) based at the University of Adelaide in South Australia.

Daniel Bergh works at the Centre for Research on Child and Adolescent Mental Health, Karlstad University, Sweden, where he is engaged in research on how schooling and social relationships influence young peoples' mental health. That was also the topic of his doctorate published in 2011. Daniel has a particular interest in psychometric analyses based on the Rasch Model. In 2012–2013 he spent an 18-month postdoc period at the University of Western Australia, Perth, Australia, focusing on Rasch Measurement. Bergh has continuously a strong interest in Rasch Measurement Theory. His research has turned even more into the school setting now focusing on the associations between motivation and school achievement, and mental health among adolescents, where psychometric analyses based on the Rasch Model is an integral part.

Monique Bijker Ph.D. is a senior researcher at Zuyd University of Applied Sciences in the Netherlands and anAassistant Professor at the Department of Psychology and Educational Sciences at the Open University of the Netherlands. She focuses on field research in educational contexts and applies the Rasch measurement model to test the reliability, validity, dimensionality, and scale structures of the psychological measurement instruments and assessments that have been employed.

William J. Boone is Professor of Psychometrics, Department of Educational Psychology, and Distinguished Research Scholar at Miami University, Oxford, Ohio. He also serves as the Director for the Questionnaire and Test Design-Analysis Laboratory. He conducts Rasch analysis workshops in various countries around the world.

Giuliana Capasso graduated in 2015 in mathematics at the University of Naples Federico II. She teaches in secondary school and collaborates with the Physics Education group at the "Ettore Pancini" Physics Department to implement laboratory activities for secondary school students. Her research interests include inquiry-based teaching and the development of teaching–learning activities to introduce quantum mechanics at the secondary school level.

Melvin Chan is a Research Scientist at the Centre for Research in Pedagogy and Practice at the National Institute of Education at Nanyang Technological University in Singapore. He is Principal Investigator of a number of large-scale quantitative research projects that investigate school, classroom, and student factors that contribute to effective pedagogy and schooling success in Singapore. Dr. Chan also serves as Managing Editor for the Asia Pacific Journal of Education and he teaches graduate-level courses in introductory research methods and latent variable modeling. His primary research interests include examining models of student learning, outcomes, and educational pathways.

Joseph Chow currently works at the Educational Development Centre at the Hong Kong Polytechnic University. He has been awarded the Dr. Judith Torney-Purta Outstanding Paper Award. As an Educational Developer, he aims to facilitate the creation of conditions supportive of teaching and learning in higher education by (1) making assessment and evaluation information meaningful and user-accessible in practice and policy contexts for instructors and senior management, and

(2) building organizational and individual capacity in assessment and evaluation areas via professional development activities. His research interests include educational measurement, diagnostic assessment, student learning outcome assessment, and scholarship of teaching and learning with a goal to provide students, teachers, and institutions with actionable information they need, value, and trust for instructional purposes.

Arturo Colantonio is a secondary school physics teacher and a Ph.D. student at the International School of Advanced Studies of the University of Camerino in collaboration with the University of Naples Federico II. His research work focuses on the development of a teaching–learning sequence about the Universe. He is also interested in the use of multimedia to enhance students' learning in physics.

Celeste Combrinck is a South African research psychologist with a focus on social science measurement. She works at the Centre for Evaluation and Assessment (CEA) at the University of Pretoria. Her lectures include research methodology and application. She has managed several large-scale assessment studies, including the Progress in International Reading Literacy Study (PIRLS) for 2016 as well as projects for the Michael and Susan Dell Foundation (MSDF) and the Nuffield Foundation. In 2017, Celeste was the recipient of the Tim Dunne Award and presented at the Seventh International Conference on Probabilistic Models for Measurement Developments with Rasch Models in Perth, Australia. As a promoter of rigorous and fair assessment practices, Celeste presents workshops on the use of Rasch measurement theory to students, colleagues, and researchers.

Christine DiStefano is a Professor of Educational Measurement at the University of South Carolina. She teaches courses in measurement theory, scale construction, Rasch methodology, and structural equation modeling. Her research interests include analysis of ordinal (e.g., Likert scale) data using Rasch models and structural equation modeling, validity issues, and mixture modeling.

Umberto Scotti di Uccio Ph.D. is an Associate Professor in Physics of Matter at "Ettore Pancini" Physics department of the University of Naples Federico II. He is the chair of the outreach activities of the Department. Recently he switched his research interest toward physics education and in particular in the teaching and learning of quantum mechanics at secondary school and university level. He is also interested in designing research-based materials for the professional development of physics teachers.

Silvia Galano Ph.D. is a Middle School Teacher and a researcher at "Ettore Pancini" Physics department of the University of Naples Federico II. She earned her Ph.D. at the International School of Advanced Studies of the University of Camerino. Her current research work focuses on students' views on media scientific communication. She is also interested in investigating children's representations of astronomical phenomena and in developing inquiry-based teaching–learning sequences for secondary school level.

Kevin Haudek is an Assistant Professor in the Biochemistry and Molecular Biology department and the CREATE for STEM Institute at Michigan State University. He earned his Ph.D. in Biochemistry, then transitioned into undergraduate science education research for his postdoctoral studies and became engaged in Discipline-Based Education Research (DBER). His current research interests focus on uncovering student thinking about key concepts in biology using formative assessments and revealing students' mental models. As part of this work, he investigates the application of computerized tools to help evaluate student writing, focusing on short, and content-rich responses. These computerized tools facilitate both the exploration of ideas in student writing, as well as the application of machine learning techniques to automate the analysis of written responses.

Fan Huang is currently a Research Scholar at the University of Macau. Her diverse research interests include educational measurement, technology in education, and international comparative studies.

Liu Huang received her master's degree from the University of Macau in 2017. She is now working as a High School Biology Teacher at Huiyang school affiliated to SCNU. Her main research interests include students' attitudes toward science, biology teacher development, and STEM education.

Ning Jiang is a Ph.D. candidate of Educational Research and Measurement at the University of South Carolina. Her research interests include Structural Equation Modeling, Differential Item Functioning, Item Response Theory, Multilevel Modeling, and art assessment. She also works as a graduate research assistant in the Research, Evaluation, and Measurement Center (REM) at the UofSC. There, she assists with many evaluations, research, and assessment projects. Mostly, she works on a statewide arts assessment program. Her work includes reviewing, and validating each year's items, creating test forms, training test administrators, analyzing data using Classical Test Theory and Item Response Theory, and writing technical reports.

Karel Kreijns is a Full Professor at the Welten Institute at the Open University of the Netherlands. His primary research interest is the social aspects of Computer-Supported Collaborative Learning (CSCL) and networked learning (i.e., social presence, social space, and sociability). Other research interests are teachers' motivation for the use of technology in education using Self-Determination Theory and the Reasoned Action Approach, and BIE-coaching (BIE = bug-in-ear technology) of beginning teachers to reduce attrition and to improve the quality of the teacher. He uses advanced statistics (Rasch measurement model, SEM, finite mixture model, bi-factor model) wherever necessary.

Irene Marzoli Ph.D. is a researcher at the School of Science and Technology, University of Camerino. After graduating in Physics at the University of Camerino, she received her Ph.D. in Physics at the University of Milan. Her research interests span from theoretical quantum optics and ion trapping to physics education. She is currently serving as a science communication manager of the COST Action

CA17113 Trapped ions: Progress in classical and quantum applications. She is actively engaged in teaching innovation and professional development for in-service teachers with a focus on modern physics and quantum mechanics. She is a co-author of more than 50 publications in international scientific journals, conference proceedings, and book chapters.

John Merrill earned his Ph.D. in Biology from the University of Washington, Seattle, in 1985. He has been a faculty member of the Department of Microbiology and Molecular Genetics at Michigan State University since 1996. From 2003 to 2016 he served as the Director of the Biological Sciences Program, the interdepartmental program responsible for administering the core lecture and laboratory courses for majors in the wide range of life science departments. This administrative assignment coincided with his transition from bench science (biochemistry and ecophysiology of algal pigmentation) to scholarship in the Science of Teaching and Learning (SOTL). For most of the last two decades, he has focused on assessment in lower division biological science courses and the interactions between teaching and technology. His currently active research collaborations focus on application of computer machine learning techniques to automate scoring of students' textual responses to open-form assessments.

Tine Nielsen is Associate Professor at the Department of Psychology, University of Copenhagen, Denmark. Her research is focused on the fields of higher education psychology and health- and mental health-related psychology in combination with psychometrics. TN conducts research on many aspects of the development, validity, and use of tests and measurement scales, primarily within item response theory and the class of Rasch models. TN collaborates broadly in her research both nationally and internationally, and she is an active member of many education and psychometric societies and networks: the European Association for Research in Learning and Instruction (EARLI), the Psychometric Society, The European Rasch Research and Teaching Group (ERRTG), and the Danish Measurement network (DM) which she founded in 2016. She is a subject editor (higher education and psychometrics) at the Scandinavian Journal of Educational Research.

Pey-Tee Oon received her Ph.D. degree in Science Education funded on a full-time research scholarship from the Nanyang Technological University in Singapore. Currently, she is an Assistant Professor at the Faculty of Education at The University of Macau. Prior to this, she worked as a Researcher at the University of Hong Kong, a physics lecturer in Singapore and as a high school physics teacher in Penang, Malaysia. Her current research focuses on rethinking and redesigning the roles of assessments in education to support student learning, teacher improvements, and development of a coherent educational system that meets the needs of all stakeholders that are evidenced-based and can serve to improve education at all levels.

Pedro Henrique Ribeiro Santiago is a Ph.D. student at the University of Adelaide, currently studying the validity and cross-cultural validity of western developed psychological instruments for an Aboriginal Australian population. His educational background includes a bachelor's degree in Psychology and a master's degree in Public Health. In his master's degree, he investigated the feasibility of a brief mindfulness-based intervention for primary care professionals in the Brazilian national health system. Additionally, Pedro works as a Research Assistant in a project evaluating the effects of a randomized controlled trial on dietary patterns and nutrient intake among Aboriginal children (School of Public Health).

Gaspare Serroni is a chemical engineer working as a Technician at the Department of Chemical Sciences, University of Naples Federico II. His research interests include the design and validation of university entrance examination tests.

Alice Shiu is an Associate Professor in the School of Accounting and Finance at Hong Kong Polytechnic University. She teaches undergraduate and postgraduates courses in economics and econometrics. In addition to traditional teaching materials, she uses games, videos, and a mobile app to engage and motivate her students. She involves in various learning and teaching projects and is currently a committee member of departmental Learning and Teaching Committee, Teaching Council, and Faculty Learning and Teaching Committee. Her contribution to teaching is recognized by Faculty of Business and she received Faculty Award for Teaching in 2014. Her current teaching research is in the area of innovative teaching methods in economics and econometrics.

R. Subramaniam is an Associate Professor at the Natural Sciences and Science Education Academic Group at the National Institute of Education at Nanyang Technological University in Singapore. His principal interests are in the area of physics education, chemistry education, primary science education, and informal science education. He has graduated six Ph.D. students and five MA students by research. Publications include over 80 papers published in peer-reviewed international journals, 40 peer-reviewed chapters published in edited books of international publishers, 6 books published by international book publishers, and 3 guest-edited issues of international journals. He also serves on the editorial boards of a number of international journals, including International Journal of Science Education (Routledge, UK) and Journal of Research in Science Teaching (Wiley, USA).

Italo Testa Ph.D. is an Assistant Professor at "Ettore Pancini" Physics department of the University of Naples Federico II. Prior to joining the University of Naples he received his Ph.D. at the University of Udine. He currently teaches physics education methods supervising students' projects. His current research interests include quantitative methods to assess students' learning through Rasch measurements, students' interpretation of visual representation in astronomy, physics teachers' professional development, and the design of inquiry-based teaching–learning sequences at the secondary school level.

Mark Urban-Lurain Ph.D. Educational Psychology, is an Associate Professor Emeritus and Associate Director Emeritus for Engineering Education Research in the CREATE for STEM Institute, College of Education, Michigan State University. His research interests are in theories of cognition, how these theories inform the design of instruction, how we might best design instructional technology within those frameworks, and how the research and development of instructional technologies can inform our theories of cognition. His recent research has focused on using a variety of statistical and machine learning approaches in the automated analysis of student writing across STEM disciplines. He has also focused on preparing future STEM faculty for teaching, incorporating instructional technology as part of instructional design, and STEM education improvement and reform.

Joshua Weidlich is a Ph.D. student at the Department of Instructional Technology & Media at FernUniversität in Hagen and a research fellow at the Department of Technology-Enhanced Learning at Heidelberg University of Education, Germany. His Ph.D. research is concerned with understanding social presence in online distance learning and finding ways to improve learning experiences in the socio-emotional dimension.

Hye Sun You earned her B.S. in Chemistry and M.S. in science education from Yonsei University and her Ph.D. in Science Education at the University of Texas at Austin. She has since worked as a Postdoctoral fellow at New York University and Michigan State University. Prior to entering academia, she spent several years teaching middle school science. Her research interests center upon interdisciplinary learning and teaching, and technology-integrated teaching practices in STEM education. She is also interested in developing robotics-embedded curricula and teaching practices in a reform-oriented approach. Currently as a Visiting Scholar at New York University, she is guiding the development of new lessons and instructional practices for a professional development program under a DR K-12 research project funded by NSF.

Chong Ho Yu is an Associate Professor of Psychology and Adjunct Professor of Mathematics at Azusa Pacific University. He is also the quantitative research consultant, advisory committee chair of Big Data Discovery Summit, and committee chair of Data Science Consortium at the same institution. He has a Ph.D. in Psychology, specializing in measurement, statistics, and methodological studies (Arizona State University, USA), and also a Ph.D. in philosophy with a focus on the philosophy of science (Arizona State University, USA). He had published numerous articles related to measurement and statistics. Some of his articles are available in full text and can be viewed online at http://www.creative-wisdom.com/pub/pub.html.

Part I
Theoretical and Conceptual Frameworks

Chapter 1
Objective Measurement in Psychometric Analysis

Myint Swe Khine

Abstract The Rasch model, a subset of a larger group of models known as item response theory (IRT), is becoming a common way of analyzing psychometric data in educational research. There are many reasons why researchers are adopting this approach. One of the reasons for using Rasch analysis technique is that it is possible to express a person's measures on the same scale, regardless of which survey or test form the respondent completed. This chapter synthesizes the studies reported in this book and describes the potentials of using Rasch model for objective measurement.

Introduction

Psychometric evaluations using Rasch measurement are increasingly prevalent in educational and human sciences research in the past decades. Quantitative researchers use Rasch techniques to guide the development of surveys, questionnaires, rating scales, and tests and analyze the functioning and improve the precision of such instruments. Rasch measurement is known to align with the notion of objective measurement that aims to provide a common metric to express the results (Bond & Fox, 2013). The use of Rasch analysis based on item response theory (IRT) provides a versatile and effective way for examining the psychometric quality of the instruments and tests and allows validation, calibration, and further improvements. Numerous studies have been conducted to discover the properties of various scales used in the fields of psychology, human, and social sciences, and in-depth analyses are reported in the literature (Boone, Staver, & Yale, 2014). The book presents studies related to the use of the Rasch measurement model in validation studies and analysis of psychometric properties of a variety of test instruments, questionnaires, and scales in different languages and diverse contexts. This book is divided into three parts.

M. S. Khine (✉)
Emirates College for Advanced Education, Abu Dhabi, United Arab Emirates
e-mail: Dr.mkhine@gmail.com

Curtin University, Perth, Australia

M. S. Khine (ed.), *Rasch Measurement*,
https://doi.org/10.1007/978-981-15-1800-3_1

While the first part of the book presents theoretical and conceptual frameworks, the second part deals with the use of the Rasch model and analysis in education research. The last part of the book covers validation studies with Rasch analysis in psychometric evaluations of various instruments.

Theoretical and Conceptual Frameworks

Three chapters in Part I of this book serve as a primer on Rasch analysis for researchers and practitioners. In Chap. 2, William Boone presents Rasch basics for the novice. The chapter covers the basics of Rasch theory, an overview of key indices in Rasch analysis, and interpreting those indices, specific techniques, and presentation of results. Boone further explains that Rasch techniques can be used to revise a test, evaluate partial credit tests, and investigate measurement bias. The author also notes that though Rasch analysis can be complex, it allows communicating the research findings more efficiently. DiStefano and Jiang in Chap. 3 provide an introduction to the Rasch rating scale model (RSM) and how to use the methodology in analyzing questionnaires and constructing a psychometrically sound scale. The chapter also presents applied examples to assist researchers in a clear understanding of the Rasch model and decision making. The authors note that RSM is a useful model to examine the characteristics of questionnaire data and scale development. Chong Ho Yu in Chap. 4 explains the concept of objective measurement and the difference between Rasch modeling and item response theory. The major components of Rasch modeling, such as item calibration and ability estimates, item characteristics, item information function, test information function, item-person map, are explained with examples. Moreover, the author also presents the use of different software packages for Rasch modeling, including SAS and Winsteps.

Rasch Model and Analysis in Education Research

The chapters in Part II cover the use of the Rasch model and analysis on education research. This part begins with Chap. 5 by Francisco Ben, who re-examined the utility of the Individualised Classroom Environment Questionnaire (ICEQ) using the Rasch model. The ICEQ is one of the learning environment questionnaires that are designed to measures the psychosocial aspects of classroom climate. The instrument specifically measures aspects of personalization, participation, independence, and differentiation in the classrooms. The study was conducted with 306 high school students in South Australia. The author reports the findings from the evaluation of the ICEQ and the implications for future research and teaching practice.

In Chap. 6, Italo Testa and his team present the findings from the validation study on the university entrance test through Rasch analysis in Italy. The team analyzed the psychometric quality of an 80-item entrance test that was administered to 2435 science and engineering students and another 100-item test administered to 1223 students. The tests were analyzed using Rasch measurement to determine item separation, personal separation, and differential item functioning (DIF). The authors report that the tests do not match the unidimensional requirement and suggest the balancing of difficult items in the tests in a more suitable way.

Chow and Shiu describe the analysis of an elementary economics test to assess university students learning using the Rasch model in Chap. 7. The study took place with 300 first-year students in a university in Hong Kong. The study examines the unidimensionality of the items, personal and item reliabilities, item statistics, personal and item measures, and person-item map of the economics test. The results of the fit statistics in a Rasch analysis reveal the characteristics of the test and information about the level of students' achievement. The chapter concludes with the future use of the assessment information to improve a better understanding of students' mastery of the subject.

In Chap. 8, Huang, Huang, and Oon report the constructs evaluation of 30-item Student Attitudes toward Science (SAS) questionnaire that was administered to 1133 students in Grade 7–11 in China. The aim of the study is to find out whether Rasch analysis can provide psychometric information about the SAS instrument when used with students in China and what the Chinese students' attitudes toward physics and biology are. The study reports, among others, model fit and data reliability, differential item functioning (DIF), and effectiveness of response categories in each of the items. The study found that although Chinese students generally held positive attitudes toward physics and biology, they enjoyed studying physics more than biology but expressed higher confidence with biology.

Chan and Subramanian present their findings from the validation of a science concept instrument with Rasch analysis. The newly developed 22-item instrument was administered to 115 students in 16 Singapore secondary schools. The data were analyzed to explore the differential item functioning with respect to gender and academic tracks, and relationships with prior attainment and science self-efficacy.

Celeste Combrick analyzed the large-scale assessment data on the Progress in International Reading Literacy Study (PIRLS) to assess the measurement invariance in the cross-national achievement of South African participants by applying Rasch partial credit model. The study used 2006 cohort as a reference group and 2016 cohort as a focal group. The objectives of the study are to find out the differential item functioning (DIF) of the common items between cycles of participation and differential bundle functioning (DBF) between cycles of participation, particularly the common linking items and internal measurement invariances. Chapter 10 reports the findings from the study. The author concludes that Rasch models offer sufficient evidence of internal measurement variance and the assessment of the stability of item ordering and functioning.

Validation Studies with Rasch Analysis

The chapters in Part III include validation studies with Rasch analysis. Kreijns and Bilker describe a Rasch analysis approach to the development and validation of a social presence measure in Chap. 11. The researchers constructed a set of 30 items instrument to measure social presence in online educational contexts, in particular, to discover the effects of mediated communication in the social interaction and group dynamics in distributed collaborative learning environments. The questionnaire was administered to 82 students in a university in Germany. A Rasch analysis was conducted to explore the fits of items and persons, unidimensionality, and category probability curve using Winsteps software. The results show two dimensions of the social presence—awareness of others and proximity with others.

In Chap. 12, You and her colleagues report the construct validity of constructed response items to test students in undergraduate introductory biology course in two public universities in the United States. The study involves 437 students who answered the 8-item constructed-response items in the Scientific Literacy in Introductory Biology (SLIB) assessment set. The data were analyzed to evaluate the psychometric properties of polytomous constructed-response items using the partial credit model. The study attempts to find out the unidimentionality of the items, local independence, item and person fits, item and person separation indices and reliabilities, and item difficulty using item-person map. The chapter reports the results and concluded that the development of constructed response items and automatic scoring models will allow faculty to provide an opportunity for students to construct explanations instead of rote learning.

The analysis of the psychometric properties of the social responsibilities goal orientation scale is presented by Bergh in Chap. 13. The study uses data extracted from the Swedish longitudinal Evaluation Through Follow-up (ETF) project. A scale consisting of six polytomous items was administered to the students to measure the students' social responsibility and goal orientation. Rasch analysis is used as a measurement model to investigate the psychometric properties of the instrument and differential item functioning (DIF) by gender. The analysis found that DIF by gender on one item. The study also found the local dependency of the items that indicate the response to one item may be governed by the response to the other item.

In Chap. 14, Nielsen and Santiago explain the graphical log-linear Rasch model (GLLRM) that can be used to test local dependence of the items and differential item functioning (DIF). The data were collected in Australia and Denmark using the perceived stress scale (PSS). The PSS consists of two sub-scales (perceived stress and perceived lack of control), and two versions of the scale (PSS-10 and PSS-14) were used in the studies. The authors report the items they found locally dependent and DIF by gender in both countries.

Conclusion

The chapters in this book cover theoretical and conceptual frameworks for Rasch modeling, analysis of questionnaires and tests, and validation of instruments using Rasch modeling. The authors in this book explain the basics of objective measurement and Rasch modeling and its applications in simple terms. The authors critically examine the effectiveness of various surveys, questionnaires, and tests and provide new and refreshing ideas and recommendations. It is hoped that the book is informative, insightful, and relevant to those who wish to employ and keep up with the latest research in Rasch modeling approach to quantitative education research.

References

Bond, T. G., & Fox, C. M. (2013). *Applying the Rasch model: Fundamental measurement in the human sciences* (3rd ed.). Mahwah, NJ: Lawrence Erlbaum Associates.

Boone, W. J., Staver, J. R., & Yale, M. S. (2014). *Rasch analysis in the human sciences*. Dordrecht: Springer.

Chapter 2
Rasch Basics for the Novice

William J. Boone

Abstract At times it can be overwhelming for the beginner to learn how to confidently interpret Rasch results. This chapter presents (1) the basics of Rasch theory, (2) a user-friendly overview of key indices in Rasch analysis and how to interpret those indices, (3) an overview of specific types of Rasch presentation techniques that can be used to communicate Rasch analyses for peer-reviewed papers, and (4) a discussion of the common aspects of Rasch that can be hard for the beginner to grasp. Upon reading this chapter—the new Rasch learner will have a solid foundation which will enable a basic Rasch analysis to be carried out. Also, the new Rasch learner will be able to confidently read articles which have made use of Rasch analysis techniques.

Keywords Rasch analysis · Item difficulty · Multiple choice · Rating scales · Meterstick · Latent variables · Partial credit

Introduction

Rasch analysis is now being used throughout the world for when one is conducting work with tests of many kinds, as well as surveys. When tests or surveys are being developed, then Rasch can be used to guide the development process. When test data and survey data are collected, the measurement qualities of tests and surveys can be evaluated and steps are taken to revise instruments to increase their precision. When data is collected with tests and surveys, the raw score totals of respondents (Jack scored 8 pts on a 10 pt test; Katie had a raw score on a 10 item self-efficacy survey of 32 pts) can be expressed on a linear logit scale that is appropriate for statistical tests.

This introductory chapter aims to provide a nontechnical introduction to the use of Rasch techniques. It makes use of many workshops I have presented over the years, as well an introductory Rasch text book I have authored. I feel that Rasch can be mastered by almost anyone. Rasch can be easily taught to high school students. In this

W. J. Boone (✉)
Miami University, Oxford, OH, USA
e-mail: boonewjd@gmail.com

M. S. Khine (ed.), *Rasch Measurement*,
https://doi.org/10.1007/978-981-15-1800-3_2

chapter, I will provide an introduction to, as I often say in my classes, "why Rasch?", and I will present the most basic of analyses. Other chapters of this book will delve into the greater details of what it means to utilize Rasch methods. In this chapter, I use my Rasch software of choice: Winsteps (Linacre, 2019). The software is very user-friendly, constantly updated, exceedingly well-documented, and inexpensive. Of course, there are other Rasch software programs. After reading this chapter, and the other chapters of this book, readers might consider reading my introductory Rasch book: Rasch Analysis in the Human Sciences (Boone, Staver, & Yale, 2014).

Why Does One Need Rasch?

There are many reasons to use Rasch. My hope is that one day, the need for Rasch measurement will be so obvious and accepted by anyone using tests and surveys that it will be a standard part of instrument development and the use of instruments for social science research. Just as one, for many years (and to this day), a Cronbach alpha or a KR-20 are reported to "evaluate" reliability in many articles, I hope that soon it will be commonplace to see that Rasch has been used when a researcher makes use of a test or a survey.

Test Items Have Differing Difficulty, Survey Items Have Differing Difficulty

To me, the first step that can be taken in an effort to understand Rasch is to learn what is wrong with the immediate use of raw test scores (the 8 points Jack earned on a 10 point test) and the immediate use of raw survey scores (the 32 points Katie earned on a 10 item self-efficacy survey). When one sees and gains a feel for the problems with raw scores, then one has begun to understand "why Rasch".

Let us begin by considering Jack, who took a multiple-choice math test where each item was worth 1 point. For this example, let us also consider students Henry, Elisabeth, and Oliver. Also, let us imagine that all four students were 8th graders, and let us imagine that the test was authored with a total of 10 test items. Six of those test items were truly 8th grade math material, but 4 of the test items were 12th grade material. Below, I present a schematic (Fig. 2.1) showing the 4 students and their test

Fig. 2.1 The raw scores of four students completing a 10 item multiple-choice test in which items can be correctly answered (1 point) or not correctly answered (0 points). Six of the ten items were written at the 8th grade level of math. Four of the items were 12th grade level math items

scores. Before individuals understood Rasch, it was commonplace to simply use the raw scores of the four test takers, as well as any other test respondents, for statistical tests. For example, one might report that the average of male students was 7.2 points and the average of female students was 8.1 points. What is the massive error in the use of these raw scores to summarize math ability for individual students and groups of students?

First off let us look at Jack, Jack's raw score of 8 means that more than likely Jack knew all of the 8th grade math (he probably correctly answered all six 8th grade math items as well as two of the 12th grade level items). Henry, Elisabeth, and Oliver more than likely did not answer any of the 12th grade level items correctly. Now, let us compute the difference in test scores between Jack and Henry, as well as the difference between Elisabeth and Oliver's raw score. It is certainly simple math; the difference is 2 points between Jack and Henry, and it is also a 2 point difference between Elisabeth and Oliver. Before Rasch, researchers would have immediately asserted that the difference in math knowledge between Jack and Henry is the same difference as between Elisabeth and Oliver. However, there is a fatal flaw in such an assertion. The problem is that such a calculation ignores "item difficulty". In our example, one can see that the difference in knowledge between Jack and Henry is very large (Jack was able to answer some 12th grade items). However, the difference between Elisabeth and Oliver is much smaller, in that their performance indicates a difference in "ability level" at the 8th grade level. This brief example should help readers appreciate that it is important to use analysis techniques that take into consideration the "difficulty" of test items. When Rasch analysis is used, there is not the assumption of all test items having the same difficulty. Rasch takes into consideration item difficulty.

The same issue is present with rating scale data. For example, a survey in which students can answer "Agree" or "Disagree". When survey data is evaluated it is important to note that not all survey items are, for this example, equally agreeable. For instance, if a 30 item environmental survey was administered to students and the students can answer "Agree" or "Disagree" to an item. It is important to understand that there will be some items which are the easiest to "Agree" to (perhaps "I can recycle at home") and there are items that are harder to "Agree" to (perhaps "It is important for all students to take 3 classes concerning Environmental Science"). Just as it is important to note that all test items are not of the same difficulty, survey items also are not all of the same agreeability (in Rasch we refer to survey items in terms of "item difficulty" as well).

Some good articles considering problems with raw scores are the following brief articles by Wright (1993), Marosszeky (2013), and Wright and Linacre (1989). I use these in my classes.

Rating Scales Can Not Be Assumed to Be Equal-Distant

There is another problem which Rasch confronts—just as Rasch helps one deal with the fact that test/survey items should not be assumed to be of the same difficulty,

Rasch confronts that rating scale data cannot be assumed to be linear. It is a common step to code the answers of a respondent to a rating scale survey. For example, if a 13 item survey used a rating scale of "Strongly Disagree" (SD), "Disagree" (D), "Barely Disagree" (BD), "Barely Agree" (BA), "Agree" (A), and "Strongly Agree" (SA). A coding scheme in a spreadsheet might use a "1" to indicate a respondent selected a "Strongly Disagree", a "2" to indicate a respondent selected "Disagree", and so on. Unfortunately, it is common practice for researchers using surveys such as this, to add up the coded responses of a survey taker. That number then is used to summarize the overall attitude of the survey taker. Then statistics are used to compare respondents. What are the flaws in this process? First off, it is completely acceptable to label a respondent's answer to a rating scale survey item with a number. That is fine. The problem with conducting mathematics immediately with these numbers is rating scales should not be assumed to be linear. Also, it is critical not to treat each survey item as having the same level of agreeability. To consider this issue review Fig. 2.2. I provide a schematic as if the rating scale is linear, and also two alternatives. Note that in all cases, in terms of agreeability, SA > A > BA > BD > D > SD. When Rasch is used, there is no assumption made about the spacing between rating scale categories. All that is assumed is that the rating scales present an ordinal scale. This means there is no assumption that the jump between a "Strongly Agree" and an "Agree," is the same as the jump from "Agree" to "Barely Agree" and so on. Another aspect of "why Rasch" with rating scale data is that items may not have the same level of agreeability, which means that in terms of a person's overall attitude, a rating of "Strongly Agree" (a 6) for one item might actually in reality have the same meaning as a "Barely Agree" (a 4) for a very hard to agree with item. When Rasch is used, we can begin with a spreadsheet full of numbers (1, 2, 3, 4, 5, 6) representing what each person selected for each survey item. But, we then have to use those numbers for our Rasch analysis. We do not simply add up the numbers of each respondent and use the raw score total to summarize their attitude.

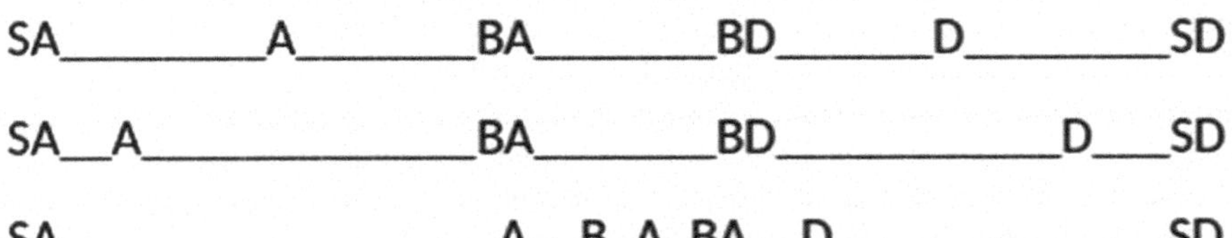

Fig. 2.2 Rating scale data is always ordinal. All that is known is the order of the rating scales. Coding can be used to indicate what rating scale category was selected to answer an item. But those numbers should not be immediately used for summarizing the attitude of a respondent

Why the Confusion?

To finish up this brief presentation on the errors that have been made in the past, it is helpful to think through why it has been so very tempting for social science researchers to use raw tests scores (e.g., Elizabeth's score of 4), and why social science researchers conduct analyses of raw rating scale data. I feel there is a temptation because of our everyday experiences; we know that the difference between 20 euros and 22 euros is 2 euros. We know the difference between 30 and 32 euros is 2 euros. And we know the amount of coffee we can buy with each 2 euro difference is the same. We also know that if we line up a pile of paper money in a row (if there were paper money for low denominations of euros), and we placed the one euro bill one meter away from the two euro bill, and we placed the two euro bill one meter away from the three euro bill, we would feel that this spacing showed the true difference between 1 euro, 2 euro, and 3 euro. The problem is, with test data and rating scale data, we cannot make the assumption that all items are of the same difficulty, and we cannot assume the rating scale is linear. Rasch methods allow one to consider these, and other, important issues.

Understanding Rasch Measurement Theory by Considering a Meterstick

To work toward finishing up an introduction to the theory of Rasch and the functioning of Rasch, I now make use of a meterstick to help readers understand some of what is gained through the use of Rasch. Ben Wright, my Ph.D. Director at the University of Chicago, often would talk about metersticks when he would discuss Rasch. Below I present a number of metersticks. I also provide a number of objects whose length we wish to measure. As readers will be able to see, meterstick A has 10 marks on it, meterstick B also has 10 marks, and meterstick C has 10 marks. Start off by observing how well each of the metersticks does in terms of measuring the length of glass #1. Also, do the same with glass #2. Make sure to align the base of the glass to the 0 mark on the meterstick. What do you observe? The accuracy of your glass measurement is greatly dependent upon the length of your glass and also upon the distribution of marks on the meterstick. With some of the metersticks glass #1 is poorly measured (when there is a great gap in the location of marks with respect to the top of the glass), but in some cases glass #1 is well marked. The same is true of glass #2.

Notice that there are really three important issues at play. First is that you are measuring one variable (one trait) which is length. This is very important in that you want to make sure you know what you are measuring. Measuring one trait is an important requirement of Rasch, we always want to make sure we measure one trait. A second and third intertwined issue is that, depending on the length of the glass and the distribution of marks, some of the metersticks work better than others. With Rasch we always think of our items (test items and survey items) as marking our meterstick. We also think about how well our meterstick will work with glasses of varied lengths. If we know that all of our glasses will always be of a particular limited range of length, then we understand that marks outside of that range will be wasted marks. Also, we understand that if we don't know the range of glass length, then we better try to have a range of marks along the meterstick. These ideas of marks on a meterstick, where marks are located on the meterstick, and the location of objects on the meterstick is something that I feel was almost totally ignored before Rasch. Sadly, there are still researchers in social sciences who do not carefully define the variable they wish to measure, and they do not think where marks on their meterstick need to be. In our work in this chapter we need to think of multiple-choice test takers being the glasses of different lengths. Some students will be the long glasses, these will be the high-ability students. And some students will be the short glasses, the low-ability students. The marks on the meterstick for the multiple-choice test are the items. The items at the high end of the meterstick are those items of higher difficulty. The items at the low end of the meterstick are those items of lower difficulty. The same thinking can be used for surveys. A set of survey items should only involve one trait. For example, items defining self-efficacy. Those survey items should mark different parts of the self-efficacy trait. This means there should be a range of items marking the self-efficacy trait for the range one would expect to see for survey respondents (these are the glasses of our example). With a rating scale survey, we are helped in our measurement by being able to supply items which can be answered with a rating scale. But for now if you are thinking about multiple-choice tests or surveys, start with the meterstick idea. Wright and Stone consider this idea in Best Test Design (Wright & Stone, 1979), as well as other authors, such as Bond and Fox (2007) (Fig. 2.3).

As readers progress in their Rasch work there are a number of good references for those interested in the theory of Rasch measurement (Rasch, 1960; Wright & Stone, 1979).

The Mathematics of the Rasch Model

Up until this point in this chapter, I have been attempting to explain some of the reasons for the Rasch model. Certainly there are added reasons, but let us now briefly consider the mathematics of the model. In Fig. 2.4, I present the Rasch model for dichotomous test data. Think of this as test data in which items are graded as correct (1) or wrong (0). Also, I provide the Rasch model for rating scales. These models can be written using other mathematics, but I find this form of the model much easier to explain to new learners of Rasch.

Let us start with the dichotomous Rasch model where B_n is the ability of a person, and D_i is the difficulty of an item. Notice that there is a subtraction between B_n and D_i. This means we are looking at the difference between the ability of a person taking a test and the test item that a person takes. So, we could pretend that we are looking at Jack taking test item 2 of a test. We can of course also look at Jack taking test

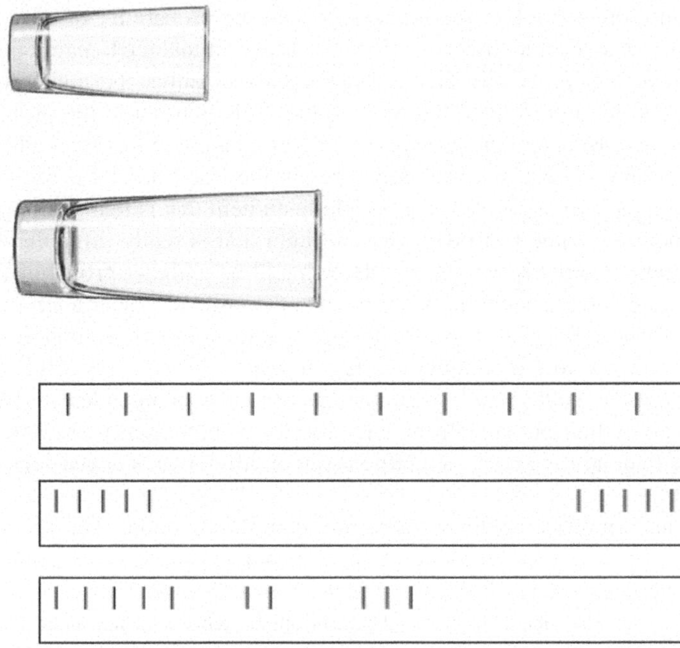

Fig. 2.3 Glasses of different lengths and metersticks with different distribution and marks. The accuracy of measuring the length of the glass will depend upon the length of the glass and the location of marks on the meterstick. It is advantageous to have marks on a meterstick near the length of the glass. The glasses are analogous to the Rasch person measure (the Rasch person ability) of the test data of this chapter. The marks are analogous to the Rasch item measure (the Rasch item difficulty) of this chapter. Plotting the glasses and marks in a single picture is similar to the Wright Map discussed later in this chapter

$$\ln\left(P_{ni}/(1-P_{ni})\right) = B_n - D_i$$

$$\ln\left(P_{nij}/P_{ni(j-1)}\right) = B_n - D_i - F_j$$

Fig. 2.4 The dichotomous Rasch model (top) and the Rasch rating scale model (bottom) as presented by Planinic et al. (Planinic et al., in press)

item 4 of a test, just as we can look at Elisabeth taking item 2 of the test (thinking about our example with the differing metersticks, Jack and Elisabeth are glasses of different lengths, the test items these two students are taking are the marks on one meterstick).

Also note that the terms B_n and D_i are in the same units. We are subtracting the two terms from each other, and we can only do so if we have the same units. The left side of the equation presents the probability of a particular test taker getting a specific item correct (look at the numerator) and the probability of that same test taker getting that same item incorrect (look at the denominator). Because probability ranges from 0 to 1, once you have the probability of either the numerator or the denominator, you can calculate the other value. This is because the probability of getting an item correct and the probability of getting an item incorrect adds up to 1. The next step that is helpful as one learns about the Rasch model is to think about what should happen when a test taker is taking an item that is really easy, and what happens when that same test taker takes an item that is really difficult. When the test taker attempts a really easy item, there should be a higher probability of them getting the item correct in comparison to when the same test taker attempts a much more difficult item. So, if Jack is a really good student and he attempts to solve an item that is easy, we would predict there is a high probability of his solving the item correctly and there would be a low probability of his not being able to solve the test item. Now, go to the right side of the equation for dichotomous data. When Jack is much better than an item there is a large positive difference between Jack (B_n) and the item (D_i).

Now let us turn our attention to the rating scale Rasch model. This model was an extension of the initial Rasch model, which considered dichotomous data. As you look at the equation you will see that there are some similarities, as well as some additions. This model also considers a respondent B_n who is taking a survey item D_i. Let us again pretend the survey item is about environmental attitudes. Remember the B_n means any person's attitude—so, B for Jack or B for Oliver, and D_i means the difficulty of an item, so D_i might be the difficulty of item 3 or item 7. Also, notice there is a new term F_j. To understand this term we cite Plannic, Boone, Susac, and Ivanjek (2019):

> In a rating scale model each item will have several rating scale categories….the probability of a person *n* endorsing category *j* over previous category (*j-1*), or being observed in category *j* of item *i*, can be expressed in a Rasch–Andrich rating scale model as…where F_j is the Rasch-Andrich threshold (step calibration), or the point on the latent variable where the probability of person *n* being observed in category *j* of item *i* equals the probability of the same person being observed in category (*j*–1). F_j is estimated from the category frequency, and the difficulty of the item is now located at the point where the highest and the lowest categories are equally probable.

Thus, for the rating scale Rasch model we have the survey taker, this could be Jack, and Jack is somewhere along the trait of environmental attitude. The survey taker can also be thought of as one of the glasses from Fig. 2.3. Glasses of great length represent survey respondents with a high environmental attitude. The marks on the ruler helping us measure the glass are the items of the survey. Some are easier to answer than others. Also, coming into play with the rating scale Rasch model is that we not only need to think of the overall attitude of the survey taker, we must not only think of the item being taken, but we must think of the probability of a respondent's (who is taking a specific item) rating scale answer. What is their probability of answering "Strongly Agree" to a specific item given their overall attitude? What is their probability of answering "Agree" to that same item, given their overall attitude? These issues are considered in Rasch and are expressed in the rating scale formula.

This issue of a respondent, Jack, answering a survey item #4 and the probability of his selecting a specific rating scale category is expressed by the term F_j.

Conducting a Rasch Analysis with Test Data

For the remainder of this chapter, I will help the readers to understand better the results of a simple Rasch analysis. For this introduction, I will use the RaschWinsteps program (Linacre, 2019). Readers can download the free RaschMinisteps program which is identical to the Winsteps program except that the free program can analyze only 25 items and 75 people. The full Winsteps program is inexpensive and can be used to evaluate survey and test data with thousands of items and millions of respondents. There are thousands of analyses which have been reported using Winsteps, and the program is exceedingly well-documented in a detailed users' manual. Mike Linacre, the author, has worked with Rasch analyses for decades.

To begin, we will start with a test item data set. That data set has the results of 75 students who completed a 10 item multiple-choice test. Each item can be correctly or incorrectly answered. Students are awarded a "1" for a correct answer and a "0" for an incorrect answer. In Fig. 2.5, I provide a picture of how that data set is organized.

To run the Rasch analysis, a so-called "control file" needs to be created. This control file tells the Winsteps program many things, for example, that each row of data is a respondent and each column is an item. Winsteps cannot read English (or any other language) so it would not know if a column is for an item or for a person. In my book, Rasch Analysis in the Human Sciences (Boone et al., 2014), I take the readers through the simple steps needed to create a control file, so in this chapter we will not cover that material. However, it only takes a few seconds to create the control file—just a few clicks within the program. Feel free to email me for this control file and the data set.

Please remember from the "get go" in a Rasch analysis, one is conducting an analysis of a set of items if one feels, from a theoretical perspective, that it makes

	A	B	C	D	E	F	G	H	I	J	K
1	Person ID	Q1	Q2	Q3	Q4	Q5	Q6	Q7	Q8	Q9	Q10
2	1	1	1	1	0	1	1	1	1	1	1
3	2	1	1	0	1	1	1	1	1	1	1
4	3	1	1	1	1	1	1	1	1	1	1
5	7	1	1	1	1	1	1	1	1	1	1
6	9	0	0	1	1	1	0	0	0	1	1
7	10	1	1	1	1	1	1	1	1	1	1
8	11	1	1	0	1	1	0	0	1	1	1
9	12	1	1	1	1	0	1	0	1	0	1
10	14	1	1	1	1	1	1	1	0	1	0

Fig. 2.5 An excel sheet showing the organization of raw data for a multiple-choice test which was administered and graded. A total of ten items were presented to students. Each row of data presents the performance of each student on each test item

Entry Number	Total Score	Total Count	Measure (Logits)	Model S.E.	Infit MNSQ	Outfit MNSQ	PT Measure Corr.	Item
1	61	75	-.11	.34	1.05	1.14	.41	Q1
2	65	75	-.61	.38	0.70	0.50	.59	Q2
3	63	75	-.34	.35	1.02	0.95	.42	Q3
4	63	75	-.34	.35	1.39	1.75	.16	Q4
5	61	75	-.11	.34	1.01	0.94	.45	Q5
6	56	75	.40	.31	0.80	0.73	.61	Q6
7	46	75	1.26	.28	0.84	0.79	.65	Q7
8	60	75	.00	.33	1.06	1.16	.41	Q8
9	64	75	-.47	.36	1.12	1.38	.32	Q9
10	57	75	.31	.31	1.00	0.96	.49	Q10

Fig. 2.6 Part of the item entry table from Winsteps. The name of each of the test items is presented in the far right column entitled "ITEM". The column with the heading of "TOTAL SCORE" indicates how many students correctly answered the test item, the column "TOTAL COUNT" lists the number of students attempting the item. The "MEASURE" column is the test item difficulty in Rasch logit units. The column "MODEL S.E." lists the error of the test item difficulty. Of great use are the columns "INFIT MNSQ" and "OUTFIT MNSQ" which provide fit statistics to evaluate the behavior of the test items

sense to pool items together for an overall measure of someone on a single trait. This means, if you are going to conduct a Rasch analysis of the test data, you feel that the items together should provide an appraisal of where a person falls on the trait. This is a requirement of Rasch analysis.

Below I provide the first table (Fig. 2.6) from Winsteps I usually look at when I conduct a Rasch analysis. This is a so-called item entry table. I have not included all the columns that are produced by the program.

Item Entry Table

Let us start with the far right column, that column lists the names of the test items, this column is entitled "ITEM". One can see names that range from Q1 to Q10. The left most column is entitled "ENTRY NUMBER". This column tells the analyst the order in which the data was read into the program. It is possible, in some data sets, for the item names not to match up with the entry number. For example, let us pretend that we were not going to review the data for Q2. In that case Q1 would have an entry number of 1 and Q3 would have an entry number of 2, as that item was the second item read into the program.

The “TOTAL SCORE” column lists the number of test takers who correctly answered each item. So, we can see that 61 students correctly answered Q1. We can see that 65 students correctly answered Q2. The “TOTAL COUNT” column lists the number of respondents who answered each item. In our data set, we can see that each item was answered by 75 respondents.

So far in this table we have not really been looking at Rasch things, but now we will. The “MEASURE” column lists the item difficulty of the item. The numbers may look a little strange to the beginner because these values range from negative values to positive values. The units are named “logits”. This is short for log odds units. Please remember these values express how difficult the item is, and this is done in linear Rasch units. These are the values that you need to use in any of your work. These values do not have the errors that are present when using raw scores.

In the coding we used for this data set (0 for a wrong answer, 1 for a correct answer), the more positive an item, the more difficult an item. Do not panic when you see negative values, think of temperature in degrees Celsius. When you see that it is −9 °C outside, although it is cold, you know how to appropriately interpret that number. The most difficult item is Q7 (it has an “item difficulty” value of 1.26 logits) and the easiest item is Q2 (it has an “item difficulty” value of −0.61 logits). In some reports/articles/talks you will see Rasch item difficulty reported on a scale that might range from 0 to 1000, from 0 to 10,000, and many other scales. Those values are logit values that have been rescaled. You can think of rescaling as akin to Celsius temperatures being converted to Fahrenheit temperatures. However, for our work in this chapter we will use the logit values from Winsteps.

The next column is entitled “MODEL S.E.”. This column presents the standard error of the item difficulty measure. Think of this as the uncertainty in the number that is reported for the item difficulty. There will always be uncertainty in the item difficulty. A number of factors can impact item error. Before Rasch was used, I feel most researchers not only ignored the nonlinearity of raw data scales but also ignored the error.

The next two columns are “INFIT MNSQ” and “OUTFIT MNSQ”. These two columns report a mean square statistic. Both statistics can be used to identify items that may not be behaving as required for the Rasch model. If an item misbehaves, it may mean a number of things. The most serious being that the item may not fall on the same trait as the other items. If there is conclusive evidence that an item does not fall on the trait, then one should remove that item from an analysis. There are a number of rules of thumb that have been used in Rasch measurement for acceptable MNSQ values. One rule that has been used is a range from 0.5 to 1.5 (O’Connor, Penney, Alfrey, Phillipson, & Phillipson, 2016). There have been proposed ranges that are narrower, it will be up to you which range you wish to select. In our data set you can see that using this criterion, one item might “misfit”—that item is Q4. There are some researchers who favor using Infit MNSQ, there are some that favor using Outfit MNSQ, and there are some that use both Infit and Outfit. I used to only look at Outfit, as outfit picks up extreme behavior of items, but now I have moved toward looking at both Infit and Outfit. When Rasch researchers look at fit, they are looking at whether or not the data fit the Rasch model.

It is important for researchers to know that when data does fit the Rasch model (all items have acceptable fit), then a Rasch analyst would say that there is evidence of "unidimensionality". I think of unidimensionality as meaning one is looking at one dimension, one variable, and one trait. Remember our example with the glasses of Fig. 2.3? The data we collect with our meterstick is only helpful if we are only looking at one dimension. If we want to compare our glasses we must decide upon what trait will our comparison be based.

The last column that I present is the Point Measure Correlation column ("PT MEASURE CORR."). A rule of thumb that researchers have reported is that a value above 0.30 should be observed. When that value is observed, it is the evidence of measuring one construct (Li et al., 2016).

I have found that an additional helpful use of this column is when one observes a negative value. If there is a negative value, then that can be evidence of miscoding. Maybe an incorrect answer key was used to grade the item? Using an incorrect answer key would mean that there would be unexpected answers on the part of respondents.

Also, when evaluating and reporting the data of Fig. 2.6, I suggest reporting the average MNSQ Outfit, the average MNSQ Infit, the average item difficulty, and the average item error. A perfect MNSQ outfit and MNSQ Infit that one would expect from theory would be 1.00. Sometimes in an analysis it is helpful to report that average value. In this analysis the average item difficulty is 0.00. You can set the location of the average item difficulty to any logit value. I find that setting the value to 0.00 is the most easy to use—that is the default value used in Winsteps.

Person Entry Table

Another key table (Fig. 2.7) used in a Rasch analysis is the so-called person entry table. As we have 75 respondents in our data set, I will not provide the entire table, but rather the table for some respondents.

For the person entry table, you will notice that most of the columns have the same headings as what was seen for the item entry table. The far right column "PERSON" lists the person ID. This ID can be any numbers, letters, or combination of letters and numbers you wish to use. The far left column, "ENTRY NUMBER", is a heading we have seen for the item table. This column tells us the order in which the person data was read into the program. So one can see, for instance, that the 10th piece of person data read into the program was for the person with the ID of 16 (the entry number of the person with an ID of 16 is 10). The "TOTAL SCORE" column reports the number of test items that were correctly answered by each respondent. Thus person 16 (entry number 10) correctly answered 8 items. The "TOTAL COUNT" column lists the number of items attempted by the test taker. You can see for the students presented in the table, all of the students have a "MEASURE". This is the "person ability" of each person. This value is reported in units of logits. With how we have

Entry Number	Total Score	Total Count	Measure	Model S.E.	Infit MNSQ	Outfit MNSQ	PT Measure Corr.	Person
1	9	10	2.31	1.07	1.15	1.53	-.22	1
2	9	10	2.31	1.07	1.15	1.53	-.22	2
5	5	10	-.01	0.65	.94	.92	.37	9
7	7	10	0.89	0.71	.83	.82	.56	11
8	7	10	0.89	0.71	.96	1.01	.29	12
9	8	10	1.46	0.81	1.08	.96	.15	14
10	8	10	1.46	0.81	1.14	1.15	-.02	16

Fig. 2.7 The person entry table from Winsteps. The name of each person is presented in the far right column entitled "PERSON". The column with the heading of "TOTAL SCORE" indicates how many items were correctly answered by each student, the column "TOTAL COUNT" lists the number of items attempted by the student. The "MEASURE" column is person ability in Rasch logit units. The column "MODEL S.E." lists the error of each person's ability level. Of great use are the columns "INFIT MNSQ" and "OUTFIT MNSQ" which provide fit statistics to evaluate the behavior of the test takers

coded the data a higher logit value means a higher ability respondent. Thus, if you compare student ID 2 and student ID 9, student ID 2 has the higher ability (2.31) in comparison to student ID 9 (ability level −0.01). Notice, just as with items, you can have persons with a negative measure. This takes a little time to get used to. All I normally do is remind myself that a higher person measure on this test, means a higher performing student. If you are going to compare students using statistics (for example, using a t-test to compare male and female test takers) you can use the person measures "as is" and you will get the correct statistical results. For example, you might report that a t-test was conducted comparing the average measure of males (−0.60 logits) and females (0.22 logits), and a statistical difference was observed. However, if you are reporting the data to the public, no one will understand what it means for a test taker to have a negative person measure. So you may want to add the same logit number (maybe a 5) to all of your person measures. That will make all your person measures positive.

Let us quickly go through the other columns which have the same headings as with the item entry table: MODEL S.E., INFIT MNSQ, OUTFIT MNSQ, PT MEASURE CORR. The "MODEL S.E." provides an assessment of the measurement error of the respondent. Notice that the value is much larger than that we saw for the item entry table. One way to think about why this value is higher for this data set is that there are 75 student answers that are used to figure out how difficult or easy each item is. So, 75 bits of information, student answers to each item (as well as other bits of information in the data set), are used to figure out the item difficulty measure. But for the persons, there are only 10 items that can be used to figure out the test taker's person ability. Having such a small number of items in this data set means there is really a lot of error in how well we can compute a person's ability level (the Rasch person measure).

The OUTFIT MNSQ and the INFIT MNSQ values also can be used in a similar manner, as with items, to identify if there is strange answering behavior on the part of respondents. For example, if a student is a poorly performing student, then it would be unusual for the student to correctly answer a very hard item—that would be one potential cause of a high person MNSQ. Other examples of strange answering patterns would be a student who concentrates for a while (getting items right and wrong matching to their ability level), but then goes through a period of not concentrating, thus missing items they should correctly answer.

Reliability and Validity

Within the field of Rasch measurement there are numerous techniques by which the instrument validity can be assessed and the reliability evaluated. When a Rasch analysis is conducted, a table within Winsteps allows the computation of what is referred to as an item reliability and a person reliability. That value ranges from a low of 0 to a high of 1.00, a higher value is better. This statistic is similar to that that from a Cronbach alpha, but the computations are based upon an understanding that raw data is not linear. Thus in a Rasch analysis one can talk of a person reliability for a test and the item reliability of a test. Target values which have been cited in the literature for person reliability and item reliability are 0.8 and 0.9 (Malec et al., 2007). Figure 2.8 presents those values. Also, often reported in a Rasch analysis are item separation and person separation. Target values that have been reported in the literature are a person separation of 2.0 and an item separation of 4.0 (Malec et al., 2007).

There are, of course, many types of validity that can be evaluated. Some of those types of validity are not unique to Rasch. One type of validity that can be evaluated through Rasch techniques is construct validity. In Fig. 2.9, I present what is termed a "Wright Map". On the right side of the Wright Map are the difficulties of test items, along the logit scale. On the left side of the Wright Map are the person abilities. A

	Total Score	Count	Measure	Model S.E.	Infit MNSQ	Outfit MNSQ	Separation	Reliability
Persons	7.4	10.0	1.30	.86	1.00	1.03	.51	.20
Items	59.6	75.0	.00	.33	1.00	1.03	1.17	.58

Fig. 2.8 Parts of a summary statistic table provided by Winsteps. This table can be used to evaluate and summarize the functioning of the instrument and summarize the fit of the data to the Rasch model. Of particular importance is the reporting of item reliability, item separation, person reliability, and person separation

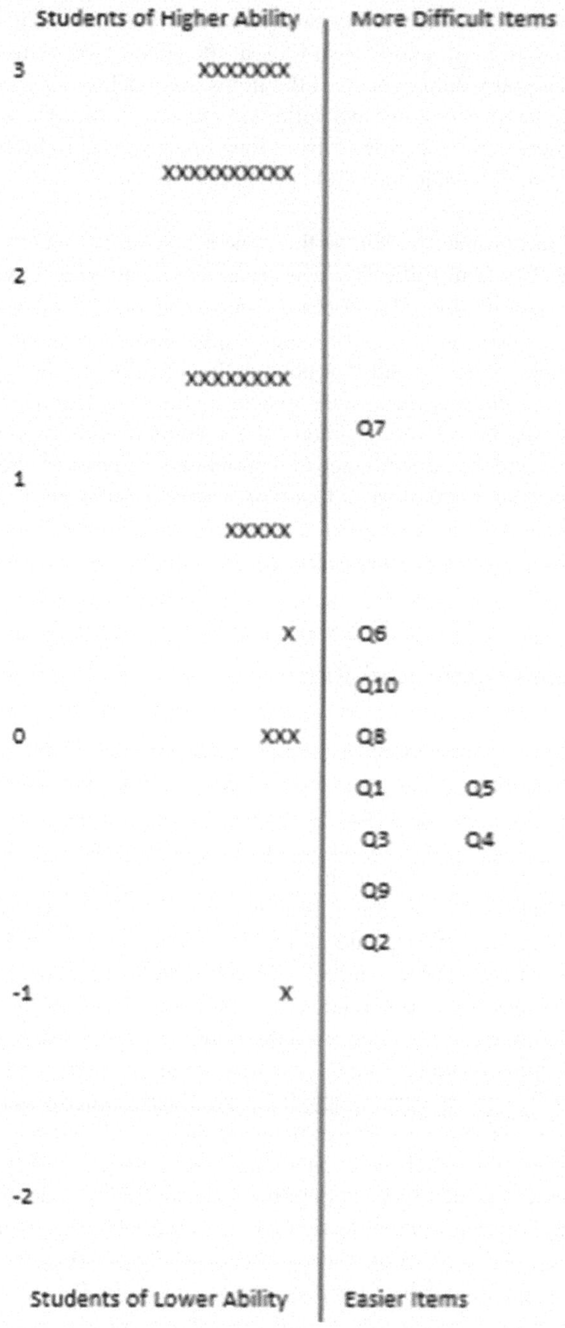

Fig. 2.9 A Wright Map presenting the results of the Rasch analysis of the test data. Items are presented on the right side of the Wright Map, and those items are organized by item difficulty. Easier items are located at the base of the Wright Map and harder items are located toward the top of the Wright Map. Persons are located on the left side of the Wright Map. Persons of lower ability are noted at the base of the scale, and higher performing students are at the top of the map

manner in which the construct validity can be evaluated is by comparing the ordering of items from easy to hard, and to also look at the spacing of items. Are the items in the order which you would expect? If the items do match what you would expect, then that is data in support of construct validity. Predictive validity can be assessed by reviewing the ordering of respondents from lower performing to higher performing. Does the ordering match what one would predict? If so, that is evidence of predictive validity.

Of particular importance is that, as the person measures (person ability) are on the same scale at the item difficulty, it is possible to summarize what items each respondent has a high likelihood of correctly answering and not answering. Take any person, and draw a horizontal line across the Wright Map. Those items below the line are those items one would predict that person should correctly answer (the student has greater than 50% chance of correctly answering the items), and those items above the line are those items one would predict the student would not correctly answer. This ability to describe the performance of respondents in terms of "items most likely correctly answered" and "items most likely not correctly answered" is an incredible aspect of using Rasch. You can explain the meaning of a person's measure, and you can explain the meaning of a group average.

Raw Scores and Logits and Error

Earlier in this chapter we considered a number of examples which I hope will convince readers of the nonlinearity of not only rating scales, but also of the nonlinearity of raw scores from a test. Thus, for example, if a 10 item multiple-choice test is administered to students where a top score is 10 points. Such a test provides nonlinear raw scores. Below we will briefly revisit this topic. In the table immediately below I provide a "raw score"-to-"measure" table (Fig. 2.10) that is provided by Winsteps. The numbers under the column named "Score" are all the possible raw scores that can be earned on the test. This does not mean that any student earned, for example, a score of 7. But this table presents all the potential scores. Also provided are the Rasch "person measures". These are the conversion from the nonlinear raw score scale to the linear Rasch scale. The units of these Rasch measures are in units of "logits".

When students first start learning about Rasch, it can sometimes be confusing to see that someone could have a negative measure. What I always ask my students to do is simply to remind themselves that it all has to do with the selection of where the 0 will be on the scale (much like temperature). At any point in an analysis one can convert the scale. For example, if we wished we could add 4 logits to each entry in the table below, and then one would have all the potential person measures expressed on a scale that has positive values for person measures (Fig. 2.11).

There are a number of added aspects of Rasch which can be better learned through review of the raw score to measure tables and the graph of Fig. 2.10. One thing I ask my students to do is to review the column with "S. E.". This value stands for standard error. This should be viewed as the uncertainty of the measure. What I ask

Score	Measure	S.E.
0	-3.58	1.86
1	-2.29	1.06
2	-1.46	.80
3	-.90	.70
4	-.44	.66
5	-.01	.65
6	.42	.67
7	.89	.71
8	1.46	.81
9	2.31	1.07
10	3.62	1.87

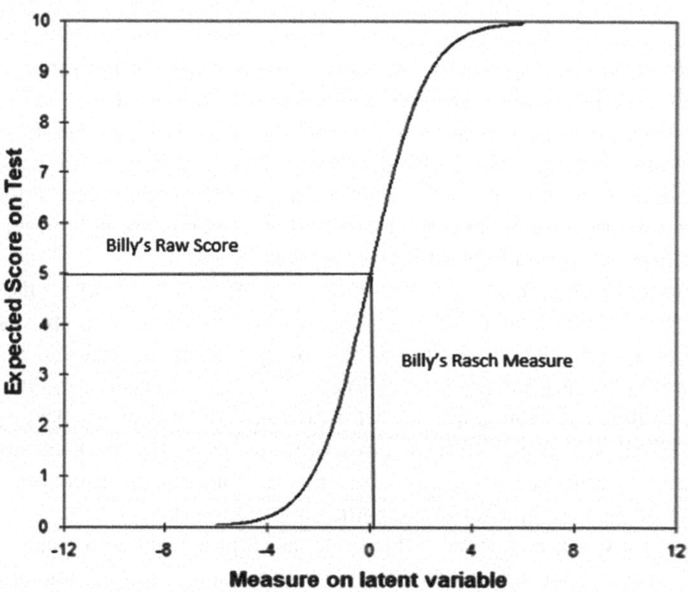

Fig. 2.10 The raw score to measure table of Winsteps. For any potential raw score, the table provides the person measure. Also provided is a plot showing the relationship between the raw scores and the measures presented in the table

Fig. 2.11 A raw score to Rasch measure table; however, all logit values for person measures are positive values. This is done in order to only have positive person measures. This step is not needed for statistical tests, but in terms of communicating the test results, it can be easier for stakeholders to understand positive person measures. Four logits have been added to all logit values in Fig. 2.10

Score	Measure	S.E.
0	0.42	1.86
1	1.71	1.06
2	2.54	.80
3	3.1	.70
4	3.56	.66
5	3.99	.65
6	4.42	.67
7	4.89	.71
8	5.46	.81
9	6.31	1.07
10	7.62	1.87

my students to do is to review the standard error column for the range of person measures that are possible for the test. Students will see that at the extreme scores (0 and 10), the standard errors are a maximum. And they will see that in the middle of the test a raw score of 5 has the smallest error. I ask my students to think through why this might be, why might persons who earn a perfect score have a lot of error in their computed person measure? Honestly, few students are able to answer this question at first, but once I explain it, they are able to get it.

Those students who receive a perfect raw score (10 of 10), we know they know a lot, but we do not know how much more they know. The same is true for the student who receives a 0 on the test. We know they do not know the material on the test, but we do not know how much less they know. Now, let us consider the student who earned a 5 on this test. Notice that their Rasch measure has the smallest error. This error is the smallest because we have a mix of items above the test taker ability, and we have a mix of items below the test takers ability. Thus one can think of our having a nice range of items to bracket in the ability of the test taker.

There are a few other aspects of this table and a plot that can be made with this table. Look at Fig. 2.10 (which has the raw score to measure table) and also look at the plot of the person measures and the raw scores possible for this test. First, notice the shape of the curve. This curve is one that is called an o-give, short for logistic o-give.

For the beginner with Rasch, I think the most useful way to use the o-give and the "raw score to measure table" is an exercise that I carry out with my students. The

Student Name	Raw Score	Measure (Logits)
Amy	0	-3.58
Katie	1	-2.29
Billy	5	-0.01
Stef	6	0.42

Fig. 2.12 The raw score and measures of 4 students making use of Fig. 2.10

first thing I have my students do is to compute the difference in raw score points, and the difference in logits, for a student who scored a 0 on the test and a student who scored a 1 on the test. I also ask my students to make the same computation for a student who earned a 5 on the test and a student who earned a 6 on the test. Above, I provide a table in which I show these calculations for 4 fictional students (Fig. 2.12).

The next step is that I then ask my students to compute the difference in raw score points and measures between Amy and Katie. Students note that the difference between these two students are 1 point and a Rasch person measure difference of 1.29 logits. I will then ask them to compute the difference between Billy and Stef. The raw point difference in performance is also 1 point, but the difference in the Rasch person measures is 0.42 logits. Then, I stress to my students, one can see that what is thought to be the same difference in test performance (a 1 point difference between Amy and Katie, and a 1 point difference between Billy and Stef) is actually not the same difference. In fact there is almost triple the difference in ability level between Amy and Katie (1.29 logits) as there is between Billy and Stef (0.43 logits). This helps my students see that indeed there are different conclusions that can be reached if one uses raw scores or the Rasch person measures. Of course, one could also add two students to the activity, for example, a student who earned 10 raw score points, and a student who earned 9 raw score points. When doing this activity, I also ask the students to mark the o-give to show the performance of each student. I have added a set of lines to the o-give plot to show the performance of Billy. If one does such plotting for all four students then one can visually see the difference between the use of raw score points for comparisons and the use of Rasch person measures.

How Do I Use Rasch for a Research Project?

There are many reasons for the use of Rasch in research, be it social science research, medical research, or market research to name a few areas. The first issue is that data collected through tests in which there is an interest to measure where a person falls on a variable should use Rasch. The same is true when surveys are used to determine where a person falls along a variable. For example, with a test of medical knowledge, how much does the person know? For a survey of confidence, what is the level of a person's confidence?

A second key reason to use Rasch is to guide the development of new instruments and to evaluate how well such instruments measure. Can you trust the measurements that are being made? For those utilizing existing instruments, Rasch is important in that it allows the researcher to evaluate if an instrument is functioning well. Believe me, just because an instrument was published, one cannot assume that the instrument is doing a good job of measuring.

A third reason to use Rasch is the person measures that you as a researcher compute. It will be those values that you will want to use for your statistical tests. For a moment, go back to Fig. 2.7 which presented the person measure from our test. In the past, before Rasch, it would have been the "total score" which would have been imported into a statistical package, and then evaluated. So the 9 for student 1, the 9 for student 2, the 7 for student 11, and so on. However, it should be the "measures" which are used for any statistical tests. This means for student 1, the value of 2.31 logits would be used, the value of 2.31 logits for student 2, the value of 0.89 logits for student 11. With the Winsteps program, it is child's play to import the measure values for each student into a spreadsheet of your choice (for example SPSS). When you run Winsteps there is a tab at the top of your screen named Output Files. Simply click on the "Output Files" tab, then you will be provided with a list of output tables. Simply click on the option "PERSON File". You will then be asked in what way you would like the person measures to be saved (e.g., Excell, SPSS, R and so on). Once you do that you will have a file with all the person measures, in the form of your choice, and you can simply run your statistical analyses using the Rasch person measures.

Are There Other Reasons to Use Rasch?

There is no way one single article or book of any length that can detail all the reasons to use Rasch. Some examples that I have found resonate with my students, colleagues, and workshop participants are the following:

Rasch techniques allow you to revise a test (add items and/or remove items) but express all test takers on the same scale regardless of which form of a test they completed. This allows you to improve your tests, and it also allows your test to include new topics, as long as you are always working with one variable.

Rasch allows you to do a much better job of communicating research findings. The Wright Map that I provided can be used to show where a student is on the trait. One can simply mark the location of a student or the average of a group of students. Those items below a student, or below the group average, are those items one would predict the student/students would have correctly answered. Those items above the student (or group average) are the items one would predict the students would not correctly answer. Wright Maps allow you to describe what it means to have a particular test performance level.

Rasch techniques can allow you to use "common person equating" in order to make use of data in which students might complete different surveys or tests (as long as you are investigating the same variable). Imagine there is a 10 item self-efficacy survey which has been developed, and also a 15 item self-efficacy survey with an entirely different set of items. By having some students complete both surveys, it is possible to put survey takers, regardless of survey completed, on the same scale.

Rasch techniques can be used to evaluate so-called partial credit tests. These are tests in which there may be some items that are worth 1 point (correct answer) or 0 point (wrong answer). But these tests also might have some items worth up to 2 points (0 points, 1 point, 2 points), and other items which might be worth up to 5 points for a correct answer. Any value of points is possible, and it is possible to analyze such data with Rasch.

Rasch techniques can be used to investigate measurement bias. For example, if one has developed a test, it is important to explore if the test is measuring female test takers in the same manner as male test takers. To make accurate comparisons of females and males, it will be important to make sure our test (our meterstick) functions in the same manner for both groups of test takers. With Rasch, one way to investigate measurement bias is through use of a DIF (Differential item functioning) investigation.

There are many added techniques beyond that described in this chapter which can be used to evaluate the functioning of an instrument (be it a test or a survey).

Finally

Rasch analysis can be complex. But it can also be easy. One can conduct a Rasch analysis at many levels of sophistication in social science research. There are still many projects which sadly use raw scores from tests or surveys. This means that statistical tests with such data are suspect. Also, there is a tendency to think that all one has to do is compute a KR-20 or an alpha for an instrument. Sadly, my experience is, computation of an alpha is not enough to evaluate if a measurement instrument can be trusted or not. Finally, Wright Maps provide a way to explain what a person's test performance means (what can they typically do, what can they not do). The same for surveys, when a person has a specific self-efficacy person measure, what does that mean in terms of their overall self-efficacy? What do they feel confident doing, what do they not feel confident doing?

My advice is to consider using Rasch in your work. Consider using the widely utilized Winsteps program. And, consider reading some introductory articles, as well as the most basic of books, Rasch Analysis in the Human Sciences (Boone, Staver & Yale, 2014) and the forthcoming Advances in Rasch Analysis in the Human Sciences (Boone & Staver, forthcoming).

References

Boone, W., Staver, J., & Yale, M. (2014). *Rasch analysis in the human sciences*. Dordrect, Netherlands: Springer.

Boone, W., & Staver, J. (forthcoming). *Advances in rasch analysis in the human sciences*. Dordrect, Netherlands: Springer.

Bond, T. G., & Fox, C. M. (2007). *Applying the Rasch model: Fundamental measurement in the human sciences* (2nd ed.). Mahwah, NJ: Lawrence Erlbaum Associates Publishers.

Li, C. Y., Romero, S., Bonilha, H. S., Simpson, K. N., Simpson, A. N., Hong, I., et al. (2016). Linking existing instruments to develop an activity of daily living item bank. *Evaluation and the Health Professions, 41*(1), 25–43.

Linacre, J. M. (2019). Winsteps® Rasch measurement computer program user's guide. Beaverton, Oregon. Winsteps.com.

Malec, J. F., Torsher, L. C., Dunn, W. F., Wiegmann, D. A., Arnold, J. J., Brown, D. A., et al. (2007). The Mayo high performance teamwork scale: Reliability and validity for evaluating key crew resource management skills. *Journal of the Society for Simulation in Healthcare, 2*(1), 4–10.

Marosszeky, N. (2013). Teaching tutorial: Building measures from raw scores—We need to use the Wright stuff! *Rasch Measurement Transactions, 27*(2), 1418–1421.

O'Connor, J. P., Penney, D., Alfrey, L., Phillipson, S., & Phillipson, S. (2016). The development of the stereotypical attitudes in the HPE scale. *Australian Journal of Teacher Education, 41*(7), 70–87.

Plannic, M., Boone, W. J., Susac, A., & Ivanjek, L. (2019). Rasch analysis in physics education research: Why measurement matters. *Physical Review Physics Education Research , 15*(2), 020111-1–020111-14.

Rasch, G. (1960). *Probabilistic model for some intelligence and achievement tests*. Copenhagen: Danish Institute for Educational Research.

Wright, B. D. (1993). Thinking with raw scores. *Rasch Measurement Transactions, 7*(2), 299–300.

Wright, B. D., & Linacre, J. M. (1989). Differences between scores and measures. *Rasch Measurement Transactions, 3*(3), 63.

Wright, B. D., & Masters, G. (1982). *Rating scale analysis*. Chicago, IL: Mesa Press.

Wright, B. D., & Stone, M. (1979). *Best test design*. Chicago, IL: Mesa Press.

Chapter 3
Applying the Rasch Rating Scale Method to Questionnaire Data

Christine DiStefano and Ning Jiang

Abstract This chapter provides an introduction to the Rasch rating scale model (RSM) and provides a primer of how to use the methodology when analyzing questionnaires. The work includes a discussion of best practices for using the RSM, how to evaluate item and person fit, and how to use the information to build a psychometrically sound scale. An applied example is provided to assist researchers with their decision making.

Keywords Rasch rating scale · Wright map · Latent construct · Probability · Infit · Outfit

Introduction

In the social sciences, questionnaires are frequently used to collect data about a variety of educational, social and behavioral construct in which responses are thought to reflect evaluations about an area of interest. Use of survey instruments in general afford many advantages to the research community including ease of distribution options through various modalities (e.g., telephone, mail, paper-pencil, on-line); the opportunity to collect a wide variety of information, from demographic characteristics to sensitive issues; and the ability to collect self-report data or proxy data (i.e., where persons complete information and reflections about someone other than themselves) from respondents. Many scales are available to use on questionnaires including items which as respondents to provide rankings on a checklist of stimuli, forced choice options, and even open-ended questions. The most popular types of survey items typically include closed-ended scales such as Likert scaled items or performance rating scales.

Ordinal scales allow respondents to select a rating according along a continuum. These scales have many advantages, such as producing data which are relatively easy to collect, summarize, and report (Fink, 2012). Likert scales are by far the most used method for collecting data, as the scales are easily adaptable to many situations,

C. DiStefano (✉) · N. Jiang
University of South Carolina, Columbia, SC, USA
e-mail: DISTEFAN@mailbox.sc.edu

M. S. Khine (ed.), *Rasch Measurement*,
https://doi.org/10.1007/978-981-15-1800-3_3

with choices of anchors that allow researchers to collect data on a wide variety of perspectives such as frequency, intensity, agreement, and likelihood (Fowler, 2013). Further, the number of scale points may be adjusted to include a greater number of scale points (producing more continuous-like data), adding a middle or neutral response category, and using few categories or even pictures to collect data from children (Fink, 2012; Fowler, 2013; Nardi, 2018).

Often, researchers use responses from an ordinal scale to represent a construct of interest by summing item responses to create a total scale score. This assumes that the items have at least interval level properties, that is, that the distance between categories is the same for all respondents. In addition, the same (unit) weight is given to all items (DiStefano, Zhu, & Mindrila, 2009). However, summing responses assumes at least interval level of data—and this assumption may be questionable when ordinal data are present (Bond & Fox, 2007; Iramaneerat, Smith, & Smith, 2008). Further, summed scores do not give additional consideration to items that may vary due to the item's placement relative to the construct (i.e., difficulty value). Finally, characteristics of items are not typically examined beyond descriptive information, such as the number of respondents per category.

As a better alternative, there are applications within the Rasch family that can be used to examine ordinal data (Smith, Wakely, De Kruif, & Swartz, 2003). The Rasch Rating Scale Model (RSM) is an optimal method for examining providing information about data fit to the model, information about characteristics of items and samples such as dimensionality of the measure, use of the rating scale, and coverage of the latent dimension (e.g., Kahler, Strong, & Read, 2005; Thomas, 2011). The purpose of this chapter is to introduce researchers to characteristics of the RSM including: the structure of the model, assumptions needed for accurate assessment, and how to evaluate results from RSM analyses. We provide information concerning these objectives and present an applied example to illustrate these characteristics in practice. The chapter closes by including additional applications for using the RSM for scale development, predicting latent scores, as well as suggestions for future research in this area.

Rasch RSM Methodology Overview

In general, Rasch methods refer to a family of mathematical models that compute the probability an individual will respond favorably to an item given the item's characteristics. The Rating Scale Model (RSM) is a specialized Rasch model for polytomously scored items; however, it follows the same perspectives (i.e., common metric, sample free measurement, linear latent scores) as with Rasch with dichotomous data (Smith, Rush, Fallowfield, Velikova, & Sharpe, 2008). In addition, the goal of RSM is the same as other Rasch models—to provide scores for each person and each item on a common, interval-level (i.e., logit or log-odds) scale.

The Rasch RSM is a specialized model for use with ordinal data, such as responses from a Likert scale. The model incorporates a threshold value into the item estimation process. For polytomous data, the number of thresholds is equal to the number of scale categories (k) minus 1. For example, a four-point scale would have three thresholds—or three points which cut the distribution of responses into four ordered categories (Bond & Fox, 2007). The threshold can be thought of as the point which moves a rating from one category into an adjacent category on the Likert scale. Thus, the threshold τ_{ki} partitions the continuum into set "categories" above and below its location. The threshold value corresponds with the location on a latent continuum at which it is equally likely a person will be classified into adjacent categories, and, therefore, likely to obtain one of two successive scores. Considering an item (i) with four categories, the first threshold of the item, τ_{1i} is the location on the continuum at which a respondent is equally likely to obtain a score of 0 or 1, the second threshold is the location at which a respondent is equally likely to obtain a score of 1 and 2, etc., through the k categories included with the ordered scale (Smith et al., 2003).

The RSM formula can be summarized as:

$$\Pr\{X_{ni} = x\} = \frac{\exp \sum_{k-0}^{x} (\beta_n - (\delta_i - \tau_k))}{\sum_{j=0}^{m} \exp \sum_{k=0}^{j} (\beta_n - (\delta_i - \tau_k))},$$

where β_n is the level of the construct for a given person, δ_i is the difficulty of item i and τ_i is the kth threshold location of the rating scale which is the same to all the items, m is the maximum score. The resulting quotient is a probability value showing the likelihood that a category will be selected given both the difficulty of the item and the individual's level of the construct under study. These probabilities can be transformed into a logit score by taking the natural odds log value. The logit score will vary if the probability is computed across all respondents for an item (item logit) or across items to compute the score for an individual (person logit).

Assumptions. The Rasch RSM includes the same assumptions as with the dichtomous Rasch model that should be met for accurate parameter estimation. These assumptions include: (1) construct unidimensionality, (2) a monotonic scale (i.e., higher latent scores represent a higher level of the latent construct), and (3) that the items fit the Rasch model (Bond & Fox, 2007; Sick, 2010). These three assumptions can be tested in the same manner with RSM as with dichtomous Rasch models. For example, unidimensionality with RSM is assessed using an unrotated Principal Component Analysis of standardized residuals to determine if there is additional variance to be explained after the latent construct has been extracted (Bond & Fox, 2007). Additional requirements (described below) are needed when using the RSM. If the requirements underlying RSM are met, the model offers the same benefits as with other Rasch models: (1) a common interval level metric for calibrated item and person measures, (2) fit statistics to evaluate items and persons which do not align with the Rasch model (i.e., misfit), (3) estimation of projected ratings for the latent construct, and (4) evaluation of the breadth of item coverage of the latent construct.

Rating Scale Diagnostics

A major benefit of the Rasch RSM is the ability to examine characteristics of category performance, frequency of category use, and interpretation of the scale (Bond & Fox, 2007). These investigations should be conducted at the start of a Rasch RSM to ensure that the scale and the categories are functioning properly. If the scales are not functioning as expected, the result is uninterpretable data. Therefore, the first step for the applied researcher utilizing RSM is to investigate rating scale performance, and, if necessary, to make improvements to the scale. The primary objective is to obtain a rating scale that produces the highest quality data for measuring the construct of interest.

Category Usage. The first step in RSM is to examine how respondents are using the categories of the rating scale. This analysis is largely descriptive and examines both the category frequencies and average measures per category. The category frequency provides the distribution of responses, indicating the number of respondents selecting a given category, summed for each category across all items on the questionnaire.

As noted by Bond and Fox (2007), researchers should investigate the shape of the distribution as well as the number of respondents per category. The shape of the distribution (e.g., normal, bimodal, uniform, skewed) provides information about the construct under study. In the social sciences, non-normal distributions are likely to be the standard rather than the exception (Finney & DiStefano, 2013; Micceri, 1989). While slight distributional anomalies are likely to be present, estimation problems may arise if the distribution is irregular, such as highly skewed or kurtotic.

In addition, the observed count in each category provides evidence of the category usage of respondents. Categories with low numbers of respondents do not provide sufficient information to allow stable estimation. Further, categories with few responses illustrate unneeded or even redundant categories, and may be collapsed into adjacent categories. It is recommended that each response category (k) has a minimum frequency of 10 respondents (Smith et al., 2003).

Another characteristic which is evaluated is the average measure value associated with each threshold. The average measure is the average of the ability estimates all persons who chose that particular response category with the average calculated across all observations in a given category. This value can be used to examine if the scale is performing adequately, including an increasing scale (e.g., persons with higher levels of the latent construct are expected to endorse higher levels of the scale).

Along with the average measure values, average Outfit measures associated with each category may also be examined using "standard" fit criteria (i.e., values less than 2.0). This investigation provides information about the quality of the rating scale. Outfit measures which are greater than 2.0 show that there is typically more misinformation than information, meaning that the category is introducing noise into the analyses (Bond & Fox, 2007; Linacre, 2004).

Threshold Values and Category Fit. Category performance may be evaluated by investigating the threshold values (or step calibrations) to determine if respondents are using the categories as expected. It is expected that rating scale categories increase in difficulty of endorsement, and that the thresholds for each item are ordered (Iramaneerat et al., 2008; Smith et al., 2003). The step measure parameter defines the location between categories, which should increase monotonically with categories. Disordering of step measures occurs when the rating scale does not function properly (Linacre, 2002). Thresholds should increase by at least 1.4 logits between categories but not more than 5 logits to avoid large gaps (Linacre, 1999).

A probability curve can be used to examine if the is performing optimally through visual inspection. This is a curve illustrating the probability of responding to a particular category given the difference in estimates between the person's level of the construct and the difficulty of the item ($\beta - \delta$). The curve plots the probability of responses on the y-axis and the person measure scores on the x-axis; individual curves for each category are presented in the body of the figure. When examining curves, researchers should note the shape and height of a given curve. Curves that are "flat" cover a large portion of the construct; however, these curves may also illustrate redundant or unneeded categories. Each curve should show a "peak". This suggests the category is the most probable response category for at least some portion of the construct measured by the questionnaire (Bond & Fox, 2007).

Figure 3.1 provides an illustration of a probability curve. Here, it can be seen that there is a four-category scale, with three threshold values noted by the asterisk (*)

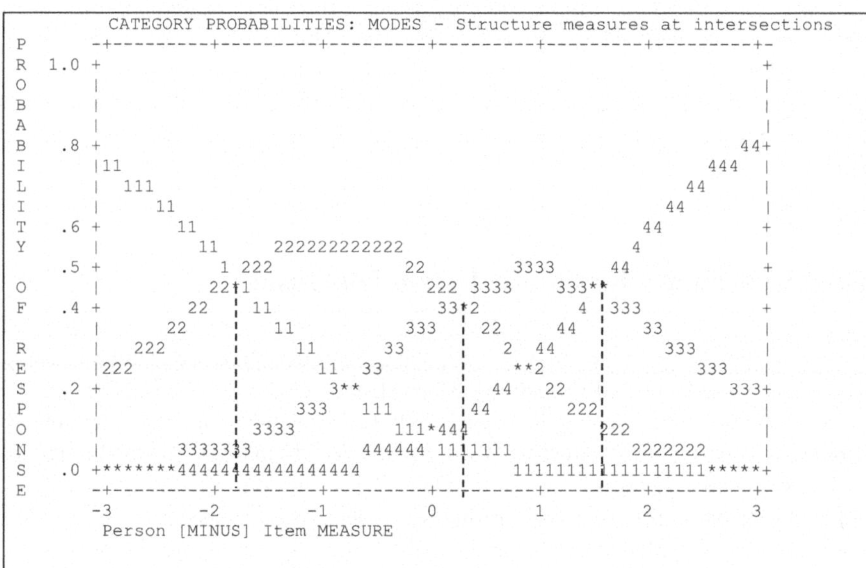

Fig. 3.1 Intensity of physical activity participation scale, 4 categories (from DiStefano et al., 2016). *Note* Threshold values are denoted by dotted lines

values. As noted below, each category displays a maximum peak, showing that it is the optimal response category (on average) for some respondents along the continuum. In addition, the dotted line shows the average construct score for a given threshold value. For example, the (approximate) threshold value between categories 1 and 2 is roughly -1.8. This can be interpreted as respondents with a person measure score that is lower than -1.8 would likely select category 1; persons with scores between -1.8 and (approximately) 0.3 would be expected to select the 2nd category. In this way, the expected category which a respondent would select, based on their overall measure, can be evaluated using the probability curve.

Using RSM Information for Scale Revision. Scale categories which are not utilized or well understood by respondents—such as: scales which include a mix of negatively and positively worded items, unclear wording on a questionnaire, or including too many response categories may show aberrant patterns. For example, Fig. 3.2a shows a scale which was originally conceptualized as an eight-category scale; however, as seen below, many of the categories were not sufficiently used, resulting in lower than recommended frequencies per category and disordered step values.

Here, the scale should be recoded to eliminate misfit and to ensure that the assumptions needed for RSM estimation are obtained. For scale development situations, this investigation can also suggest revisions to the ordinal scale to be used with future administrations of the questionnaire. Figure 3.2b recodes the same scale with three ordered categories, collapsing the scale from the original 0–7 to recoded values of 0 (0–1 from the original scale), 1 (2–3), and 2 (4–7). As can be seen here, recoding the eight-category measure to a three-category scales eliminates problems, producing a scale which functioned acceptably (i.e., no misfit). This can be observed by noting the ordered threshold values (*) between categories and a definite peak for each category included on the scale. As a reminder, any scale revisions should be conducted during the questionnaire's piloting stage to ensure that the best measurement can be obtained.

Visual Representations of the Latent Dimension

Coverage of the latent dimension and expected responses may be examined using Wright Maps and Expected Probability Maps (Bond & Fox, 2007). These maps are similar to the ones presented with other Rasch analyses, however, the plots may be helpful to interpret when conducting RSM. First, a Wright map (or Person-Item map) may be examined to determine the concordance between estimated ability levels of a sample of examinees relative to item difficulty values. These maps typically provide a picture of both calibrated abilities and difficulties along a continuum. For person and item distribution of scores, the mean (M) is provided in the center of the distribution with one (S) and two (T) standard deviations from the mean noted. Person-item maps are very useful in questionnaire development for many reasons such as identifying item redundancy and ensuring that the items on the questionnaire are focused at the

(a)

(b)

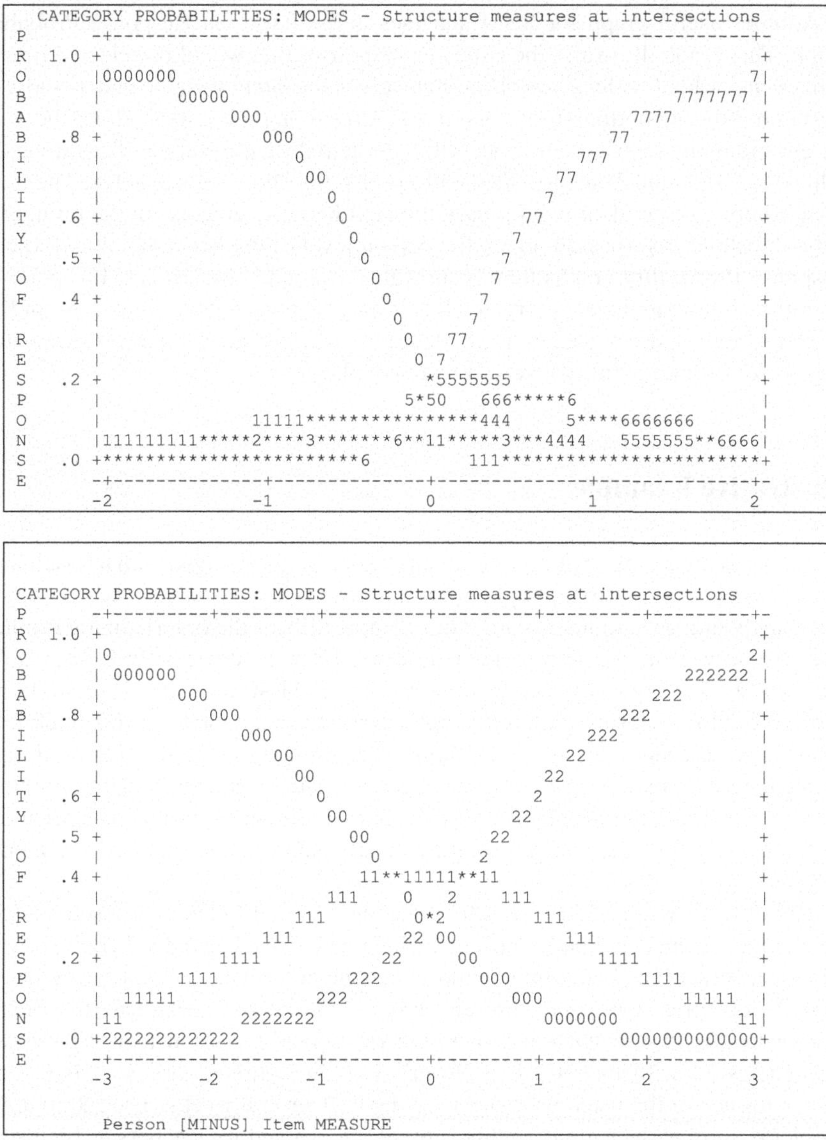

Fig. 3.2 **a** Non-optimal performing Likert scale, eight ordered categories. **b** Ordinal RSM scale recoded to three ordered categories

target level. While the same Wright map is typical in Rasch analyses, with RSM, there are "multiple" threshold estimates that are produced. Thus, multiple threshold levels for a given item are provided. The graphs allow for an examination of category endorsement relative to the distribution of levels of the construct under study.

Another useful graph for RSM analyses is the Expected Response Probability graph. This graph illustrates the expected responses that would be selected for each item on the ordinal scale, given different levels of the latent variable under study. The graph provides a continuum of person measures along the x-axis; along the y-axis are questionnaire items, ordered according to item difficulty values. The rating scale values (e.g., 0, 1, and 2) are provided with colons (threshold values) noted. The colons show where a respondent would mark the next highest category on the rating scale if the threshold is surpassed, given the person level of the latent variable. Expected Response Probability graphs may be useful to examine how expected responses to determine how examinees at targeted levels may respond to the rating scale and also of interest for test users to examine to identify what expected responses to scale items may be for different ability levels of respondents.

Illustrative Example

To assist researchers with interpretation of the decisions involved with a Rasch RSM, we provide an example to highlight information and choices that may be encountered when analyzing questionnaire data. The example utilizes the Externalizing Problems scale from the Pediatric Symptoms Checklist, 17-item screener (PSC-17, Gardner et al., 1999). The PSC-17 is a short version of the full PSC measure (35-items) which is often used to measure children's emotional and behavioral risk (Jellinek et al., 1988). The screener consists of 17 items, measuring three kinds of mental health problems: internalizing problems, attention problems, and externalizing problems. Both the Internalizing Problems subscale and the Attention Problems subscale are represented by five items each; seven items are used for determining Externalizing Problems.

The PSC-17 was rated by preschool teachers from 12 elementary schools/child development centers in South Carolina that were involved in a federal grant project to provide information about young children's behavioral risk upon entry to school. A total of 1,000 preschool-aged children's PSC-17 ratings were obtained. Responses to items were provided for each student within a preschool classroom using a three-point frequency scale with anchors: 0 = "Never", 1 = "Sometimes", or 2 = "Often" based on occurrence of the listed behavior over the past several weeks. The Externalizing Problems subscale was used as this subscale was noted by teachers to be the area which teachers report as most problematic to the classroom environment (Greer, Wilson, DiStefano, & Liu, 2012). The PSC-17 Externalizing Problems are reported in Appendix A. Winsteps (version 4.4.1; Linacre, 2019) was used for all Rasch RSM analyses.

To assess unidimensionality of the Externalizing Problems subscale, an unrotated PCA of standardized residuals and the standardized residual contrast plot were examined. This analysis is used to determine if there is additional variance to be explained after the latent construct has been extracted (Linacre, 1992). As recommended, the construct should account for at least 50% of the total variance to be explained and,

Table 3.1 Category frequencies and average measures for PSC-17 screener, Externalizing Problems subscale

Category label	Observed count	Average measure[a]	Infit MNSQ	Outfit MNSQ	Threshold
0—Never	4884	−2.69	1.01	1.01	None
1—Sometimes	1654	−0.85	0.97	0.90	−1.37
2—Often	454	0.99	1.05	1.12	1.37

[a]Average Measure = sum (person measures—item difficulties)/count of observations in category

after accounting for the model, remaining extracted components should account for a small percentage of the remaining variance (less than 5%; Linacre, 1992). The PCA of the standardized residuals showed that the dimension extracted by the Rasch model account for 47.8% of the variance by the persons and items, slightly lower than recommendations. In addition, the unexplained variance in the first extracted component was 11.7% which was higher than the recommended value of 5%. Part of the reason for the high level of unexplained variance was thought to be due to the small number of items on the Externalizing Subscale. Overall, the results showed that the Externalizing Problems subscale shows some characteristics of dimensionality; however, we recognize that this assumption tentatively holds, allowing this subscale to be used to illustrate the Rasch RSM.

Externalizing Subscale: Category Usage. Table 3.1 showed the example output for the three-category rating scale. As we can see that all three category frequencies were larger than 10 responses, and the distribution of responses per category was right-skewed. The right-skewness in this situation shows that most of the students are not demonstrating externalizing problems.

The average measure for category 0 was −2.69 logits, and increased monotonically, moving from category 1 (: at −0.85 logits), to category 2 at 0.99 logits. It was expected that the higher the category selected, the higher the student's average measures. Category Infit and Outfit results were within the acceptable range. Thresholds results illustrated that the PSC-17 rating scale met the criteria that thresholds should increase by at least 1.4 logits between categories but not more than 5 logits (Linacre, 1999).

Externalizing Subscale: Response Probabilities and Thresholds. The graph in Fig. 3.3 illustrates the probability of responding to each category, given the difference in estimates between person ability and any item difficulty (Bond & Fox, 2007). As noted, each category has a definite peak, showing it is the most probable response for teachers at least some of the time. The threshold estimates were identified in Fig. 3.3 by dashed lines between curves. For ratings of 0, 1, 2, the threshold estimates were −1.37 and 1.37, respectively. In sum, this information suggests that the 0–2 rating scale is functioning appropriately.

Externalizing Subscale: Wright Map. Calibrated scores for both children and items are provided in the Wright map shown in Fig. 3.4. On the left side of the Wright map are the person measures, showing the placement of children by their estimated

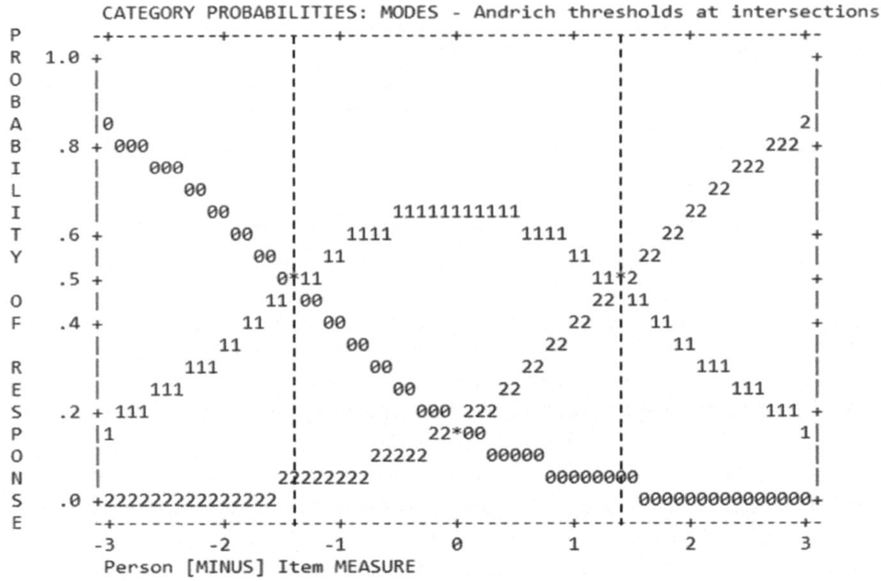

Fig. 3.3 Response category probability curves for the Externalizing Problems subscale of PSC-17

"externalizing problem" scores, and information about the relationship between items and construct is presented on the right side. Both person measures and item measures are on the same scale which children's latent scores can be interpreted related to the placement of the items. For person and item distribution of scores, the mean (*M*) of distribution is noted, with one (*S*) and two (*T*) standard deviations from the mean noted.

The left side of the graph provides information about the distribution of children rated by teachers. As we can see that most preschoolers were rated by teachers are relatively well-behaved—this is seen by the low average value of the person latent score (reported as −0.4) and the majority of children noted by a code of "X" or "." (relative to the number of cases) at the lower end of the scale. On the right side, the PSC-17 Externalizing items can be compared to the distribution of child ratings. These items are used for identifying a range of severe externalizing problems included on the screener. Items at the top of the item distribution are more sever and harder for teacher to frequently observe in the classroom, and items at the bottom of the scale (i.e., "Fights with other children" and "Does not listen to rules") are easier for teachers to observe. These two items are between 1 (*S*) and 2 (*T*) standard deviations below the item measure mean. Also, the three items at the top of the Wright map at the same "line" are not providing unique information regarding externalizing problems in young children. These items all are at roughly 1 standard deviation above the item mean; future revisions of the PSC-17 Externalizing Problems subscale may want to consider incorporating different items that help to identify children along the latent continuum.

```
MEASURE    Person - MAP - Item
                <more>|<rare>
    4             . +
                    |
                    |
                    |
                  . |
                    |
                    |
    3               +
                    |
                    |
                  . |
                    |
                    |
                    |
    2             . +
                    |T
                    |
                    |
                  . |
                   T|
                    |
    1               +S
                  . |  Refuse share    Take things    Tease Other
                    |
                    |
                  . |  Dont Undsd Feelin
                  . |
                    |
    0            .# +M
                 . S|
                  . |  Blames others
                .## |
                    |
                    |
                 .# |
   -1               +S
                    |
                    |  Dont listen
               .### |
                    |  Fights
                 . M|
               .### |T
   -2               +
                    |
                    |
                    |
               .### |
                    |
                    |
   -3               +
                   S|
                    |
                  . |
            .###### |
                    |
                    |
   -4 .############ +
                <less>|<freq>
```

Fig. 3.4 Wright map for the PSC-17 Externalizing Problems subscale

Figure 3.5 presents the Wright map when there are ordinal scales. The right-hand column shows the items positioned at the measures where the expected score on the item is equal to the category number. It is also the measure at which the category has the highest probability. The left-hand column shows the distribution of person ability measures along the variable. As we can see, children with low externalizing problems

```
MEASURE    Person - MAP - Item - Measures for category scores (maximum probability of observing a category)
               <more>|<rare>        never           sometimes                 often
   4               . +
                     |
                     |
                   . |
                    ||                                                 Takes things.2
                                                                       Refuse share.2
                                                                      Teases others.2
                     |
   3                 +                                              Does not unders.2
                     |
                     |
                   . |
                     |                                                Blames others.2
                     |
   2               . +
                     |T
                     |
                     |
                   . T|                                             Does not listen.2
                     |
   1                 +S                                             Fights with oth.2
                   . |                          Takes things.1
                                                Refuse share.1
                                               Teases others.1
                     |
                   . |                       Does not unders.1
                     |
                   . |
   0              .# +M
                  . S|                         Blames others.1
                     |
                 .## |
                     |
                  .# |
  -1                 +S
                     |
                .### |                       Does not listen.1
                     |                       Fights with oth.1
                  . M|        Takes things.0
                              Refuse share.0
                             Teases others.0
                .### |T
  -2                 +  Does not unders.0
                     |
                     |
                .### |
                     |
                     |   Blames others.0
  -3                 +
                    S|
                     |
             .###### |
                     |
                     |  Does not listen.0
  -4                 +  Fights with oth.0
                     |
                     |
                     |
                    T|
                     |
  -5  .############  +
               <less>|<freq>        never           sometimes                 often
 EACH "#" IS 26: EACH "." IS 1 TO 25
```

Fig. 3.5 Wright map measures by category scores, PSC-17 Externalizing Problems subscale

```
-5    -4    -3    -2    -1     0     1     2     3     4
|-----+-----+-----+-----+-----+-----+-----+-----+-----| NUM   Item
0                   0     :        1        :     2   2   7 Take things
0                   0     :        1        :     2   2   1 Refuse share
0                   0     :        1        :     2   2   6 Tease Other
|                                                     |
0                 0     :        1        :    2      2   2 Dont Undsd Feelings
|                                                     |
|                                                     |
0            0     :         1        :     2         2   4 Blames others
|                                                     |
|                                                     |
0      0     :        1         :     2               2   5 Dont listen
0     0     :        1        :     2                 2   3 Fights
|-----+-----+-----+-----+-----+-----+-----+-----+-----| NUM   Item
-5    -4    -3    -2    -1     0     1     2     3     4

3        1         1
3        6     9   0  8  4 5  5 1 1  1
2   1    5     7  21  1  8 5 111 9 2  5   8  8     2  1 Person
  S          M           S          T
0 30    40    50  60 70 80     90            99           PERCENTILE
```

Fig. 3.6 Expected scores on the "Externalizing Problems subscale" of PSC-17 by child measure

(at the bottom of the Wright map) are likely to be rated zero by teachers using PSC-7 Externalizing Problem items; children with moderate externalizing problems (in the middle of the Wright map) are likely to be rated one by teachers; and children with high externalizing problems (on the top of the Wright map) are likely to be rated two by teachers using the seven PSC-17 Externalizing Problems items. By looking at the ordering of the item categories and the children's measures, we can conclude that all the items perform well and match what they are intended to be measured.

Figure 3.6 presents the expected item endorsements for children at various risk levels. Along the x-axis, preschoolers' risk levels are shown; along the y-axis are items from the PSC-17, ordered according to item difficulty values. Values correspond to the rating scale 0, 1, and 2, and colons correspond to threshold values, where a teacher would mark the next highest category on the rating scale if the threshold is surpassed. The response scales are approximately of equal distance apart, showing that the responses are spread among the different categories. Also, the response scale categories display a logical ordering of values (e.g., 0:1:2), illustrating that the categories are being used appropriately.

Determining Between Using the Rasch RSM and PCM

The Rasch RSM is not the only method available for analyzing ordinal data. The Rasch Partial Credit Model (PCM; Wright & Masters, 1982) is another option that researchers may consider. The PCM is similar in the sense that it accommodates ordinal by including threshold values in its estimation. However, there are distinct differences between the RSM and PCM. RSM is typically used when all items on a questionnaire follow the same response scale (e.g., all items employ a 5-category Likert scale). PCM can be used in situations where the response scale differs across the questionnaire. Thus, each item is thought to have a unique rating scale. By allowing the items to have unique rating scales, the number of parameters to be estimated with the PCM increases by $(L - 1) * (m - 2)$, where L is the number items and m the number of categories in the rating scale (Linacre, 2000). While increasing the number of parameters may help to reduce misfit, generally, fewer rating scale parameters is preferred for stability and the communication of results.

To determine between use of RSM or PCM, Linacre (2000) recommends the following steps. First, examine the number of responses per category with the PCM. If there are categories with fewer than recommended responses (i.e., <10 ratings), estimates of difficulty of the parameters may be compromised. Second, communication of the results is facilitated if all items (or groups of items) share the same response format, (e.g., Strongly Disagree, Disagree, Agree, Strongly Agree). In such situations, the questionnaire/test developer and the respondents generally perceive the set of items to share the same rating scale. To attempt to explain a separate parameterization for of each item would hinder communication of the results. If there are only a few items that have a different scale (e.g., True/False), it may be easier to omit the non-conforming items than to argue that a separate scale exists for every item.

Future Directions. As with other areas of measurement, there are many unanswered questions which may be investigated using the Rasch RSM. For example, guidelines exist about the number of cases needed for stable estimation, including roughly 10 cases per category. An interesting avenue of investigation would be to examine the differences in estimated parameters with different numbers of sample sizes to determine how the minimum requirements change when scale usage follows patterns that may be observed with empirical studies, such as negatively and positively worded items on the same scale, respondents using the end points or the middle category of a Likert scale and investigation of parameter bias when items are skewed in opposite directions.

In addition, various software packages (e.g., IRTPRO, Xcalibre, the R-extended Rasch modeling package [eRm]; WinGen, Stata) are available to run the Rasch RSM. Differences among packages, including fit information and estimated parameters may be of interest to researchers. Such evaluations would not only compare results across software packages, but allow a thorough investigation of the drawbacks, benefits, and unique features offered by different software packages and programs. Finally, it may be of interest for researchers to include validity studies as part of the support for scaling decisions made from Rasch RSM. For example, examining relations between person-measure scores and relevant outcomes may provide quantitative data to support deleting misfitting items, changing the number of scale responses, and eliminating items which do not provide unique information to a scale.

In summary, the Rasch RSM is a useful model to use to examine characteristics of questionnaire data and for use in scale development. The methodology provides an opportunity for researchers to investigate category usage, distributions of person-item measures for a scale, and estimate responses given characteristics of a person and item. In addition, visual representations of these procedures aid researchers and help to convey complex information with ease. We hope that this chapter will help to encourage more applied researchers to consider incorporating the Rasch RSM as part of their own investigations with questionnaire data.

Acknowledgements The research reported here was supported in part by the Institute of Education Sciences, U.S. Department of Education, through Grant #R305A150152 to South Carolina Research Foundation. The opinions expressed are those of the authors and do not represent views of the Institute of Education Sciences or the U.S. Department of Education.

Appendix: PSC-17 Externalizing Problem Subscale Items (Gardner et al., 1999)

1. Refuses to share
2. Does not understand other people's feelings.
3. Fights with other children.
4. Blames others for his or her troubles.
5. Does not listen to rules.
6. Teases others
7. Takes things that do not belong to him or her.

References

Bond, T. G., & Fox, C. M. (2007). *Applying the Rasch model: Fundamental measurement in the human sciences*. Mahwah, NJ.

DiStefano, C., Pate, R., McIver, K., Dowda, M., Beets, M., & Murrie, D. (2016). Creating a physical activity self-report form for youth using Rasch methodology. *Journal of Applied Measurement, 17*(2), 125–141.

DiStefano, C., Zhu, M., & Mindrila, D. (2009). Understanding and using factor scores: Considerations for the applied researcher. *Practical Assessment, Research & Evaluation, 14*(20), 1–11.

Fink, A. (2012). *How to ask survey questions* (Vol. 4). Thousand Oaks, CA: Sage Publishers.

Finney, S., & DiStefano, C. (2013). Non-normal and categorical data in structural equation modeling. In G. R. Hancock & R. O. Mueller (Eds.), *Structural equation modeling: A second course* (2nd ed., pp. 439–492). Greenwich, CT: Information Age.

Fowler, F. J. (2013). *Survey research methods*. Thousand Oaks, CA: Sage Publishers.

Gardner, W., Murphy, M., Childs, G., Kelleher, K., Pagano, M., Jellinek, M., …, & Chiappetta, L. (1999). The PSC-17: A brief pediatric symptom checklist with psychosocial problem subscales. A report from PROS and ASPN. *Ambulatory Child Health, 5*, 225.

Greer, F. W., Wilson, B. S., DiStefano, C., & Liu, J. (2012, December). Considering social validity in the context of emotional and behavioral screening. In *School psychology forum* (Vol. 6, No. 4).

Iramaneerat, C. H. E. R. D. S. A. K., Smith E. V., Jr., & Smith, R. M. (2008). An introduction to Rasch measurement. *Best Practices in Quantitative Methods*, 50–70.

Jellinek, M. S., Murphy, J. M., Robinson, J., Feins, A., Lamb, S., & Fenton, T. (1988). Pediatric symptom checklist: Screening school-age children for psychosocial dysfunction. *The Journal of Pediatrics, 112*(2), 201–209.

Kahler, C. W., Strong, D. R., & Read, J. P. (2005). Toward efficient and comprehensive measurement of the alcohol problems continuum in college students: The brief young adult alcohol consequences questionnaire. *Alcoholism: Clinical and Experimental Research, 29*(7), 1180–1189. http://dx.doi.org/10.1097/01.ALC.0000171940.95813.A5.

Linacre, J. M. (1992). *Many facet Rasch measurement*. Chicago, IL: MESA Press.

Linacre, J. M. (1999). Investigating rating scale category utility. *Journal of Outcome Measurement, 3*, 103–122.

Linacre, J. M. (2000). Comparing and choosing between "partial credit models" (PCM) and "rating scale models" (RSM). *Rasch Measurement Transactions, 14*(3), 768.

Linacre, J. M. (2002). Optimizing rating scale category effectiveness. *Journal of Applied Measurement, 3*(1), 85–106.

Linacre, J. M. (2004). Optimizing rating scale category effectiveness. Rasch measurement: The dichotomous model. In E. V. Smith & R. M. Smith (Eds.), *Introduction to Rasch measurement* (pp. 258–278). Maple Grove, MN: JAM Press.

Linacre, J. M. (2019). *Winsteps® (Version 4.4.1) [Computer Software]*. Beaverton, Oregon, Winsteps.com. Retrieved January 1, 2019, from https://www.winsteps.com/.

Micceri, T. (1989). The unicorn, the normal curve, and other improbable creatures. *Psychological Bulletin, 105*(1), 156.

Nardi, P. M. (2018). *Doing survey research: A guide to quantitative methods* (4th ed.). Philadelphia: Routledge.

Sick, J. (2010). Assumptions and requirements of Rasch measurement. *JALT Testing & Evaluation SIG Newsletter, 14*(2), 23–29.

Smith, A. B., Rush, R., Fallowfield, L. J., Velikova, G., & Sharpe, M. (2008). Rasch fit statistics and sample size considerations for polytomous data. *BMC Medical Research Methodology, 8*(1), 33.

Smith, E. V., Jr., Wakely, M. B., De Kruif, R. E., & Swartz, C. W. (2003). Optimizing rating scales for self-efficacy (and other) research. *Educational and Psychological Measurement, 63*(3), 369–391.

Thomas, M. L. (2011). The value of item response theory in clinical assessment: A review. *Assessment, 18*(3), 291–307. https://doi.org/10.1177/1073191110374797.

Wright, B. D., & Masters, G. N. (1982). *Rating scale analysis*. MESA Press.

Chapter 4
Objective Measurement: How Rasch Modeling Can Simplify and Enhance Your Assessment

Chong Ho Yu

Abstract Although Rasch modeling is a powerful psychometric tool, for novices its functionality is a "black box." Some evaluators still prefer classical test theory (CTT) to Rasch modeling for conceptual clarity and procedural simplicity of CTT, while some evaluators conflate Rasch modeling and item response theory (IRT) because many texts lump both together. To rectify the situation, this non-technical, concise introduction is intended to explain how Rasch modeling can remediate the shortcomings of CTT, and the difference between Rasch modeling and item response theory. In addition, major components of Rasch modeling, including item calibration and ability estimates, item characteristic curve (ICC), item information function (IIF), test information function (TIF), item-person map, misfit detection, and item anchoring, are illustrated with concrete examples. Further, Rasch modeling can be applied into both dichotomous and polytomous data, and hence different modeling methods, including normal ogive model, partial credit model, graded response model, nominal response model, are introduced. The procedures of running these models are demonstrated with SAS and Winsteps.

Keywords Rasch modeling · Classical test theory · Item response theory · Unidimensionality · Rating scale · Item information function · Test information function

Introduction

Although Rasch modeling (Rasch, 1980) is a powerful psychometric tool, for novices its functionality is a "black box." In reaction most quantitative researchers favor classical test theory (CTT) for its conceptual clarity and procedural simplicity (Hutchinson & Lovell, 2004). One problem involved with using Rasch modeling is that it is often confused with item response theory (IRT), and as a result users cannot decide

C. H. Yu (✉)
Azusa Pacific University, Azusa, CA, USA
e-mail: cyu@apu.edu

M. S. Khine (ed.), *Rasch Measurement*,
https://doi.org/10.1007/978-981-15-1800-3_4

what assessment approach is suitable for their data. To rectify the situation, this non-technical introduction starts with an explanation of how Rasch modeling can remediate the shortcomings of CTT. Next, theoretical assumptions and major procedural components of Rasch modeling are illustrated with concrete examples. Further, Rasch modeling can be applied using both dichotomous and polytomous data; hence, different modeling methods, including the partial credit model and the graded response model, are introduced. Because comparison of Rasch modeling and IRT requires the preceding information, their differences are discussed at the end. Finally, the merits and shortcomings of two powerful software applications for Rasch analysis—namely, SAS (SAS Institute, 2018) and Winsteps (Winsteps & Rasch measurement Software, 2019)—are discussed.

Classical Test Theory Versus Rasch Modeling

The root of classical test theory (CTT), also known as the true score model (TSM), could be traced back to Spearman (1904). Conceptually and procedurally speaking CTT is very straight-forward. According to this approach, item difficulty and person ability are conceptualized as relative frequencies. For instance, if a student is able to correctly answer 9 out of 10 questions in a test, according to the total score his or her ability would be quantified as 9/10 = 0.9 or 90%. The item attribute can also be computed by percentage. For example, if only 2 out of 10 students can correctly answer a particular item in a test, obviously this question would be considered very challenging: 2/10 = 0.2 or 20%. However, this approach of assessing student ability is item-dependent. If the test is composed of easy items, even an average student might look very competent. In a similar vein, the CTT approach of evaluating the psychometric properties of test items is sample-dependent. If the students are very good at the subject matter in the test, then even challenging items might seem easy. This issue is called *circular dependency*. Rasch modeling, which estimates item difficulty and person ability simultaneously, is capable of overcoming this circular dependency. Because comparison of person ability is unaffected by the choice of items and comparison of items is also unbiased by the choice of participants, Rasch modeling is said to be a form of *objective measurement* that can yield invariant measurement properties across various settings (Wright, 1992). Details regarding the estimation are discussed in the section on item calibration and ability estimation.

In addition, CTT is built upon the philosophy of true score model (TSM). True score model is so named because its equation is expressed as: $X = T + E$, where:

X = fallible, observed score
T = true score
E = random error

Ideally, a true score reflects the exact value of a respondent's ability or attitude. The theory assumes that traits are constant and the variation in observed scores are caused by random errors, which result from numerous factors, such as guessing and fatigue.

These random errors over many repeated measurements are expected to cancel each other out (e.g. sometime the tester is so lucky that his or her observed scores are higher than his or her true scores, but sometimes he or she is unlucky and his or her observed scores are lower). In the long run, the expected mean of measurement errors should be zero. When the error term is zero, the observed score is the true score: $X = T + 0 \rightarrow X = T$.

On the other hand, some modern Rasch modelers do not assume that there exists a true score for each person. Rather, they subscribe to the notion that uncertainty is an inherent property of any estimation, and that there might thus be a score distribution within the same person. For example, in large-scale international assessments, such as the Programme for International Student Assessment (PISA) and the Programme for International Assessment of Adult Competencies (PIAAC), for every participant there are ten plausible scores, known as *plausible values* (PV) (OECD, 2013a, 2013b). These plausible values represent the estimated distribution for a student's θ (student ability). In psychometrics, this distribution is known as the posterior distribution (Wu, 2004, 2005).

Assumptions of Rasch Modeling

Unidimensionality

One of the foundational assumptions of Rasch modeling is *unidimensionality*, meaning that all items in the scale are supposed to measure a single construct or concept. A typical example is that a well-written math test should evaluate the construct of mathematical capability. This approach can come with limitations. For example, if a test designer uses a long passage to illustrate a math problem, this item may end up simultaneously challenging both math and comprehension abilities, thereby becoming multidimensional rather than unidimensional. This is problematic because it complicates the interpretability of results; to explain, if a student receives a low score on a test, it will be difficult to determine whether this score is due to deficits in this student's mathematical or reading ability.

Some psychometricians argue that many assessment tests are multidimensional in nature. Returning to the example of a math test—this type of test might include questions about algebra, geometry, trigonometry, statistics, and calculus. By the same token, a science test may include questions about physics, chemistry, and biology. Bond and Fox (2015) noted that psychometricians must choose the level of aggregation that can form a coherent and unidimensional latent construct. While it may be reasonable to lump algebra, geometry, trigonometry, statistics, and calculus into a construct of mathematical reasoning, and to lump physics, chemistry, and biology into the construct of scientific logic, it can be problematic to lump GRE-verbal, GRE-quantitative, and GRE-analytical together into a single construct.

Local Independence

Another major assumption of Rasch modeling is *conditional independence*, also known as *local independence*. It is assumed that there is no relationship between items that is not accounted for by the Rasch model. In CTT, psychometricians usually employ factor analysis to explore and confirm *construct validity*. In the context of Rasch modeling, Borsboom and Markus (2013) used the following analogy to illustrate the notion of construct validity in measurement: Variations in the construct must cause variations in the scores yielded by the instrument. For instance, changes in the temperature should cause the rise or fall of the mercury level in a thermometer. Conditional independence specifies that after the shared variance among the observed items has been captured, the unique variance (i.e. the residuals or random errors) should be independent. In this case, there should be a covariation between the latent trait and the observed items. Simply put, the latent construct causes variation in the item scores. This is how construct validity can be established, using a valid Rasch model (Baghaei, Shoahosseini, & Branch, 2019).

One may argue that in CTT the same mechanism can be provided by item-total correlation, such as point-biserial correlation. Baghaei et al. (2019) argued against this classical approach by pointing out that while Rasch modeling estimates the latent ability score, also known as the theta, there is no such thing in CTT (The concept of theta will be explained in the next section). In item-total correlation the total score is nothing more than a summation of item scores; there is no advanced algorithm to take item difficulty and person ability into account. At most the total score can represent content validity only.

Item Calibration and Ability Estimation

Unlike CTT, in which test scores of the same examinees may vary from test to test (depending upon test difficulty), in IRT item parameter calibration is sample-free, while examinee proficiency estimation is item-independent. In a typical process of item parameter calibration and examinee proficiency estimation, the data are conceptualized as a two-dimensional matrix, as shown in Table 4.1.

In this example, Person 1, who answered all five items correctly, is tentatively considered as having achieved 100% proficiency, Person 2 is treated as having achieved 80% proficiency, Person 3 is treated as having achieved 60%, etc. These percentages are considered tentative because: (1) in Rasch analysis there is a specific set of terminology and scaling scheme for proficiency, and (2) a person's ability cannot be based solely on the number of correct items he or she obtained, as item attributes should also be taken into account. In this highly simplified example, no examinees have the same raw scores. But what would happen if there was an examinee (e.g. Person 6) whose raw score was the same as that of another examinee (e.g. Person 4)? (see Table 4.2).

Table 4.1 5 × 5 person by item matrix

	Item 1	Item 2	Item 3	Item 4	Item 5	Average
Person 1	1	1	1	1	1	1
Person 2	0	1	1	1	1	0.8
Person 3	0	0	1	1	1	0.6
Person 4	0	0	0	1	1	0.4
Person 5	0	0	0	0	1	0.2
Average	0.8	0.6	0.4	0.2	0	

Table 4.2 Example of two people with the same raw score

	Item 1	Item 2	Item 3	Item 4	Item 5	Average
Person 4	0	0	0	**1**	**1**	0.4
Person 6	**1**	**1**	0	0	0	0.4

We cannot draw a firm conclusion that these two people have the same level of proficiency because Person 4 answered two easy items correctly, whereas Person 6 answered two hard questions instead. Nonetheless, for the simplicity of this illustration, we will stay with the five-person example. This neat five-person example illustrates an ideal case in which proficient examinees succeed on all items, less competent examinees succeed on the easier items and fail on the hard ones, and poor students fail on all items (see Table 4.1). This ideal case is known as the *Guttman pattern* (Guttman, 1944), but it rarely happens in reality. If it happened, the result would be considered an *overfit*. In non-technical terminology, this result would simply be "too good to be true."

We can also make a tentative assessment of the item attribute based on this ideal-case matrix. Let's look back at Table 4.1. Item 1 seems to be the most difficult because only one person out of five could answer it correctly. It is tentatively asserted that the difficulty level in terms of the failure rate for Item 1 is 0.8, meaning that 80% of students were unable to answer the item correctly. In other words, the item is so difficult that it can "beat" 80% of students. The difficulty level for Item 2 is 60%, Item 3 is 40% … etc. Please note that for person proficiency we count the number of successful answers, but for item difficulty we count the number of failures. While this matrix is nice and clean, the issue would be very complicated when some items have the same pass rate but are passed by examinees of different levels of proficiency.

In Table 4.3, Item 1 and Item 6 have the same level of difficulty. However, Item 1 was answered correctly by a person with high proficiency (83%) whereas Item 6 was not (the person who answered it had 33% proficiency). If the text in Item 6 confuses good students, then the item attribute of Item 6 would not be clear-cut. For convenience of illustration, we call the portion of correct answers for each person "tentative student proficiency" (TSP) and the pass rate for each item "tentative item

Table 4.3 Two items share the same pass rate

	Item 1	Item 2	Item 3	Item 4	Item 5	Item 6	Average
Person 1	1	1	1	1	1	0	0.83
Person 2	0	1	1	1	1	0	0.67
Person 3	0	0	1	1	1	0	0.5
Person 4	0	0	0	1	1	0	0.33
Person 5	0	0	0	0	1	1	0.33
Average	**0.8**	0.6	0.4	0.2	0	**0.8**	

difficulty" (TID). Please do not confuse these "tentative" numbers with the item difficulty parameter and the person theta in the final Rasch model.

In short, when conducting item calibration and proficiency estimation, both item attribute and examinee proficiency should be taken into consideration. This is an iterative process in the sense that tentative proficiency and difficulty derived from the data are used to fit the model, and the model is employed to predict the data. Needless to say, there will be some discrepancy between the model and the data in the initial steps. It takes many cycles to reach *convergence*.

Given the preceding tentative information, we can predict the probability of answering a particular item correctly given the proficiency level of an examinee using the following equation:

$$\text{Probability} = \exp(\text{proficiency} - \text{difficulty})/(1 + \exp(-(\text{proficiency} - \text{difficulty})))$$

where

Exp is the Exponential Function; $e = 2.71828$.

By applying the above equation, we can give a probabilistic estimation about how likely a particular person is to answer a specific item correctly. As mentioned before, the data and the model do not necessarily fit together. This residual information can help a computer program to further calibrate the estimation until the data and the model converge. In this sense, parameter estimation in Rasch modeling is a form of *residual analysis*.

Information Provided by Rasch Modeling

Item Characteristic Curve (ICC)

From this point on, we give proficiency a special name: *Theta*, which is usually denoted by the Greek symbol θ. Rasch modeling is characterized by its simplicity, meaning that only one parameter is needed to construct the ICC. This parameter is called the *B parameter*, also known as the *difficulty parameter* or the *threshold*

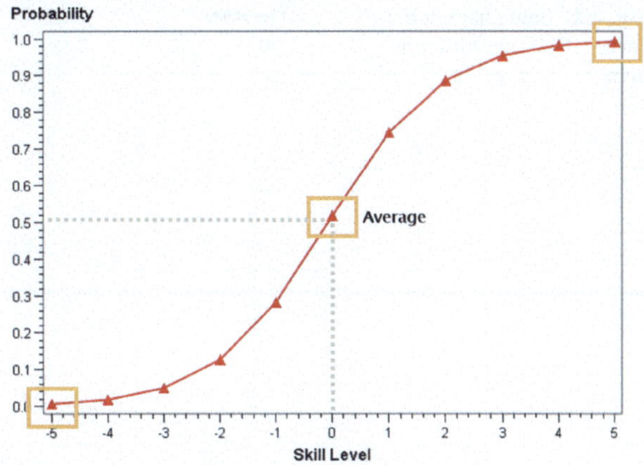

Fig. 4.1 Item characteristic curve (ICC) of an average item

parameter. This value tells us how easy or how difficult an item is and can be utilized to model the response pattern of a particular item, using the following equation:

$$\text{Probability} = \exp(\text{proficiency} - \text{difficulty})/(1 + \exp(-(\text{theta} - \text{difficulty})))$$

After the probabilities of giving the correct answer across different levels of θ are obtained, the relationship between the probabilities and θ can be presented as an Item Characteristic Curve (ICC), as shown in Fig. 4.1.

In Fig. 4.1, the x-axis is the theoretical θ (proficiency) level, ranging from -5 to $+5$. Please keep in mind that this graph represents theoretical modeling rather than empirical data. To be specific, there may not be examinees who are deficient or proficient enough to reach a level of -5 or $+5$. Nevertheless, in order to study the "performance" of an item, we are interested in knowing—for a person whose θ *is* $+5$, what the probability of giving a correct answer might be. Figure 4.1 shows a near-ideal case. The ICC indicates that when θ is zero (i.e. average), the probability of answering the item correctly is almost 0.5. When θ is -5, the probability is almost zero. When θ is $+5$, the probability increases to 0.99.

Figure 4.2 shows the ICC of a difficult item. When the skill level of a student is average, the probability of scoring this item correctly is as low as 0.1. If θ is -5, there is no chance of scoring this item correctly. Figure 4.3 depicts the opposite scenario, in which an average student ($\theta = 0$) has a 95% chance of answering the question correctly, whereas an unprepared student ($\theta = -5$) has a 10% chance.

Item Information Function and Test Information Function

In Fig. 4.1, when the θ is 0 (average), the probability of obtaining the right answer is 0.5. When the θ is 5, the probability is 1; when the θ is -5, the probability is 0. The last two cases raise the problem of missing information. To illustrate—if

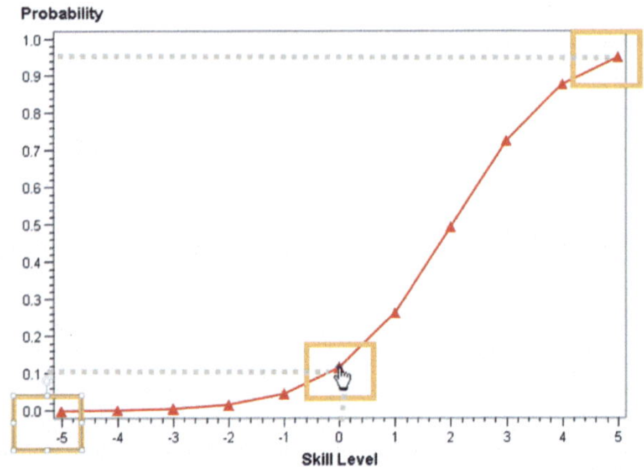

Fig. 4.2 Item characteristic curve (ICC) of a difficult item

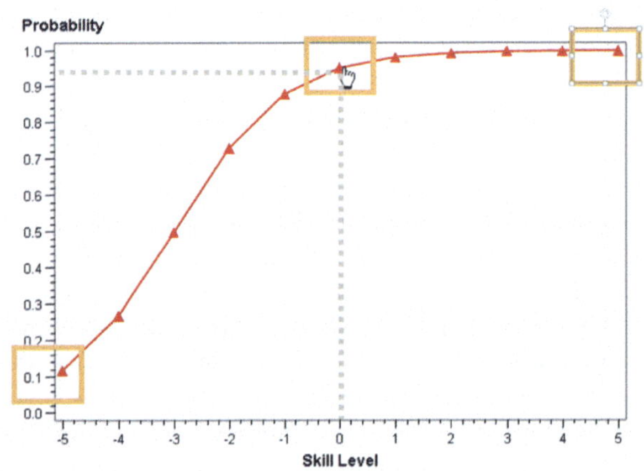

Fig. 4.3 Item characteristic curve (ICC) of an easy item

ten competent students answered the item in this example correctly, it would be impossible to determine which student was more competent than the others, with respect to domain knowledge. Similarly, if ten incompetent students failed the item in this example, it would be impossible to determine which student was less competent than the others, with regard to the subject matter. In other words, we have virtually no information about the θ in relation to the item parameter at the extreme poles, and increasingly less information as the θ moves away from the center toward the two ends. Not surprisingly, if a student was to answer all items in a test correctly, his or her θ could not be estimated. Similarly, if an item was to be answered correctly by all candidates, the difficulty parameter for this item could not be estimated. To summarize, the same problem occurs when all students fail or pass the same item; in either case, the result is that the item parameter cannot be computed.

There is a mathematical way to compute how much information each ICC can yield. This method is called the *Item Information Function (IIF)*. The meaning of

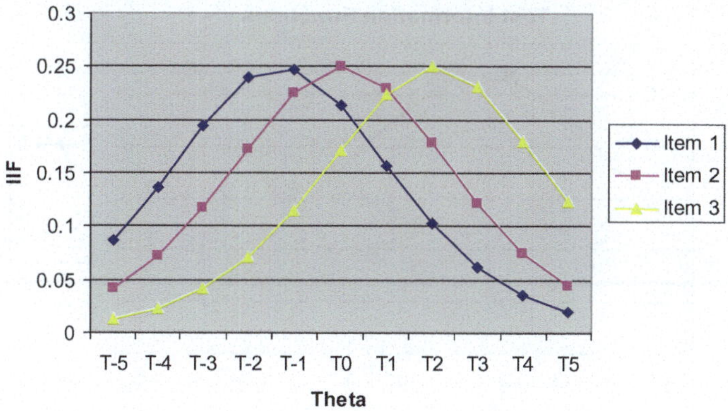

Fig. 4.4 Item information functions

"information" in this term, can be traced back to R. A. Fisher's notion that information is defined as the reciprocal of the precision with which a parameter is estimated. If one can estimate a parameter with precision, one can know more about the value of the parameter than if one had estimated it with less precision. The precision is a function of the variability of the estimates around the parameter value—it is the reciprocal of the variance, and the formula is: Information = 1/(variance).

In a dichotomous situation, the variance is $p(1 - p)$ where $p =$ parameter value. Based on the item parameter values, one can compute and plot the IIFs for the items, as shown in Fig. 4.4.

Obviously, these IIFs differ from each other. In Item 1 (the line with diamonds), the maximum amount of information can be obtained when the θ is -1. When the θ is -5, there is still some amount of information (0.08). But there is virtually no information when the θ is 5. In item 2 (the line with squares), the maximum amount of information is centered at $\theta = 0$, while the amount of information in the lowest θ is the same as that in the highest θ. Item 3 (the line with triangles) is the opposite of Item 1. On this item one might have much information near the higher θ, but information would drop substantively as the θ approached the lower end.

The *Test Information Function (TIF)* is simply the sum of all IIFs in the test. While IIF can provide information on the precision of a particular item parameter, the TIF can provide this information at the exam level. When there is more than one form of the same exam, the TIF can be used to balance the forms. One of the purposes of using alternate test forms is to avoid cheating. For example, consider the written portion of the driver license test. Usually different test-takers receive different sets of questions and it is futile for a test-taker to peek at his/her neighbor. However, it is important to ensure that all alternate forms carry the same values of TIF across all levels of theta, as shown in Fig. 4.5.

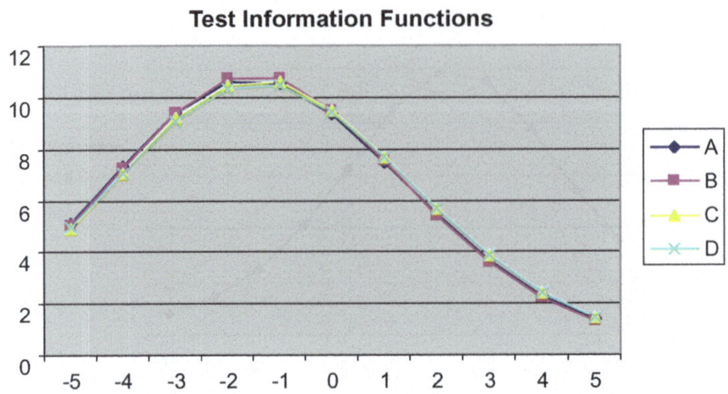

Fig. 4.5 Balancing form A to D using the Test information function (TIF)

Logit and Item-Person Map

One of the beautiful features of the Rasch modeling is that item and examinee attributes can be presented on the same scale (i.e. the *logit* scale). Before explaining the logit, it is essential to explain *odds*. The odds for the item dimension is the ratio of the number of the non-desired events (Q) to the number of the desired events (P). The formula can be expressed as: Q/P. For example, if the pass rate of an item is four of out five candidates, the desired outcome of passing the item would be 4 counts, and the non-desired outcome would be failing the question (1 count). In this case, the odds would be 1:4 = 0.25.

The odds can also be conceptualized as the probability of non-desired outcomes, relative to the probability of a desired outcome. In the above example, the probability of answering the items correctly is 4/5, which is 0.8, and the probability of failing is 1−0.8 = 0.2. Thus, the odds is 0.2/0.8 = 0.25. In other words, the odds can be expressed as $(1 - P)/P$. The relationships between probabilities (p) and odds are expressed in the following equations:

$$\text{Odds} = P/(1 - P) = 0.20/(1\text{–}0.20) = 0.25$$
$$P = \text{Odds}/(1 + \text{Odds}) = 0.25/(1 + 0.25) = 0.20$$

The logit is the natural logarithmic scale of the odds, which is expressed as: Logit = Log(Odds).

In Rasch modeling we can list item and examinee attributes on the same scale. How can one compare apples and oranges? The trick is to convert the values from two measures into a common scale: the logit. One of the problems of scaling is that spacing in one portion of the scale is not necessarily comparable to spacing in another portion of the same scale. To be specific, the difference between two items in terms of difficulty near the midpoint of the test (e.g. 50% and 55%) does not equal the gap between two items at the top (e.g. 95% and 100%) or at the bottom (5% and 10%). Consider weight reduction as a metaphor: It is easier for me to reduce my

Table 4.4 Spacing in the original and the log scale

Original	Subtraction	Unequal spacing	Log transformation of original	Subtraction	Equal spacing
1	N/A		0	N/A	
2	2−1	1	0.30103	0.30103−0	0.30103
5	5−2	3	0.69897	0.69897−0.30103	0.39794
10	10−5	5	1	1−0.69897	0.30103
20	20−10	10	1.30103	1.30103−1	0.30103
50	50−20	30	1.69897	1.69897−1.30103	0.39794

weight from 150 to 125 lbs, but it is much more difficult to trim my weight from 125 to 100 lbs. However, people routinely misperceive that distances in raw scores are comparable. By the same token, spacing in one scale is not comparable to spacing in another scale. Rescaling by logit solves both problems. In short, log transformation can turn scores measured in an ordinal scale into interval-scaled scores (Wright & Stone, 1979). However, it is important to point out that while the concept of logit is applied to both person and item attributes, the computational method for person and item metrics are slightly different. For persons, the odds for persons is calculated as $P/(1 - P)$ whereas for items it is $(1 - P)/P$. In the logit scale, the original spacing is compressed. As a result, equal intervals can be found on the logit scale, as shown in Table 4.4.

The item difficulty parameter and the examinee theta are expressed in the logit scale, and their relationships are presented in the *Item-Person Map* (IPM), also known as the *dual plot* or *Wright's map*, in which both types of information can be evaluated simultaneously. Figure 4.6 is a typical example of IPM. In Fig. 4.6, observations on the left hand side are examinee ability whereas those on the right hand side are item parameter values. This IPM can tell us the "big picture" of both items and students. The examinees on the upper right are said to be "better" or "smarter" than the items on the lower left, which means that those easier items are not difficult enough to challenge those highly proficient students. On the other hand, the items on the upper left outsmart examinees on the lower right, which implies that these tough items are beyond their ability level. In this example, the ability level of the highlighted students on the upper right is 1.986. It is no wonder that these students can "beat" all the items in this exam.

Misfit

In Fig. 4.6, it is obvious that some students are situated at the far end of the distribution. In many statistical analyses we label them as "outliers." In psychometrics there is a specific term for this type of outliers: *Misfit*. It is important to point out that the

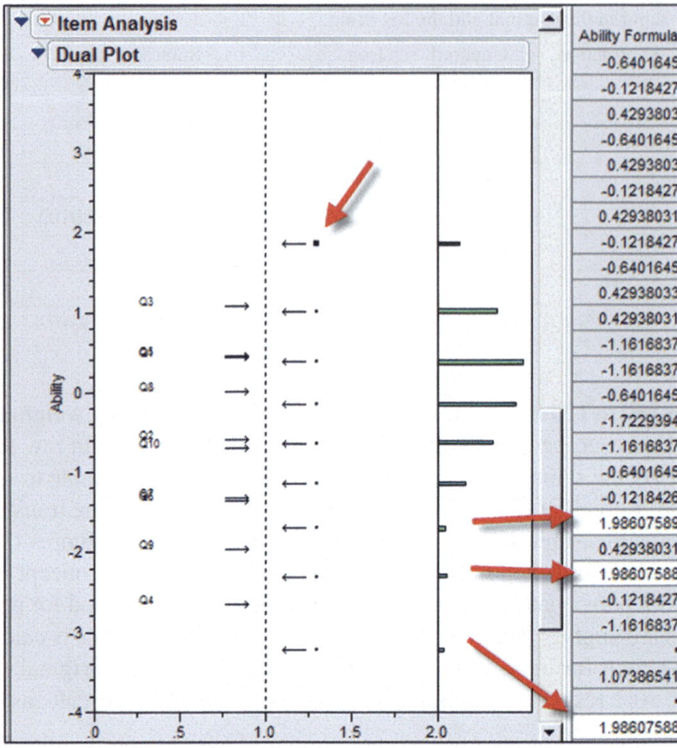

Fig. 4.6 Item-person map

fitness between data and model during the calibration process is different from the misfit indices for item diagnosis. Many studies show that there is no relationship between item difficulty and item fitness (Dodeen, 2004; Reise, 1990). As the name implies, a misfit is an observation that cannot fit into the overall structure of the exam. Misfits can be caused by many reasons. For example, if a test developer attempts to create an exam pertaining to American history but accidentally includes an item about European history in this exam, then it is expected that the response pattern for the item on European history will differ substantially from that of the other items. In the context of classical test theory, this type of item is typically detected either by point-biserial correlation or by factor analysis. In Rasch modeling, this issue is identified by examining misfit indices.

Model Fit

SAS's IRT outputs five global or model fit indices: the log likelihood, Akaike information criteria (AIC), Bayesian information criterion (BIC), likelihood ratio Chi-square G^2 statistic, and Pearson's Chi-square. AIC and BIC are useful when the analyst wants to compare across multiple tests or different sections of the same test in terms of model goodness. It is important to note that neither AIC nor BIC has an absolute cut-off. Rather, these values are used as relative indices in *model comparison*. The principle that underlies both AIC and BIC is in alignment with Ockham's razor: Given the equality of all other conditions, the simplest model tends to be the best; and simplicity is a function of the number of adjustable parameters. Thus, a smaller AIC or BIC suggests a better model. However, Cole (2019) argued that when there are only a few items in the test, these overall model fit statistics are not suitable for test calibration.

Another way to check model fit is to utilize item fit information, meaning that all individual item fit statistics are taken into account as a whole. This can be accomplished by looking into infit and outfit statistics yielded by Winsteps. In a typical Winsteps output, "IN.ZSTD" and "OUT.ZSTD" stand for "infit standardized residuals" and "outfit standardized residuals." To explain their meanings, regression analysis can be used as a metaphor. In regression a good model is expected to have random residuals. A residual is the discrepancy between the predicted position and the actual data point position. If the residuals form a normal distribution with the mean as zero, with approximately the same number of residuals above and below zero, we can tell that there is no systematic discrepancy. However if the distribution of residuals is skewed, it is likely that there is a systematic bias, and the regression model is invalid. While item parameter estimation, like regression, will not yield an exact match between the model and the data, the distribution of standardized residuals informs us about the goodness or badness of the model fit. The easiest way to examine the model fit is to plot the distributions, as shown Fig. 4.7.

In this example, the fitness of the model is in question because both infit and outfit distributions are skewed. The darkened observations are identified as "misfits." The rule of thumb for using standardized residuals is that a value >2 is considered bad.

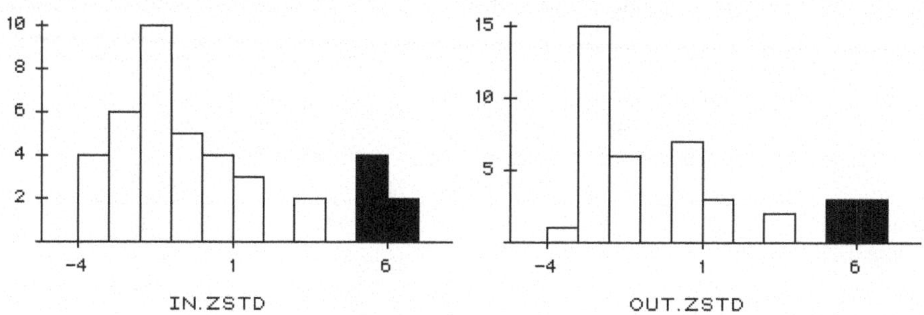

Fig. 4.7 Distributions of infit standardized residuals (left) and outfit standardized residuals (right)

However, Lai, Cella, Chang, Bode, and Heinemann (2003) asserted that standardized residuals are still sample size dependent. When the sample size is large, even small and trivial differences between the expected and the observed may be statistically significant. Because of this, they suggested putting aside standardized residuals altogether.

Item Fit

Model fit takes the overall structure into consideration. If one was to remove some "misfit" items and re-run the Rasch analysis, the distribution would look more normal; however, there would still be items with high residuals. Because of this, the "model fit" approach is not a good way to examine item fit. A better way is to check the mean square. Unlike standardized residuals, the mean square is sample-size independent when data noise is evenly distributed across the population (Linacre, 2014). In a typical Winsteps output, "IN.MSQ" and "OUT.MSQ" stand for "infit mean square" and "outfit mean square." "Mean square" is the Chi-square statistics divided by the degrees of freedom (*df*), or the mean of the squared residuals (Bond & Fox, 2015).

Table 4.5 is a crosstab 2 × 3 table showing the number of correct and incorrect answers to an item categorized by the skill level of test takers. At first glance this item seems to be problematic because while only 10 skilled test-takers were able to answer this item correctly, 15 less skilled test-takers answered the question correctly. Does this mean that the item is a misfit? To answer this question, the algorithm performs a Chi-square analysis. If the Chi-square statistic is statistically significant, meaning that the discrepancy between the expected cell count and the actual cell count is very large, then it indicates that the item might be a misfit.

It is important to keep in mind that the above illustration is over-simplified. In the actual computation of misfit, examinees are not typically divided into only three groups; rather, more levels should be used. There is no common consent about the optimal number of intervals. Yen (1981) suggested using 10 grouping intervals. It is important to point out that the number of levels is tied to the degrees of freedom, which affects the significance of a Chi-square test. The degrees of freedom for a Chi-square test is obtained by (the number of rows) × (the number of columns). Whether

Table 4.5 2 × 3 table of answer and skill level

	More skilled (theta > 0.5)	Average (theta between −0.5 and +0.5)	Less skilled (theta < −0.5)	Row total
Answer correctly (1)	**10**	5	**15**	30
Answer incorrectly (0)	5	10	5	20
Column total	15	15	20	Grand total: 50

the Chi-square is significant or not highly depends on the degrees of freedom and the number of rows/columns (the number of levels chosen by the software package). Hence, to generate a sample-free fit index, the mean-square (i.e. the Chi-square divided by the degrees of freedom) is reported.

Infit and Outfit

The infit mean-square is the Chi-square/degrees of freedom with weighting, in which a constant is put into the algorithms to indicate how much certain observations are taken into account. As mentioned before, in the actual computation of misfit there may be many groups of examinees partitioned by their skill level, but usually there are just a few observations near the two ends of the distribution. Do we care much about the test takers at the two extreme ends? If not, then we should assign more weight to examinees near the middle during the Chi-square computation (see Fig. 4.8). The outfit mean square is the converse of its infit counterpart: unweighted Chi-square/df. The meanings of "infit" and "outfit" are the same in the context of standardized residuals. Another way of conceptualizing "infit mean square" is to view it as the ratio between observed and predicted variance. For example, when infit mean square is 1, the observed variance is exactly the same as the predicted variance. When it is 1.3, it means that the item has 30% more unexpected variance than the model predicted (Lai et al., 2003).

The objective of computing item fit indices is to spot misfits. Is there a particular cutoff to demarcate misfits and non-misifts? The following is a summary of

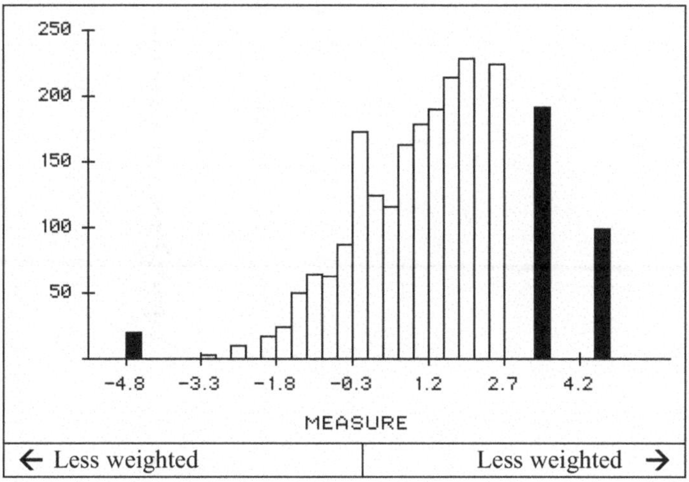

Fig. 4.8 Distribution of examinees' skill level

how different levels of mean-square value should be interpreted (Linacre, 2017) (Table 4.6).

Many psychometricians do not recommend setting a fixed cut-off (Wang & Chen, 2005). An alternate practice is to check all mean squares visually. Consider the example shown in Fig. 4.9. None of the mean squares displayed in the dot plot is above 1.5 by looking at the numbers alone, we may conclude that there is no misfitted items in this example. However, by definition, a misfit is an item whose behavior does not conform to the overall pattern of items, and it is obvious from looking at the

Table 4.6 Interpretation of different levels of mean-square values

Mean-square value	Implications for measurement
>2.0	Distorts or degrades the measurement system. Can be caused by only one or a few observations. By removing them it might bring low mean-squares into the productive range
1.51–2.0	Unproductive for construction of measurement, but not degrading
0.5–1.5	Productive for measurement
<0.5	Less productive for measurement, but not degrading. May produce misleadingly high reliability and separation coefficients

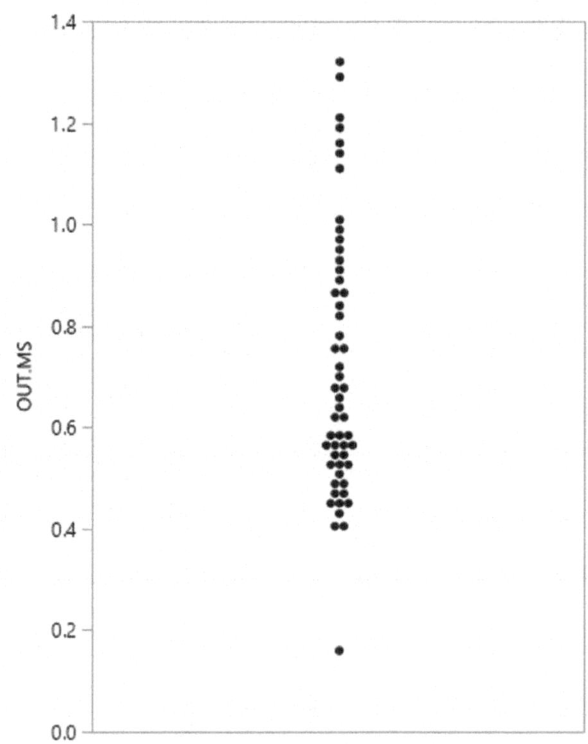

Fig. 4.9 Dot plot of outfit mean squares

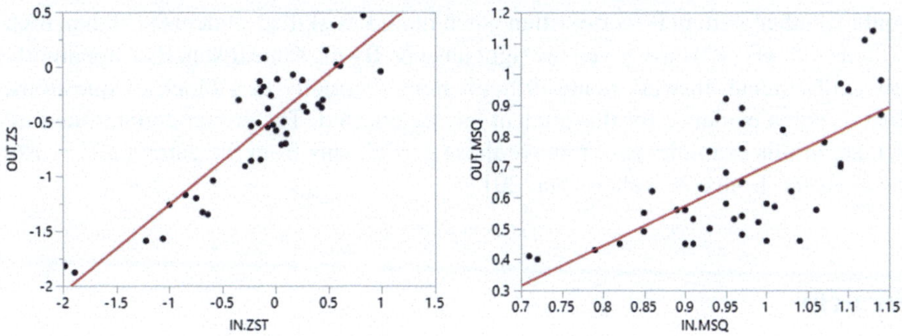

Fig. 4.10 Scatterplot of the infit and outfit statistics

pattern of the data that one particular item departs from the others. As such, further scrutiny for this potential misfit is strongly recommended.

According to Winsteps and Rasch Measurement Software (2010), if the mean square values are less than 1.0, the observations might be too predictable due to redundancy or model overfit. Nevertheless, high mean squares are a much greater threat to validity than are low mean squares. As such, it is advisable to focus on items with high mean squares while conducting misfit diagnosis (Bond & Fox, 2015; Bonne, Staver, & Yale, 2014).

A common question to ask may be whether these misfit indices agree with each other all the time, and which one we should trust when they differ from one another. Infit is a weighted method while outfit is unweighted. Because some difference will naturally occur, the question to consider is not whether items are different from one another. Rather, the key questions are: (1) To what degree do items differ from one another? (2) Do differences lead to contradictory conclusions regarding the fitness of certain items? Checking the correspondence between infit and outfit can be done by a scatterplot and Pearson's *r*. Figure 4.10 shows that in this example there is a fairly good degree of agreement between infit and outfit statistics.

Person Fit

As mentioned before, a Rasch output contains two clusters of information: a person's theta and item parameters. In the former the skill level of the examinees is estimated, whereas in the latter the item attributes are estimated. The preceding illustration uses the item parameter output only, but a person's theta (θ) output may also be analyzed, using the same four types of misfit indices. It is crucial to point out that misfits among person thetas are not just outliers, which represent over-achievers who obtained extremely high scores or under-achievers who obtained extremely low scores. Instead, misfits among person thetas represent people who have an estimated ability level that does not fit into the overall pattern. In the example of item misfit, we doubt whether an item is well-written when more low skilled students (15) than high skilled students (10) have given the right answer. By the same token, if an apparently low-skill student answers many difficult items correctly in a block of questions, there is some evidence for this student having cheated. The proper countermeasure to take, in this example, is to remove these participants from the dataset and re-run the analysis (Bonne & Noltemeyer, 2017).

Strategy

Taking all of the above into consideration, the strategy for examining the fitness of a test for diagnosis purposes is summarized as follows:

1. Evaluate the person fit to remove suspicious examinees. Use outfit mean squares, because when you encounter an unknown situation, it is better not to perform any weighting on any observation. If the sample size is large (e.g. >1,000), removing a few subjects is unlikely to make a difference. However, if a large chunk of person misfits must be deleted, it is advisable to re-compute the Rasch model.
2. If there are alternate forms or multiple sections in the same test, compare across these forms or sections by checking their AIC and BIC. If there is only one test, evaluate the overall model fit by first checking the outfit standardized residuals and second checking the infit standardized residuals. Outfit is more inclusive, in the sense that every observation counts. Create a scatterplot to see whether the infit and outfit model fit indices agree with one another. If there is a discrepancy, determining whether or not to trust the infit or outfit will depend on what your goal is. If the target audience of the test consists of examinees with average skill-level, an infit model index may be more informative.
3. If the model fit is satisfactory, examine the item fit in the same order with outfit first and infit second. Rather than using a fixed cut-off for mean square, visualize the mean square indices in a dot plot to detect whether any items significantly depart from the majority, and also use a scatterplot to check the correspondence between infit and outfit.
4. When item misfits are found, one should check the key, the distracters, and the question content first. Farish (1984) found that if misfits are mechanically deleted just based on chi-square values or standardized residuals, this improves the fit of the test as a whole, but worsens the fit of the remaining items.

Specialized Models

Partial Credit Model

Traditionally Rasch modeling was employed for dichotomous data only. Later it was extended to polytomous data. For example, if essay-type questions are included in a test, then students can earn partial credits. The appropriate Rasch model for this type of data is the *partial credit model* (PCM) (Masters, 1982). In a PCM the analyst can examine the *step function* for diagnosis. For example, if an item is worth 4 points, there will be four steps:

Step 1: from 0 to 1
Step 2: from 1 to 2
Step 3: from 2 to 3
Step 4: from 3 to 4

Between each level, there is a step difficulty estimate, also known as the *step threshold*, which is similar to the item difficulty parameter (e.g. How hard is it to reach 1 point from 0? How hard is it to reach 2 points from 1? …etc.). Because the difficulty estimate uses logit, distances between steps are comparable. For instance, if step3–step2 = 0.1 and step2–step1 = 0.1, then the two numbers are equal. Table 4.7 shows an example of the step function.

If the number of the step difficulty is around zero, this step is considered average. If the number is above 0.1, this step is considered hard. If the number is below zero, this step is considered easy. In this example, going from score = 0 to score = 1 is relatively challenging (Step difficulty = 0.6), reaching the middle step (score = 2) is easy (Step difficulty = −0.4), reaching the next level (score = 3) is even easier (Step difficulty = 0), but reaching the top (Score = 4) becomes very difficult (Step difficulty = 0.9). For example, for a Chinese student who doesn't know anything about English, it will be challenging for him/her to start afresh , with no prior knowledge of English

Table 4.7 Step function

Score	Frequency	Step difficulty	Step	Decision
0	50	NA	NA	NA
1	30	0.6	1. Difficulty of reaching 1 point from 0	Relatively difficult
2	40	−0.4	2. Difficulty of reaching 2 points from 1	Relatively easy
3	40	0	3. Difficulty of reaching 3 points from 2	Average
4	5	0.9	4. Difficulty of reaching 4 points from 3	Relatively difficult

grammar. After he/she has built up a foundational knowledge in English, it will be easier to gradually improve his/her proficiency, but for him/her to master the English language at the level of Shakespeare, it would be very difficult.

Rating Scale Model

If the data are collected from a Likert-scaled survey, the most appropriate model is the *rating scale model* (RSM) (Andrich, 1978). Interestingly, although originally Andrich intended to develop RSM for evaluating written essays, like PCM it is now routinely used for Likert-scaled data (Bond & Fox, 2015). When a 4-point Likert scale is used, then "strongly agree" is treated as 4 points whereas the numeric value "1" is assigned to "strong disagree." This approach models the response outcome as the probability of endorsing a statement. Figure 4.11 is an output by SAS's graded response modeling. In each graph there are five ICCs corresponding to the numeric values from "strongly agree" to "strongly disagree." In this case the θ represented by the X-axis (-4 to 4) is the overall endorsement of the idea or the construct. For example, if the survey aims to measure the construct "computer anxiety" and Question 1 is: "I am so afraid of computers I avoid using them," it is not surprising to

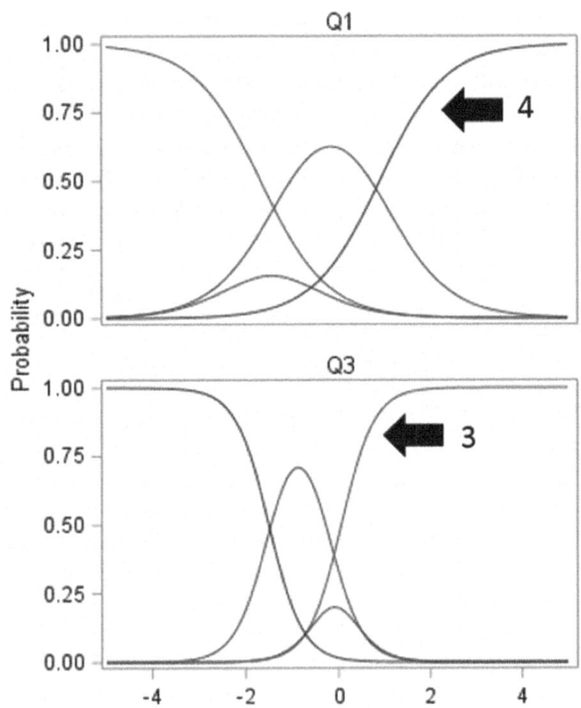

Fig. 4.11 ICCs in the graded response model

see that students who are very anxious about computing has a higher probability of choosing “strongly agree” (4). Question 3 is “I am afraid that I will make mistakes when I use my computer.” Obviously, this statement shows a lower fear of computers (the respondent still uses computers) than does Statement 1 (The respondent does not use computers at all), and thus it is more probable for students to choose “agree” (3) than “strongly agree” (4). However, in CTT responses from both questions would contribute equal points to the computer anxiety score. This example shows that Rasch modeling is also beneficial to survey analysis (Bond & Fox, 2015).

In SAS there is no direct specification of the partial credit model. PCM is computed through the generalized partial credit model (Muraki, 1992), in which the discrimination parameter is set to 1 for all items. In Winsteps both RSM and PCM are under the rating-scale family of models and therefore for both models the syntax is “Models = R.” Moreover, the average of the item threshold parameters is constrained to 0.

Debate Between Rasch and IRT

Rasch modeling has a close cousin, namely, item response theory (IRT). Although IRT and Rasch modeling arose from two independent movements in measurement, both inherited a common intellectual heritage: Thurstone’s theory of mental ability test in the 1920s (Thurstone, 1927, 1928). Thurstone realized that the difficulty level of a test item depends on the age or the readiness of the test-taker. Specifically, older children are more capable of answering challenging items than their younger peers. For this reason it would be absurd to assert that a 15-year old child who scored a ‘110’ on an IQ test is better than his 10-year old peer who earned 100 points on the same test. Hence, Thurstone envisioned a measurement tool that could account for both item difficulty and subject ability/readiness. Bock (1997), one of the founders of the IRT school, explicitly stated that his work aimed to actualize the vision of Thurstone. By the same token, Wright (1997), one of the major advocates of Rasch modeling, cited Thurstone’s work in order to support claims regarding the characteristics of Rasch modeling (e.g. uni-dimensionality and objective measurement).

The debate over Rasch versus IRT has been ongoing for several decades (Andrich, 2004). This debate reflects a ubiquitous tension between parsimonies and fitness in almost all statistical procedures. Since the real world is essentially “messy,” any model attempting to accurately reflect or fit “reality” will likely end up looking very complicated. As an alternative, some researchers seek to build elegant and simple models that have more practical implications. Simply put, IRT leans toward fitness whereas Rasch leans toward simplicity. To be more specific, IRT modelers might use up to three parameters. When the data cannot fit into a one-parameter model, additional parameters (such as the discrimination parameter (a) and the guessing parameter (g)) are inserted into the model in order to accommodate the data. Rasch modelers, however, stick with only one parameter (the item difficulty parameter), dismissing the unfit portion of their data as random variation. When the discrepancy between the data and the model exceeds minor random variation, Rasch modelers believe that something went wrong with the data and that modifying the data collection approach might produce a more plausible interpretation than changing the model (Andrich, 2011). In other words, IRT is said to be *descriptive* in nature because it aims to fit the model to the data. In contrast, Rasch is *prescriptive* for it emphasizes fitting the data into the model. Nevertheless, despite their diverse views on model-data fitness, both IRT and Rasch modeling have advantages over CTT.

Using additional parameters has been a controversial issue. Fisher (2010) argued that the discrimination parameter in IRT leads to the paradox that one item can be more and less difficult than another item at the same time. This phenomenon known as the *Lord's paradox*. In the perspective of Rasch modeling, this outcome should not be considered a proper model because construct validity requires that the item difficulty hierarchy is invariant across person abilities. Further, Wright (1995) asserted that the information provided by the discrimination parameter is equivalent to the Rasch INFIT statistics and therefore Rasch modeling alone is sufficient. When guessing occurs in an item, in Wright's view (1995) this item is poorly written and the appropriate remedy is to remove the item.

Historically, Rasch modeling has gained more popularity than IRT, because of its low demand in sample size, relative ease of use, and simple interpretation (Lacourly, Martin, Silva, & Uribe, 2018). If Rasch modeling is properly applied, a short test built by Rasch analysis can provide more reliable assessments than a longer test made by other methods (Embretson & Hershberger, 1999). Prior research showed that even as few as 30 items administered to 30 participants can produce valid assessment (Linacre, 1994). On the other hand, psychometricians warned that complex IRT models might result in variations of scoring. In some peculiar situations three-parameter IRT models might fail to properly estimate the likelihood functions (Hambleton, Swaminathan, & Rogers, 1991).

There is no clear-cut answer to this debate. Whichever model is more suitable depends on the context and the desired emphasis. For instance, many educators agree that assessment tests are often multidimensional rather than unidimensional, which necessitates multidimensional IRT models (Cai, Seung, & Hansen, 2011; Han & Paek, 2014; Hartig & Hohler, 2009). Further, 3-parameter modeling is applicable to educational settings, but not to health-related outcomes, because it is hard to imagine how guessing could be involved in self- or clinician-reported health measures (Kean, Brodke, Biber, & Gross, 2018). Nonetheless, when standardization is a priority (e.g. in an educational setting), Rasch modeling is preferred, because its clarity facilitates quick yet informed decisions.

Software Applications for Rasch Modeling

There are many software applications for Rasch modeling on the market (Rasch.org, 2019), but it is beyond the scope of this chapter to discuss all of them. This chapter only highlights two of these applications: SAS and Winsteps. SAS is by far the world's most popular statistical package; needless to say, it is convenient for SAS users to utilize their existing resources for assessment projects. In addition, SAS offers academicians free access to the University Edition, which can be run across Windows and Mac OS through a Web browser. Winsteps has its merits, too. Before SAS Institute released PROC IRT, the source code of Winsteps was considered better-built than its rivals (Linacre, 2004); therefore it is highly endorsed by many psychometricians. The differences between SAS and Winsteps are discussed as follows.

As its name implies, PROC IRT includes both IRT and Rasch modeling, based on the assumption that Rasch is a special case of a one-parameter IRT model, whereas Winsteps is exclusively designed for Rasch modeling. PROC IRT in SAS and Winsteps use different estimation methods. Specifically, SAS uses marginal maximum likelihood estimation (MMLE) with the assumption that the item difficulty parameter follows a normal distribution, while Winsteps uses joint maximum likelihood estimation (JMLE). In SAS there are no limitations on sample size and the number of items, as long as the microprocessor and the RAM can handle them. In Winsteps the sample size cannot exceed 1 million and the maximum number of items is 6,000.

Both SAS and Winsteps have unique features that are not available in other software packages. For example, in CTT, dimensionality of a test is typically examined by factor analysis whereas unidimensionality is assumed in Rasch modeling (Yu, Osborn-Popp, DiGangi, & Jannasch-Pennell, 2007). In SAS's PROC IRT an analyst can concurrently examine factor structure and item characteristics (Yu, Douglas, & Yu, 2015). In Winsteps good items developed in previous psychometric analysis can be inserted into a new test for *item anchoring*. By doing so all other item attributes would be calibrated around the anchors. Further, these item anchors can be put into alternate test forms so that multiple forms can be compared and equated based on a common set of anchors (Yu & Osborn-Popp, 2005).

In a simulation study, Cole (2019) found that there was virtually no difference between SAS and Winsteps for identifying item parameters (in data sets consisting of all dichotomous or all polytomous items, and in terms of average root mean squared errors (RMSE) and bias). Taking all of the above into consideration, the choice of which software application should be used depends on the sample size, the number of items, availability of resources, and the research goals, rather than upon accuracy of the output. SAS and Winsteps codes for different modeling techniques are shown in the appendix.

Conclusion

Rasch modeling is a powerful assessment tool for overcoming circular dependency observed in classical test theory. Based on the assumptions of uni-dimensionality and conditional independence, Rasch is capable of delivering objective measurement in various settings. Rasch analysis calibrates item difficulty and person ability simultaneously, in the fashion of residual analysis. After the data and the model converge by calibration, Rasch modelers can visualize the probability of correctly answering a question or endorsing a statement through item characteristic curves

(ICC). In addition, the test designer can utilize item information functions (IIF) and test information function (TIF) to create alternate forms. One of the wonderful features of Rasch analysis is that the item and person attributes are put on the same scale (i.e. logit) and thus an analyst can examine whether a student and an exam can "match" each other, using the item-person map (IPM). Like every other analytical tool, diagnosis is an essential step in Rasch analysis. All Rasch modeling software packages, including SAS and Winsteps, provide users with both model-level and item-level fit indices. In addition to the Rasch dichotomous model, both SAS and Winsteps can run specialized models, such as the partial credit model (PCM) and the graded response model (GSM). Readers are encouraged to explore the functionality of these model by experimenting with the source codes at the appendix. Last but not least, the debate over Rasch vs. IRT has been ongoing for decades and the issue remains inconclusive. Different problems and different settings necessitate different solutions. It is advisable to keep an open mind to the strengths and the limitations associated with various modeling techniques.

Appendix

SAS syntax

```
ods graphics on;
proc irt data=dataset_name out=output_file_name itemfit plots=all;
      var i1-i50;
      model i1-i50 /resfunc=rasch;
      /* resfunc stands for response function. For generalized partial credit model, use
      resfunc=gpc; for graded response model, use resfunc=graded; */
run;
```

Winsteps codes: For Rasch Dichotomous Model

```
&INST
Batch = yes; allow the program to run in a command prompt
NI = 50; Number of items
ITEM1 = 6; Position of where the first item begins.
CODES = 01; Valid data, 1 = 1 point, 0 = no point
key = 11111111111111111111111111111111111111111111111111
UPMEAN = 0; Set the mean (center) of student ability to 0.
NAME1 = 1; The first position of the subject ID.
NAMELEN = 4; Length of the subject ID
; output file names
IFILE = output.que; que is the question file for item parameters.
```

PFILE = output.per; per is the person file for person theta.
; Prefix for person and item. They are arbitrary.
PERSON = S
ITEM = I
DATA = data.txt; Name of the raw data file
&END

For partial credit model or rating scale model

&INST
Batch = yes; allow the program to run in a command prompt
NI = 50; Number of items
ITEM1 = 6; Position of where the first item begins.
CODES = 01234; Valid data, 1 = 1 point, 4 = 4 points
key1 = **44
key2 = **33
key3 = **22
key4 = 11111111111111111111111111111111111111111111111111
KEYSCR = 4321; the answers are compared against the above key in the order of 4, 3, 2, 1. "*": skip it and go to the next key.
ISGROUPS = 0; If ISGROUPS = 0 then the PCM is used. If ISGROUPS is more than 0, then the grouped RSM is used.
MODELS = R; Both PCM and RSM are run under the family of rating scale models
UPMEAN = 0; Set the mean (center) of examinees' ability to 0.
NAME1 = 1; The first position of the subject ID.
NAMELEN = 4; Length of subject ID
; output file names
SFILE = output.sf; sf is the step function file for partial-credit or rating-scale.
IFILE = output.que; que is the question file for item parameters.
PFILE = output.per; per is the person file for person theta.
; Prefix for person and item. They are arbitrary.
PERSON = S
ITEM = I
DATA = data.txt; Name of the raw data file
&END

References

Andrich, D. (1978). A rating scale formulation for ordered response categories. *Psychometrika, 43,* 561–573.

Andrich, D. (2004). Controversy and the Rasch model: A characteristic of incompatible paradigms? *Medical Care, 42,* 7–16. https://doi.org/10.1097/01.mlr.0000103528.48582.7c.

Andrich, D. (2011). *Rasch models for measurement.* Thousand Oaks, CA: Sage.

Baghaei, P., Shoahosseini, R., & Branch, M. (2019). A note on the Rasch model and the instrument-based account of validity. *Rasch Measurement Transactions, 32,* 1705–1708.

Bock, R. D. (1997). A brief history of item response theory. *Educational Measurement: Issues and Practice, 16*(4), 21–33. https://doi.org/10.1111/j.1745-3992.1997.tb00605.x.

Bond, T., & Fox, C. M. (2015). *Applying the Rasch model: Fundamental measurement in the human sciences* (3rd ed.). New York, NY: Routledge.

Bonne, W. J., & Noltemeyer, A. (2017). Rasch analysis: A primer for school psychology researchers and practitioners. *Cogent Education, 4*(1) Article 1416898. https://doi.org/10.1080/2331186X.2017.1416898.

Boone, W. J., Staver, J. R., & Yale, M. S. (2014). *Rasch analysis in the human sciences*. Dordrecht: Springer. https://doi.org/10.1007/978-94-007-6857-4.

Borsboom, D., & Markus, K. A. (2013). Truth and evidence in validity theory. *Journal of Educational Measurement, 50,* 110–114.

Cai, L., Seung, J., & Hansen, M. (2011). Generalized full-information item bifactor analysis. *Psychological Methods, 16,* 221–248.

Cole, K. (2019). Rasch model calibrations with SAS PROC IRT and WINSTEPS. *Journal of Applied Measurements, 20,* 1–45.

Dodeen, H. (2004). The relationship between item parameters and item fit. *Journal of Educational Measurement, 41,* 261–270.

Embretson, S. E., & Hershberger, S. L. (Eds.). (1999). *The new rules of measurement. What every psychologists and educator should know*. Mahwah, NJ: Lawrence, Erlbaum.

Farish, S. (1984). *Investigating item stability* (ERIC document Reproduction Service No. ED262046).

Fisher, W. (2010). IRT and confusion about Rasch measurement. *Rasch Measurement Transactions, 24,* 1288.

Guttman, L. A. (1944). A basis for scaling qualitative data. *American Sociological Review, 91,* 139–150.

Hambleton, R. K., Swaminathan, H., & Rogers, H. J. (1991). *Fundamentals of item response theory*. Newbury Park, CA: Sage.

Han, & Paek, I. (2014). A review of commercial software packages for multidimensional IRT modeling. *Applied Psychological Measurement, 38,* 486–498.

Hartig, J., & Hohler, J. (2009). Multidimensional IRT models for the assessment of competencies. *Studies in Educational Evaluation, 35,* 57–63.

Hutchinson, S. R., & Lovell, C. D. (2004). A review of methodological characteristics of research published in key journals in higher education: Implications for Graduate research training. *Research in Higher Education, 45,* 383–403.

Kean, J., Brodke, D. S., Biber, J., & Gross, P. (2018). An introduction to item response theory and Rasch analysis of the eating assessment tool (EAT-10). *Brain Impairment, 19,* 91–102. https://doi.org/10.1017/BrImp.2017.31.

Lacourly, N., Martin, J., Silva, M., & Uribe, P. (2018). IRT scoring and the principle of consistent order. Retrieved from https://arxiv.org/abs/1805.00874.

Lai, J., Cella, D., Chang, C. H., Bode, R. K., & Heinemann, A. W. (2003). Item banking to improve, shorten, and computerize self-reported fatigue: An illustration of steps to create a core item bank from the FACIT-Fatigue scale. *Quality of Life Research, 12,* 485–501.

Linacre, J. M. (1994). Sample size and item calibration [or person measure] stability. *Rasch Measurement Transactions, 7*(4), 328. Retrieved from https://www.rasch.org/rmt/rmt74m.htm.

Linacre, J. M. (2004). From Microscale to Winsteps: 20 years of Rasch software development. *Rasch Measurement Transactions, 17,* 958.

Linacre, J. M. (2014, June). Infit mean square or infit zstd? *Research Measurement Forum*. Retrieved from http://raschforum.boards.net/thread/94/infit-mean-square-zstd.

Linacre, J. M. (2017). Teaching Rasch measurement. *Rasch Measurement Transactions, 31,* 1630–1631.

Masters, G. N. (1982). A Rasch model for partial credit scoring. *Psychometrika, 47,* 149–174.

Muraki, E. (1992). A generalized partial credit model: Application of an EM algorithm. *Applied Psychological Measurement, 16,* 159–176.

Organization for Economic Co-operation and Development [OECD]. (2013a). PISA 2012 assessment and analytical framework: Mathematics, reading, science, problem solving, and financial literacy. Retrieved from http://www.oecd.org/pisa/pisaproducts/PISA%202012%20framework%20e-book_final.pdf.

Organization for Economic Co-operation and Development [OECD]. (2013b). Technical report of the survey of adult skills (PIAAC). Retrieved from https://www.oecd.org/skills/piaac/_Technical%20Report_17OCT13.pdf.

Rasch, G. (1980). *Probabilistic models for some intelligence and attainment tests*. Chicago, IL: University of Chicago Press.

Rasch.org. (2019). Rasch measurement analysis software directory. Retrieved from https://www.rasch.org/software.htm.

Reise, S. (1990). A comparison of item and person fit methods of assessing model fit in IRT. *Applied Psychological Measurement, 42,* 127–137.

SAS Institute. (2018). *SAS 9.4 [Computer software]*. Cary, NC: SAS Institute.

Spearman, C. (1904). General intelligence: Objectively determined and measured. *American Journal of Psychology, 15,* 201–293.

Thurstone, L. L. (1927). A Law of comparative judgment. *Psychological Review, 34,* 273–286.

Thurstone, L. L. (1928). Attitudes can be measured. *American Journal of Sociology, 33,* 529–554.

Wang, W. C., & Chen, C. T. (2005). Item parameter recovery, standard error estimates, and fit statistics of the Winsteps program for the family of Rasch models. *Educational and Psychological Measurement, 65,* 376–404.

Winsteps & Rasch measurement Software. (2010). Misfit diagnosis: Infit outfit mean-square standardized. Retrieved from https://www.winsteps.com/winman/misfitdiagnosis.htm.

Winsteps & Rasch measurement Software. (2019). *Winsteps 4.4. [Computer software]*. Chicago, IL: Winsteps and Rasch measurement Software.

Wright, B. D. (1992). The international objective measurement workshops: Past and future. In M. Wilson (Ed.), *Objective measurement: Theory into practice* (Vol. 1, pp. 9–28). Norwood, NJ: Ablex Publishing.

Wright, B. D. (1995). 3PL IRT or Rasch? *Rasch Measurement Transactions, 9,* 408.

Wright, B. D. (1997). A history of social science measurement. *Educational Measurement: Issues and Practice, 16*(4), 33–45, 52. http://dx.doi.org/10.1111/j.1745-3992.1997.tb00606.x.

Wright, B. D., & Stone, M. (1979). *Best test design*. Chicago, IL: Mesa Press.

Wu, M. (2004). Plausible values. *Rasch Measurement Transactions, 18,* 976–978.

Wu, M. (2005). The role of plausible values in large-scale surveys. *Studies in Educational Evaluation, 31,* 114–128.

Yen, W. M. (1981). Using simulation results to choose a latent trait model. *Applied Psychological Measurement, 5,* 245–262.

Yu, C. H., Douglas, S., & Yu, A., (2015, September). *Illustrating preliminary procedures for multi-dimensional item response theory*. Poster presented at Western Users of SAS Software Conference, San Diego, CA.

Yu, C. H., & Osborn-Popp, S. (2005). Test equating by common items and common subjects: Concepts and applications. *Practical Assessment Research and Evaluation, 10*. Retrieved from http://pareonline.net/pdf/v10n4.pdf.

Yu, C. H., Osborn-Popp, S., DiGangi, S., & Jannasch-Pennell, A. (2007). Assessing unidimensionality: A comparison of Rasch modeling, parallel analysis, and TETRAD. *Practical Assessment, Research and Evaluation, 12*. Retrieved from http://pareonline.net/pdf/v12n14.pdf.

Part II
Rasch Model and Analysis in Education Research

Chapter 5
Re-examining the Utility of the Individualised Classroom Environment Questionnaire (ICEQ) Using the Rasch Model

Francisco Ben

Abstract Attempts have been made to develop tools to assess classroom environment since the late 1960s. These have generated a huge interest and growth in research studies that examined how school classroom environment impact on student learning and achievement in, and attitudes towards, a particular subject. The assessment of classroom learning environments saw the development of several tools that can be used for this purpose. One of them, particularly used by educational researchers in Australia, is Barry Fraser's Individualised Classroom Environment Questionnaire (ICEQ). For years, the ICEQ has been deployed and rigorously validated by its author using statistical methods within the classical test theory (CTT). However, a number of published works have highlighted the shortcomings of the CTT in establishing the reliability and validity of survey instruments as measuring tools in social science and education research. Within the context of the physics classroom in South Australian schools, this chapter reports on the evaluation of the short version of the ICEQ using the Rasch model. Fraser's findings were confirmed indicating that the ICEQ scales exhibited adequate scale independence, although one misfitting item was removed from the preferred classroom ICEQ. This chapter concludes with relevant implications for classroom environment research and teaching practice.

Keywords Individualised classroom environment questionnaire · Classical test theory · Item response theory · Item fit · Rasch rating scale model · Infit · Outfit

Introduction

Learning environments research, particularly classroom environment, has gained the attention of education researchers since the 1960s (see, e.g., Walberg & Anderson, 1968). The assessment of classroom environments involved the development of instruments that included constructs and scales that could be used in a variety of applications within educational settings. Consequently, through these instruments,

F. Ben (✉)
Tabor College of Higher Education, Millswood, SA, Australia
e-mail: FBen@adelaide.tabor.edu.au

M. S. Khine (ed.), *Rasch Measurement*,
https://doi.org/10.1007/978-981-15-1800-3_5

numerous research studies have associated classroom environment with student outcomes. Examples of instruments developed to assess classroom environments include *learning environment inventory* (LEI) (Fraser, Anderson, & Walberg, 1982) and the *classroom environment scale* (CES) (Moos & Tricket, 1974). There is also the *my class inventory* (MCI) (Fisher & Fraser, 1981), the *questionnaire on teacher interaction* (QTI) that originated in The Netherlands, to focus on the nature and quality of interpersonal relationships between the teachers and the students (Wubbels, Brekelmans, & Hooymayers, 1991). Further, an instrument that combined the most salient scales from a range of existing scales has been developed and called as *what is happening in this class* (WIHIC) questionnaire (Fraser, Fisher, & McRobbie, 1996).

In Australia, the *individualised classroom environment questionnaire* (ICEQ) appears to have been used primarily by education researchers who assessed classroom environments. The author of this chapter has used the ICEQ to examine classroom environments in Australian school physics classrooms.

Barry Fraser developed the ICEQ. Like the examples of instruments to assess classroom environments given above, the ICEQ has been deployed in different school contexts, both locally and internationally, and has gone through rigorous validation to ascertain the measurement properties of its scales that were robust. However, it appears that the authors of the different classroom environment scales, including the ICEQ, used statistical approaches classified under the classical test theory (CTT). Recent research studies relating to educational and social science measurement have established shortcomings of the CTT approaches compared to newer techniques found under the umbrella of the item-response theory (IRT). Hence, the ICEQ scales were re-examined using the IRT, particularly the Rasch rating scale model (RSM). This paper reports on the findings of analysing an ICEQ dataset using the Rasch RSM. Brief information about the development of the ICEQ is first presented, followed by previous analytic practices used to examine its psychometric properties. A brief background information about the dataset used is also provided. Analysis of the ICEQ scales using the Rasch RSM is detailed along with the analysis findings. Thus, this paper aims to:

- Add to ICEQ's previous validation findings which were based on some Australian and international samples; and
- To re-examine the ICEQ's measurement properties and, therefore, its utility.

This paper concludes with how the assessment of classroom environments implicates research in this topic, and the teaching practice.

The Individualised Classroom Environment Questionnaire (ICEQ)

Barry Fraser began developing the ICEQ in the 1970s (see Fraser, 1980). This was in the midst of having a few existing instruments used in assessing classroom environments. However, Fraser (1990) had established that many of these existing instruments including the LEI and CES "…are limited in that they exclude dimensions which are important in open or individualised classrooms" (p. 1). Thus, the aim of developing the ICEQ was to fill the voids of the shortcomings of the instruments that were considered to be widely used in assessing classroom environment.

The ICEQ has noteworthy characteristics separating it from other classroom environment questionnaires. First, the ICEQ assesses five constructs that represent different classroom dimensions. These include: *personalisation*, *participation*, *independence*, *investigation*, and *differentiation*. These are important dimensions to consider in examining the extent of students' positive or negative experiences in a classroom environment. Second, the ICEQ has forms to enable assessment of the actual classroom environment as observed by students, and students' preferred classroom environment. Third, the ICEQ can be administered to either teachers or students. Fourth, Fraser designed the ICEQ to permit hand scoring. And fifth, the ICEQ has a short form that can be used to provide a rapid, more economical measure of the classroom environment. However, the long form is generally preferred over the short form for its reliability, as classical test theory recognises that longer scales are more reliable than shorter ones, partly because they more adequately sample the identified construct or behaviour (Alagumalai & Curtis, 2005).

The following is Fraser's (1990, p. 5) description of each of the five scales in his ICEQ:

- *Personalisation*—emphasis on opportunities for individual students to interact with the teacher and on concern for the personal welfare and social growth of the individual.
- *Participation*—extent to which students are encouraged to participate rather than be passive listeners.
- *Independence*—extent to which students are allowed to make decisions and have control over their own learning and behaviour.
- *Investigation*—emphasis on the skills and processes of inquiry and their use in problem solving and investigation.
- *Differentiation*—emphasis on the selective treatment of students on the basis of ability, learning style, interests, and rate of working.

This paper reports on the examination of the short form. This is following the principle of keeping survey questionnaires short and simple to minimise what Roszkowski and Bean (1990) termed as "low response rate", enabling participants to be more genuine or honest about their questionnaire item responses. Hence, it is likely that the short form will be used by more classroom environment researchers. The actual classroom and the preferred classroom short forms each comprise of 25 items covering the five dimensions (i.e., five items for each scale dimension) of the classroom environment.

Each item in the ICEQ shows a classroom experience related statement and five Likert-type response choices, including *almost never*, *seldom*, *sometimes*, *often*, and *very often*. These choices are coded 1, 2, 3, 4, and 5, respectively. Statements are either positively (16 of them) or negatively worded (nine of them). Appendices A and B show item statements for the ICEQ actual and preferred classroom, respectively. Also included in the tables are the item codes used in the validation presented in this paper.

Previous ICEQ Validation

Barry Fraser has comprehensively and rigorously tested the ICEQ scales for a number of years in different contexts using different groups of samples from Australia and overseas since its inception. Internationally, Indonesia, the Netherlands (Fraser, 1990), and the UK (Burden & Fraser, 1993) were among the countries that he visited and used for his ICEQ instrument cross-validation. Information about the ICEQ's short and long form's internal reliability and scale independence was obtained through this cross-validation. For the ICEQ's short form (which is the focus of this paper), Fraser's (1990) validations obtained an alpha coefficient ranging from 0.63 to 0.85, pointing towards "…typically 0.1 smaller than the reliability of the long form" (p. 16). These values, according to Fraser, suggest satisfactory reliability for applications based on class means. For the ICEQ's between scales independence (i.e., correlation between scales), Fraser found the mean correlations to range from 0.13 to 0.36, which is comparable with those of the long form. Fraser (1990) suggested that these values show an adequate level of scale independence which means that the "ICEQ measures distinct although somewhat overlapping aspects of classroom environment" (p. 14). Test–retest reliability coefficients for the five scales (personalisation = 0.78, participation = 0.67, independence = 0.83, investigation = 0.75, and differentiation = 0.78) in the ICEQ were found to be satisfactory according to Fraser (1980). These statistics for the ICEQ short form resulted from the following total number of samples used by Fraser in his studies: actual classroom form = 1083 students and preferred classroom form = 1092 students.

Fraser's (1990) ICEQ handbook outlined how researchers and teachers from several different contexts and countries used the ICEQ for different purposes including:

- Associations between student outcomes and classroom environment;
- Differences between scores of various groups on the ICEQ;
- Evaluation of innovations in classroom individualisation;
- Study of teachers' attitudes to classroom individualisation;
- Person–environment fit studies; and
- Practical attempts to improve classroom environments.

Wheldall, Beaman, and Mok (1999) carried out a study that surveyed (using the ICEQ) 1467 high school students in New South Wales, Australia to measure classroom climate (or classroom environment). Their instrument analysis findings indicated that the ICEQ could be considered a relatively good instrument to measure classroom climate. In their study, Wheldall, Beaman, and Mok have derived intraclass correlations through multilevel variance analysis components models to determine the degree to which ICEQ scores may reasonably measure aspects of classroom climate against individual student attitude. Furthermore, they have added that their analysis results showed that the class variable accounted for large and noteworthy proportions of overall variance in all five ICEQ scales and that subsequent analyses showed that only small and non-significant proportions of variance were attributable to the school variable.

However, it is noteworthy that early classroom environment researchers such as Fraser, Walberg, and Moos have used statistical techniques classified under classical test theory (CTT) to establish the validity and reliability of their instruments. With no intention to undermine these researchers' important works, research has shown that CTT has a number of shortcomings that could adversely affect the results of analysing data to establish measurement reliability and validity (see, e.g., Alagumalai & Curtis, 2005; Piquero, MacIntosh, & Hickman, 2000). Alagumalai and Curtis (2005) asserted that CTT methods have limited effectiveness in educational measurement because

> When different tests that seek to measure the same content are administered to different cohorts of students, comparisons of test items and examinees are not sound. Various equating processes have been implemented, but there is little theoretical justification for them (p. 10).

This also applies to attitudinal survey items used in different cohorts and contexts. Thus, also making them exposed to the shortcomings of the procedures under CTT. Recently, researchers have used contemporary statistical analysis techniques to examine classroom environment instruments (see, e.g., Dorman, 2003; Aldridge, Dorman, & Fraser, 2004). Included in these contemporary analytic techniques is the Rasch model which belongs to a family of techniques classified under item-response theory. However, there appears to be no mention of the ICEQ being subjected to these kinds of analyses. For this reason, the author of this chapter has taken this opportunity to investigate the validity of the different dimensions of the ICEQ using the Rasch model. It is the author's aim to add value to what has already been established by Fraser in terms of the utility of his ICEQ, particularly the short form.

The Rasch Model

Rasch (1960), a Danish mathematician, developed the one-parameter item-response model called the Rasch model. This was in response to educational and social science researchers' decades-long challenges in scoring survey responses and test items. Rasch (1960) proposed a simple formulation to fit the parameters of test item difficulty and person ability to a measurement model for responses to test questions.

In fact, the Rasch model demonstrates flexibility in its use as it is not only confined to dichotomous items but can also handle polytomous items (Masters, 1982). The model defines the probability of a specified response in relation to the ability of the test taker (or survey respondent) and the difficulty of a test (or survey) item (Hailaya, Alagumalai, & Ben, 2014). Thus, the Rasch model scales persons and test (or survey) items on the same continuum (Van Alphen, Halfens, Hasman, & Imbos, 1994). The person and item parameters are both sample independent (Van Alphen et al., 1994; Hambleton & Jones, 1993). In other words, in a scaling process using the Rasch model, the scale is independent of both the test or survey items and the sample of persons employed in the calibration (Keeves & Masters, 1999).

Specific objectivity and unidimensionality are two of the Rasch model's special properties. Specific objectivity underscores the independence between the estimation of item parameter and person parameter (Bond & Fox, 2007). Unidimensionality requires a factor, construct, or attribute to be measured one at a time (Bond & Fox, 2007). In a test or a survey scale, items that fit the Rasch model are expected to follow a structure that has a single dimension. According to Alagumalai and Curtis (2005), the Rasch model has a "unique property that embodies measurement" (p. 2) that, when trying to understand how a construct operates, provides a probabilistic insight into how a set of data operates within a unidimensional model. The Rasch model is largely considered to be an objective approach that fulfils measurement requirements resulting in enhanced measurement capacity of a test or survey instrument (Cavanagh & Romanoski, 2006). The Rasch model enables for a more detailed, item-level examination of the structure and operation of tests and survey scales.

The Rasch model can be used to examine the scale items at the pilot or validation stage (Wu & Adams, 2007), or to review psychometric properties of existing scales (Tennant & Conaghan, 2007) such as the ICEQ. It determines whether the item responses conform to the requirements of a measurement model (Hailaya, Alagumalai, & Ben, 2014). Items are judged based on fit indicators that are provided by the model. Those which do not conform to measurement requirements are kept and those that do not satisfy the requirements are removed (Ben, Hailaya, & Alagumalai, 2012).

Data Used to Re-examine the Utility of the ICEQ

The ICEQ formed part of the *students' uptake of physics study questionnaire* that was used in a study that the author of this chapter conducted in 2010. This study examined several factors that could influence school students' attitudes towards, and subsequent decision to study physics (Ben, 2010). The dataset used to review the measurement properties of the ICEQ was drawn from this study. The participants for the study were senior (years 11 and 12) school students from selected government, independent, and catholic schools in South Australia. A total of 306 students from 12 schools participated in the study. Table 5.1 provides details about the distribution of

Table 5.1 Summary of number of student participants and schools per sector in South Australia

School sector	Number of schools	Number of students (N)
Government schools	4	108
Independent schools	6	157
Catholic schools	2	41
		Total N = 306

study participants' schools, and the number of participating students. The short version ICEQ (both *actual* and *preferred* versions) was used to collect data concerning students' experiences in a physics classroom covering all the five different dimensions of the classroom environment (*personalisation*, *participation*, *independence*, *investigation*, and *differentiation*). Since the students sampled in the study were at the time already enrolled in a physics subject, the ICEQ was also used to examine their experiences in the physics classroom and their impact on subsequent decision to continue doing physics or physics-related courses at university.

Data were collected using paper questionnaires. They were distributed to student participants to fill out. Numerical data entry was carried out using Microsoft Excel. Data saved in Excel was exported to IBM SPSS for "data cleaning" (checking up for errors or mistyped numbers). The data saved in the IBM SPSS format became the raw data for the study.

Addressing Missing Data

In any large-scale surveys, it is inevitable that respondents may "skip", for whatever reason, responding to survey items. This results to having a dataset with missing data. Missing values in datasets can affect inferences and reporting of studies. There are some standard or "more traditional" statistical techniques that can be used to handle data with missing values. However, these methods have some identified disadvantages that could adversely affect the study. Hence, a more contemporary approach without the identified disadvantages was used.

The multiple imputation (MI) approach was employed to handle missing values in the collected dataset. The MI was developed by Rubin (1977, 1987, as cited in Patrician, 2002) to address the problems encountered using single imputation methods. This is a predictive approach to handling missing data in a multivariate analysis (Patrician, 2002).

In the last three decades, the MI methods have been progressively developed and used to handle missing values in datasets by social science and medical researchers (see, e.g., Huque, Carlin, Simpson, & Lee, 2018; Lee & Carlin, 2010). A complete dataset resulting from using MI methods allows a researcher to use standard complete-data procedures just as if the imputed data were the real data obtained from non-respondents (Rubin, 1987).

Analysis of the ICEQ Items Using the Rasch Rating Scale Model

The Rasch model is a broad classification of a family of different measurement models. Two of these models are the rating scale model (Andrich, 1978) and the partial credit model (Masters, 1982). The study from which this chapter was drawn employed the rating scale model (RSM). The rating scale model can be used for the analysis of questionnaires that use a fixed set of response alternatives with every item like "strongly disagree", "disagree", "agree", and "strongly agree" (Masters, 1999). Although questionnaires of this type can also be analysed using the partial credit model, Masters (1999, p. 103) pointed out that:

> …the fact that the response alternatives are defined in the same way for all items introduces the possibility of simplifying the partial credit model by assuming that, in questionnaires of this type, the pattern…will be the same for all items on the questionnaire and that the only difference between items will be a difference in location on the measurement variable (e.g., difficulty of endorsement).

Hence, the rating scale model was chosen over the partial credit model.

The ICEQ dataset was subjected to Rasch RSM analysis using the ConQuest 2.0 software (Wu, Adams, Wilson, & Haldane, 2007). All items in the scale used the same five response categories. All 25 items in the ICEQ were included in the initial analysis.

Item Analysis Using the Rasch Rating Scale Model

Using the dataset described above, all of the 25 items from the ICEQ short form (both *actual* and *preferred*) were subjected to item analysis using the rating scale model (RSM). These items are distributed to the five constructs that represent different classroom dimensions (*personalisation*, *participation*, *independence*, *investigation*, and *differentiation*). There are five items in each construct. This involved examining each item's fit statistics. More specifically, the infit mean-square (INFIT MNSQ) statistic was used as a basis for model fitting or non-fitting items. Tilahun (2004, p. 69) describes the function of INFIT MNSQ as one that "measures the consistency of fit of the students to the item characteristic curve for each item with weighted consideration given to those persons close to the 0.05 probability level." In examining the ICEQ items using the RSM, a range of values of this statistic was taken to be from 0.60 to 1.40 (Wright & Linacre, 1994). There was a degree of leniency in the chosen range because of the low stakes nature of a survey instrument (such as the

ICEQ). Items whose INFIT MNSQ values fall above 1.40 are generally considered underfitting and do not discriminate well, while below 0.60 are overfitting or too predictable (Wright & Linacre, 1994), hence, provide redundant information. Items with INFIT MNSQ values outside the accepted range, and therefore not fitting the model, were made candidates for deletion from the analysis. However, care was taken in removing items. Item deltas—the set of parameters that are associated with the category choices for an item that have estimates with numerical values in order that mirrors the same order as the categories—for items that do not fit the model were also examined. Disordered (or reversed) deltas could represent data incompatibility with the underlying intentions of Rasch measurement (Andrich, 2005). Hence, items with INFIT MNSQ values outside the accepted range whose item deltas exhibit disorder were readily removed. When items have an INFIT MNSQ values outside the range but exhibit item deltas in order, item statements/wordings were examined carefully to identify whether they appeared to have purpose in relation to what was needed in the study. If not, then they were removed. In other words, caution was strongly exercised in removing items that do not fit, as they may be valuable in providing other important information, or findings, that might arise from the study.

Tabulated results include item estimate, error, and the weighted fit statistics which show the INFIT MNSQ and *T* statistic. The range for the *T* statistic taken to indicate acceptable item fit was from −2 to +2 (Wu & Adams, 2007). The separation reliability index for each scale and significance level are also included. Adams and Khoo (1993) defined separation reliability index as an indication of the proportion of the observed variance that is considered true. Generally, there is a preference for high separation reliability index because this means that measurement error is smaller.

It should be noted that each of the five constructs representing the classroom dimensions was treated as a single scale. Thus, there were five items subjected to the Rasch rating scale analysis for each scale. This follows what Barry Fraser had established that the whole ICEQ is not unidimensional but multidimensional (hence, the five distinct constructs).

Results

Tables 5.2 and 5.3 show the response model parameter estimates of the actual ICEQ and the preferred ICEQ, respectively. It should be noted that the analysis results shown includes all the ICEQ items (for both the actual and preferred classroom forms).

For the actual classroom ICEQ, each misfitting item was carefully examined for its infit statistics, the item's deltas, and the item statement. As shown in Table 5.2, a total of two items became candidates for removal when the data was fitted to the Rasch RSM (see Table 5.2). These were *Item 11* (PERSN75R with INFIT MNSQ = 1.72) and *Item 7* (PARTI71R with INFIT MNSQ = 1.42).

Item 11's (PERSN75R) text reads "*The teacher is unfriendly to students.*" The item's INFIT MNSQ is well above the upper threshold value of 1.40. The item deltas

Table 5.2 Table of response model parameter estimates of the *actual classroom* ICEQ (scales analysed separately and no items removed)

Item number	Scale items and codes	Estimates	Error	Weighted fit		
				INFIT MNSQ	CI	T
Personalisation (PERSN) *(Separation reliability = 0.991; Significance level = 0.000)*						
1	PERSN65	0.511	0.057	0.82	(0.84, 1.16)	−2.0
6	PERSN70	1.161	0.055	1.18	(0.84, 1.16)	2.0
11	PERSN75R	−1.725	0.116	1.72	(0.84, 1.16)	2.0
16	PERSN80	−0.354	0.063	0.91	(0.84, 1.16)	−1.1
21	PERSN85	0.407	0.058	0.86	(0.84, 1.16)	−1.7
Participation (PARTI) *(Separation reliability = 0.995; Significance level = 0.000)*						
2	PARTI66	0.057	0.055	0.81	(0.84, 1.16)	−2.0
7	PARTI71R	0.065	0.110	1.42	(0.84, 1.16)	2.0
12	PARTI76	0.513	0.054	0.94	(0.84, 1.16)	−0.7
17	PARTI81	−0.864	0.058	0.94	(0.84, 1.16)	−0.7
22	PARTI86	0.229	0.054	1.06	(0.84, 1.16)	0.8
Independence (INDEP) *(Separation reliability = 0.997; Significance level = 0.000)*						
3	INDEP67R	−1.229	0.050	0.97	(0.84, 1.16)	−0.4
8	INDEP72	−0.187	0.044	1.06	(0.84, 1.16)	0.7
13	INDEP77R	0.713	0.040	0.91	(0.84, 1.16)	−1.1
18	INDEP82R	−0.474	0.046	1.03	(0.84, 1.16)	0.3
23	INDEP87R	1.176	0.091	0.95	(0.84, 1.16)	−0.5
Investigation (INVES) *(Separation reliability = 0.989; Significance level = 0.000)*						
4	INVES68R	−0.073	0.097	1.21	(0.84, 1.16)	2.0
9	INVES73	−0.546	0.049	0.96	(0.84, 1.16)	−0.5
14	INVES78	0.324	0.048	0.92	(0.84, 1.16)	−0.9
19	INVES83	−0.187	0.048	1.01	(0.84, 1.16)	0.1
24	INVES88	0.481	0.048	0.89	(0.84, 1.16)	−1.4
Differentiation (DFFER) *(Separation reliability = 0.972; Significance level = 0.000)*						
5	DFFER69	−0.144	0.050	1.01	(0.84, 1.16)	0.2
10	DFFER74R	−0.237	0.050	0.82	(0.84, 1.16)	−2.4
15	DFFER79	−0.038	0.051	1.07	(0.84, 1.16)	0.9
20	DFFER84	−0.239	0.050	1.02	(0.84, 1.16)	0.3
25	DFFER89R	0.658	0.100	1.11	(0.84, 1.16)	1.4

for *Item* 11 were also examined and found their values to be in order indicating that there was no swapping of choice categories. No issue was found in the item text, either. However, it is noteworthy that most (92%) of the respondents indicated that they either "strongly disagree" (77%) or "disagree" (15%) with the statement that could lead to a conclusion that the item did not discriminate well (item discrimination

Table 5.3 Table of response model parameter estimates of the *preferred classroom* ICEQ (scales analysed separately and no items removed)

Item number	Scale items and codes	Estimates	Error	Weighted fit		
				INFIT MNSQ	CI	T
Personalisation (PRSN) *(Separation reliability = 0.988; Significance level = 0.000)*						
1	PRSN90	0.436	0.055	0.84	(0.84, 1.16)	−2.0
6	PRSN95	0.872	0.052	1.19	(0.84, 1.16)	2.0
11	PRSN100R	−1.175	0.117	1.31	(0.84, 1.16)	1.8
16	PRSN105	−0.430	0.068	0.81	(0.84, 1.16)	−2.0
21	PRSN110	0.298	0.059	1.03	(0.84, 1.16)	0.3
Participation (PRTI) *(Separation reliability = 0.986; Significance level = 0.000)*						
2	PRTI91	0.147	0.054	0.89	(0.84, 1.16)	−1.3
7	PRTI96R	0.087	0.111	1.64	(0.84, 1.16)	3.6
12	PRTI101	0.431	0.053	0.84	(0.84, 1.16)	−2.0
17	PRTI106	−0.668	0.059	0.87	(0.84, 1.16)	−1.6
22	PRTI111	0.003	0.056	0.87	(0.84, 1.16)	−1.5
Independence (INDP) *(Separation reliability = 0.994; Significance level = 0.000)*						
3	INDP92R	−0.808	0.049	1.18	(0.84, 1.16)	2.0
8	INDP97	−0.322	0.046	1.16	(0.84, 1.16)	1.9
13	INDP102R	0.557	0.042	0.86	(0.84, 1.16)	−1.8
18	INDP107R	−0.324	0.046	0.97	(0.84, 1.16)	−0.4
23	INDP112R	0.896	0.091	1.01	(0.84, 1.16)	0.1
Investigation (INVS) *(Separation reliability = 0.945; Significance level = 0.000)*						
4	INVS93R	0.209	0.104	1.43	(0.84, 1.16)	2.0
9	INVS98	−0.381	0.052	0.79	(0.84, 1.16)	−2.0
14	INVS103	0.095	0.052	0.76	(0.84, 1.16)	−1.1
19	INVS108	0.068	0.052	1.12	(0.84, 1.16)	1.4
24	INVS113	0.009	0.052	0.93	(0.84, 1.16)	−0.8
Differentiation (DFER) *(Separation reliability = 0.971; Significance level = 0.000)*						
5	DFER94	0.095	0.049	0.83	(0.84, 1.16)	−1.2
10	DFER99R	−0.074	0.048	0.86	(0.84, 1.16)	−1.7
15	DFER104	0.014	0.050	0.97	(0.84, 1.16)	−0.3
20	DFER109	−0.548	0.048	1.32	(0.84, 1.16)	1.5
25	DFER114R	0.514	0.098	1.14	(0.84, 1.16)	1.6

index = 0.43), which is also shown in Fig. 5.1, hence, obtaining an INFIT MNSQ statistic that is well beyond the threshold value. However, Linacre (2002) identified that the mean-square values between 1.5 and 2.0 may be unproductive for measurement construction, but not degrading. In addition, the item's T value sits within the acceptable range suggested by Wu and Adams (2007).

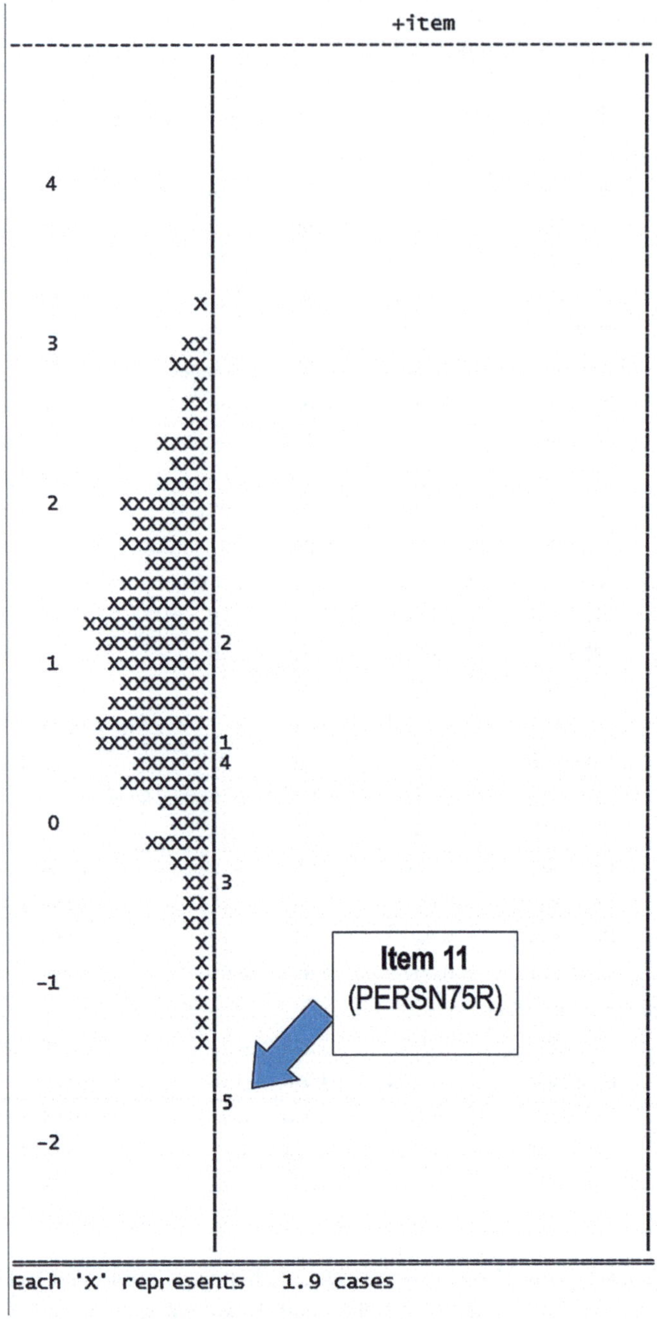

Fig. 5.1 Map of latent distributions and response model parameter estimates (actual ICEQ—personalisation scale)

Item 7 (PARTI71R: "*The teacher lectures without students asking or answering questions.*") was likewise examined due to its INFIT MNSQ (1.42) being greater than the upper limit of the threshold. However, the item was also kept due to its item deltas being in order, and that the mean-square value is only a tiny fraction over the limit. In addition, according to Linacre (2002), the mean-square values between 0.5 and 1.5 are productive for measurement. Furthermore, the *T* value for *Item 7* shows a value within the acceptable range indicated by Wu and Adams (2007).

Misfitting items in each scale of the preferred classroom ICEQ were also examined. The same procedure for examining items in the actual classroom ICEQ scales was employed—checking INFIT MNSQ, *T* values, items deltas, and item statements—to check the preferred classroom ICEQ items. A total of two items appeared to misfit when data was fitted to the Rasch RSM. Items include *Item 7* (PRTI96R: "*The teacher would lecture without students asking or answering questions.*"); and *Item 4* (INVS93R: "*Students would find out the answers to questions from textbooks rather than from investigations.*"). *Item 4* satisfies the criteria of having ordered item delta values despite its mean-square values beyond the set upper limit of 1.40. In addition, *Item 4* was kept in its scale following Linacre's (2002) assertion that items with the mean-square values between 0.5 and 1.50 could be considered useful (productive) in measurement. *Item 7* (PRTI96R) was removed due to its disordered (or reversed) item delta values, which indicate swapping category choices which could pose a problem in establishing measurement. In addition, *Item 7*'s *T* value at 3.6 is beyond the maximum value of +2 which could indicate the item having a highly determined response pattern that violates the Rasch model measurement requirements (Bond & Fox, 2007).

For both the actual classroom and the preferred classroom ICEQ, it can be observed that the scales generally have very high separation reliability. This indicates high discriminating power and small measurement error (Alagumalai & Curtis, 2005), which further shows measurement precision and reliability (Wright & Stone, 1999). In addition, based on the analysis results, the actual and preferred classroom ICEQ short forms show a high level of construct validity.

Discussion and Conclusion

The results of analysing the ICEQ data using the Rasch RSM provide evidence of robust measurement properties of both the actual and preferred classroom ICEQ. Although one item from the preferred classroom ICEQ was ultimately removed, the findings generally support Barry Fraser's claim of his instrument's reliability, validity, and multidimensionality with adequate scale independence. Thus, the ICEQ can be used by teachers to evaluate their classroom environment covering the different aspects of teaching and learning.

Although it has been shown in this paper that the use of the Rasch model added value to Fraser's assertions about the utility of his ICEQ, the following suggestions are put forward:

- Using datasets collected from different contexts (i.e., education systems from different countries, in addition to Australia) and analysed using the Rasch RSM will further add value by enabling further calibration of the different ICEQ scales and their corresponding items. This will establish a more robust structure of the ICEQ, especially enhancing its portability across contexts.
- For the same reasons stated above, the long form actual and preferred classroom ICEQ items should also be subjected to the same analysis using the Rasch RSM.
- Removal of a scale item due to its disordered (or reversed) deltas needs further consideration and examination. More recent publications on disordered deltas have illuminated some reasons why Andrich's (2005) assertions that disordered category thresholds indicate a problem should be reconsidered. Adams, Wu, and Wilson (2012) have pointed out that parameter disorder and order of response categories are separate phenomena. They have argued that disordered deltas are not necessarily indication of a problem of item fit, but of "specific patterns in the relative numbers of respondents in each category" (p. 547).

Teachers are constantly being reminded and required to be in tune with their students' needs in the classroom. Hence, being "in tune" consequently drives setting up an optimum classroom climate where students could engage in learning. Producing an optimum classroom climate could likewise be determined by the teacher's pedagogy and classroom activities. In the Australian education system, the *Australian Institute for Teaching and School Leadership* requires teachers, first and foremost, to "Know students and how they learn" (see www.aitsl.edu.au). It is recognised, however, that there are ways in which a teacher could establish being "in tune" with their students. One of the ways could be by evaluating their current classroom environment. The ICEQ could provide teachers a couple of valid and reliable tools (the short and long forms) to help obtain a holistic picture of their classroom environment as it covers aspects of learning that are important in gauging what students actually experience in their classroom, and what they would prefer to happen in their classroom. Narrowing the gap between the actual experience of students in the classroom and what they want to experience in the classroom could only result to enhanced learning, hence, resulting to a more enjoyable classroom experience—for both the students and their teacher.

Appendix 1

Individualised classroom environment questionnaire (actual classroom) items and their corresponding statements:

Item number	Item code	Nature of statement	Item code to indicate reverse scoring	Item text
1	PERSN65	Positive	*None*	The teacher talks with each student
2	PARTI66	Positive	*None*	Students give their opinions during discussions
3	INDEP67	Negative	INDEP67R	The teacher decides where students sit
4	INVES68	Negative	INVES68R	Students find out the answers to questions from textbooks rather than from investigations
5	DFFER69	Positive	*None*	Different students do different work
6	PERSN70	Positive	*None*	The teacher takes a personal interest in each student
7	PARTI71	Negative	PARTI71R	The teacher lectures without students asking or answering questions
8	INDEP72	Positive	*None*	Students choose their partners for group work
9	INVES73	Positive	*None*	Students carry out investigations to test ideas
10	DFFER74	Negative	DFFER74R	All students in the class do the same work at the same time
11	PERSN75	Negative	PERSN75R	The teacher is unfriendly to students
12	PARTI76	Positive	*None*	Students' ideas and suggestions are used during classroom discussion
13	INDEP77	Negative	INDEP77R	Students are told how to behave in the classroom

(continued)

(continued)

Item number	Item code	Nature of statement	Item code to indicate reverse scoring	Item text
14	INVES78	Positive	*None*	Students carry out investigations to answer questions coming from class discussions
15	DFFER79	Positive	*None*	Different students use different books, equipment, and materials
16	PERSN80	Positive	*None*	The teacher helps each student who is having trouble with the work
17	PARTI81	Positive	*None*	Students ask the teacher questions
18	INDEP82	Negative	INDEP82R	The teacher decides which students should work together
19	INVES83	Positive	*None*	Students explain the meanings of statements, diagrams, and graphs
20	DFFER84	Positive	*None*	Students who work faster than others move on to the next topic
21	PERSN85	Positive	*None*	The teacher considers students' feelings
22	PARTI86	Positive	*None*	There is classroom discussion
23	INDEP87	Negative	INDEP87R	The teacher decides how much movement and talk there should be in the classroom
24	INVES88	Positive	*None*	Students carry out investigations to answer questions which puzzle them

(continued)

(continued)

Item number	Item code	Nature of statement	Item code to indicate reverse scoring	Item text
25	DFFER89	Negative	DFFER89R	The same teaching aid (e.g., blackboard or overhead projector) is used for all students in the class

Appendix 2

Individualised classroom environment questionnaire (preferred classroom) items and their corresponding statements:

Item number	Item code	Nature of statement	Item code to indicate reverse scoring	Item text
1	PRSN90	Positive	*None*	The teacher would talk to each student
2	PRTI91	Positive	*None*	Students would give their opinions during discussions
3	INDP92	Negative	INDP92R	The teacher would decide where students will sit
4	INVS93	Negative	INVS93R	Students would find out the answers to questions from textbooks rather than from investigations
5	DFER94	Positive	*None*	Different students would do different work
6	PRSN95	Positive	*None*	The teacher would take personal interest in each student

(continued)

(continued)

Item number	Item code	Nature of statement	Item code to indicate reverse scoring	Item text
7	PRTI96	Negative	PRTI96R	The teacher would lecture without students asking or answering questions
8	INDP97	Positive	*None*	Students would choose their partners for group work
9	INVS98	Positive	*None*	Students would carry out investigations to test ideas
10	DFER99	Negative	DFER99R	All students in the class would do the same work at the same time
11	PRSN100	Negative	PRSN100R	The teacher would be unfriendly to students
12	PRTI101	Positive	*None*	Students' ideas and suggestions would be used during classroom discussion
13	INDP102	Negative	INDP102R	Students would be told how to behave in the classroom
14	INVS103	Positive	*None*	Students would carry out investigations to answer questions coming from class discussions
15	DFER104	Positive	*None*	Different students would use different books, equipment, and materials
16	PRSN105	Positive	*None*	The teacher would help each student who was having trouble with the work

(continued)

(continued)

Item number	Item code	Nature of statement	Item code to indicate reverse scoring	Item text
17	PRTI106	Positive	*None*	Students would ask the teacher questions
18	INDP107	Negative	INDP107R	The teacher would decide which students should work together
19	INVS108	Positive	*None*	Students would explain the meanings of statements, diagrams, and graphs
20	DFER109	Positive	*None*	Students who worked faster than others would move on to the next topic
21	PRSN110	Positive	*None*	The teacher would consider students' feelings
22	PRTI111	Positive	*None*	There would be classroom discussion
23	INDP112	Negative	INDP112R	The teacher would decide how much movement and talk there should be in the classroom
24	INVS113	Positive	*None*	Students would carry out investigations to answer questions which puzzled them
25	DFER114	Negative	DFER114R	The same teaching aid (e.g., blackboard or overhead projector) would be used for all students in the class

References

Adams, R. J., & Khoo, S. (1993). *Quest—The interactive test analysis system*. Melbourne: Australian Council for Educational Research.

Adams, R. J., Wu, M. L., & Wilson, M. (2012). The Rasch rating model and the disordered threshold controversy. *Educational and Psychological Measurement, 72*(4), 547–573.

Alagumalai, S., & Curtis, D. D. (2005). Classical test theory. In S. Alagumalai, D. D. Curtis, & N. Hungi (Eds.), *Applied Rasch measurement: A book of exemplars* (pp. 1–14). The Netherlands: Springer.

Aldridge, J. M., Dorman, J. P., & Fraser, B. J. (2004). Use of multitrait-multimethod modeling to validate actual and preferred forms of the technology-rich outcomes-focused learning environment inventory (TROFLEI). *Australian Journal of Educational & Developmental Psychology, 4,* 110–125.

Andrich, D. (1978). A rating formulation for ordered response categories. *Psychometrika, 43*(4), 561–573.

Andrich, D. (2005). The Rasch model explained. In S. Alagumalai, D. D. Durtis, & N. Hungi (Eds.), *Applied Rasch measurement: A book of exemplars* (pp. 308–328). Berlin, Germany: Springer-Kluwer.

Ben, F. (2010). *Students' uptake of physics: A study of South Australian and Filipino physics students* (Unpublished PhD Thesis). The University of Adelaide, Adelaide, Australia.

Ben, F., Hailaya, W., & Alagumalai, S. (2012). *Validation of the technical and further education—South Australia (TAFE-SA) Assessment of basic skills instrument (TAFE-SA Commissioned Report)*. Adelaide, Australia: TAFE-SA.

Bond, T. G., & Fox, C. M. (2007). *Applying the Rasch model: Fundamental measurement in the human sciences*. New York, NY: Lawrence Erlbaum Associates.

Burden, R., & Fraser, B. J. (1993). Use of classroom environment assessments in school psychology: A British perspective. *Psychology in the Schools, 30,* 232–240.

Cavanagh, R. F., & Romanoski, J. T. (2006). Rating scale instruments and measurement. *Learning Environment Research, 9,* 273–289.

Dorman, J. P. (2003). Relationship between school and classroom environment and teacher burnout: A LISREL analysis. *Social Psychology of Education, 6,* 107–127.

Fisher, D. L., & Fraser, B. J. (1981). Validity and use of the my class inventory. *Science Education, 65*(2), 145–156.

Fraser, B. J. (1980). *Criterion validity of an individualised classroom environment questionnaire*. Retrieved from https://files.eric.ed.gov/fulltext/ED214961.pdf.

Fraser, B. J. (1990). *Individualised classroom environment questionnaire: Handbook and test master set*. Brisbane: Australian Council for Educational Research.

Fraser, B. J., Anderson, G. J., & Walberg, H. J. (1982). *Assessment of learning environments: Manual for Learning Environment Inventory (LEI) and My Class Inventory (MCI)*. Perth: Western Australian Institute of Technology.

Fraser, B. J., Fisher, D. L., & McRobbie, C. J. (1996, April). *Development, validation, and use of personal and class forms of a new classroom environment questionnaire*. Paper presented at the annual meeting of the American Educational Research Association, New York.

Hailaya, W., Alagumalai, S., & Ben, F. (2014). Examining the utility of Assessment Literacy Inventory and its portability to education systems in the Asia Pacific region. *Australian Journal of Education, 58*(3), 297–317.

Hambleton, R. K., & Jones, R. W. (1993). Comparison of classical test theory and item-response theory and their applications to test development. *Educational Measurement: Issues and Practice, 12,* 38–47.

Huque, H., Carlin, J. B., Simpson, J. A., & Lee, K. J. (2018). A comparison of multiple imputation methods for missing data in longitudinal studies. *BMC Medical Research Methodology, 18*(168), 1–16.

Keeves, J. P., & Masters, G. N. (1999). Issues in educational measurement. In G. N. Masters & J. P. Keeves (Eds.), *Advances in measurement in educational research and assessment* (pp. 268–281). The Netherlands: Pergamon Press.

Lee, K. J., & Carlin, J. B. (2010). Multiple imputation for missing data: Fully conditional specification versus multivariate normal imputation. *American Journal of Epidemiology, 171*(5), 624–632.

Linacre, J. M. (2002). What do infit and outfit, mean-square and standardized mean? *Rasch Measurement Transactions, 16*(2), 878.

Masters, G. N. (1982). A Rasch model for partial credit scoring. *Psychometrika, 47*(2), 149–174.

Masters, G. N. (1999). Partial Credit Model. In G. N. Masters & J. P. Keeves (Eds.), *Advances in Measurement in educational research and assessment* (pp. 98–109). The Netherlands: Pergamon.

Moos, R. H., & Trickett, E. J. (1974). *Classroom environment scale manual* (1st ed.). Palo Alto, California: Consulting Psychologists Press.

Patrician, P. A. (2002). Focus on research methods: Multiple imputation for missing data. *Research in Nursing & Health, 25*, 76–84.

Piquero, A. R., MacIntosh, R. & Hickman, M. (2000). Does self-control affect survey response? Applying exploratory, confirmatory, and item response theory analysis to Grasmick et al.'s Self-Control Scale. *Criminology, 38*(3), 897–929.

Rasch, G. (1960). *Probabilistic models for some intelligence and attainment tests* (Reprint, with Foreword and Afterword by B. D. Wright, Chicago: University of Chicago Press, 1980). Copenhagen, Denmark: Danmarks Paedogogiske Institut.

Roszkowski, M. J., & Bean, A. G. (1990). Believe it or not! Longer questionnaires have lower response rates. *Journal of Business and Psychology, 4*(4), 495–509.

Rubin, D. B. (1977). Assignment to treatment group on the basis of a covariate. *Journal of Educational Statistics, 2*(1), 1–26.

Rubin, D. B. (1987). *Multiple imputations for nonresponse in surveys*. New York: Wiley.

Tennant, A., & Conaghan, P. G. (2007). The Rasch measurement model in rheumatology: What is it and why use it? When should it be applied, and what should one look for in a Rasch paper? *Arthritis Care & Research, 57*, 1358–1362.

Tilahun M. A. (2004). Monitoring mathematics achievement over time: A secondary analysis of FIMS, SIMS and TIMS: A Rasch analysis. In S. Alagumalai, D. D. Curtis, & N. Hungi (Eds.), *Applied Rasch measurement: A book of exemplars—Papers in honour of John P. Keeves* (pp. 63–79). The Netherlands: Springer.

Van Alphen, A., Halfens, R., Hasman, A., & Imbos, T. (1994). Likert or Rasch? Nothing is more applicable than good theory. *Journal of Advanced Nursing, 20*, 196–201.

Walberg, H. J., & Anderson, G. J. (1968). Classroom climate and individual learning. *Journal of Educational Psychology, 59*, 414–419.

Wheldall, K., Beaman, R., & Mok, M. (1999). Does the individualized classroom environment questionnaire (ICEQ) measure classroom climate? *Educational and Psychological Measurement, 59*(5), 847–854.

Wright, B. D., & Linacre, J. M. (1994). Reasonable mean-square fit values. *Rasch Measurement Transactions, 8*(3), 370.

Wright, B. D., & Stone, M. H. (1999). *Measurement essentials* (2nd ed.). Wilmington, Delaware: Wide Range Inc.

Wu, M. L., & Adams, R. J. (2007). *Applying the Rasch model to psycho-social measurement: A practical approach*. Melbourne: Educational Measurement Solutions.

Wu, M. L., Adams, R. J., Wilson, M. R., & Haldane, S. A. (2007). ConQuest Version 2.0 [Generalised Item Response Modeling Software]. Camberwell, Victoria: ACER Press.

Wubbels, Th, Brekelmans, M., & Hooymayers, H. P. (1991). Interpersonal teacher behaviour in the classroom. In B. J. Fraser & H. L. Walberg (Eds.), *Educational environments: Evaluation, antecedents and consequences* (pp. 141–160). Oxford, England: Pergamon Press.

Chapter 6
Validation of University Entrance Tests Through Rasch Analysis

Italo Testa, Giuliana Capasso, Arturo Colantonio, Silvia Galano, Irene Marzoli, Umberto Scotti di Uccio and Gaspare Serroni

Abstract Initial preparation of first-year university students is often assessed by means of an entrance examination, which tests their knowledge of mathematics and science as well as their reading skills. This paper illustrates how we used Rasch analysis to: (i) investigate the reliability and construct validity of a typical university entrance test administered in Italy; (ii) explore the extent to which mathematics, science, and reading items differ in their difficulty. Two studies were set up. In study 1, we analyzed the psychometric quality of an 80-item test administered in 2016 to $N = 2435$ science and engineering freshmen. In study 2, we analyzed the responses of $N = 1223$ students to a 100-item entrance test administered in 2017, 2018, and 2019 to an extended population of students. Results of both studies show that the analyzed entrance tests do not match unidimensional requirement, as proficiency in mathematics, science, and reading capability correspond to distinct latent traits. Moreover, items on different scientific topics have significantly different difficulty. The study shows a need for revising the analyzed tests to meet unidimensionality requirements. Moreover, the analysis of items' difficulty suggests balancing in a more suitable way the difficulty of the different content areas.

Keywords Entrance exam · Rasch analysis · Unidimensionality · Psychometric quality · Differential item functioning

---

Electronic supplementary material The online version of this chapter (https://doi.org/10.1007/978-981-15-1800-3_6) contains supplementary material, which is available to authorized users

---

I. Testa (✉) · G. Capasso · S. Galano · U. Scotti di Uccio
Department of Physics "E. Pancini", University of Naples Federico II, Complesso M.S. Angelo, Via Cintia, 80126 Napoli, Italy
e-mail: italo.testa@unina.it

A. Colantonio · I. Marzoli
School of Science and Technology, Università di Camerino, Piazza dei Costanti, 4, 62032 Camerino, Italia

G. Serroni
Dipartimento di Scienze Chimiche, Università di Napoli 'Federico II', Complesso Monte S. Angelo, Via Cintia, 80126 Napoli, Italia

M. S. Khine (ed.), *Rasch Measurement*,
https://doi.org/10.1007/978-981-15-1800-3_6

Introduction

Universities and higher education institutions worldwide use scores from entrance tests for selective purposes and as criteria for assigning students to remedial and credit-bearing courses (Davey, De Lian, & Higgins, 2007; Kuramoto & Koizumi, 2018). Hence, results of these tests deeply impact not only on the individuals' careers, but also on institutions' strategic decisions. For instance, since late 2000s in many European countries, such as Italy, public funding policies establish goals and standards for higher education institutions, which should try to improve students' performances and to reduce drop-out rates over a determined range of time (Ortiz-Lozano, Rua-Vieites, Bilbao-Calabuig, & Casadesús-Fa, 2018). To this aim, the entrance examination tests must provide the university board with valid and reliable evidence about the initial preparation of enrolling students (Thomas, 2011; Thomas & Hovdhaugen, 2014) and the prerequisites for academic success (Vivo & Franco, 2008). This is particularly crucial, for instance, in STEM (Science, Technology, Engineering, and Math) degrees, where competencies in mathematics and reading, usually targeted in common admission tests, play a relevant role for a successful university career, thus lowering the risk for students being underprepared in specific content areas (Kyoung Ro, Lattuca & Alcott, 2017). Initial content knowledge is also deemed as relevant for medicine studies, since knowledge in biology, chemistry, and physics is usually assessed in admission tests for these degrees. In particular, findings from previous research studies show that the predictive power of such entrance tests lies most in the sections whose items address scientific content knowledge (Emery & Bell, 2009; McManus, Ferguson, Wakeford, Powis, & James, 2011). Hence, to improve the quality of entrance exams, it is important to explore how freshmen perform in different content areas of a typical admission test. However, very few studies have addressed this issue in depth. Thus, the research questions that guided this study were: RQ1) what is the reliability and construct validity of a typical university entrance test administered in Italy? RQ2) to what extent does the item difficulty vary across three content areas (mathematics, science, and reading)? The first question aims to establish whether the university admission tests actually measure student preparation in the content areas under evaluation. The second one is aimed at assessing whether the preparation of the students at the end of secondary education is the same in the three content areas targeted by the test. To answer our research questions, we used Rasch measurement since reliability indices allow to establish if the test can discriminate the sample into enough levels of proficiency and to precisely locate the items along the latent variable continuum. Moreover, Rasch measurement allows us to compare the difficulty of different content areas using the same scale.

The University Entrance Examination Test in Italy

Since 1999, the assessment of the initial preparation of the enrolling students has become mandatory for all universities in Italy (Italian Ministry of Education, University and Research, 1999). To this aim, each university had to define, for each undergraduate course, the knowledge level required to freshmen and the corresponding evaluation criteria. Whenever the entrance knowledge level, as measured by the entrance test, is not adequate and does not meet the agreed criteria, students must attend specific additional remedial and credit-bearing courses. Since 2005, about 44 out of 77 Italian public universities have adopted the entrance evaluation system developed by the interuniversity agency "Consorzio Interuniversitario Sistemi Integrati per l'Accesso" (CISIA). The main mission of the CISIA consortium is to design and validate the entrance test, develop guidance tools and make available the results to the participating universities. The CISIA test is used in many STEM degrees, especially engineering and science. In the academic year 2017–18, it was administered to about 120,000 students across Italy.

Methods

Assessed Tests

To answer our research questions, two studies were set up. In study 1, we analyzed the psychometric quality of a CISIA test, administered in academic year 2016, consisting of 80 questions divided into 5 content sections: logic (15 questions, labeled as L1, …, L15), reading comprehension (15 questions, from T1 to T15), mathematics 1 (20 questions, M1.1, …, M1.20), sciences (20 questions, F1, …, F15, CH1, …, CH5), mathematics 2 (10 questions, M2.1, …, M2.10). The choice of the content areas is related to the relevance they have for engineering and science undergraduates. However, we realized that the distributions of items across the sections were not fair and that relevant areas as biology, chemistry, and physics were not adequately targeted. Therefore, we set up a second study, in which we analyzed the psychometric properties of an extended CISIA-like test, compiled by our group on the basis of previous CISIA tests and research-based concept inventories, consisting of 100 questions distributed across 6 content sections as follows: logic (10 questions, L1, …, L10), biology (20 questions, B1, …, B20), chemistry (20 questions, CH1, …, CH20), mathematics (20 questions M1, …, M20), physics (20 questions, F1, …, F20), reading comprehension (10 questions, T1, …, T10). This test was administered in academic years 2017, 2018, and 2019. Anonymous data in both studies were accessed through formal request to the University "Federico II" of Naples.

Data Analysis

As mentioned in the introduction, multiple-choice tests are commonly employed as entrance evaluation instruments. However, tests used in such evaluations are not always favorably regarded because they lack theoretical foundations, as well as psychometric and statistical evidence (Deygers, Zeidler, Vilcu, & Carlsen, 2018; Sternberg et al., 2004). Doubts about their validity may lead to looking at the test-based university admission as a nontransparent or even fraught-laden process (Killgore, 2009). To further complicate the issue, raw scores of different samples could not be directly compared due to the lack of linearity and to the dependency between subjects' scores and items' difficulty. Considering such limitations, it is necessary to validate admission tests using a robust measurement approach. Extensive prior work in science education (Liu, 2010; Neumann, Neumann, & Nehm, 2011) suggests that the Rasch model may be useful to better characterize the psychometric properties of assessment instruments. Thus, we analyzed students' responses in both study 1 and 2 using Rasch measurement (Bond & Fox, 2007; Boone, Staver, & Yale, 2014). The Rasch model aims to determine the probability for a particular individual to correctly answer a given item. Under the following hypotheses:

- questions are designed to evaluate the same variable, called the latent trait;
- the measurement process is not influenced by the characteristics of the individual other than the ability to respond to questions, nor by the peculiarities of the instrument;
- the item score is dichotomous (0 = wrong answer, 1 = correct answer);

this probability is given by

$$P(\beta_i, \theta_j) = \frac{\exp(\beta_i - \theta_j)}{1 + \exp(\beta_i - \theta_j)} = \frac{1}{\exp(\theta_j - \beta_i) + 1}$$

where β_i is the estimation of the ability of the ith individual, θ_j is the estimate of the difficulty of the jth item, and with $-\infty < \beta_i, \theta_j < +\infty$. According to Rasch measurement, ability is defined as the extent to which a student possesses the trait targeted by the questionnaire, in our case the knowledge of basic aspects of logic, mathematics, sciences, and the reading skills. The numerical values of θ_j and β_i are measured in *logit* since they are obtained by fitting the data to the logistic characteristic curve. By default, the mean item difficulty is set to 0. Therefore, if the sample mean ability is about 0, the students, on average, have 50% chance to correctly answer the items of the questionnaire. Mean ability values slightly above (below) 0 indicate that the questionnaire was slightly less (more) difficult for the sample as a whole. Mean ability values much larger (smaller) than 0 indicate that the questionnaire was very easy (difficult) for the sample. Results of Rasch analysis are graphically represented using a Wright map, which displays, in the same plot, the persons' ability and items' difficulty. In such a way, it is possible to readily explore the students' ability distribution across the questionnaire's items.

We adopted Rasch analysis also because it allows to evaluate the quality of the data obtained by the measurement tool, and hence, to evaluate also the quality of the measurement tool (Wright & Masters, 1982). In particular, to establish the validity and reliability of the administered questionnaires, we considered the following indices: Person reliability, Item Separation, Person Separation, Infit, and Outfit mean square (MNSQ). Person reliability is similar to classic Cronbach's alpha and it is defined as the ratio between the true and observed variance, with acceptable values above 0.5. Item separation indicates whether the sample was able to discriminate between the items according to their difficulty. Acceptable values are above 3. Person separation is defined as the ratio between true variance and error variance; it ranges from 0 to infinity. Person separation thus indicates the distribution of person-abilities across the questionnaire's items, so it can be used to investigate if the sample can be divided into levels of increasing ability. Acceptable values are above 2. MNSQ outfit and infit can be used to investigate the goodness of the model fit. Basically, they indicate whether students' responses showed more or less randomness than expected. Acceptable MNSQ infit values are between 0.7 and 1.3. For instance, an item with MNSQ infit of 1.4 has a variability that is 40% greater than expected. Similarly, an item with MNSQ infit of 0.6 has a predictability that is 40% greater than expected.

All calculations and statistical analysis were carried out using WINSTEPS® software (Linacre, 2012).

To verify unidimensionality of the two administered instruments, we first performed an exploratory factor analysis (EFA) using principal axis factoring with promax rotation to look for underlying latent traits, other than the hypothesized one. To determine the number of factors to be retained we used parallel analysis (Horn, 1965). According to this technique, the eigenvalues of the prevalent factors extracted from the EFA should be larger than the eigenvalues of the corresponding factors generated from random data. To conduct parallel analysis, we simulated a data set with the same sample size and the same number of items. Then, since the eigenvalues of the real data should be larger than those of the random set—namely the observed eigenvalues are supposed to account for more variance than expected from the random analysis—we retained only the factors with an eigenvalue significantly greater than the mean of the corresponding factors from the simulated data set. Second, we compared the EFA results with those obtained from the Rasch principal component analysis (PCA) of residuals. A residual is the variability not foreseen by the Rasch model and is subdivided into components (contrasts) that depend on factors other than the difficulty of the items and the ability of the students. Contrarily to EFA, the aim of PCA of residuals is to falsify the hypothesis that the unexplained variance is at the noise level. Moreover, in PCA, differently from EFA, the eigenvalue of a contrast can be interpreted as the number of items that share a common trait. If two (or more) items share such a common trait, they likely determine a possible "secondary dimension" (Linacre, 2012). Therefore, a contrast needs to have an eigenvalue of at least two to be above the noise level. A useful representation to identify secondary dimensions in a dataset is the residuals plot, in which the items are identified by two coordinates, the difficulty measured by the fit procedure (*x-axis*) and the saturation coefficient of the item in the first contrast (*y-axis*). By convention, if the items are randomly distributed in the graph, with saturation values between −0.1 and +0.1 there are no secondary dimensions. If, instead, some items have a saturation with absolute value larger than 0.4 and are separated from the others along the vertical axis, then it is likely that there is a secondary dimension in the test.

Finally, we scanned the tests used in both studies for potential differential item functioning (DIF) across the sample (Linacre, 2012). DIF is a technique to establish whether items' responses are biased with respect to a given sociocultural trait of the sample (e.g., gender, ethnicity). For instance, differences can be due to a higher degree of familiarity of various groups of individuals within the sample with the topics addressed in the questionnaire. See next section for the sample description.

To answer RQ2—namely to investigate whether the studied entrance admission tests are able to discriminate the preparation of the students of the sample in the different content areas—we compared the difficulties of the questions in the various areas, starting from the estimates obtained from Rasch analysis. We also compared the ability of the various groups of individuals within the sample in the different content areas by performing an analysis of variance (ANOVA) of the abilities as measured through Rasch analysis. The advantage of using Rasch difficulty and ability measures instead of raw scores is that, typically, the CISIA test score is calculated as follows: 1 point for each correct answer; 0 points for each answer not given; −0.25 for each wrong answer. The choice of such scoring method is to reduce the guessing effect. However, such a choice does not allow to discriminate between students who did not respond. For instance, student A could have decided not to answer a question because, after performing some calculations, their result did not match any answer choice, whereas student B could have skipped the question simply because they did not study that topic. Both students get the same score (0 points) even though, student A is likely more proficient than student B. Hence, the scoring method typically adopted by the CISIA consortium is not sensitive enough to measure the differences between students A and B and provides only a qualitative description of the students' ability to answer the proposed questions.

Sample

Overall $N = 2435$ students participated in study 1. Students were either enrolled in an engineering degree ($N = 1803$) or in a science degree ($N = 632$) at the University "Federico II" in Naples (Italy). Science degrees include: Chemistry, Physics, Computer Science, Mathematics, Optics and Optometry, Science and Technology for Nature, and Geological Sciences. The average final grade point (FGP)[1] was 85 ± 12. Due to the lack of more information on this sample, we could only evaluate DIF and ANOVA of abilities with respect to the above variables.

[1]FGP in Italy is a score obtained at the end of secondary school on the basis of three concurrent evaluations: last 3-year grades (25%), written exam (45%), and oral exam (30%). Minimum score is 60, maximum is 100. The score is not used to determine university admission.

In study 2, we involved $N = 1223$ students, who voluntarily chose to take the extended CISIA-like test as an entrance evaluation at the beginning of their university degree. In such a way, we were able to include students enrolled in different university degrees and to measure contextual and attitudinal constructs for which we performed DIF and ANOVA of abilities (see Table 6.1).

Table 6.1 Variables of the sample involved in Study 2 ($N = 1223$)

	Percentage of students (%)
Gender	
Female	42.3
Male	57.7
Ranking of secondary school[a]	
Above median	62.9
Below median	37.1
University degree	
Engineering	27.1
Medicine	22.3
Science	18.8
Other	31.8
Participation to extracurricular activities in science[b]	
Yes	30.1
No	69.9
Attitude toward school science[c]	
More positive	75.6
Less positive	24.4
Interest toward career in science[c]	
High interest	85.1
Low interest	14.9

[a]Ranking according to Agnelli Foundation "Eduscopio". Score ranges from 0 to 100 and it is based on the grade point average obtained by the students of the school enrolled in all faculties and is updated each year. Median for the schools of the students taking the test is 64.3, according to 2018 ranking. For more information, see www.eduscopio.it
[b]Activities include laboratory tasks for a total of six hours in small groups and seminars at the university for at least one of the following areas: biology, chemistry, geology, mathematics, and physics
[c]Constructs were measured through a 5-item questionnaire on a 6-point Likert scale

Results

Study 1

The analysis was conducted on a subset of 78 questions, since responses to two logic questions (L1, L4) had to be discarded because the printed text was unreadable.

EFA and Parallel Analysis

Kaiser–Meyer–Olkin measure of sampling adequacy and Bartlett sphericity test were calculated to investigate whether EFA was appropriate in our case. Obtained values were 0.890 and $\chi^2 = 19367$, $df = 3003$, $p < 10^{-4}$, respectively, which suggest that coherent factors can be identified. The EFA results show that the first eigenvalue is three times as big as the second eigenvalue. Out of the remaining factors with eigenvalue bigger than 1, only three have eigenvalues that clearly emerge above those extracted from the parallel analysis (see Fig. 6.1). Therefore, we retained the solution with four factors, which account for 17% of the variance. We report in the electronic supplementary materials how questionnaire's items load into these four factors. In Table 6.2, we summarize, for each section of the test, the number of items with a loading greater than 0.10 into each of the extracted factors. We note that all reading ability items load in the same factor, while the remaining items are distributed among the three other factors: logic items load more onto factor 2, mathematics items

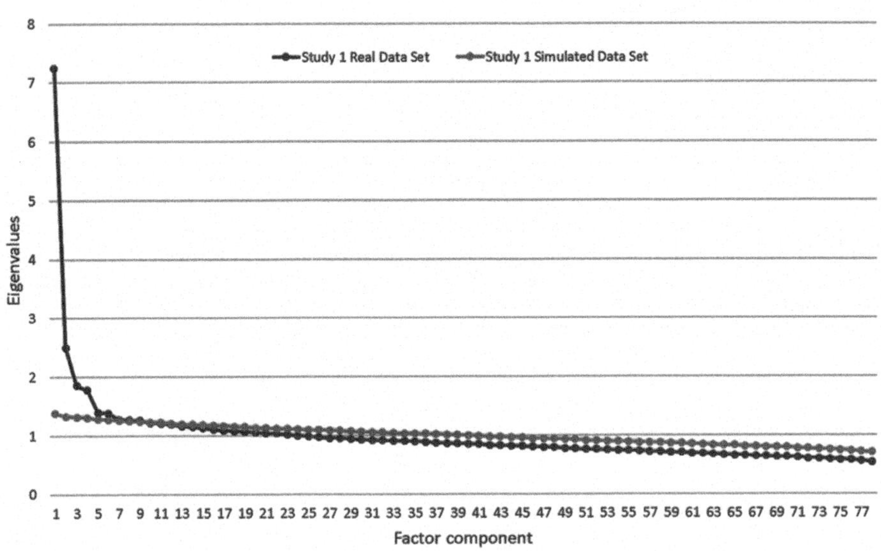

Fig. 6.1 Parallel analysis of real and simulated data set for Study 1

Table 6.2 Item distribution of the CISIA questionnaire used in Study 1 across the four factors

Section of the test (number of items)	Factor 1	Factor 2	Factor 3	Factor 4
Logic (13)	1	10	2	0
Reading ability (15)	0	0	0	15
Mathematics 1 and 2 (30)	15	9	6	0
Sciences (20)	4	5	11	0
Overall (78)	20	24	19	15

onto factor 1, while science items load mainly onto factor 3. This pattern suggests that the CISIA questionnaire used in study 1 investigates more than a single latent trait.

PCA of Residuals

Results of Rasch PCA of residuals seem to confirm the above results. About 34% of the variance is explained by Rasch measures (persons: 6.5%, items: 27.3%). In the unexplained variance, we found only a contrast with eigenvalue greater than 2 (2.46), while the second and third contrasts have eigenvalues smaller than 2 (1.97 and 1.89, respectively). We report the residual plots in Fig. 6.2. In the upper area of the plot (loading >0.2) there are only mathematics and science (specifically, physics) items. In

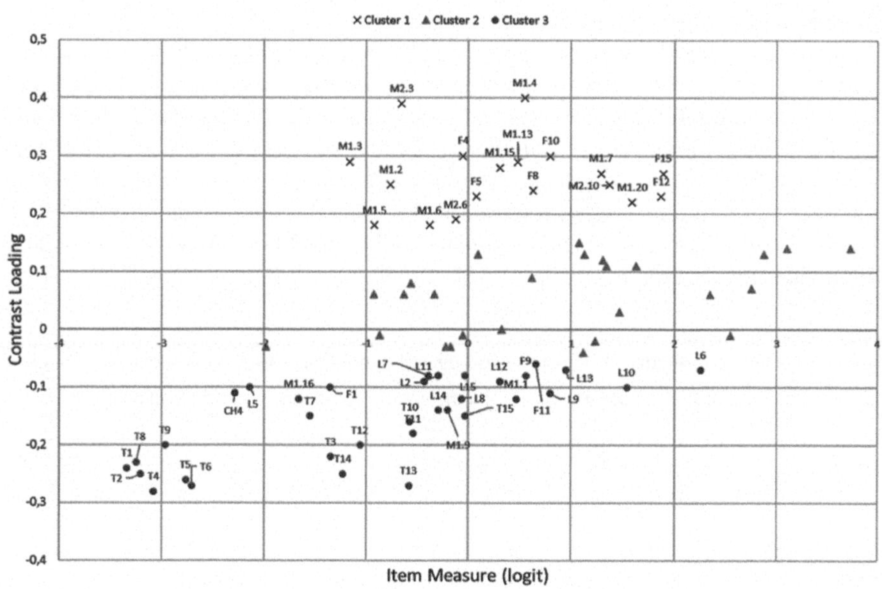

Fig. 6.2 Residual plot for CISIA questionnaire used in Study 1. Items in cluster 2 are not labeled

the bottom area of the plot (loading <−0.2) only reading ability items appear. These items show strongest contrast to each other and cluster amongst themselves more than they do with the remaining items of the test. The disattenuated correlation between these clusters of items is 0.61, which is very close to the cutoff value suggested by Linacre (0.57) for which a secondary dimension begins to be noticeable. However, given also the results of the factor analysis we can conclude that likely reading ability items and mathematics/physics items measure two different latent traits of the sample.

Rasch Measures

The person reliability index is 0.84, which can be considered excellent. Item Separation is 22.93 while Person Separation is 2.39. Both values are satisfactory. The value of the Person Separation index suggests that at least two groups of students can be identified. Only three items have MNSQ outfit values greater than 1.3 (L6, L9, F3) and only one item a value smaller than 0.7 (M1.18). In the electronic supplementary material, we provide the complete statistics for the items of the CISIA questionnaire. Table 6.3 reports the item difficulty according to the addressed content area. First, we note that the average item difficulty of targeted content areas, except reading ability, is greater than 0, suggesting that the CISIA questionnaire was difficult for the students. Reading ability items have statistically different difficulty in comparison to the other items, while the difficulty of logic, mathematics and science questions is not statistically different. Such evidence confirms that, likely, the CISIA questionnaire measures two different latent traits of the sample.

Figure 6.3 shows the Wright map of the CISIA test used in study 1. The average ability is -1.15 ± 0.79 logit. Only 7% of students have ability greater than 0. Table 6.4 shows the average abilities of the students according to the faculty of enrollment and their FGP. The differences are statistically significant for both variables. Note that the average FGP of individuals enrolling in engineering is greater than the average FGP of individuals enrolling in science (85.9 vs. 84.0, $t = 3.282$, $df = 1055.234$, $p = 0.001$). This result suggests that estimated ability and FGP may vary significantly within the sciences group.

Table 6.3 Average difficulty of content areas targeted in the CISIA questionnaire used in Study 1

	Reading ability	Logic	Mathematics 1	Sciences	Mathematics 2	F
Avg. difficulty (logit)	-1.88 ± 0.31	0.15 ± 0.30	0.34 ± 0.27	0.63 ± 0.32	0.68 ± 0.47	10.383[a]

[a] $df = 4; p < 10^{-4}; \eta^2 = 0.36$

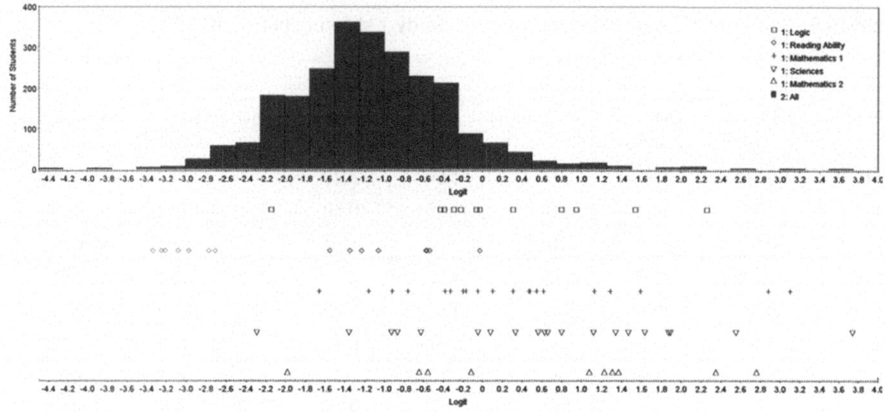

Fig. 6.3 Wright map of the CISIA questionnaire used in Study 1

Table 6.4 Distribution of students' abilities among groups of Study 1

	Engineering ($N = 1803$)	Sciences ($N = 632$)	t	FGP > 90/100 ($N = 972$)	FGP < 90/100 ($N = 1463$)	t
Avg. ability (logit)	-1.19 ± 0.75	-1.02 ± 0.89	-4.336^{a}	-0.86 ± 0.85	-1.34 ± 0.69	14.982^{b}

[a] $df = 962.907; p < 10^{-4}$
[b] $df = 1777.074; p < 10^{-4}$

Differential Item Functioning (DIF)

Table 6.5 reports the main findings. Overall, 17 items exhibit potential DIF as a function of faculty enrollment and secondary school FGP.

Concerning the faculty enrollment, we found three mathematics items with significant difference ($p < 0.05$) and large DIF contrast (>0.64, Linacre, 2012). Four other items exhibit a significant difference ($p < 0.05$) and moderate DIF contrast (>0.50). Note that CH2 and M1.18 are the most difficult items of the test. All items, except M2.1, favor science students. Concerning secondary school performance as measured by FGP, four items display a significant difference and large contrast; three of them favor students with higher FGP. Two of these items, L6 and L9, were also misfitting items. Six other items display moderate contrast but still significant difference, evenly favoring students with higher and lower FGP, respectively. Overall, 13 out of the 17 items showing potential DIF concern logic and mathematics (about one-third of the items in this content area), while 4 concern physics and chemistry (one-fifth of the items in this area). To obtain more insight, we then performed a new analysis removing the 17 items showing potential DIF and inspected again the differences between the abilities of the groups. Table 6.6 reports the results of this analysis. While, as expected, the test becomes easier (average ability $= -0.90 \pm 0.80$), we

Table 6.5 Items of CISIA questionnaire used in Study 1 showing potential DIF

		Faculty enrollment				Final grade point (FGP)	
Item	Difficulty (logit)	DIF contrast[a]	Probability	Item	Difficulty (logit)	DIF contrast[b]	Probability
M1.18[c]	3.10	0.71	0.02	L6[c]	2.26	0.89	$<10^{-4}$
M2.8	1.31	0.68	$<10^{-4}$	L9[c]	0.80	0.72	$<10^{-4}$
M2.4	−0.56	0.64	$<10^{-4}$	L10	1.54	0.66	$<10^{-4}$
CH2	3.74	0.58	0.15	M2.5	2.35	0.61	0.005
F11	0.66	0.51	$<10^{-4}$	F4	−0.05	0.59	$<10^{-4}$
M1.20	1.59	0.50	$<10^{-4}$	CH3	−0.87	0.59	0.0122
M2.1	−1.98	−0.54	$<10^{-4}$	M1.7	1.29	−0.55	0.0001
				F10	0.80	−0.63	0.0007
				M1.15	0.31	−0.63	$<10^{-4}$
				M1.3	−1.16	−0.67	$<10^{-4}$

[a]Negative values indicate a difference in favor of engineering students
[b]Negative values indicate a difference in favor of students with lower FGP
[c]Misfitting item

note that differences between groups are still significant: students enrolling in a science faculty are more able than engineering students, and students with higher FGP are more able than students with a lower FGP.

Study 2

The analysis was carried out for all items, except those pertaining to reading ability (total analyzed items = 90). The reason for excluding such items is that the EFA previously performed in study 1 provided clear evidence of a uniform loading of such items into a single factor.

EFA and Parallel Analysis

The values of Kaiser–Meyer–Olkin measure of sampling adequacy and Bartlett sphericity test are 0.828 and $\chi^2 = 13295$, $df = 4005$, $p < 10^{-4}$, respectively, which suggest that coherent factors can be identified. The EFA results show that the first eigenvalue is 2.3 times as big as the second eigenvalue. Out of the remaining factors with eigenvalue bigger than 1, only three have eigenvalues distinguishable in size from those extracted from the parallel analysis (see Fig. 6.4). Therefore, we retained the solution with four factors, which account for 16% of the variance, a very similar value to that of study 1. We report in the electronic supplementary materials how questionnaire's items load into the extracted four factors. In Table 6.7 we

Table 6.6 Distribution of students' abilities in Study 1 after removing items showing potential DIF

	Engineering ($N = 1803$)	Sciences ($N = 632$)	t	FGP > 90/100 ($N = 972$)	FGP < 90/100 ($N = 1463$)	t
Avg. ability (logit)	−0.94 ± 0.77 (st. dev.)	−0.80 ± 0.90 (st. dev)	−3.616[a]	−0.62 ± 0.86 (st. dev.)	−1.09 ± 0.71 (st.dev.)	14.300[b]

[a] $df = 971.447; p < 10^{-4}$
[b] $df = 1798.961; p < 10^{-4}$

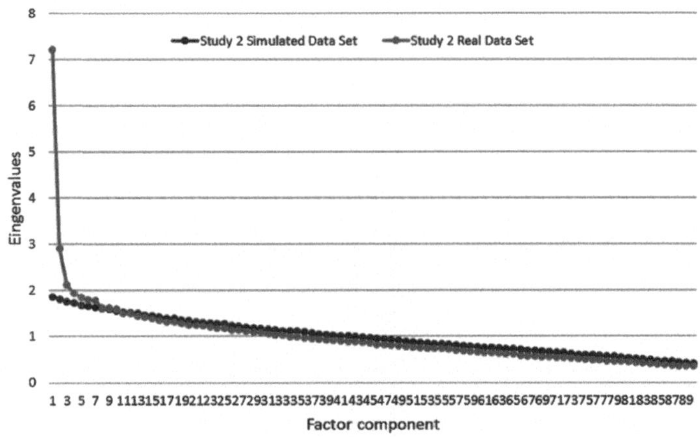

Fig. 6.4 Parallel analysis of real and simulated data set for Study 2

Table 6.7 Item distribution of the extended CISIA-like questionnaire used in Study 2 across the four factors

Section of the test (number of items)	Factor 1	Factor 2	Factor 3	Factor 4
Biology (20)	19	1	0	0
Chemistry (20)	10	0	3	7
Physics (20)[a]	2	3	14	0
Mathematics (20)[b]	0	3	14	2
Logic (10)	1	8	1	0
Overall (90)[c]	32	15	32	9

[a,b]One item does not load into any factor
[c]Overall, two items do not load into any factor

summarize, for each targeted content area of the test, the distribution of items with a loading greater than 0.10 into the extracted factors. Biology items load exclusively onto factor 1, chemistry items load mainly in factors 1 and 4, logic items onto factor 2, while mathematics and physics items load mainly onto factor 3. The emergent pattern suggests that also the extended CISIA-like questionnaire used in study 2 likely investigates different latent traits, most notably knowledge in biology and chemistry, and knowledge in mathematics and physics.

PCA of Residuals

About 28% of the variance is explained by Rasch measures (persons: 4.7%, items: 23.2%). In the unexplained variance, we found two contrasts with eigenvalue greater than 2 (3.0 and 2.4, respectively), while the third, fourth, and fifth contrasts have

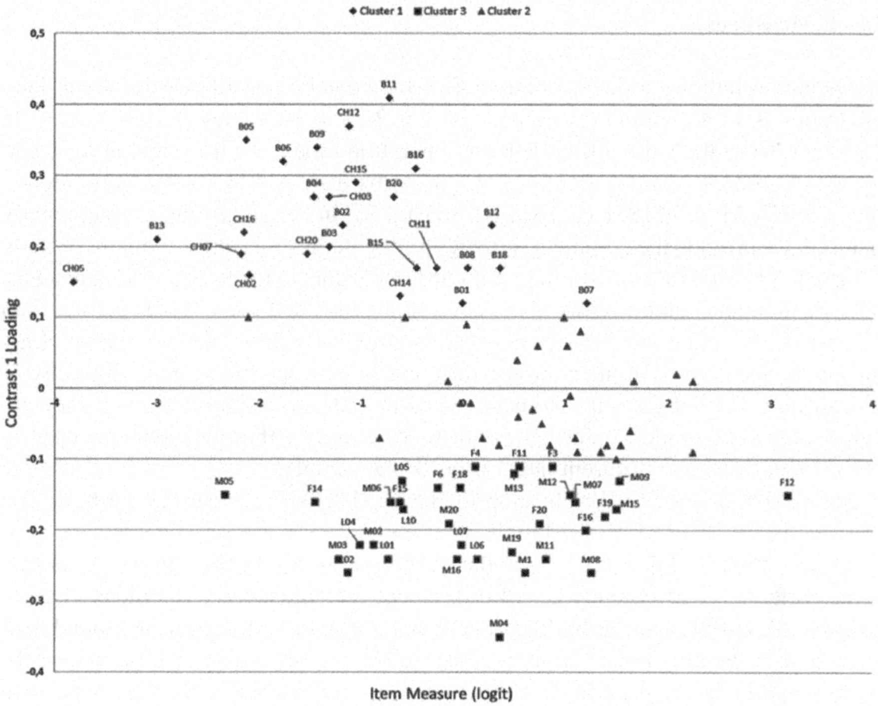

Fig. 6.5 Plot of residual loadings for CISIA questionnaire used in Study 2. Only items with loadings—in absolute value—greater than 0.1 (cluster 1 and 3) are labeled

eigenvalues equal or smaller than 2 (2.0, 1.8 and 1.7, respectively). Such results confirm that the extended CISIA-like questionnaire in study 2 could be not unidimensional. To gain some insight about which items contribute to such non-unidimensionality, we report the residual plot for the first contrast in Fig. 6.5. Three clusters, each with roughly the same number of items, can be identified. In particular, items with absolute value of loading greater than ±0.1 form two distinct clusters. Items with positive loading (>0.1) are all biology and chemistry items, while items with negative loadings (<−0.1) are all mathematics and physics items. Moreover, the disattenuated correlation between these two clusters of items is 0.4272; namely, person measures on these two clusters of items have less than half variance in common as they have independently (Linacre, 2012). Overall, such evidence suggests that mathematics/physics items and biology/chemistry items likely measure different latent traits of the sample.

Rasch Measures

The person reliability index is about 0.83, which can be considered excellent. Item Separation is 14.80 while Person Separation is 2.25. Both values are satisfactory. In particular, from the value of the Person Separation index, we infer that at least two groups of students can be identified. Eight items have MNSQ outfit value greater than 1.3 (F2, M14, M18, F12, F13, F1, M10, L3). In the electronic supplementary material, we provide the complete statistics for the items of the questionnaire in study 2. Table 6.8 reports the average item difficulty according to the targeted content areas. Only mathematics and physics items have an average difficulty that is greater than 0. In particular, math and physics items are significantly more difficult than biology and chemistry items. On the contrary, differences between the average difficulty of biology and chemistry items, and between math and physics items are not statically significant. Such evidence further confirms that, likely, the questionnaire used in study 2 measures two different latent traits of the sample.

Figure 6.6 shows the Wright map of the CISIA-like test used in study 2. The average ability is -1.19 ± 0.70 logit. We note that only 5% of students have ability greater than 0. Table 6.9 shows the average abilities of the sample according to the variables used in study 2. All differences are statistically significant, except male-female differences on biology and chemistry items. Moreover, we found that, regardless of the targeted content area, the ranking of secondary school, the enrollment in a STEM faculty, the participation in extracurricular activities, a positive attitude toward school science and the interest in pursuing a science-related career are all positively associated with the test performance.

Differential Item Functioning (DIF)

To investigate whether statistical differences among students of different groups in the sample were due to unintended biases in the formulation of the items, we inspected items for potential DIF across the variables of study 2. The criterion to flag the items was the same as the one used in study 1. Table 6.10 reports the main findings. Overall, we found that less than 6% of the items exhibit DIF when considering the following variables: participation in extracurricular activities (4 items: 1 biology, 2 math, 2 physics), attitude toward school science (2 items: 1 biology, 1 physics), and interest toward a career in science (5 items: 1 chemistry, 2 math, 2 physics). The results for the remaining variables are reported in Tables 6.10 and 6.11. Given that we found 35 items exhibiting potential DIF for at least one of the variables of study 2, we proceeded to remove such items to look for changes in item difficulty and students' abilities. Results are shown in Tables 6.12 and 6.13. The ranking of content areas according to their difficulty does not change (physics items are still the most difficult ones, while chemistry items the easiest). Similarly, all the differences among groups are still significant after removing the items, except that the test itself becomes more affordable for the subjects (average ability = -0.82 logit).

Table 6.8 Average difficulty of content areas targeted in the extended CISIA-like questionnaire used in Study 2

	Biology	Chemistry	Physics	Mathematics	Logic	F
Avg. difficulty (logit)	−0.5 ± 1.1 (st.dev)	−0.6 ± 1.4 (st.dev)	0.8 ± 1.0 (st.dev)	0.5 ± 1.1 (st.dev)	−0.29 ± 0.80 (st.dev)	6.195[a]

[a] $df = 4; p < 10^{-4}; \eta^2 = 0.23$

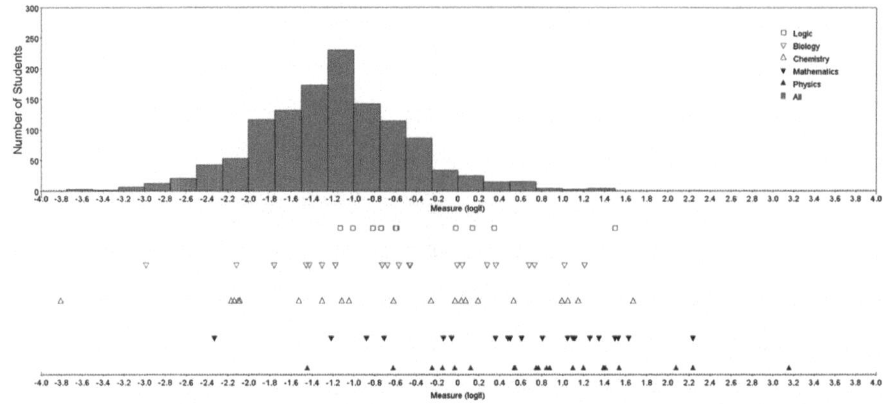

Fig. 6.6 Wright map of the extended CISIA-like questionnaire used in Study 2

Discussion and Conclusions

The aim of this study was to illustrate how Rasch analysis can assess the psychometric properties of a typical entrance test used in several Italian universities, and how such evidence may help policy makers and test designers to improve validity and reliability of such an instrument. In the following, we discuss the extent to which our aims have been achieved.

What is the reliability and construct validity of a typical university entrance test administered in Italy?

In study 1, person reliability is excellent, while item and person separation indices are satisfactory. When investigating how well data fit the Rasch model, the test has only four misfitting items out of 78. Hence, it can be concluded that the CISIA test is substantially valid and reliable. However, the results of EFA and Rasch PCA of residuals also suggest that the test may be not unidimensional. In particular, by examining the unexplained variance, we found that two sets of measures, reading ability and mathematics/physics knowledge, are not well correlated because they showed strong contrasts with each other (Linacre, 2012). Hence, collected evidence suggests that these two sets of items likely measure distinct latent traits. Looking more into the details of reading ability items, we note that they basically test the extent to which the students are able to recognize if a given claim is present in the text rather than the capability to infer conclusions from the text. Hence, it is reasonable that the reading ability, as measured by this CISIA test, is different from the capability to perform mathematical calculations or the ability to apply scientific concepts to everyday situations. When exploring DIF, 17 items may be potentially

Table 6.9 Distribution of students' abilities among groups of Study 2

	Avg. ability on all items (logit)	Avg. ability on chemistry and biology items (logit)	Avg. ability on math and physics items (logit)
Whole sample	−1.19 ± 0.70	−0.65 ± 0.95	−1.92 ± 0.90
Gender			
Female	−1.31 ± 0.63	−0.70 ± 0.94	−2.14 ± 0.79
Male	−1.10 ± 0.74	−0.61 ± 0.97	−1.76 ± 0.93
t	−5.399[a]	−1.623[ns]	6.876[b]
Ranking of secondary school			
Above median	−1.05 ± 0.69	−0.49 ± 0.95	−1.79 ± 0.90
Below median	−1.43 ± 0.66	−0.91 ± 0.91	−2.15 ± 0.85
t	−9.535[b]	−7.608[b]	6.876[b]
Enrollment faculty			
Engineering	−1.17 ± 0.69	−0.70 ± 0.92	−1.78 ± 0.87
Medicine	−1.06 ± 0.67	−0.34 ± 0.94	−1.97 ± 0.78
Science	−1.04 ± 0.73	−0.47 ± 0.95	−1.8 ± 1.0
Other	−1.37 ± 0.68	−0.92 ± 0.92	−2.06 ± 0.88
F	15.387[c]	23.735[c]	6.752[c]
Extracurricular activities in science			
Yes	−1.01 ± 0.79	−0.5 ± 1.0	−1.70 ± 1.01
No	−1.26 ± 0.65	−0.71 ± 0.91	−2.02 ± 0.82
t	−5.324[d]	−3.435[e]	−5.395[f]
Attitude toward school science			
More positive	−1.13 ± 0.71	−0.59 ± 0.96	−1.87 ± 0.91
Less positive	−1.34 ± 0.66	−0.82 ± 0.93	−2.10 ± 0.82
t	4.364[b]	−3.637[b]	−3.979[b]
Interest toward a career in science			
High interest	−1.15 ± 0.70	−0.60 ± 0.95	−1.89 ± 0.90
Low interest	−1.42 ± 0.69	−0.90 ± 0.93	−2.13 ± 0.84
t	4.808[b]	−3.982[b]	3.355[b]

[a] $df = 1193.26, p < 10^{-4}$
[b] $df = 1221, p < 10^{-4}$
[c] $df = 3, p < 10^{-4}$
[d] $df = 592.47, p < 10^{-4}$
[e] $df = 623.068, p = 0.001$
[f] $df = 584.016, p < 10^{-4}$

Table 6.10 Items of extended CISIA-like questionnaire used in Study 2 showing potential DIF when considering gender and ranking of secondary school

		Gender				Ranking of secondary school	
Item	Difficulty (logit)	DIF contrast[a]	Probability	Item	Difficulty (logit)	DIF contrast[b]	Probability
L6	0.14	0.65	$<10^{-4}$	CH04	1.67	0.63	0.0349
CH09	1.15	0.59	0.0067	CH06	1.05	−0.51	0.0077
M1	0.61	0.87	$<10^{-4}$	M10[c]	1.35	−0.82	0.0001
F5	−0.15	0.74	$<10^{-4}$	M18[c]	1.12	−0.54	0.0058
F7	2.08	0.78	0.02	F1[c]	1.10	−0.76	0.0001
F9	0.85	0.53	0.0059	F6	−0.25	−0.67	$<10^{-4}$
F16	1.20	0.52	0.017	F13[c]	1.54	−0.79	0.0005
F19	1.39	0.51	0.00295				
F20	0.75	0.94	$<10^{-4}$				

[a]Positive values indicate a difference in favor of male students
[b]Positive values indicate a difference in favor of students from schools with lower ranking
[c]Misfitting items

biased according to FGP and students' faculty of enrollment. DIF of the 10 items for FGP may be justified by the fact that low-achievement students may understand differently the same item due to unfamiliar wording. In the second case (faculty enrollment), the seven items (six are math items) showing DIF are mostly biased toward science students. Such evidence could be justified with a greater degree of familiarity with math of students enrolling in a science degree. However, a further content analysis did not highlight specific features of the above items that could justify DIF. Hence, we cannot conclude that these specific items were formulated in an unfamiliar way in comparison to the others. Moreover, since differences between the groups remain unaltered after removal of the items that exhibit potential DIF, we conclude that the items can be safely retained since they do not alter the measurement properties of the test.

Also in study 2 person reliability is excellent, with satisfactory values of item and person separation indices. We found eight items that have MNSQ outfit value greater than 1.3 (F2, M14, M18, F12, F13, F1, M10, L3). Given that the average ability of students is lower than the mean difficulty of these items, likely, such misfits may be due to ambiguous or unclear wording, rather than guessing. Hence, these items need to be improved. However, since 82 out of the 90 analyzed items do not present misfitting behavior and are well distributed along the student-ability continuum, we can conclude that the extended CISIA-like questionnaire used in study 2 possesses certain degrees of validity and reliability. However, unidimensionality issues arise also for this test. Having removed the reading ability items, we explored in more detail the extent to which mathematics and science items measure the same latent trait. Evidence from EFA and Rasch PCA of residuals suggests that math/physics items, and biology/chemistry items, likely measure two distinct latent traits. Such subdivision may be related to the fact that, at secondary school level in Italy, mathematics and

Table 6.11 Items of extended CISIA-like questionnaire used in Study 2 showing potential DIF when considering faculty enrollment

Item	Difficulty (logit)	DIF contrast	Probability	Favors	Bias against
B07	1.21	0.90	0.0029	Medicine	Science
B10	0.73	0.58	0.0224	Medicine	Science
B11	−0.73	−0.59	0.0013	Science	Others
B12	0.28	−0.51	0.0247	Science	Engineering
B13	−2.99	−0.61	0.0247	Science	Others
B13	−2.99	−0.58	0.0248	Science	Engineering
B19	1.02	0.91	0.0009	Medicine	Science
CH10	0.03	−0.53	0.0099	Science	Others
CH12	−1.12	−0.53	0.0032	Science	Others
CH18	0.19	−0.64	0.0026	Science	Others
CH20	−1.53	−0.51	0.0067	Science	Engineering
M1	0.61	−0.72	0.0072	Science	Medicine
M5	−2.33	0.90	$<10^{-4}$	Engineering	Science
M7	1.10	−0.54	0..0422	Science	Engineering
M7	1.10	−0.56	0.0348	Science	Others
M10[a]	1.35	0.82	0.0143	Medicine	Science
M14[a]	2.24	0.90	0.0363	Other	Science
F1[a]	1.10	0.77	0.0042	Other	Science
F9	0.85	−0.85	0.0021	Science	Medicine
F11	0.55	−0.92	0.0002	Science	Medicine

[a]Misfitting items

physics are often taught by the same teacher, as it happens for biology and chemistry. These school subjects have very different approaches, goals, and methodologies: in mathematics and physics, emphasis is on demonstrating and deploying formulas and on solving quantitative problems, while in biology and chemistry, emphasis is on more qualitative aspects of natural phenomena involving life and matter, respectively. The differences between how these couples of subjects are taught may be reflected in the two different latent traits measured by the questionnaire. More insight could be inferred when looking at items exhibiting potential DIF. When considering gender, nine items exhibit potential DIF, all biased toward male students. Seven items target physics; however, detected items concern all areas of physics, from kinematics to astronomy, and do not present graphical or verbal features that are different in comparison to the other physics items. Hence, we can infer that such differences may be inherent to the test. When considering the ranking of secondary school, seven items exhibit potential DIF, all except one biased toward students from school with higher ranking: two address chemistry, two math, and three physics. Since the difficulty of these items range from −0.25 toward 1.67 logit, we cannot infer any significant

Table 6.12 Average difficulty of content areas targeted in the extended CISIA-like questionnaire used in Study 2 after removing items showing potential DIF

	Biology ($N = 13$)	Chemistry ($N = 13$)	Physics ($N = 9$)	Mathematics (N = 11)	Logic (N = 9)	F
Avg. difficulty (logit)	−0.47 ± 0.76 (st.dev)	−0.70 ± 1.4 (st.dev)	0.81 ± 1.1 (st.dev)	0.70 ± 1.0 (st.dev)	0.04 ± 0.84 (st.dev.)	4.759[a]

[a] $df = 4; p < 0.002; \eta^2 = 0.28$

Table 6.13 Distribution of students' abilities in Study 2 after removing items showing potential DIF

	Avg. ability on all items (logit)
Whole sample	-0.82 ± 0.72
Gender	
Female	-0.92 ± 0.67
Male	-0.74 ± 0.75
t	-4.553^{a}
Ranking of secondary school	
Above median	-0.66 ± 0.71
Below median	-1.07 ± 0.67
t	-9.910^{a}
Enrollment faculty	
Engineering	-0.79 ± 0.71
Medicine	-0.71 ± 0.72
Science	-0.69 ± 0.73
Other	-0.99 ± 0.70
F	12.301^{b}
Extracurricular activities in science	
Yes	-0.66 ± 0.80
No	-0.88 ± 0.67
t	-5.136^{a}
Attitude toward school science	
More positive	-0.77 ± 0.72
Less positive	-0.97 ± 0.69
t	-4.344^{a}
Interest toward career in science	
High interest	-0.77 ± 0.71
Low interest	-1.06 ± 0.72
t	-4.918^{a}

$^{a}df = 1221, p < 10^{-4}$
$^{b}df = 3, p < 10^{-4}$

trend from such evidence. Finally, when considering faculty enrollment, we find 18 items that exhibit potential DIF: six items target biology, four target chemistry, four math, and four physics. The analysis shows that three biology items favored medicine students, the other three science students. The four chemistry items and three physics items favored science students, while math items do not present a clear pattern. Likely, such potential DIF may be due to specific areas deepened by the students in relation to their future academic path. Finally, when removing items showing potential DIF, the order relationships between the difficulty of targeted areas and students' abilities do not change. Thus, as in the case of study 1, the DIF cannot be due to a higher degree of familiarity of one group with respect to the others with the topics addressed but rather it can be considered inherent to the test and the sample, so the items can be safely retained. Our evidence adds to a growing body of literature that aims at investigating reasons for DIF in typical entrance tests (Kalaycioglu & Berberoglu, 2011). We are currently investigating whether a different formulation of the same item could bias the responses of a specific group of students according to the type of attended high school.

To what extent does the item difficulty vary across three content areas (mathematics, science and reading)?

In study 1, the difficulty of the underlying latent traits is significantly different: reading ability items are the only ones with a negative average value of difficulty, namely, they are easy items. Advanced mathematics and science items have a 2.6-logit distance on the latent continuum from reading ability average difficulty, namely they are difficult items. Because the CISIA questionnaire focus on what the students have learned during secondary school, as other admission tests (Atkinson, 2009), our study supports the conclusion that secondary school students have significantly different preparations in these areas of the Italian curriculum. In particular, it emerges that secondary school math curriculum does not offer enough support to students to reach an acceptable level at the university admission test in this subject area. The analysis of students' scores confirms a significant difference between students who chose an engineering degree and those who chose a science degree, and between students with good and below average school grades. Such difference may be likely linked to the different ways in which students are evaluated during their secondary school path and at the end of such path. A suitable follow-up study should aim at establishing more rigorously whether the evaluation of the reading ability and the capability of reasoning in math/science actually aim at significantly different learning objectives and target different competences.

Similarly, also in study 2, we found that the targeted latent traits have significantly different difficulties. In particular, math/physics items have an average difficulty of $+0.76$ logit, while biology/chemistry items a value of -0.59 logit. Although the questionnaire used in study 2 was designed by our group as an extension of the CISIA test used in study 1, the obtained results confirm that students at the end of the secondary school are underprepared in math/physics for the standards of a typical CISIA admission test. A possible reason is that math/physics items in the questionnaire targeted topics that are not deepened enough during secondary school. Thus, inclusion or elimination of math/physics items may considerably change the final result of the test and hence the results of the students' selection. While secondary school teaching cannot become a test preparation program (Changbin, 1995), a greater alignment between student ability and item difficulty is needed in order to make university entrance tests fairer for the Italian student population.

As a final implication, our study shows that Rasch analysis of university admission questionnaires can offer valid information about students' proficiency in reading ability, math/physics and chemistry/biology when entering in STEM degrees. Thus, the results of the two studies may be used by secondary school teachers and university instructors as a resource for identifying students' main gaps in math and science, so to design more focused and responsive teaching interventions.

Acknowledgements This study was funded by the Italian Ministry of Education, University and Research under the national project "Piano nazionale Lauree Scientifiche" (PLS).

References

Atkinson, R. (2009). The new SAT: A test at war with itself. Invited presidential address at the annual meeting of the American Educational Research Association, 15 April, San Diego, CA. Retrieve 04-24-2019 at http://rca.ucsd.edu/speeches/aera_041509_speech_reflections_on_a_century_of_college_admissions_tests.pdf.

Bond, T., & Fox, C. M. (2007). *Applying the Rasch Model: Fundamental Measurement in the Human Sciences*. Mahwah, NJ: Lawrence Erlbaum.

Boone, W. J., Staver, J. R., & Yale, M. S. (2014). *Rasch Analysis in the Human Sciences*. Dordrecht, The Netherlands: Springer.

Changbin, Z. (1995). The National University Entrance Examination and its influence on secondary school physics teaching in China. *Physics Education, 30*(2), 104–108. https://doi.org/10.1088/0031-9120/30/2/010.

Davey, G., De Lian, C., & Higgins, L. (2007). The university entrance examination system in China. *Journal of Further and Higher Education, 31*(4), 385–396. https://doi.org/10.1080/03098770701625761.

Deygers, B., Zeidler, B., Vilcu, D., & Carlsen, C. H. (2018). One Framework to Unite Them All? *Use of the CEFR in European University Entrance Policies, Language Assessment Quarterly, 15*(1), 3–15. https://doi.org/10.1080/15434303.2016.1261350.

Emery, J. L., & Bell, J. F. (2009). The predictive validity of the Biomedical Admissions Test for pre-clinical examination performance. *Medical Education, 43,* 557–564. https://doi.org/10.1111/j.1365-2923.2009.03367.x.

Horn, J. L. (1965). A rationale and test for the number of factors in factor analysis. *Psychometrica, 30*(2), 179–185.

Italian Ministry of Education, University and Research (1999) Rules for admission at University degrees. http://www.miur.it/0006Menu_C/0012Docume/0098Normat/2056Norme__cf2.htm.

Kalaycioğlu, D. B., & Berberoğlu, G. (2011). Differential item functioning analysis of the science and mathematics items in the university entrance examinations in Turkey. *Journal of Psychoeducational Assessment, 29*(5), 467–478. https://doi.org/10.1177/0734282910391623.

Killgore, L. M. (2009). Merit and competition in selective college admissions. *Review of Higher Education, 32,* 469–488. https://doi.org/10.1353/rhe.0.0083.

Kuramoto, N., & Koizumi, R. (2018). Current issues in large-scale educational assessment in Japan: focus on national assessment of academic ability and university entrance examinations. *Assessment in Education: Principles, Policy & Practice, 25*(4), 415–433. https://doi.org/10.1080/0969594X.2016.1225667.

Kyoung Ro, H., Lattuca, L. R., & Alcott, B. (2017). Who goes to graduate school? Engineers' math proficiency, college experience, and self-assessment of skills. *Journal of Engineering Education, 106,* 98–122. https://doi.org/10.1002/jee.20154.

Linacre J. M. (2012). Winsteps® Rasch Tutorial 4. Available at http://www.winsteps.com/a/winsteps-tutorial-4.pdf.

Liu, X. (2010). *Using and developing measurement instruments in science education: A Rasch modeling approach*. Charlotte: Information Age Publishing.

McManus, I. C., Ferguson, E., Wakeford, R., Powis, D., & James, D. (2011). Predictive validity of the Biomedical Admissions Test: An evaluation and case study. *Medical Teacher, 33*(1), 53–57. https://doi.org/10.3109/0142159X.2010.525267.

Neumann, I., Neumann, K., & Nehm, R. (2011). Evaluating Instrument Quality in Science Education: Rasch-based analyses of a Nature of Science test. *International Journal of Science Education, 33*(10), 1373–1405. https://doi.org/10.1080/09500693.2010.511297.

Ortiz-Lozano, J. M., Rua-Vieites, A., Bilbao-Calabuig, P., & Casadesús-Fa, M. P. (2018). University student retention: Best time and data to identify undergraduate students at risk of dropout. *Innovations in Education and Teaching International*. https://doi.org/10.1080/14703297.2018.1502090.

Sternberg, J. R., & The Rainbow Project Collaborators & The University of Michigan Business School Project Collaborators. (2004). Theory-based university admissions testing for a new millennium. *Educational Psychologist, 39*(3), 185–198. https://doi.org/10.1207/s15326985ep3903_4.

Thomas, L. (2011). Do Pre-entry Interventions such as 'Aimhigher' impact on student retention and success? A review of the literature. *Higher Education Quarterly, 65,* 230–250.

Thomas, L., & Hovdhaugen, E. (2014). Complexities and challenges of researching student completion and non-completion of HE programmes in Europe: A comparative analysis between England and Norway. *European Journal of Education, 49,* 457–470.

Vivo, J.-M., & Franco, M. (2008). How does one assess the accuracy of academic success predictors? *ROC analysis applied to university entrance factors, International Journal of Mathematical Education in Science and Technology, 39*(3), 325–340. https://doi.org/10.1080/00207390701691566.

Wright, B. D., & Masters, G. N. (1982). *Rating scale analysis*. Chicago, IL: Mesa Press.

Chapter 7
Examining an Economics Test to Inform University Student Learning Using the Rasch Model

Joseph Chow and Alice Shiu

Abstract This paper describes a quantitative analysis from an educational measurement approach to evaluating a multiple-choice test used in an introductory economics course in a Hong Kong university. The assessment was used in an undergraduate course on elementary economics topics with an enrolment of over 300 first-year students from various engineering disciplines. The results of a Rasch analysis showed how the assessment analysis provided information for evaluating students' understanding of economics concepts at the end of the course. Investigations were made and reported on the quality of the test for assessing student mastery of the economic concepts. Benefits for university instructors to use the assessment evidence to support more targeted and effective teaching and achieve better understanding of student mastery were discussed. Recommendations and implications for future use of the assessment information were also discussed.

Keywords Teacher-constructed assessment · Higher education · Economics education · Rasch modeling · Multiple-choice test · Educational measurement

Introduction

To support student learning with assessment, it is important for instructors in higher education institutions to master relevant skills in assessment. Instructors are expected to utilize the information derived from student assessment results for monitoring and improving their teaching practices. To do this, instructors need to professionally review, evaluate, and make evidence-based decision regarding student assessment performance.

J. Chow (✉)
Educational Development Centre, The Hong Kong Polytechnic University, Hung Hom, Hong Kong
e-mail: joseph.chow@polyu.edu.hk

A. Shiu
School of Accounting and Finance, The Hong Kong Polytechnic University, Hung Hom, Hong Kong

M. S. Khine (ed.), *Rasch Measurement*,
https://doi.org/10.1007/978-981-15-1800-3_7

This article illustrates with an empirical example of how university instructors can obtain useful and actionable information from assessment results to better understand student learning. Specifically, obtaining the diagnostic information from assessment and making it visible to instructors is crucial in supporting them to make informed instructional decisions that lead to higher learning effectiveness. Analysis of the assessment data is the initial step that helps instructors obtain useful assessment information, including overall quality of the test and the difficulty of the individual items.

Purposes of Analyzing Student Assessment Data

To inform teaching and learning, there are at least two perspectives from which instructors can obtain valuable insights based on the assessment results: from evaluating the student performance and evaluating the items administered in the test.

Assessment information includes the performance of individual students, performance of the whole class, difficulty of individual items in specific content domains, and overall difficulty and characteristics of the test. By looking at both information of the items and the information of the student performance together, instructors can understand student learning more holistically.

In addition to the various indicators of the quality of test based on the student responses to the test items, there is additional information that instructors can make use of data at different levels to guide instructional decisions and actions. For example, at the student level, the assessment results can show the strengths and weaknesses of individual students in a class. It also helps instructors to make reflection about classroom teaching effectiveness. At the course level, the assessment information can support instructors to make evidence-based evaluative judgements such as alignment between the assessment standards and curriculum standards, potential areas for improvement of assessment items, and level of course effectiveness.

Making use of student assessment data for teaching and learning enhancement is not something new to instructors in higher education. Common uses included analysis of student assessment data for evaluating assessment tools, understanding student learning progress, as well as enhancing teaching practices. This paper outlines some techniques of how the assessment data can be analyzed and offers some indicators for instructors to examine information about the test items and students. It will illustrate collecting useful information from analyzing an empirical assessment test used in a university economics course. Assessment information will be presented by interpreting the analysis results to inform the above-mentioned assessment purposes.

In the current study, Rasch analysis was applied to provide diagnostic information about the test items and students that can be used to enhance teaching and learning. One of the advantages of applying the Rasch model to analyze the assessment data is its ability to consider and analyze the assessment items and the students as test takers together and present the results jointly. It can thus provide an objective measure of student ability that is independent of the difficulty of the item in the assessment task (Bond & Fox, 2015).

Method

Participants

This was a part of a larger study on assessment feedback in mobile learning of economics of university engineering students. Participants for the current study comprised of more than 250 engineering students in a university in Hong Kong.

Instrument

A 25-item economics test was developed with careful examination of the course learning outcomes, the assessment requirements, and consultation with the instructor on the applicability of the test for the engineering students enrolled in the course.

The test was administered to the students toward the end of the course in the second semester in 2017/2018 academic year. All the test items were multiple-choice items with four response options while only one option was correct response and the other three options were distractors. The test items fell into four domains with reference to the four major areas of economics knowledge standards intended in the course. See Table 7.1.

Data Analysis

The assessment test and items analyzed in this study were designed by the instructor of the economics course. Rasch analysis was applied to the analyzing test to inform the test quality as well as student achievement.

Table 7.1 Topics and number of items of the multiple-choice test

Topic	Number of items
1	6
2	6
3	6
4	7

The Rasch Model

Developed by Rasch (1960), the Rasch model specifies that the probability that a person with ability (b) succeeds on an item with difficulty (d) is a logistic function of the relative difference between item difficulty and person ability. Rasch analysis can be used to calibrate person parameters (ability) and item parameters (difficulty) on the same unidimensional scale (Bond & Fox, 2015). The parameters are expressed in log-odd units (logits) which is the natural algorithm of the odd ratio (probability of the desired outcomes against the probability of the non-desired outcome). Under Rasch measurement, when person ability is greater than item difficulty, the greater their difference, the higher the probability of answering an item correctly. When person ability is lower than the item difficulty, the greater the difference, the lower the probability of answering an item correctly.

The Rasch analysis was performed with the analysis software Winsteps (Linacre, 2011). The student responses to the multiple-choice (four choices) items were scored either correct (if the student chose the right option) or incorrect (if the student chose any one of the three wrong options), the dichotomous Rasch model was applied to estimate both the item difficulties and student cognitive abilities regarding economics knowledge under assessment.

The Rasch analysis provided several statistical indices for examining the knowledge test under examination: person separation index, person reliability index, item separation index, and item reliability index. Person reliability referred to the replicability of person placements along the latent trait scale while item reliability referred to the replicability of item placement along the measured construct for samples from the same population (Bond & Fox, 2015, p. 363 and 369). Person separation and item separation indices indicated the spread of the person measures and item measures, respectively (Bond & Fox, 2015). The separation index estimated the number of measurably different levels of item measures or person measures that can be distinguished on the measurement scale. It was considered acceptable if it was higher than 2.0 (Wright & Stone, 2004).

Findings

As mentioned above, the results of the Rasch analysis can provide information in two main aspects: (a) characteristics of the test as the assessment tool, and (b) information about the achievement of student learning outcomes. Regarding the characteristics of the test, the first criterion for examination is the degree of model-data fit, i.e., the extent to which the assessment data fit to the requirements of the Rasch model. This can be empirically evaluated by the fit statistics provided from the Rasch analysis. Besides, other statistics informing the quality of the test were also reported and examined, such as the person and item separation indices, and person and item reliabilities.

Regarding the information about student learning outcomes, the distribution of student ability measures, their relative positions in relation to the test and item difficulty measures were reported. The item difficulties were also presented across the four content domains. Such information would be useful for instructors making evidence-based decisions about the assessment test, such as whether some items showing good psychometric properties should be kept for future use (e.g., be retained in an item bank).

The Rasch analysis findings were first summarized below, followed by a more detailed discussion of the results.

Unidimensionality of the Items

For examination of unidimensionality, a Principal Component Analysis (PCA) of Rasch residuals was performed. It was performed to examine whether the assessment data can be explained adequately by a single Rasch dimension. In other words, this examined whether there is more than one dimension possibly explaining the data after the Rasch dimension was extracted.

Previous simulations reported acceptable ranges of eigenvalues of the first contrast of the PCA as being around two eigenvalues: from 1.4 to 2.1 (Raîche, 2005) or below 2.0 (Linacre, 2011). In this analysis, the PCA showed eigenvalues of the first contrast to be 2.1, while 37.8% of variance in the data were explained by the Rasch measure. It indicated that the economics test showed adequate fit to the Rasch model, providing a unidimensional measurement of the underlying construct.

Person and Item Reliabilities

The results showed that the MC test consisting of 25 items had satisfactory item reliability (0.92) and item separation index (3.33). The person separation index was 1.91 while person reliability was 0.74. The corresponding measure of internal consistency according to the classical test theory, the Cronbach's alpha, was 0.80, which was acceptable. These results mean that based on the assessment data, the items could be separated into around four difficulty strata and the students could be divided into almost two ability strata.

The number of students (more than 100) and the number of items (less than 30) analyzed should be taken into consideration when interpreting the item/person separation measures reported here. Compared to dividing more than 100 students into discrete levels of ability by 25 items only, it is easier to divide 25 items into discrete levels of difficulty by more than 100 students.

Item Statistics

Table 7.2 showed the item statistics for each of the 25 items, which included the measures: item difficulty, standard error of measurement, fit statistics (both infit and outfit), and point-measure correlation.

All the items showed fit statistics ranging from 0.5 to 1.5, which was an acceptable fit. The items were located across a wide range of difficulties, ranging from −1.0 to +1.2 logits. Overall, the levels of test item difficulties matched well with the levels of student ability. These statistics showed that these 25 items had good psychometric

Table 7.2 Item difficulty, standard error, fit, and point-measure correlation

Item	Difficulty	Standard error	Infit		Outfit		PTME corr.
			MnSq	ZStd	MnSq	ZStd	
1	−0.83	0.33	1.18	0.90	1.31	0.90	0.20
2	0.78	0.25	1.06	0.70	1.02	0.20	0.36
3	0.30	0.26	0.81	−1.70	0.73	−1.60	0.57
4	−0.16	0.28	0.86	−1.00	0.77	−1.00	0.52
5	−0.25	0.29	1.33	2.00	1.17	1.40	0.03
6	−0.52	0.30	1.00	0.10	0.82	−0.50	0.40
7	−0.72	0.32	0.86	−0.70	0.66	−1.00	0.50
8	1.04	0.25	0.99	−0.10	0.97	−0.10	0.42
9	0.73	0.25	0.94	−0.60	0.88	−0.80	0.47
10	−0.62	0.31	0.87	−0.70	0.73	−0.80	0.49
11	1.11	0.25	1.20	2.10	1.21	1.30	0.23
12	−0.72	0.32	1.05	0.30	0.93	−0.10	0.33
13	−2.49	0.59	1.18	0.50	1.23	0.53	0.06
14	0.15	0.27	1.09	0.80	1.08	0.50	0.32
15	−2.15	0.52	0.81	−0.30	1.19	0.50	0.36
16	−0.95	0.34	0.83	−0.70	0.69	−0.70	0.49
17	−0.25	0.29	0.88	−0.80	0.70	−1.20	0.52
18	−0.08	0.28	0.94	−0.40	0.83	−0.70	0.46
19	1.11	0.25	1.11	1.20	1.18	1.20	0.29
20	0.30	0.26	1.01	0.10	0.96	−0.20	0.40
21	−0.62	0.22	0.85	−1.30	0.72	−1.40	0.53
22	0.72	0.18	1.16	2.20	1.17	1.50	0.37
23	2.52	0.23	1.10	0.70	1.20	0.80	0.42
24	0.57	0.19	0.92	−1.10	0.88	−1.10	0.53
25	1.00	0.19	0.93	−1.00	0.92	−0.70	0.53
Mean	0.00	0.29	1.00	0.05	0.96	−0.12	0.39
SD	1.07	0.09	0.14	1.08	0.20	0.95	0.14

properties and an adequate fit to the Rasch model. This in turn meant that those items could be regarded as a test measuring students' level of proficiency in economics knowledge of concern.

Person and Item Measures

Table 7.2 shows the item difficulties range from −2.49 logits to 2.52 logits. The standard error of measurement is small and at the order of 0.2–0.3. The hardest item (item estimate >2.00 logits) was Q23 (Topic 3) whereas the easiest items (item estimates <−2.00 logits) were Q13 and Q15 (both Topic 3).

While all the three questions deal with the concepts in Topic 3, Q23 is most difficult because the distractors among the available response options appear to be the trickiest, and it was the only one item in the entire test that there was a greater number of students who got it incorrect than number of students who answered it correctly.

The other three items which were also relatively more difficult are Q8, Q11, and Q19 (all item measures were at around 1.00 logit). In particular, similar with the most difficult item (Q23), Q11 was also an item from Topic 3, receiving over 40% student responses in one of its distractors. The distractor attracted most of the wrong responses in this item because a content analysis showed that it displayed a conception that students commonly found difficult to differentiate from the correct understanding of the underlying economics concept.

Q19, a Topic 4 item, was answered correctly by 47% of the students but received 21% and 26% of responses, respectively in two of its distractors. A similar finding is observed in Q8, a Topic 2 item, which received 20% and 24%, respectively, in two of its distractors.

In contrast, the results showed that students performed relatively well in Q13 and Q15. Overall, the levels of test item difficulty matched well with the levels of student ability in terms of the relative distributions of the difficulty and ability measures.

The student ability measures ranged from −2.39 to 3.66 logits. The standard error of measurement is small and at the order of 0.2 to 0.3. As summarized in Table 7.2, the mean of the student ability estimates was 0.96 logits, which was much higher than the mean of the item estimates (=0.00 logit), indicating a relatively high economics proficiency of the students.

Item-Person Map

The Rasch analysis reported the difficulty estimates of the test items and ability estimates of the students. Figure 7.1 showed an item-person map that displayed a graphical distribution of the item difficulties and person abilities. The student ability measures were located on the left of the map while the item difficulty measures

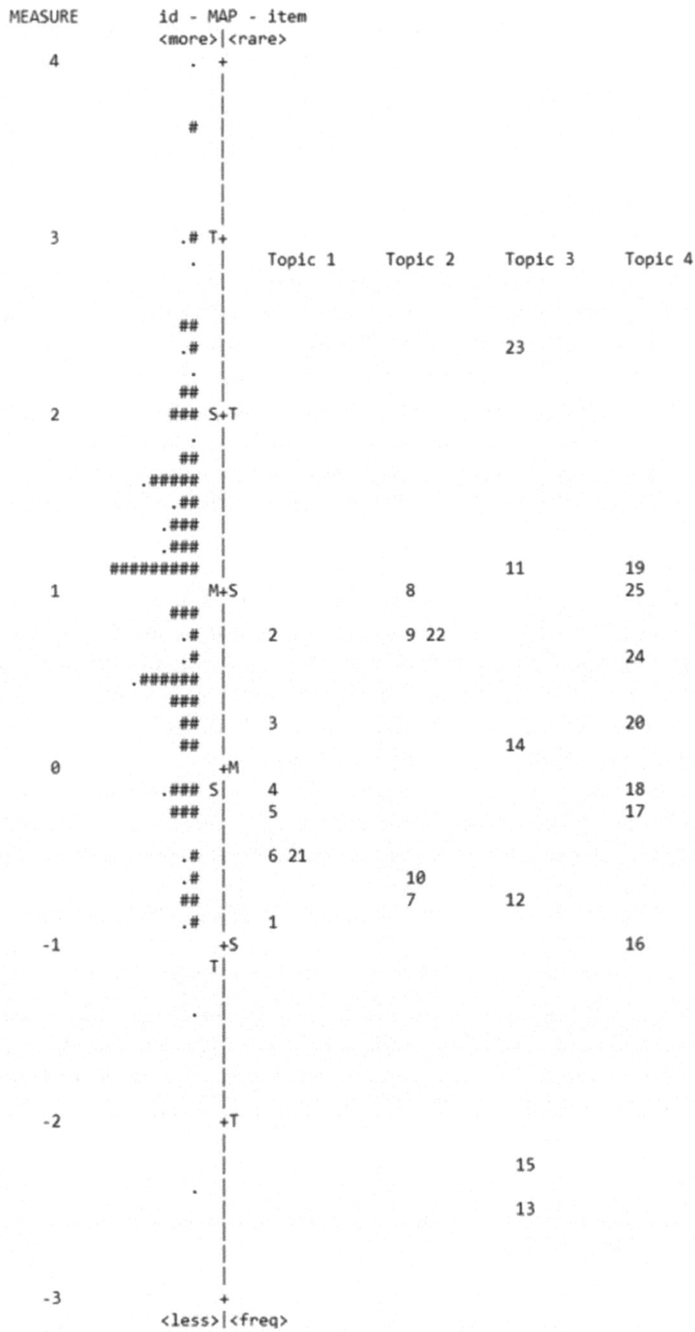

Fig. 7.1 Item-person map provided from the Rasch analysis of the data shown by items clustered in topics

were located on the right. The items (students) of lower difficulties (abilities) were located at the bottom of the continuum whereas items (students) of higher difficulties (abilities) were located at the top.

The item difficulties ranged from −2.49 logits to 2.52 logits, showing an adequate range of difficulty levels covered. However, the item-person map showed relatively few test items are difficult. There was a gap between the mean of the item difficulty (denoted by "M" on the right panel of the item-person map) and the mean of the person difficulty (denoted by "M" on the left panel of the item-person map). This suggested a possible room for improvement in alignment of the test item difficulty with the student ability: more items of above-average difficulty (e.g., >1 logits) could be added to better differentiate students of relatively higher abilities.

The item-person map showed that Topic 4 contained the items of smaller range of difficulties with all seven items receiving item difficulty estimates between −1.0 and 1.0 logits. In contrast, Topic 3 showed the largest range of item difficulties because it contained both the two most difficult items (Q11 and Q23), which showed highest item estimates, and the two easiest items (Q13 and Q15), which showed lowest item estimates.

In the item-person map in Fig. 7.1, the items were re-arranged in clusters in accordance with the content domains of the economics knowledge assessed. The item-person map showed a small gap between the item difficulty measures and student ability measures, with the location of the mean student ability measure a little bit above that of the mean item difficulty measure. Overall, this assessment instrument is a relatively easy test for measuring the economics understanding of this group of students.

Most of the items received difficulty estimates in the middle range of the continuum and stayed within the range between the average difficulty level and one standard deviation of the average difficulty (denoted by "S" on the right panel). As mentioned above, the hardest item was Q23 (Topic 3) whereas the easiest items are Q13 and Q15 (both Topic 3). The hardest item had a difficulty estimate that was two standard deviations above the mean item difficulty (denoted by "T" on the right panel). Similarly, the two easiest items (Q13 and Q15) showed difficulty estimates that were two standard deviations below the mean item difficulty level.

Item Fit

The statistical indices infit and outfit mean squares (MnSq) indicated construct validity of the assessment test in its ability to differentiate students with varying levels of economics knowledge (Table 7.2). The infit and outfit statistics of all the items were smaller than 2.0 which suggested no misfit. All items show goodness-of-fit values between 0.5 and 1.5, and thus were considered as showing adequate fit to the Rasch model (Linacre, 2011).

The Rasch analysis also reported other statistical indices, such as the point-measure correlation, which was a measure of the association of the response to a single item and the total score of the test, and positive values were considered support for internal coherence of the item in contributing to the assessment test.

Q5 and Q13 had low point-measure correlations 0.03 and 0.06, respectively, while other items showed correlation values from 0.2 to 0.57. This result suggested that except for Q5 and Q13, items in the test were internally coherent.

As discussed earlier, students might have failed Q13 because of the way the question was presented, which did not directly connect with knowledge and skills in the Topic. Nevertheless, student performance in these two items revealed deficiencies in the area, and highlighted possible direction for enhancement in future instruction.

Discussion

Implications for the Course Instructor's Use

This study reported an analysis of the student assessment data using a Rasch measurement approach, which provides item-level statistics for the examination of test quality in measuring student knowledge proficiency.

Traditional reporting of the assessment results provides an overview of the student performance; however, this is more difficult for instructors, especially those in their early career with less experience, to draw diagnostic information from the assessment results. Unlike the classical test theory approach to analyzing student assessment data, the analysis results presented above have provided multiple frames of reference, including the performance of the whole class, performance of particular students, the difficulty of the whole test, difficulty of specific domains and items within a domain. The information obtained from looking from those multiple perspectives allow the instructors to better understand the student proficiency levels and their learning profiles.

The results provided the instructors with empirical assessment information to support evaluation of the students' proficiency level of economics knowledge upon completion of the course. It also provided a comparison between the item difficulty levels and the student proficiency levels. It thus allows an objective account of comparison between the content standards as intended by the curriculum and the performance standards as expected from the students.

In particular, students found some items, as reported above, trickier than the others. It also meant most students did not show an adequate mastery in the economics concepts tapped by those tricky questions. Based on the assessment information, the course instructors in the course had managed to clarify with the students in this class the correct understanding of the underlying concept.

Overall, the diagnostic information derived from the analyses can support instructors to identify the strengths and weaknesses of the whole class or individual students. The results also showed, as illustrated above with the characteristics of some selected items (including most difficult items, easiest items, and tricky items) and student responses, that instructors can identify any learning gaps between expected and actual student learning outcomes, and make informed decisions in aligning subsequent instructional activities to meet student learning needs (Schmid et al., 2016).

The information about student performance on the test items was especially instructionally useful when the distractors were closely connected to some underlying misconceptions. The results showed the level of "instructional actionability," which describes "the degree to which a test's results indicate whether a test taker needs additional instruction regarding whatever is being measured" (Popham, 2014, p. 190). For example, item Q23, the most difficult item as shown on the item-person map (Fig. 7.1), was answered incorrectly by most of the students (78%). Similar high difficulty level was also found in items Q11 and Q19, in both of which more than one of their respective distractors attracted over 20% of overall student responses. This highlights that the underlying concepts to be assessed in these items needed to be further explained to students through additional instruction. In addition, further examination of the incorrect response patterns and associated misconceptions provided the instructor with actionable information to identify the learning gap and rectify student misconceptions in subsequent teaching. The course instructor had therefore reminded the class revisiting the reading notes supplemented with explanations on the concept of concern. In general, the results thus enable instructors to make better decisions in aligning student needs with effective instructional strategies and resources. Further use of the results can be fostered by the course instructor. For example, the instructor may improve the instructional actionability of the knowledge test by designing assessment items with stronger link between the distractors and common misconceptions hindering student learning. The instructor may also include distractors which appear to students as plausible choices alternative to the unique correct option that shows mastery of underlying economics concept.

Implications and Recommendations in Future Use

The use of Rasch analysis in this study demonstrated how university instructors can evaluate the psychometric quality of a knowledge test in measuring student knowledge proficiency in an undergraduate course. The analysis results supported that the knowledge test created to fit the instructor's own teaching contexts was psychometrically sound.

The knowledge test can also serve as a diagnostic tool that instructors can use to uncover their students' conceptual understanding of the topics and can be applied for multiple purposes, including using it for formative assessment, building customized assessment instrument, and monitoring course effectiveness.

First, the Rasch-based measures of item difficulty and student ability, being test-and-sample independent, can serve as a baseline measure for tracking or monitoring of student learning. At the student level, this can be done by either longitudinal or group comparisons, the learning progress of the students across multiple deliveries of the same course across cohorts. At the course level, this is also useful for instructors with management role, such as subject coordinator, who can use the analysis results based on student performance across multiple cohorts to identify and monitor the trend across multiple deliveries of the course over time.

Second, this study showed that given the knowledge test and the functioning of the individual items, instructors can make use of the assessment test for future use. For example, instead of administering the test at the end of the course and using the information as an evaluation of the student achievement, instructors can use the test in the middle of the course (with a suitable choice of items) to obtain information about the progress of student learning. With a more accurate understanding of the student learning progression, instructors are in a better position to make timely and formative alignment in subsequent teaching activities to achieve more targeted and effective teaching for the rest of the semester. The course instructors are thus able to use the test items as a formative assessment tool that supports subsequent teaching and learning decisions and arrangements.

Third, the results of this analysis have implications for teachers to develop customized and flexible cognitive tests (Knight, 2006; Scully, 2017). The literature has examples of making use of a combination of existing assessment items from validated instruments and additional items generated by teachers to form a new, reliable assessment tool for use by instructors in higher education (Schultz et al., 2017). The assessment items analyzed in this study showed sound psychometric properties and can be building blocks for creating longer assessment test with broader scope of knowledge and extended content domains.

Fourth, the current analysis of MCQ assessment results has potential to provide professional learning for university course instructors in developing their assessment capacity (Crisp & Palmer, 2007). The analysis performed can be adopted by instructors with interest in fostering evidence-based assessment improvement.

Conclusion

In this study, Rasch modeling was used to examine a 25-item economics knowledge test for university engineering students. Based on the student responses to the test items, the psychometric analysis provided useful assessment information to evaluate the quality of the test in measuring student proficiency in economics knowledge. The findings showed that the test showed adequate fit to the Rasch model and measurement properties at acceptable levels, which provided support to the validity and reliability of interpretation of assessment results. As a summary, the results demonstrated the utility of student classroom assessment data from the Rasch measurement approach.

References

Bond, T. G., & Fox, C. M. (2015). *Applying the Rasch Model: Fundamental measurement in the human sciences*. New York and London: Routledge.

Crisp, G. T., & Palmer, E. J. (2007). Engaging academics with a simplified analysis of their multiple-choice question (MCQ) assessment results. *Journal of university teaching & learning practice, 4*(2), 88–106.

Knight, P. (2006). The local practices of assessment. *Assessment & Evaluation in Higher Education, 31*(4), 435–452.

Linacre, J. M. (2011). *A user's guide to Winsteps/Ministep Rasch-model computer program*. Chicago, IL: Winsteps.com.

Popham, W. J. (2014). Looking at assessment through learner-coloured lens. In C. Wyatt-Smith, V. Klenowski, & P. Colbert (Eds.), *Designing assessment for quality learning* (pp. 183–194). NY: Springer.

Raîche, G. (2005). Critical eigenvalue sizes in standardized residual principal components analysis. *Rasch Measurement Transactions, 19*(1), 1012.

Rasch, G. (1960). *Probabilistic models for some intelligence and achievement tests*. Copenhagen, Denmark: Danish Institute for Educational Research. Expanded. 1980. Chicago, IL: The University of Chicago Press.

Schmid, S., Schultz, M., Priest, S., O'Brien, G., Pyke, S., Bridgeman, A., et al. (2016). Assessing the assessments: Development of a tool to evaluate assessment items in chemistry according to learning outcomes. In Madeleine Schultz, Siegbert Schmid, & Thomas Holme (Eds.), *Technology and assessment strategies for improving student learning in chemistry* (pp. 225–244). Washington: American Chemical Society.

Schultz, M., Lawrie, G. A., Bailey, C. H., Bedford, S. B., Dargaville, T. R., O'Brien, G., … & Wright, A. H. (2017). Evaluation of diagnostic tools that tertiary teachers can apply to profile their students' conceptions. *International Journal of Science Education*, 1–22.

Scully, D. (2017). Constructing multiple-choice items to measure higher-order thinking. *Practical Assessment, Research & Evaluation, 22,* 1–13.

Wright, B. D., & Stone, M. H. (2004). *Making measures*. Chicago: Phaneron Press.

Chapter 8
Constructs Evaluation of Student Attitudes Toward Science—A Rasch Analysis

Fan Huang, Liu Huang and Pey-Tee Oon

Abstract The research on students' attitudes toward science (SAS) is well-documented in the science education literature. Many studies examine SAS through the use of survey rating scales. The incorporation of SAS constructs; however, is affected by the subjective judgments of the researchers. We report here the examination of the three constructs in the measure of SAS based on the Asian student attitudes toward science (ASATSC) instrument. A total of 1,133 7th to 11th graders from China completed the ASATSC survey instrument. The Rasch measurement model was used to analyze the resulting student data. The findings indicated that psychometric properties of data collected from ASATSC were sufficient in the measure of SAS. The present study found that though Chinese students generally held positive attitudes toward physics and biology, they enjoyed studying physics more than biology and expressed higher confidence with biology.

Keywords Science attitudes · Rasch measurement · PISA · Model fit · Differential item functioning · Chinese students

Background

The discussion of SAS has attracted the attention of many scholars (Bathgate, Schunn, & Correnti, 2014; Brophy, 1998; Bryan, Glynn, & Kittleson, 2011; George, 2006; Tuan, Chin, & Shieh, 2005) over the past decades and still does (Wan & Lee, 2017). However, most studies have been focused on Western societies and most survey SAS instruments were designed and developed in Western societies (Boone, 1997; Potvin & Hasni, 2014). Chinese students continue to exhibit outstanding performance in international assessments such as Programme for International Student Assessment (PISA). This has seized the attention of international educators and researchers. As such, it is important to look at the measurement of SAS within a Chinese context.

Biggs (1994) indicates the conflicts between Chinese students' consistent excellent performance in international assessments and the stereotypical impression of

F. Huang · L. Huang · P.-T. Oon (✉)
University of Macau, Macau, China
e-mail: peyteeoon@um.edu.mo

M. S. Khine (ed.), *Rasch Measurement*,
https://doi.org/10.1007/978-981-15-1800-3_8

the public about them being passive, unconfident, and exam-driven. A recent study (Li & Chen, 2016) which used a modified instrument from the 2006 Programme for International Student Assessment (PISA) indicated that high school students in China exhibited superficial science knowledge although they obtained higher scores than the OECD averages. The authors stated that students expressed high interest in science but they had low interest in joining science clubs. A second study (Ma & Chen, 2014) conducted in Changzhou city, Jiangsu Province, China, examined 1,334, 9th grade students' attitudes toward science (SAS) found that students with high achievements in science suffered low confidence in science. The findings are corroborated with other Asia studies (e.g., Oon & Subramaniam, 2013).

China is facing an increasing demand to cultivating students' scientific literacy for citizenship, and to increase students' interest and positive attitudes toward science in this age of globalization (Boone, 1997; Zhang & Campbell, 2011). The Ministry of Education (MOE) issued the Guidelines for Curriculum Reform of Basic Education to shift the curriculum to adapt to the needs of individuals and society (Tao, Oliver, & Venville, 2013). Some researchers referred to this change as a shift (Chiu & Duit, 2011; Scott, 2008, as reported in Tao et al., 2013) that leads to reforming the actions of school teaching and learning with global approaches (Tao et al., 2013). The current study provides insights that may provide a glimpse of the impacts of such educational reform in China from the Chinese perspective.

Western Students generally perceive the various branches of science (physics, biology, and chemistry) differently. As expected, physics is often perceived to be the least favored among the science subjects (Barmby & Defty, 2006; Bennett, Lubben, & Hampden-Thompson, 2013; Hemmo & Love, 2008; Lyons, 2006; Owen, Dickson, Stanisstreet, & Boyes, 2008; Spall, Barrett, Stanisstreet, Dickson & Boyes, 2003; Williams, Stanisstreet, Spall, Boyes, & Dickson, 2003) while biology is perceived as a more popular subject among secondary school students (Rabgay, 2018; Uitto, 2014). Despite the finding that students entering secondary are reported to have equal liking for the science subjects but the numbers who find physics interesting decreased as they progressed through the secondary years (Gill & Bell, 2013; Politis, Killeavy, & Mitchell, 2007; Spall, Stanisstreet, Dickson, & Boyes, 2004; Wang, Chow, Degol, & Eccles, 2017). Spall, Stanisstreet, Dickson, and Boyes (2004) employed a survey method involving 1,395 secondary school students aged between 11 and 16 in England. The purpose of the study was to compare students' views about physics and biology over the school years. The number of students advocating liking for physics decreased over the school years, this did not occur for biology (Spall, et al., 2004). This has led to an interesting question of what made students enjoy physics less than other science subjects as grade levels progressed. Could it be due to poor curriculum planning, teacher factor, or the nature of physics itself? The current study sets to probe possible reasons.

In addition to the foregoing, the issues of validity and reliability of SAS instruments are of concern. As evident in the pertinent literature, most SAS instruments are Likert-type scales comprising of various sub-scales (e.g., Angell, Guttersrud, Henriksen, & Isnes, 2004; Pell & Jarvis, 2001; Stokking, 2000; Wang & Berlin,

2010). Most of the scales assume linearity. In other words, where Likert scale survey approaches are used, the prevalent form of analysis is to assume that the data obtained are interval in nature. This is, in fact, an erroneous assumption given that the data obtained are ordinal in nature but is often assumed to be linear (Wright & Linacre, 1989). Our intention in the current study is to measure students' attitudes toward physics and biology in a way that allows us to compare SAS estimates for these two subjects on an unequivocal linear and invariant scale by Rasch Model that is capable of such a comparison.

Research Questions

In this study, the following two research questions were explored:

RQ1: Can Rasch analysis can be used to provide psychometric information to validate Wang and Berlin (2010)'s SAS instrument in China and can such information help to improve the psychometric quality of the SAS instrument?

RQ2: What are Chinese students' attitudes toward physics and biology?

Method

Instrument

Wang and Berlin (2010)'s survey instrument entitled "*Asian Student Attitudes Towards Science Class (ASATSC)*" was used to explore SAS in a Chinese context. It consists of 30 items in three constructs: (1) science enjoyment, (2) science confidence, and (3) importance of science (Table 8.1).

The survey is divided into two sections. The first section asks demographic information on students' genders and school levels and the second section contains 16 positively worded and 14 negatively worded SAS items and uses a five-point Likert-type response format (1 = strongly disagree, 2 = disagree, 3 = undecided, 4 = agree, 5 = strongly agree).

The original ASATSC in English (Wang & Berlin, 2010) was translated by the first and third authors into Chinese. The translated survey was sent to two postgraduate students specialized in English–Chinese translation and two academic staff to validate and proofread the translations. Wordings were refined according to their feedback to achieve 95% of agreement on the translations' appropriateness. Two surveys, one on physics and one on biology were used for the current study.

Research ethics has been obtained and approved by the University of Macau prior to data collection.

Table 8.1 Items to SAS constructs for the current study (Wang & Berlin, 2010)

Construct	Items
Science enjoyment	1. I like when the teacher teaches our Bio/Phy outdoors 2. In Bio/Phy class, listening to lectures from the teacher is interesting 3. In science class, watching the Bio/Phy film on TV is boring 4. My Bio/Phy class is interesting 6. I would enjoy school more if there was no Bio/Phy class 7. During Bio/Phy class, I like to read science posters 8. I look forward to Bio/Phy class 9. In science class, doing experiments is boring 10. I do not like Bio/Phy class 17. I enjoy reading the Bio/Phy textbook 19. I like to do experiment in Bio/Phy class 20. I do not like answering the questions in my Bio/Phy workbook 28. I do not like field trips in my Bio/Phy class
Science confidence	11. The material in the Bio/Phy textbook is hard for me 12. I am afraid to answer the questions in Bio/Phy class 15. In Bio/Phy class, experiments are difficult 18. I usually understand what is taught in my Bio/Phy class 22. Bio/Phy class is hard for me 23. It is easy for me to understand the teacher's lectures in Bio/Phy class 25. I usually get good scores in Bio/Phy class 30. The questions in the Bio/Phy workbook are easy for me
Importance of science	5. In Bio/Phy class, I learn more science when I work in a group 13. Bio/Phy class provides me with knowledge to use in my daily life 14. The experiments I do in Bio/Phy class are useful 16. In Bio/Phy e class, science poster does not help me to learn science 21. In my Bio/Phy class, field trips do not help me to learn science 24. The material in the Bio/Phy textbook help me to learn science 26. The questions in the Bio/Phy workbook do not help me to learn science 27. In Bio/Phy class, watching science film on TV helps me to learn science 29. Bio/Phy class is a waste of time

Note Bio = biology; Phy = physics

Participants and Data Collection Procedures

The study was conducted in Guangzhou, China. Of 514 secondary schools in Guangzhou (Guangzhou Education Bureau, 2017), eight secondary schools from Tianhe district, Panyu district, Huadu district, and Yuexiu district agreed to participate in the current study. Among these participating schools, one of them was a nonprofit private school and the rest were public schools; three of them were senior high schools and the rest were junior high schools. Two classes of students from each grade from each school completed the survey. A total of 1,133 7th to 11th science students completed the survey (Table 8.2). Of these students, 55% were male and 45% were female students. Twelfth graders were not invited to take this survey because

Table 8.2 Demographic information of the student samples (N = 1,133)

		Number	%
Gender	Male	622	54.90
School level	Female	511	45.12
	7th grade	239	21.11
	8th grade	371	32.71
	9th grade	67	5.91
	10th grade	157	13.91
	11th grade	299	26.42

they needed to prepare for the university entrance examination. The participants and the participating schools were assured that the collected responses would be kept confidentially and the consolidated data would be used strictly for research purposes only.

The surveys were sent to the science teachers of the eight schools that agreed to participate in this study in June 2016. A briefing session was held by the first author with the participating students. Each student was given 15 min to answer the survey. Science teachers collected the completed surveys and returned the completed survey to the second author.

Data Analyses

Data from the 30 items were subjected to WINSTEPS (version 3.81.0) for Rasch analysis (Linacre, 2014) that assess the invariant relationship between student agreeability and SAS item difficulty using the following:

$$\ln[P_{ni}/(P_{ni-1})] = B_n - D_i$$

which states that the log-odds of observed success for student *n* on item *i* is equal to the difference between the estimate B of student *n*'s ability and the difficulty estimate D of item *i* (Andrich, 2010; Rasch, 1960; Wright & Masters, 1982). This allows group comparison on item estimates between physics and biology to be made on the same interval scale of logit.

The higher the item difficulty estimate, the lower the endorsement (harder to be agreed with). The converse holds true the lower the item difficulty estimate, the higher the endorsement (easier to be agreedwith). Each item estimate is accompanied by an error statistic showing the precision of the estimate (Table 8.3).

Table 8.3 Item statistics for the 30 SAS items

	All students						Physics						Biology					
	(N = 2024)						(N = 891)						(N = 1133)					
	Item		Infit		Outfit		Item		Infit		Outfit		Item		Infit		Outfit	
No	Estimate	Err	MnSq	Zstd	MnSq	Zstd	Estimate	Err	MnSq	Zstd	MnSq	Zstd	Estimate	Err	MnSq	Zstd	MnSq	Zstd
1	−0.67	0.02	1.19	5.9	1.18	5.2	−0.68	0.03	1.10	2.0	1.09	1.9	−0.65	0.03	1.27	6.0	1.24	5.3
2	−0.38	0.02	0.90	−3.6	0.91	−3.4	−0.47	0.03	0.88	−3.0	0.88	−2.9	−0.32	0.03	0.92	−2.3	0.92	−2.2
3	0.49	0.02	1.20	7.4	1.23	8.0	0.60	0.03	1.20	4.5	1.23	5.1	0.42	0.03	1.20	5.7	1.22	6.1
4	−0.48	0.02	0.87	−4.9	0.88	−4.2	−0.51	0.03	0.86	−3.5	0.86	−3.4	−0.46	0.03	0.87	−3.4	0.90	−2.6
5	−0.41	0.02	0.90	−3.5	0.91	−3.4	−0.45	0.03	0.90	−2.4	0.89	−2.5	−0.39	0.03	0.91	−2.6	0.91	−2.3
6	0.61	0.02	1.31	9.9	1.34	9.9	0.69	0.03	1.28	6.0	1.31	6.5	0.55	0.03	1.33	8.4	1.36	8.8
7	−0.32	0.02	0.86	−5.5	0.88	−4.7	−0.35	0.03	0.88	−3.1	0.88	−2.9	−0.30	0.03	0.85	−4.5	0.87	−3.6
8	−0.34	0.02	0.89	−4.4	0.89	−4.2	−0.39	0.03	0.88	−3.1	0.88	−3.0	−0.31	0.03	0.89	−3.1	0.90	−2.9
9	0.80	0.02	1.12	3.9	1.20	6.0	0.81	0.03	1.20	4.1	1.29	5.7	0.81	0.03	1.07	1.8	1.14	3.1
10	0.67	0.02	1.13	4.3	1.17	5.5	0.67	0.03	1.17	3.7	1.21	4.6	0.67	0.03	1.10	2.5	1.14	3.4
11	0.24	0.02	1.06	2.6	1.07	2.9	0.22	0.03	1.06	1.7	1.07	1.8	0.26	0.03	1.06	2.0	1.08	2.3
12	0.29	0.02	1.07	2.7	1.09	3.5	0.24	0.03	1.11	3.0	1.13	3.4	0.32	0.03	1.03	1.0	1.06	1.7
13	−0.63	0.02	0.92	−2.5	0.93	−2.2	−0.67	0.03	0.95	−1.1	0.95	−1.1	−0.61	0.03	0.91	−2.3	0.92	−1.9
14	−0.57	0.02	0.90	−3.3	0.90	−3.4	−0.59	0.03	0.89	−2.5	0.89	−2.5	−0.55	0.03	0.92	−2.1	0.91	−2.3
15	0.49	0.02	0.92	−3.1	0.96	−1.3	0.50	0.03	0.98	−0.6	1.02	0.5	0.49	0.03	0.88	−3.5	0.93	−2.1
16	0.48	0.02	0.93	−2.6	0.97	−1.2	0.49	0.03	0.94	−1.6	0.97	−0.8	0.48	0.03	0.93	−2.0	0.97	−0.8
17	−0.40	0.02	0.84	−6.3	0.84	−6.1	−0.36	0.03	0.83	−4.4	0.84	−4.1	−0.43	0.03	0.84	−4.5	0.83	−4.5
18	−0.41	0.02	0.78	−8.4	0.79	−8.1	−0.37	0.03	0.82	−4.7	0.81	−4.8	−0.45	0.03	0.76	−7.0	0.77	−6.5

(continued)

Table 8.3 (continued)

	All students						Physics						Biology					
	(N = 2024)						(N = 891)						(N = 1133)					
	Item		Infit		Outfit		Item		Infit		Outfit		Item		Infit		Outfit	
No	Estimate Err		MnSqZstd		MnSqZstd		Estimate Err		MnSqZstd		MnSqZstd		Estimate Err		MnSqZstd		MnSqZstd	
19	−0.57	0.02	0.98	−0.6	0.98	−0.5	−0.66	0.03	0.92	−1.7	0.91	−1.9	−0.51	0.03	1.02	0.5	1.03	0.7
20	0.21	0.02	1.06	2.3	1.08	3.1	0.26	0.03	1.04	1.2	1.06	1.7	0.17	0.02	1.07	2.1	1.09	2.7
21	0.54	0.02	1.14	4.9	1.15	5.4	0.57	0.03	1.15	3.6	1.17	4.0	0.52	0.03	1.13	3.5	1.14	3.8
22	0.35	0.02	1.09	3.6	1.12	4.7	0.38	0.03	1.08	2.1	1.12	2.9	0.34	0.03	1.10	3.0	1.13	3.8
23	−0.11	0.02	0.82	−7.9	0.82	−7.6	−0.10	0.03	0.79	−6.0	0.79	−5.8	−0.12	0.03	0.84	−5.2	0.84	−4.9
24	−0.56	0.02	0.80	−7.0	0.80	−7.1	−0.60	0.03	0.80	−4.8	0.80	−4.8	−0.54	0.03	0.81	−5.1	0.80	−5.2
25	−0.10	0.02	0.88	−5.0	0.89	−4.6	−0.08	0.03	0.87	−3.6	0.88	−3.1	−0.12	0.03	0.89	−3.4	0.89	−3.4
26	0.46	0.02	0.91	−3.8	0.91	−3.5	0.46	0.03	0.92	−2.2	0.92	−1.9	0.45	0.03	0.90	−3.0	0.90	−2.8
27	−0.67	0.02	0.88	−3.9	0.87	−4.1	−0.72	0.03	0.94	−1.3	0.94	−1.3	−0.63	0.03	0.84	−4.0	0.83	−4.3
28	0.60	0.02	1.17	5.9	1.17	5.9	0.69	0.03	1.13	2.9	1.12	2.7	0.54	0.03	1.20	5.2	1.20	5.3
29	0.66	0.02	1.14	4.9	1.34	9.9	0.70	0.03	1.17	3.7	1.35	7.2	0.63	0.03	1.13	3.3	1.34	7.9
30	−0.26	0.02	1.23	8.2	1.61	9.9	−0.28	0.03	1.22	5.2	1.64	9.9	−0.24	0.03	1.23	6.4	1.59	9.9

Results

Psychometric Assessments

Model Fit and Data Reliability

Table 8.3 presents item statistics for the 30 SAS items for all, physics and biology calibrations. The mean square information-weighted (infit) and outlier-sensitive (outfit) model fit statistics (Wright & Masters, 1982) are between 0.60 and 1.40 ranges which are expected from a good quality assessment. However, one exception is on item 30 (*The questions in the Bio/Phy workbook are easy for me*) with a misfit for both, physics only and biology only outfit mean square statistics –1.61, 1.64 and 1.59, respectively. Standardized fit (Zstd) ranging from −2 to +2 are regarded as acceptable in assessing the quality of data (Bond & Fox, 2001). Most of the items reported misfit Zstd with Zstd statistics with all students(N = 2024) reporting largest misfit (−8.1 to 9.9), followed by biology students (N = 1133) (−6.5 to 9.9) then physics students (N = 891) (−5.8 to 9.9) (Table 8.3). The literature suggest that Zstd statistics should be interpreted with caution as it is influenced by sample size (Smith, Rush, Fallowfield, Velikova, & Sharpe, 2008) as evident in the current study.

Person and item reliabilities were 0.55 and 1.00, respectively. A lower person reliability (<0.80) indicates that the SAS items may not be sufficient in distinguishing students' agreeability level. More SAS items are needed to better measure students' SAS. The high item reliability indicates that the SAS items estimates are reproducible by another subgroup of samples (Bond & Fox, 2001, p. 32). In other words, high item reliability indicates a sufficient sample for the current study for the SAS measurement (Linacre, 2009).

Differential Item Functioning

The item difficulties estimated from the physics items correlated 0.992 (disattenuated, 0.995) with the biology items (Fig. 8.1) which indicated that the results from the two scales (physics and biology) remain invariant and thus are comparable.

Effectiveness of Response Categories

A criterion of Rasch analysis was used to verify the effectiveness of each of the 5-point response categories (1 = strongly disagree, 2 = disagree, 3 = undecided, 4 = agree, 5 = strongly agree). A minimum of ten observations were made and the outfit MNSQ for each category reported values were below 2.00.

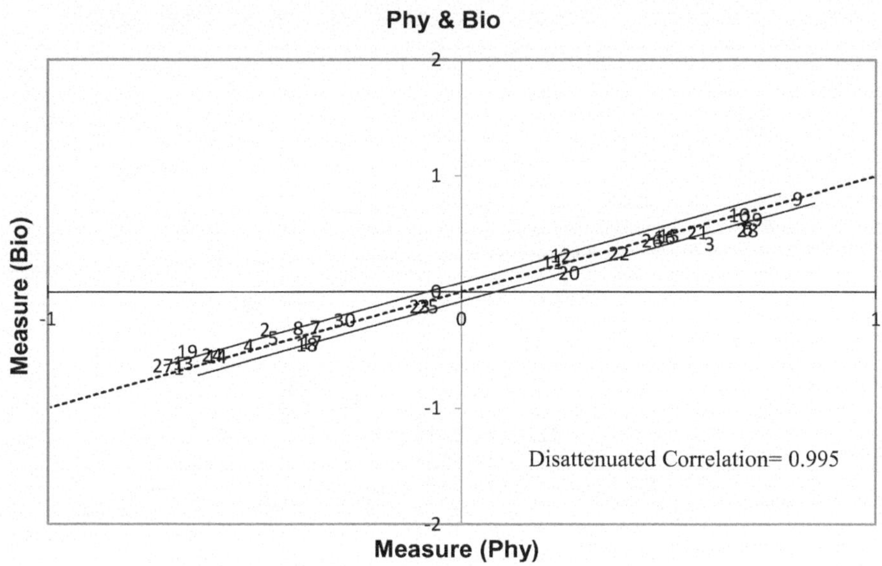

Fig. 8.1 Compare statistics: scatter plot between physics and biology estimates

The average measure increased monotonically from −0.42 (Strong Disagree) to 0.42 (Strong Agree). The threshold calibration also increased monotonically (Table 8.4). The results suggested that each category worked optimally as intended (Linacre, 2002). Although each category had an obvious peak (Fig. 8.2), the distance of threshold calibration between Category 2 (Disagree) and Category 3 (Undecided) was.14 as such these two categories should be collapsed to increase the reliability of the data (Linacre, 2002).

Since the category function did not meet Linacre's criteria requirement, an attempt was made to reorganize the five-point scale (1-2-3-4-5) to four-point scale (1-2-2-3-4). Category 2 and Category 3 were collapsed as one category threshold. Table 8.5 summarizes the adequacy of the original and collapsed categories. However, the other Rasch index did not show significant improvement (Table 8.5). The results prompted the use of the original categories for results interpretations.

Table 8.4 Summary of category structure of 5−point rating scales for the student SAS scale

Category	Observed count (%)	Average measure	Outfit MNSQ	Threshold calibration
1	9991(17)	− 0.42	1.09	NONE
2	11576(19)	− 0.31	0.81	−0.50
3	14571(24)	0.00	0.96	−0.36
4	14303(24)	0.29	0.84	0.14
5	9928(16)	0.42	1.19	0.72

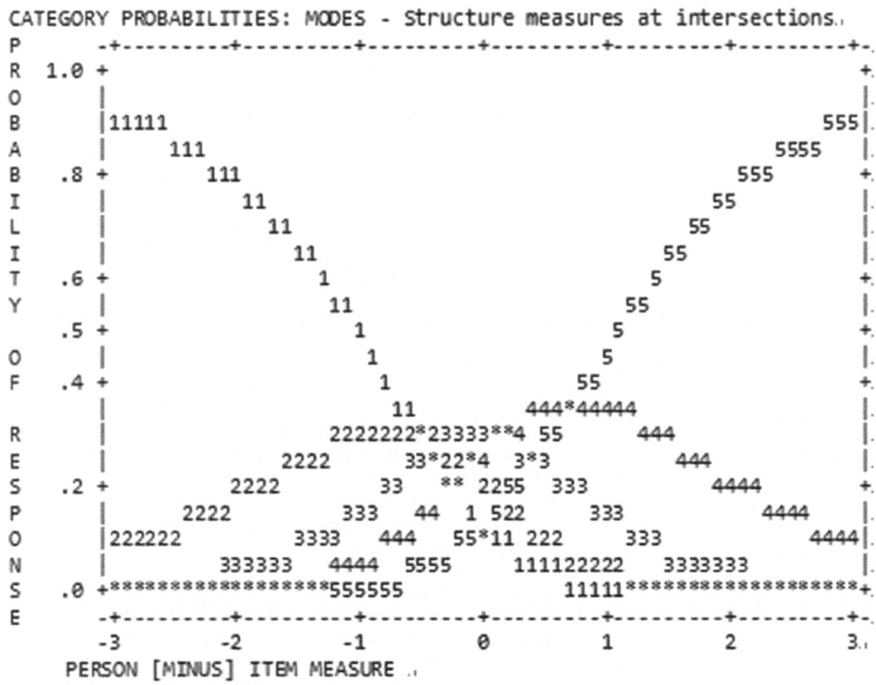

Fig. 8.2 Category probability curves for the 5-point rating scale

Table 8.5 Summary of analysis for original and collapsed scales

	Rating scale	
	Original (1-2-3-4-5)	Revised (1-2-2-3-4)
Fit statistics		No improvement
Reliabilities		
Person	0.55	0.59
Item	1.00	1.00
Raw variance explained by measure	30%	28.5%
DIF contrast		No improvement
Linacre's criteria		
N > 10	✓	✓
$M(q)_{increase}$	✓	✓
MS < 2	✓	✓
$\tau_{increase}$	✗	✗
Curves $_{peak}$	✓	✓

Note ✓ indicates satisfied; ✗ indicates not satisfied

On Findings on Students' Attitudes Toward Various Aspects of Physics and Biology

The standardized difference (t) (Fig. 8.3) was used to indicate the significant difference in item estimates between physics and biology subjects. If t values were outside the range of −2 and 2, it means there were significant differences in item estimates between the two subjects. For example, the two subjects reported significant difference on item 2 ($t > 2$) but not on item 7 ($0 < t < 2$) (Fig. 8.3).

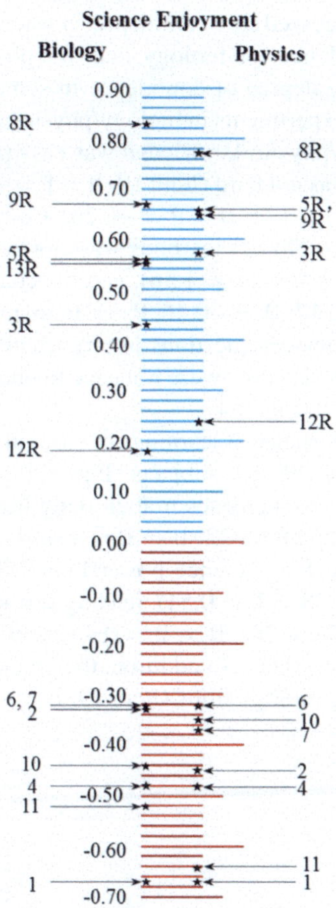

Item No.	1	2	3R	4	5R	6	7	8R	9R	10	11	12R	13R
Biology	-0.67	-0.33	0.43	-0.48	0.56	-0.32	-0.32	0.83	0.67	-0.44	-0.52	0.18	0.55
Physics	-0.67	-0.45	0.57	-0.48	0.66	-0.32	-0.37	0.77	0.65	-0.35	-0.64	0.24	0.66
t	0.00	2.91	-3.52	0.00	-2.50	0.00	1.38	1.23	0.54	-2.28	2.74	-1.73	-2.58

Fig. 8.3 Science enjoyment

The Chinese students perceived the learning of physics to be more fun than the learning of biology. They preferred attending physics lectures (Item 2: B = −0.33, P = -0.45, t = 2.91) (Fig. 8.3), watching science film (Item3R: B = 0.43, P = 0.57, t = −3.52) (Fig. 8.3), enjoying school with physics (Item 5R: B = 0.56, P = 0.66, t = −2.50) (Fig. 8.3), doing experiment in physics class (Item 11: B = -0.52, P = -0.64, t = 2.74) (Fig. 8.3), and enjoying field trips in physics class (Item 13R: B = 0.55, P = 0.66, t = −2.58) (Fig. 8.3) compared of those in biology subject. However, it is of interest that they preferred to read biology textbooks more than physics textbooks (Item 10: B = −0.44, P = −0.35, t = −2.28) (Fig. 8.3). There were no significant differences in the other items.

Overall, Chinese students expressed low confidence in science. Figure 8.4 indicates students had higher confidence for biology than for physics (Item 14–21). However, students held the same degree of confidence in some activities for both biology and physics, e.g., doing experiments in biology/physics was easy (Item 16R: B = P = 0.49), learning biology/physics knowledge was easy (Item 18R: B = P = 0.35), learning biology/physics was not hard (Item 19: B = P = −0.11), questions in biology/physics class were easy (Item 21: B = P = −0.26). Compared with biology, the Chinese students stated that the physics textbook was more challenging for them to read (Item 14R: B = 0.27, P = 0.21, t = 1.56), and the content in physics was more difficult to understand (Item 17: B = −0.46, P = −0.36, t = −2.54) (Fig. 8.4). In addition, they were afraid to answer questions in physics class (Item 15R: B = 0.33, P = 0.23, t = 2.56), and good scores were not easy to obtain in physics (Item 20: B = 0.1, P = 0.08, t = −0.60) (Fig. .84).

Chinese students rated the importance of learning activities in science class highly with no significant difference for the two subjects (Fig. 8.5). They embraced the usefulness of activities in biology and physics in their daily life(Item 23: B = P = −0.63), such as, working in groups(Item 22: B = P = −0.41), doing experiments (Item 24: B = P = −0.57), watching science poster(Item 25R: B = P = 0.49), participating field trips(Item 26R: B = P = 0.54), reading textbook(Item 27: B = P = −0.56), answering questions(Item 28r: B = P = 0.46), and having biology and physics classes (Item 30r: B = P = 0.66). In addition, they found watching physics films more helpful than watching biology films (Item 29: B = −0.65, P = −0.69, t = 1.07).

Discussions

This study explored psychometric information of a translated Wang and Berlin's (2010)'s SAS instrument in a Mainland Chinese population and analyzed how Chinese students perceive physics and biology. It contributes to the under-researched pertinent literature on SAS study within a Chinese context.

ASATSC-SAS items stayed within acceptable fit indices with exception on item 30 (*The questions in the Bio/Phy workbook are easy for me*). We speculate the term "workbook" may sound vague to the participating students as they might have

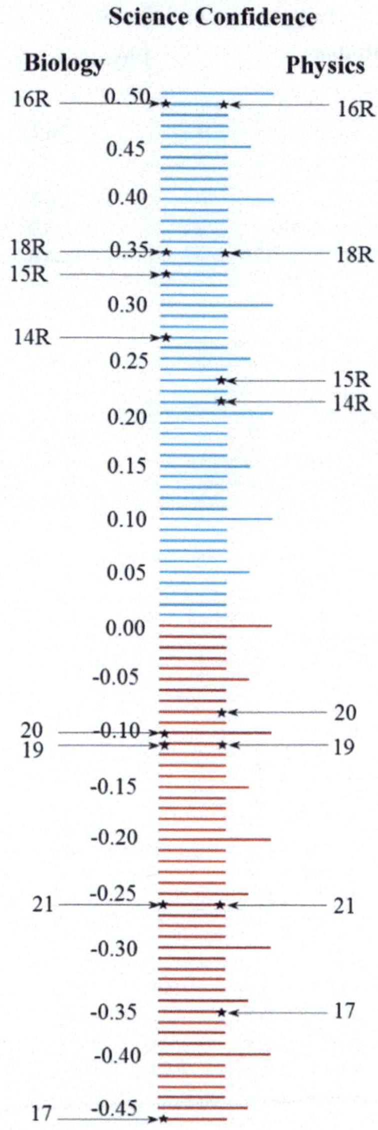

Item No.	14R	15R	16R	17	18R	19	20	21
Biology	0.27	0.33	0.49	-0.46	0.35	-0.11	-0.10	-0.26
Physics	0.21	0.23	0.49	-0.36	0.35	-0.11	-0.08	-0.26
t	1.56	2.56	0.00	-2.54	0.00	0.00	-0.60	0.00

Fig. 8.4 Science confidence

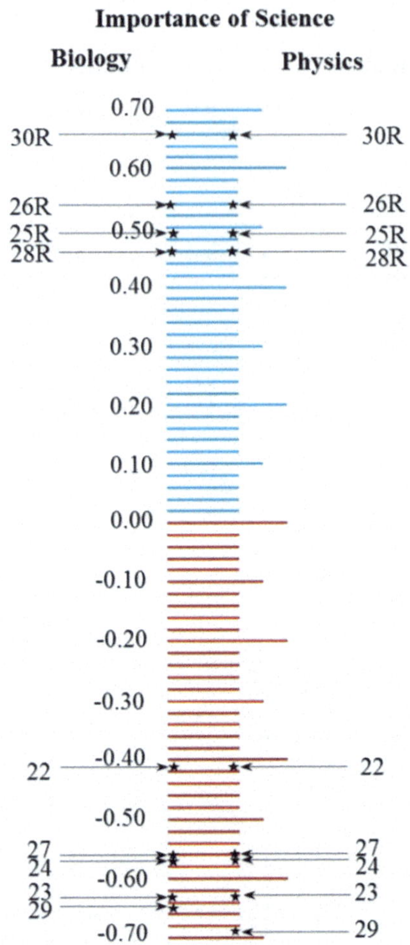

Item No.	22	23	24	25R	26R	27	28R	29	30R
Biology	-0.41	-0.63	-0.57	0.49	0.54	-0.56	0.45	-0.65	0.66
Physics	-0.41	-0.63	-0.57	0.49	0.54	-0.56	0.45	-0.69	0.66
t	0.00	0.00	0.00	0.00	0.00	0.00	0.00	1.07	0.00

Fig. 8.5 Importance of science

interpreted it to be "textbook" or "exercise book". In China, textbooks usually contain factual information with some simple exercises while exercise books or reference books consist of more sophisticated test items of different levels of difficulty in addition to factual information. Teachers from different schools are free to choose which exercise or textbooks to be used in class. This means that students from different schools are likely to use different exercises or textbooks. The translated term "workbook" in the question might have confused them as to which book it is referred to. Future research ought to clarify this ambiguity. Scores on the scale showed high item reliability but lower person reliability. The former indicates sufficient samples in the current study but more items are desirable to increase the person reliability SAS (Bond & Fox, 2001; Linacre, 2009). In addition, the high disattenuated correlation between physics and biology estimates reflects an invariant relationship between the SAS item measures between physics and biology are thus comparable. The five-point response categories can be kept as it functions adequately although it failed to satisfy one of Linacre's six criteria. Collapsing the "*Disagree*" and "*Undecided* categories did not improve the fit. Inclusion of the "*Undecided*" category may have encouraged some respondents to not think deeply about the meaning of the items before choosing one that best reflected their view. This may affect responses in other categories as well. We recommend the removal of this category but it was replaced with "*Slightly Disagree*" and "*Slightly Agree*" in the future research.

The findings to the current study corroborated previous SAS studies (Li & Chen, 2016; Ying & Zhang, 2016) which reported that Chinese students held positive attitudes toward science in general, as is found in other cultures (Jocz, Zhai, & Tan, 2014; Li & Chen, 2016; Osborne, Simon, & Collins, 2003; Williams, Stanisstreet, Spall, Boyes, & Dickson, 2003; Ying & Zhang, 2016). In contrast to the other reports (Osborne, Simon, & Collins, 2003; Zhou, 2008), the present study found that Chinese students enjoyed studying physics more than biology. This reveals potential success of incorporating participatory approach in many physics classroom in China (Wu, Gao, & Hu, 2010) stemming from the New Curriculum which requires teachers to adopt a more diverse pedagogy that emphasizes students' active participation and collaborative learning styles so as to cultivate learning interest in senior high school physics (Liu, 2016).

In this study, students expressed low confidence in physics and higher confidence in biology. Pertinent literature pointed out that the poorer grades they received in physics and the nature of physics being perceived as difficult may have attributed to the low confidence in the subject (Duan, 2009; Nie, 2015). It is important to note that the sampled students in the current study also found physics to be more difficult. The major reason for finding physics more difficult could be due to the often abstract nature vs.concrete examples of physics content (Oon & Subramaniam, 2013), and the need for mathematical skills (Spall, Stanisstreet, Dickson, & Boyes, 2004).

The current study found Chinese students rated the importance of science highly, similar to the findings in Du and Guo (2012) and elsewhere (OECD, 2007). The importance of science was stressed in the policy of Deng Xiaoping beginning in 1988 and is still evident in the current policy. Science curriculum in China has experienced several waves of changes including; the implementation of Science Technology Society (STS) education, HPS (History, Philosophy, and Sociology of Science) education, Compulsory Education Primary School Science Curriculum Standard (Grade 3–6) (experimental draft) (Ministry of Education of the People's Republic of China, 2017), The National Medium- and Long-term Plan for Scientific and Technological Development (2006–2020) (The Central People's Government of the People's Republic of China, 2006), and Outline of the National Action Plan for Scientific Literacy (2006–2010–2020) (The State Council of the People's Republic of China,

2006) highlight the vital importance of science to Chinese society and development. Included is a pedagogy that has shifted from passive to participatory approaches, contents revisions, and assessment methods improved to be in line with participatory pedagogy.

Conclusion

Chinese students perceived physics and biology positively as reported in Ying and Zhang (2016) and Li and Chen (2016) though physics was perceived more favorably than biology. However, the message that physics is more difficult than biology is evident in the current study as corroborated with other studies reported elsewhere in Asian context (Oon & Subramaniam, 2013). In addition, Chinese students were found to be not confident in physics (Nie, 2015).

References

Andrich, D. (2010). Sufficiency and conditional estimation of person parameters in the polytomous Rasch model. *Psychometrika, 75*(2), 292–308.

Angell, C., Guttersrud, Ø., Henriksen, E. K., & Isnes, A. (2004). Physics: Frightful, but fun. Pupils' and teachers' views of physics and physics teaching. *Science Education, 88*(5), 683–706.

Barmby, P., & Defty, N. (2006). Secondary school pupils' perceptions of physics. *Research in Science & Technological Education, 24*(2), 199–215.

Bathgate, M. E., Schunn, C. D., & Correnti, R. (2014). Children's motivation toward science across contexts, manner of interaction, and topic. *Science Education, 98*(2), 189–215.

Bennett, J., Lubben, F., & Hampden-Thompson, G. (2013). Schools that make a difference to post-compulsory uptake of physical science subjects: Some comparative case studies in England. *International Journal of Science Education, 35*(4), 663–689.

Biggs, J. (1994). Asian learners through Western eyes: An astigmatic paradox. *Australian and New Zealand Journal of Vocational Educational Research, 2*(2), 40–63.

Bond, T. G., & Fox, C. M. (2001). *Applying the Rasch model: Fundamental measurement in the human sciences*. Lawrence Erlbaum Associates.

Boone, W. J. (1997). Science attitudes of selected middle school students in China: A preliminary investigation of similarities and differences as a function of gender. *School Science and Mathematics, 97*(2), 96–103.

Brophy, J. (1998). *Motivating students to learn*. Madison, WI: McGraw Hill.

Bryan, R. R., Glynn, S. M., & Kittleson, J. M. (2011). Motivation, achievement, and advanced placement intent of high school students learning science. *Science Education, 95*(6), 1049–1065.

Chiu, M. H., & Duit, R. (2011). Globalization: Science education from an international perspective. *Journal of Research in Science Teaching, 48*(6), 553–566.

Du, X., & Guo, L. (2012). On secondary school students' attitudes toward science and relevant factors. *Chinese Journal of Special Education,* (12), 86–91. (in Chinese)杜秀芳, &郭玲霄. (2012). 中學生對科學的態度影響因素研究. *中國特殊教育,* (12), 86–91.

Duan, S. F. (2009). Can interdisciplinary teaching improve students' interests? – A questionnaire from Denmark. *Modern Primary and Secondary Education,* (6), 70–74. (in Chinese). 段素芬. (2009). 跨學科教學能提高學生的興趣嗎?——一項來自丹麥的問卷調查. *現代中小學教育,* (6), 70–74.

George, R. (2006). A cross-domain analysis of change in students' attitudes toward science and attitudes about the utility of science. *International Journal of Science Education, 28*(6), 571–589.

Gill, T., & Bell, J. F. (2013). What factors determine the uptake of A-level physics? *International Journal of Science Education, 35*(5), 753–772.

Guangzhou Education Bureau (2017). *2016 Guangzhou Education Statistics Handbook*. Retrieved from http://www.gzedu.gov.cn/gzeduxxgk/0803/201710/06063d43ba114b9a94d335c9481972ca/files/fe00fd7712f34bffb3999f7fdd88082d.pdf (in Chinese). 廣州市教育局 (2017). 2016廣州市教育統計手冊.

Hemmo, V., & Love, P. (2008). *Encouraging student interest in science and technology studies*. Paris: Organisation for Economic Co-operation and Development., & Global Science Forum.

Jocz, J. A., Zhai, J., & Tan, A. L. (2014). Inquiry learning in the Singaporean context: Factors affecting student interest in school science. *International Journal of Science Education, 36*(15), 2596–2618.

Li, X., & Chen, L. (2016). An empirical study of senior high school students' attitudes towards science. *Science Popularization, 11*(2), 31–35 (in Chinese). 李秀菊, &陳玲. (2016). 我國高中生科學態度的實證研究. *科普研究, 11*(2), 31–35.

Linacre, J. M. (2002). Optimizing rating scale category effectiveness. *Journal of Applied Measurement, 3*(1), 85–106.

Linacre, J. M. (2009). *WINSTEPS* (Version 3.69.0) [Computer Software]. Beaverton, OR: Winsteps.com. Retrieved from http://www.winsteps.com.

Linacre, J. M. (2014). WINSTEPS (version 3.81.0) [Computer Software]. Chicago, IL: Winsteps.com.

Liu, J. H. (2016). Taking "Newton's Third Law" as an example to discuss the development of participatory learning. *Middle School Physics: High School Edition, 5*, 40–41 (in Chinese). 劉嘉慧 (2016). 以「牛頓第三定律」教學為例談參與式學習的開展. *中學物理:高中版,5*, 40–41.

Lyons, T. (2006). The puzzle of falling enrolments in physics and chemistry courses: Putting some pieces together. *Research in Science Education, 36*(3), 285–311.

Ma, J. H., & Chen, G. (2014). An empirical study on factors affecting students' attitudes to science. *Ke Cheng. Jiao Cai. Jiao Fa, (7)*, 15–28 (in Chinese). 馬宏佳&陳功 (2014).影響學生對科學態度因素的實證研究. *課程. 教材. 教法, (7)*, 15–28.

Ministry of Education of the People's Republic of China (2017). Compulsory education primary school science curriculum standard. Retrieved from http://www.moe.edu.cn/srcsite/A26/s8001/201702/t20170215_296305.html?authkey=pjcyn (in Chinese). 教育部 (2017). 科學 (3–6) 年級課程標準 (實驗稿).

Nie, Z. D. (2015). A survey of rural senior middle school students' attitudes towards Physics learning—A case study of Guangdong rural high school. *Journal of Guangxi College of Education, 04*, 192–196. (in Chinese). 聶卓丹 (2015). 農村高中生物理學習態度調查研究——以廣東一所農村高中為例. *廣西教育學院學报, 04*, 192–196.

OECD (Organisation for Economic Co-operation and Development). (2007). *PISA 2006. Science competencies for tomorrow's world*. Paris: Author.

Oon, P. T., & Subramaniam, R. (2013). Factors influencing Singapore students' choice of Physics as a tertiary field of study: A Rasch analysis. *International Journal of Science Education, 35*(1), 86–118.

Osborne, J., Simon, S., & Collins, S. (2003). Attitudes towards science: A review of the literature and its implications. *International Journal of Science Education, 25*(9), 1049–1079.

Owen, S., Dickson, D., Stanisstreet, M., & Boyes, E. (2008). Teaching physics: Students' attitudes towards different learning activities. *Research in Science & Technological Education, 26*(2), 113–128.

Pell, T., & Jarvis, T. (2001). Developing attitudes to science scales for use with children of ages from five to eleven years. *International Journal of Science Education, 23*(8), 847–862.

Politis, Y., Killeavy, M., & Mitchell, P. I. (2007). Factors influencing the take-up of physics within second-level education in Ireland—The teachers' perspective. *Irish Educational Studies, 26*(1), 39–55.

Potvin, P., & Hasni, A. (2014). Interest, motivation and attitudes towards science and technology at K-12 levels: a systematic review of 12 years of educational research. *Studies in Science Education, 50*(1), 85–129.

Rabgay, T. (2018). The effect of using cooperative learning method on tenth grade students' learning achievement and attitude towards biology. *International Journal of Instruction, 11*(2), 265–280.

Rasch, G. (1960). Probabilistic models for some intelligence and attainment tests (Reprint, with Foreword and Afterword by B. D. Wright, Chicago: University of Chicago Press, 1980). Copenhagen, Denmark: Danmarks Paedogogiske Institut.

Scott, D. (2008). *Critical essays on major curriculum theorists*. Milton Park, UK: Routledge.

Smith, A.B., Rush, R., Fallowfield, L.J., Velikova, G., & Sharpe, M. (29 May 2008). Rasch fit statistics and sample size considerations for polytomous data. *BMC Medical Research Methodology, 8*(33), Retrieved August 1, 2009, from http://www.biomedcentral.com/1471–2288/8/33.

Spall, K., Barrett, S., Stanisstreet, M., Dickson, D., & Boyes, E. (2003). Undergraduates' views about biology and physics. *Research in Science & Technological Education, 21*(2), 193–208.

Spall, K., Stanisstreet, M., Dickson, D., & Boyes, E. (2004). Development of school students' constructions of biology and physics. *International Journal of Science Education, 26*(7), 787–803.

Stokking, K. M. (2000). Predicting the choice of physics in secondary education. *International Journal of Science Education, 22*(12), 1261–1283.

Tao, Y., Oliver, M., & Venville, G. (2013). A comparison of approaches to the teaching and learning of science in Chinese and Australian elementary classrooms: Cultural and socioeconomic complexities. *Journal of Research in Science Teaching, 50*(1), 33–61.

The Central People's Government of the People's Republic of China (2006). Outline of the national medium and long-term plan for scientific and technological development (2006–2020). *Xinhua News Agency*. Retrieved from http://www.gov.cn/jrzg/2006-02/09/content_183787.htm (in Chinese). 中華人民共和國中央人民政府 (2006). 國家中長期科技發展規劃綱要 (2006–2020).

The State Council of the People's Republic of China (2006). Outline of the national action plan for scientific literacy (2006–2010–2020). *Department of State Bulletin, 10*. Retrieved from http://www.gov.cn/gongbao/content/2006/content_244978.htm (in Chinese). 國務院 (2006). 全民科學素質行動計畫綱要 (2006–2010–2020年).

Tuan, H. L., Chin, C. C., & Shieh, S. H. (2005). The development of a questionnaire to measure students' motivation towards science learning. *International Journal of Science Education, 27*(6), 639–654.

Uitto, A. (2014). Interest, attitudes and self-efficacy beliefs explaining upper-secondary school students' orientation towards biology-related careers. *International Journal of Science & Mathematics Education, 12*(6), 1425–1444.

Wan, Z. H., & Lee, J. C. K. (2017). Hong Kong secondary school students' attitudes towards science: A study of structural models and gender differences. *International Journal of Science Education, 39*(5), 507–527.

Wang, T. L., & Berlin, D. (2010). Construction and validation of an instrument to measure Taiwanese elementary students' attitudes toward their science class. *International Journal of Science Education, 32*(18), 2413–2428.

Wang, M. T., Chow, A., Degol, J. L., & Eccles, J. S. (2017). Does everyone's motivational beliefs about physical science decline in secondary school?: Heterogeneity of adolescents' achievement motivation trajectories in physics and chemistry. *Journal of Youth and Adolescence, 46*(8), 1821–1838.

Williams, C., Stanisstreet, M., Spall, K., Boyes, E., & Dickson, D. (2003). Why aren't secondary students interested in Physics. *Physics Education, 38*(4), 324–329.

Wright, B. D., & Linacre, J. M. (1989). Observations are always ordinal; measurements, however, must be interval. *Archives of Physical Medicine and Rehabilitation, 70*, 857–860.

Wright, B. D., & Masters, G. N. (1982). *Rating Scale Analysis. Rasch Measurement*. MESA Press, 5835 S. Kimbark Avenue, Chicago, IL 60637.

Wu, J. Y., Gao, G. Z., & Hu, X. L. (2010). An empirical study on the relationship between physics learning interest and academic performance of high school students. *Education Practice and*

Research, 31(22), 3–4. (in Chinese).吳靖媛, 高光珍, &胡象嶺. (2010). 高中生物理學習興趣與學習成績關係的實證研究.*教育實踐與研究, 31*(22), 3–4.

Ying, X., & Zhang, X. Y. (2016). A study on the characteristics of middle school students' scientific attitudes—A case study of freshmen from two universities in Wenzhou city, Zhejiang province. *Ke Cheng. Jiao Cai. Jiao Fa, (1)*, 110–115. (in Chinese).應向東, &張曉岩 (2016). 中學生科學態度特點的調查研究——以浙江省温州市兩所高校的理科新生為例. *課程. 教材. 教法, (1)*, 110–115.

Zhang, D., & Campbell, T. (2011). The psychometric evaluation of a three-dimension elementary science attitudes survey. *Journal of Science Teacher Education, 22*(7), 595–612.

Zhou, J. R. (2008). Investigation and analysis on the attitudes of junior middles students to study Biology curriculum. *Inner Mongolia Education,* (19), 44–46. (in Chinese). 周建榮. (2008). 初中生學習生物課程態度的調查與分析. *內蒙古教育*, (19), 44–46.

Chapter 9
Validation of a Science Concept Inventory by Rasch Analysis

Melvin Chan and R. Subramaniam

Abstract The purpose of this study was to describe the Rasch analysis of a newly developed 22-item science concept instrument, which was administered to grade 7 students ($N = 2163$) across a large sample of classrooms ($N = 115$) in secondary schools ($N = 16$) in Singapore. In view of the broad domain-specificity of science education, and in consideration of students' prior knowledge, the topic of cell system was identified as a suitable theme for the concept test. First, we used item analysis to investigate the psychometric properties and adequacy of the test items, following which we proceeded to assess the overall fit of the test to the Rasch model. Results indicate that the instrument is reasonably robust with respect to the Rasch model. Differential item functioning was investigated with respect to gender and academic track, and relationships with external related variables (e.g., prior attainment, science self-efficacy) were also examined. Implications are discussed in light of the findings, with recommendations for areas for improvement.

Keywords Rasch analysis · Science education · Differential item functioning · Fit statistics · Science concept test

Introduction

Science concept inventories represent useful instruments to explore students' understanding of particular topics. For example, a concept inventory on forces in physics in MCQ format can not only ascertain students' understanding of forces but also diagnose misconceptions on the topic. The availability of concept inventories on a range of topics provides teachers with an additional tool to map the state of understanding of their students on these topics.

For the purpose of our funded study, we sought to develop and validate an instrument that can assess lower secondary students' understanding of the cell system using the Rasch model. Validation of such instruments using the Rasch model is an under-explored area in science education research.

M. Chan · R. Subramaniam (✉)
National Institute of Education, Nanyang Technological University, Singapore, Singapore
e-mail: subramaniam.r@nie.edu.sg

M. S. Khine (ed.), *Rasch Measurement*,
https://doi.org/10.1007/978-981-15-1800-3_9

According to Messick (1989), a robust test that is constructually valid must be assessed for content relevance, representativeness, and technical quality. Essentially, this means that the cognitive processes involved in answering items on the test, as well as respondents' responses to these items, should be relevant and representative of the cognitive domains being assessed. To this end, Messick outlined six aspects of construct validity: *substantive* (i.e., purposefulness), *content* (i.e., representativeness), *structural* (i.e., use of appropriate scoring and functional distractors), *generalizability* (i.e., stability of score interpretation within and across populations), *external* (i.e., external validation of test score with related variables), and *consequential* (i.e., socio-educational impact of the test results).

Literature Review

Whether it is physics, chemistry, biology or general science, the respective discipline is characterized by a diversity of topics of varying difficulty levels, depending on the grade. Content proficiency of students in a topic can be determined by a number of modes of assessment. In recent times, more rigorous appraisal of students' proficiency in a topic, in contradistinction to the discipline of the topic, has been facilitated by the development of concept inventories. Though a concept inventory has been defined as an MCQ-based instrument that probes students' conceptual understanding of a topic (Lindell, Peak, & Foster, 2007), the testing mode has also evolved to other assessment modes such as, for example, 2-tier (Treagust, 1988), 3-tier (Caleon & Subramaniam, 2010a) and 4-tier Caleon & Subramaniam, 2010b) formats. One of the reasons for the evolution of other formats is that in the MCQ-based format, it is possible for students to answer a question correctly using guesswork, partial knowledge or elimination of unlikely options. That is, the scores obtained by using MCQ-based testing may have a component due to inflation. In other words, the true score of students is likely to be less than the actual score obtained even if the distracters all seem challenging. Items in a concept inventory are generally pitched at higher levels of the revised Bloom's Taxonomy, and thus permit a more accurate characterization of students' conceptual understanding of a topic that goes beyond the recall level of knowledge. This is one of the reasons for the rise in number of concept inventories in science for various topics. Typically, a concept inventory includes a modest number of items that can be taken by students in one sitting—the idea is that testing, whilst reasonably comprehensive, should not lead to respondent fatigue.

Examples of some concept inventories in Physics include Force Concept Inventory, (Hestenes, Wells, & Swackhamer, 1992), Mechanics Baseline Test (Hestenes & Wells, 1992), Conceptual Survey of Electricity & Magnetism (Planinic, 2006), and Wave Diagnostic Instrument (Caleon & Subramaniam, 2010a). In Chemistry, we can cite the following: Quantum Chemistry Concept Inventory (Dick-Perez, Luxford, Windus, & Holme, 2016), and Thermodynamics Diagnostic Instrument (Sreenivasulu & Subramaniam, 2013), In Biology, examples include: Conceptual Inventory of

Natural Selection (Anderson, Fisher, & Norman, 2002), Genetics Literacy Assessment Instrument (Bowling, et al. 2008), and Enzyme-Substrate Interactions Concept Inventory (Bretz & Linenberger, 2012).

A concept inventory must possess good psychometric properties. The conventional practice, which is still prevalent, is to make use of face validity as well as standard statistical measures such as facility index, discrimination index and reliability to assess its utility for diagnostic testing. While this is a defensible practice, the availability of other tools allows for a more robust appraisal of the psychometric properties of the inventory. Conventional practices, however, do not allow for a number of issues to be addressed—for example, are the questions in the instrument well targeted with respect to the sample's ability level, do they all conform to a unidimensional construct, and so on. This can be reasonably addressed using the Rasch model.

In recent times, a number of concept inventories or diagnostic instruments have been the subject of validation using the Rasch model. The most common concept inventory in Physics, the Force Concept Inventory, though originally validated using conventional approaches, has been the subject of quite a number of studies using the Rasch model (Planinic, Ivanjek, & Susac, 2010; Morris, et al., 2012; Fulmer, 2015). The Light Diagnostic Instrument has also been the subject of a Rasch validation study (Fulmer, Chu, Treagust, & Neumann, 2015). However, it has to be noted from the literature that only a small number of well-known inventories have undergone rigorous validation using the Rasch model. Proper validation of concept inventories using the Rash model endows the instrument with enhanced psychometric validity.

There are very few, if any, concept inventories that probe primary or lower secondary students' understanding of a science topic. A possible reason for this could be that at these levels, content covered in a topic do not have much breadth and depth, thus presenting difficulties in coming up with an instrument with a modest number of thinking questions. It could also be due to curriculum constraints and the need for a learning progression whereby content is presented at greater breadth and depth as students advance across grade levels.

Review of the literature suggests that there is a gap which can be filled—development of a concept inventory that can test students' understanding of a science topic at the lower secondary level as well as its validation by the Rasch model.

For the purpose of this study, we have chosen to focus on the topic of cells. There are two reasons for this: feedback from teachers indicate that this topic is prone to learning difficulties and misconceptions; and the topic is of sufficient breadth and depth to come up with a concept inventory comprising a reasonable number of items. We selected the MCQ format for the mode of assessment as this format allows for a greater number of items to be included for testing as compared to questions in 2-tier, 3-tier or 4-tier formats, where the number of items need to be necessarily fewer for a given duration owing to the greater cognitive processing needed by students.

Rasch Measurement

The Rasch model is a stochastic model that allows raw test items to be subjected to a linear transformation so as to generate a standardized score that locates student ability and item difficulty on a common logit scale. The dichotomous Rasch model is defined mathematically by the following equation:

$$ln\left(\frac{P_{ni}}{1 - P_{ni}}\right) = \theta_n - \delta_i$$

where P_{ni} is the probability that a student with ability θ_n will provide the correct answer with an item difficulty of δ_i. Put simply, the probability that a given student will provide the correct answer is a logistic function of the difference in the students' ability and the item's difficulty. For example, when student ability matches exactly the difficulty of the item, the probability of a correct response is 0.5. For students with very low ability, the probability of getting a correct answer is virtually zero, while those with very high ability will have a probability of almost 1 in providing a correct answer to the item. As the difference between a student's ability and the difficulty of an item can be translated to the probability of getting a correct answer using the exponential function, a student with an ability of 1.0 logit higher than the difficulty of the item has a 73% chance of answering the item correctly.

Method

Samples

The samples ($N = 2163$) comprised Secondary One students (Grade 7)) drawn from 16 secondary schools in Singapore and that were selected by stratified sampling. About 58% of the samples were males. In terms of academic track, about 10%, 24% and 66% belonged to the normal technical (NT), normal academic (NA) and express (EXP) tracks, respectively. The NT track focuses on a "technical" oriented curriculum, whereas the NA track is academically less rigorous than EXP.

Instrument Development

In the following section, our description of test development and procedure addresses the first of Messick's six standards for construct validity, while the main analyses attend to the second to fifth standards. The final aspect of consequential validity—the differential social and institutional impact of the test—is addressed in the section on differential item functioning (e.g., see Engelhard, 2009, for similar approaches, and Behizadeh & Engelhard, 2015; Kane, 2013, for related reviews).

Prior to the development of the science concept test, several logistical and practical conditions were adhered to. First, the length of the test has to be kept to a maximum of 30 minutes (a standard class period) so as to minimize lesson disruption. Second, given the brevity of the test, the focus of the test has to be limited to 1-2 topics. Third, the format for assessment needs to be MCQ since the intent was to use items from text books, assessment books and examination papers, of which many can be found in this commonly used format, and not to develop items from scratch.

To ensure that the test fulfilled strong content- and construct-relevance, we reviewed the official science syllabus (Ministry of Education, 2013) and a range of academic assessment guides and textbooks published by local authors and publishers (e.g., EPH, 2015). Next, based on our review of the two sets of resources, we determined "Cell System" to be a common topic. The decision to focus on the topic of Cell System was also influenced by practical considerations as we expected and confirmed with teachers and curriculum planners that Cell System, as a 'micro' topic, would likely be covered in Secondary One. Moreover, students are likely to be familiar with this topic as it was earlier covered in some depth at the primary level.

We began with an initial pool of 33 items that probed "factual" (i.e., knowing key functions, descriptors, similarities and differences) and "understanding" (i.e., understanding relationships) content knowledge. All items were face-validated by curriculum experts, as a result of which 6 items were removed due to content irrelevance and repetition. A pilot test of the 27-item instrument was administered to two classes ($N \sim 80$), each from an average mixed gender school. Overall, only a handful of students could not complete the test within the allocated time of 30 min. Given the nature of the pilot study, we asked for more time, to which the teachers accommodated. Preliminary item analysis of the pilot data was performed to identify non-functioning distractors (less than 5% selection), and problematic items at the extreme ends (i.e., item removed if more than 90% of students provided the right answer). Based on the pilot result, a further 6 items were removed and the main study proceeded with 22 items. Across the items, 9 items were categorized as items assessing "factual" knowledge (see second column of Table 9.3, though the context still calls for some thinking rather than mere recall of knowledge.

A sample "Understanding" item is shown below:

Q12. The table below shows some information about three different cells, X, Y and Z.

Parts of a cell	Cell X	Cell Y	Cell Z
cell wall	Yes	No	Yes
chloroplast	No	No	Yes
nucleus	Yes	Yes	Yes

Based on the table, which of the following statements describe(s) cells X, Y and Z correctly?

I. Cell X is able to make its own food.
II. Cell Y can be found in the stem of a plant.
III. Cell Z is able to release oxygen to the surroundings.
A. I and II only
B. II only
C. III only (*)
D. I and III only

Data Analyses

WINSTEPS program (version 4.01) was used for data analyses. Based on the Rasch model, item analysis was performed as a preliminary investigation of the test items that includes item difficulty and discrimination, which are usually accompanied by distractor analysis. Next, summary statistics and model fit to the Rasch model were examined to explore the psychometric properties of the 22-item science concept test.

More specifically, the analyses done in relation to the Rasch model were as follows:

- Person-item map
- Uni-dimensionality and local independence
- Item-person separation and reliability
- Fit statistics
- Differential item functioning
- Option probability curves for selected items in inventory

Results

We present the Rach-based validation findings in this section.

Person-Item Map

Figure 9.1 depicts a Wright map that plots the 22 items of the test ranked according to person ability. It provides a graphical summary of the distribution of item difficulty and person ability that are expressed along the same interval logit scale. A Wright map is also useful for establishing construct representativeness and determining the

```
MEASURE        PERSON - MAP - ITEM
                    <more>|<rare>
  4                      . +
                           |
                           |
                           |
                           |
                       .## |
                           |
  3                        +
                          T|
                    .##### |
                         . |
                           |
  2               .####### +
               ########### S|
                         . |T Q3
            .############  |
                         . |  Q10
              .##########  |
  1                      . +  Q21
             .###########  |S Q2
                         . M| Q4         Q5
               .#########  |  Q13
               .#########  |  Q7
                           |  Q1
                .########  |  Q8
  0               .######  +M Q11
                         . |  Q19
                  .######  |  Q17
                   .##### S|  Q18        Q6
                         . |  Q14
                    .####  |  Q20        Q22
                     .###  |S Q16
 -1                      . +  Q12
                      ###  |
                         . |  Q15        Q9
                      .## T|
                           |T
                       .#  |
                           |
 -2                      . +
                           |
                           |
                           |
                         . |
                           |
 -3                        +
                           |
                         . |
                           |
                           |
                           |
 -4                        +
                    <less>|<freq>
 EACH "#" IS 17: EACH "." IS 1 TO 16
```

Fig. 9.1 Wright map of 22 item science concept test. "M" denotes the mean. "S" denotes one standard deviation from the mean. "T" denotes two standard deviation from the mean

extent to which items align to the ability, and for identifying locations of the Rasch scale that are in need of improvement.

The right side of the plot shows the distribution of items ranked by item difficulty, with the easiest items (Q9—"functions of animal cell", and Q15—"similarities and differences about cells and parts") at the bottom to the most difficult items (Q3—"identify parts of cells between plant and animal"—and Q10—"functions of cell vacuole") at the top.

Overall, the Wright map indicates that most of the ability ranges (of students) are generally well covered, thus indicating representativeness of test items (See Table 9.3 for on overview of the item content). Moreover, content relevance is also supported as the easiest two items were related to "factual" knowledge and the hardest two items were related to "understanding" (see Table 9.3 on content type). However, the "bare" portion at the upper end of the right side of the plot makes it clear that persons of high ability (approximately 10% of the population) are not measured by any items in the test. The mean person ability is about 0.75 logits higher than the mean item difficulty for the test, thus suggesting that more difficult items are needed to improve person-item coverage. In addition, while Q3, Q10 and Q21 appear to be the most difficult items (requiring ability of 1.0 and above), these do not match person ability exactly, thus suggesting that item calibration is needed to improve its precision. Essentially, the Wright map facilitates a fundamental assessment of construct validity as it provides evidence about the relevance and representativeness of the content upon which the test matches the theory that it purports to predict (Messick, 1995).

Uni-dimensionality and Local Independence

These are two conceptually similar but fundamentally non-equivalent assumptions that must be met in modern test analysis. Uni-dimensionality refers to the existence of one dominant construct being measured. For instance, the assumption of uni-dimensionality is violated if the items in our science concept test (Cell System) measure other related constructs over and beyond what the test items are purported to measure. The assumption of local independence requires that students' responses to any items in the test are unrelated or not affected by responses to other items. Local independence is achieved when the probability of getting a right or wrong answer depends on the latent trait being measured (i.e., θ_n).

Violations of local independence and uni-dimensionality can be determined by principal components analysis of the residuals (PCAR). This analyzes the difference between the observed values and those implied by the Rasch model to determine if additional dimensions exist beyond the first Rasch dimension. Evidence for multidimensionality is supported when at least two items belong to the second dimension (i.e., an eigenvalue of >2), and the dimension contributes at least 5% of unexplained variance (Linacre, 2018).

In relation to PCAR, the Rasch component explained 25.1% of the variance, with 13.4% explained by items. The low variance explained is consistent with the lack of precision of person-item match at the higher ability levels. Importantly, although overall total unexplained variance was substantial (74.9%), those in the first and subsequent contrasts were not appreciably higher than the recommended threshold of 2 eigenvalue units and 5% unexplained variance. In PCAR analysis, it is also a common practice to examine the dis-attenuated correlations to determine if the clusters reflect the same dimension and the standardized residual correlations to determine item dependency. The results revealed corrections of 1.0 between clusters 1–3 as well as 1–2, and 0.99 between clusters 2–3. In terms of local independence, the results revealed a negligible correlation of 0.13 for items Q14 and Q16.

The PCAR results thus present reasonable evidence of a unidimensional model. In other words, the test scores sufficiently represent students' overall test performance (Table 9.1).

Table 9.1 Table of standardized residual variance (in Eigenvalue units)

	Eigenvalue	Observed (%)	(%)	Expected (%)
Total raw variance in observations	29.35	100.00		100.00
Raw variance explained by measures	7.35	25.10		25.30
Raw variance explained by persons	3.43	11.70		11.80
Raw Variance explained by items	3.92	13.40		13.50
Raw unexplained variance (total)	22	74.90	100.00	74.70
Unexplained variance in 1st contrast	1.49	5.10	6.80	
Unexplained variance in 2nd contrast	1.35	4.60	6.10	
Unexplained variance in 3rd contrast	1.21	4.10	5.50	
Unexplained variance in 4th contrast	1.18	4.00	5.40	
Unexplained variance in 5th contrast	1.15	3.90	5.20	

Item and Person Separation Reliability

Item and person separation reliability are two reproducibility statistics that are used in conjunction to evaluate the adequacy of the unidimensional Rasch model. Item separation examines the item hierarchy with respect to how well the items are located on the latent trait, whereas person separation illustrates how well the model can rank scores between persons. Separation values of above 2 are typically desired. On the other hand, item-person reliabilities are related to the reproducibility of relative item placements on the modelled latent trait. Low item reliability indicates insufficiency of the sample size of good quality (i.e., good representation along levels of the latent trait), while low person reliability indicates insufficiency of items that target the range of ability levels being assessed. Analogous to Cronbach's Alpha, higher values are indicative of high reliability with a minimum threshold of 0.70.

Table 9.2 shows the summary statistics of person-item separation and reliability. With respect to items, both the separation index and reliability were well above the

Table 9.2 Person reliability and separation reliability

			Infit		Outfit	
Persons	Measure	REALSE	IMNSQ	ZSTD	OMNSQ	ZSTD
Mean	0.69	0.55	1.00	0.1	0.98	0.1
SD	1.08	0.12	0.16	0.8	0.30	0.9
Real RMSE = 0.56; *True SD* = 0.93; *Separation* = 1.66; *Person reliability* = 0.73						
Items	Measure	REALSE	IMNSQ	ZSTD	OMNSQ	ZSTD
Mean	0.00	0.05	0.99	0.1	0.98	0.0
SD	0.79	0.00	0.10	4.3	0.18	4.4
Real RMSE = 0.05; *True SD* = 0.79; *Separation* = 14.78; *Item reliability* = 1.00						

threshold for acceptability, thus indicating stability of the item estimates across different populations (given that our sample can be considered to be large and reasonably representative). Item separation (14.78) and item reliability (1.00) suggest adequacy of sample size in revealing hierarchy and spacing of items across different samples of similar characteristics. Person separation (1.66) and reliability (0.73), however, were slightly lower than the recommended acceptability range. Of interest to note is that the average Infit and Outfit (summarizing all persons and items) hovered at 1.0, indicating optimal person-item fit of the Rasch model.

Fit Statistics

Infit and Outfit are two types of fit statistics that determine if each item matches the expectations of the Rasch model. The reported statistical values are expressed as mean squares (χ^2 mean square divided by the degrees of freedom), with an optimal expected value of 1.0. Infit signals misfit due to unexpected pattern of responses on items when there is a relative close person-item fit, whereas Outfit signals misfit due to unexpected responses to items when there is extreme person-item mismatch (e.g., high ability students providing an incorrect answer to an easy item and vice versa). Both statistics provide evidence about construct validity of the instrument, and well established guidelines exist where values of between 0.7 and 1.3 (Bond & Fox, 2007) are generally accepted as good indication that the item contributes well to the latent trait Rasch model. Values below the lower limit indicate that the item in question may exhibit non-trivial interdependence with another item, whereas, values above the upper limit indicate that the item may not fit well under the unidimensional model.

Table 9.3 shows the summary of person-item fit and distractor quality. Item Infit and Outfit statistics were within acceptable range (0.7–1.3; Bond & Fox, 2007). Infit ranged from 0.79 (Q16) to 1.20 (Q10), thus indicating good fit of the items to the Rasch model. This is particularly reassuring as studies have indicated that Infit values impact overall person-item estimates more than Outfit values (Bond & Fox, 2015). Outfit ranged from 0.64 (Q16) to 1.39 (Q10), indicating some evidence of person-item mismatch for the two extreme items as well as Q10 ($mnsq = 1.32$). The other 19 items were within the recommended cut-offs. Due to the large sample size, we did not interpret the sample-dependent z-standardized. Item discrimination is examined from two statistics: *point measure correlation* and *estimated discrimination*. Point measure correlation is the correlation between the difficulty of the item and the test as a whole, with values above 0.3 indicating internal coherence. Estimated discrimination values above 1 indicate that the item discriminates between persons with low or high ability better than the expected item difficulty, while the reverse is true for values below 1.0. Most of the 22 items exhibited adequate coherence, with the exception of Q10 (0.23; 0.42) and Q11 (0.26; 0.55), suggesting that these two items do not discriminate person ability very well. As these items also reported the largest Infit and Outfit values, we proceeded to perform distractor analysis (via Option Probability Curves)

Table 9.3 Summary of person-item fit and distractor quality

Item	Item content	Distractor quality				ptma corr	estim discrim	Infit		Outfit	
		(1)	(2)	(3)	(4)			mns	zstd	mns	zstd
Q1	Smallest unit of life between plant and animal [F]	59	24	14	4	0.47	1.13	0.95	−2.6	0.93	−2.3
Q2	Understand plant functions [F]	46	19	5	29	0.37	0.77	1.08	4.3	1.09	3.1
Q3	Classify parts of cells between plant and animal [U]	46	14	6	33	0.29	0.68	1.13	5.9	1.25	6.2
Q4	Identify different parts of chicken as cell [F]	48	29	4	18	0.37	0.78	1.06	3.5	1.13	4.7
Q5	Identify shape of an animal cell [F]	5	42	5	48	0.41	0.92	1.03	1.6	1.02	0.8
Q6	Identity cell structure in animal cell [F]	6	9	14	71	0.43	1.04	0.98	−1.0	0.96	−0.9
Q7	Identify substances in cell vacuole [U]	10	56	28	7	0.43	0.98	1.00	0.3	1.02	−0.8
Q8	Functions of animal cell [U]	4	13	21	62	0.50	1.20	0.93	−3.7	0.87	−4.3
Q9	Functions of animal cell [F]	2	13	83	2	0.46	1.14	0.88	−3.4	0.74	−4.1
Q10	Functions of cell vacuole [U]	10	35	39	17	0.23	0.42	1.20	9.8	1.39	9.9
Q11	Identify correct statement about functions of cell nucleus [U]	14	14	63	9	0.26	0.55	1.17	7.9	1.32	9.0
Q12	Functions of different cell types [U]	3	9	80	8	0.46	1.13	0.90	−3.0	0.83	−3.0
Q13	Identify correct statement about plant cell based on diagram [U]	3	6	37	54	0.39	0.87	1.05	2.6	1.05	1.8
Q14	Identify multicellular organism based on diagram [U]	7	74	11	7	0.54	1.26	0.84	−6.2	0.74	−6.0
Q15	Similarities and differences about cells and parts [F]	7	4	6	83	0.43	1.10	0.91	−2.4	0.81	−2.9
Q16	Comparing using flowcharts [U]	77	8	11	4	0.57	1.30	0.79	−7.6	0.64	−7.7
Q17	Make conclusion based on information given [U]	6	14	12	68	0.40	0.96	1.03	−1.1	1.01	−0.3
Q18	Make correct observations based on diagram [F]	2	71	8	19	0.40	0.98	1.01	0.3	1.03	0.8
Q19	Functions of cells [U]	11	7	67	14	0.42	1.01	1.01	0.5	0.94	−1.6
Q20	Functions of nerve [F]	12	3	76	9	0.44	1.09	0.95	−1.9	0.86	−2.8
Q21	Cell organization [U]	16	1	37	45	0.49	1.21	0.92	−4.2	0.92	−3.0
Q22	Respiratory system [U]	12	7	76	5	0.35	0.93	1.04	1.5	1.07	1.3

Note "mns" denotes mean square statistics. "zstd" denotes *z*-standardized. "ptma corr" denotes "point measure correlation". "estim discrim" denotes "estimated discrimination". Values underlined denote correct answer. [F] denotes "factual" items; [U] denotes "understanding" items of the item responses that can help to identify structural issues with the item or possible misconceptions (Sadler, 1998).

Option Probability Curves

Empirical option probability curves show the probability of selecting each response in an item as a function of students' ability. We present findings for three problematic items: Q10 and Q11 (misfit items) and Q3 (non-misfit but most difficult item).

Figure 9.2a shows the curve for Q10 (a difficult item). The question was: "Vacuoles contain…". The given options were: (1) food; (2) water; (3) cell sap; and (4) cellulose. From the figure, it is clear that the correct answer (3) (39% selected) increases monotonically along with increasing ability. Among the four answers, the curves for (1) (10%) and (4) (17%) follow a relatively similar pattern. Low to moderate ability students were more likely to select these answers, with the probability dropping to almost zero beyond the ability of 2.0 logits. Answer (2) is a strong distractor, with 35% of the students selecting this answer. Students who selected this option were those with ability −4 logits as well as those whose ability ranged between −1.5 and 0.5 logits. Further examination of the profile of this curve suggests that students' misconception that 'water is a constituent of vacuoles' is quite strong, though it dissipates as ability increases.

Figure 9.2b shows the probability curve for Q11 (of average difficulty). The question was: "Which one of the following statements about the nucleus of a cell is not true?" Given options were: (1) "It is present in all plant and animal cells"; (2) "It controls all chemical reactions in the cells"; (C) "It determines which materials can move in and out of the cell"; and (4) "It contains genetic material which are passed from one generation to another". The probability of selecting option (1) (14% selected) was highest among low ability students. However, this option was also popular among higher ability students as the probability of selection remained constant (15–20%) for students whose ability approached four logits. Since this concept is covered in upper primary science and extended further in lower secondary science, the selection of this option represents a misconception that is carried forward from primary science. In the science education literature, it is well known that misconceptions can be deeply entrenched and are often resistant to instruction (Sreenivasulu & Subramaniam, 2013). There could also be another reason why this option was chosen—the stem of the question was negatively phrased and students might have difficulties in disagreeing with the selected response. Again, this has been noted in the literature (Haladyna & Downing, 1989). The probability of the other two incorrect options (2) (14%) and (4) (9%) decreased as ability increased. Interestingly, between ability −2 and −1, students were almost equally likely to select any of the four options. However, the probability of selecting the correct option (3) (63%) increased rapidly for students with ability above −1 logit. In subsequent item revision, it would be more efficacious to rephrase the stem of this question.

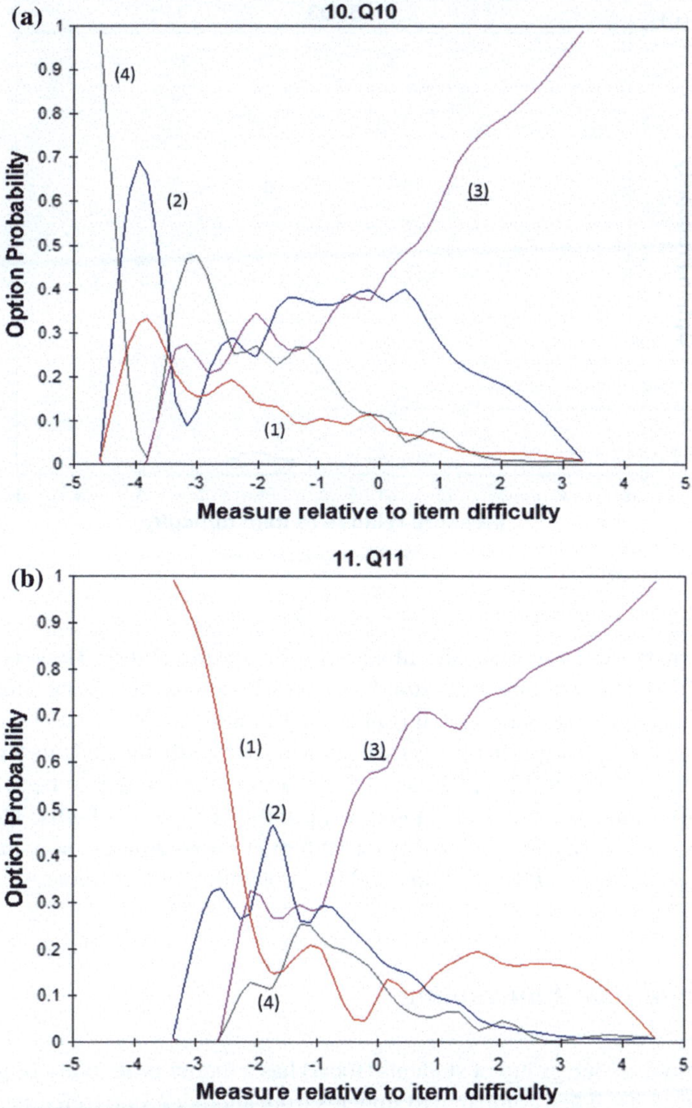

Fig. 9.2 **a** Option probability curve for Q10. **b** Option probability curve for Q11. **c** Option probability curve for Q3

To compare these results with a non-misfit item, we plotted the curve for the most difficult item (Q3) (see Fig. 9.2c). For this question, a diagram was presented that showed six different parts of plant cells. Students were asked to identify the correct combination of cell parts that can only be found in plant cells as well as the combination that can be found in animal cells. In general, the curve for the correct option is consistent with the earlier two plots. The correct answer (3), with 33%

(c)

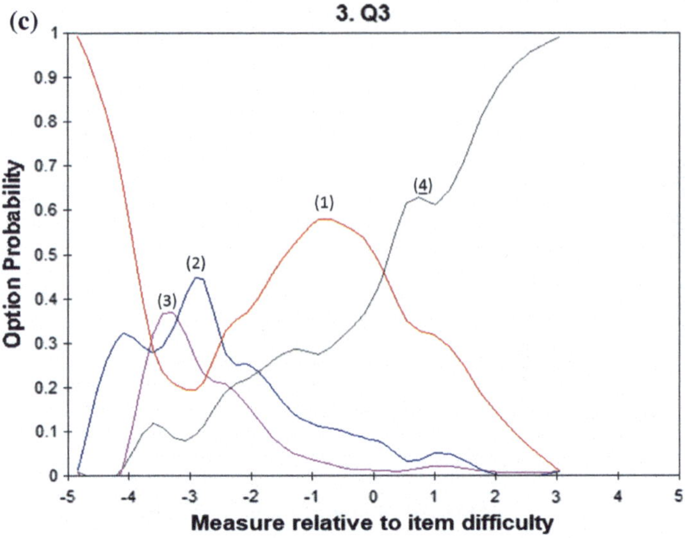

Fig. 9.2 (continued)

selection, increases monotonically along with increasing ability. However, option (1) (46%) was a very strong distractor. Students who chose this option (incorrectly) identified vacuole in an animal cell (rather than in a plant cell). The curve for this option indicates that the probability of selection drops rapidly for students with ability above −1 logit. Options (2) (14%) and (3) (6%) were more likely to be selected by lower ability students, especially those with ability below −3 logits. Unlike the above two misfit items, the probability curve for Q3 shows a much more monotonic relationship between students' ability and the probability of a correct response.

Differential Item Functioning

DIF occurs when one group of students (focal) has a higher probability of providing a correct response when compared to students from another group (reference). Stated another way, DIF is not so much concerned with real differences in item outcome, but whether the relative location of the item varies unexpectedly across the subgroups, given similar ability levels. DIF is therefore a threat to test validity as it signals the presence of construct irrelevant variance and that the item is measuring something else other than the assessed latent trait (e.g., group characteristics). Relatedly, from the perspective of measurement validity, differential item functioning also provides a heuristic assessment of consequential validity (Behizadeh & Engelhard, 2015; Kane, 2013) by examining test and item appropriateness for certain subgroups of students. In this study, we examined DIF for gender and academic track. According to Linacre (2018), two statistical values are useful to detect DIF. First is the statistical significance to identify DIF items. Second is the effect size difference associated with the offending DIF item by referring to the "DIF Contrast". Values greater than 0.64, coupled with a rejection of the null hypothesis, would provide evidence in support of DIF.

Uniform DIF analysis for gender indicated no biased items. All DIF contrasts (using Mantel-Haenszel tests) were below recommended thresholds and not statistically significant (−0.30 to 0.33 logits, $p > 0.05$) (Linacre, 2018). For academic track, however, several DIF items were found. It is important to note that differences in subgroup sample sizes can affect the precision of the DIF analysis, which we have also observed in this sample with respect to academic track. Figure 9.3 shows the person DIF plot for the three separate academic tracks. Although a number of DIF could be observed, we highlight those below the significance level of 0.001 (given our large sample size). Q3 was the only item that was differentially more difficult for NT students with a DIF contrast of −0.93 ($p < 0.001$) and −1.44 ($p < 0.001$) against NA and EXP, respectively. A positive value indicates that the item is more difficult for the focal group (i.e., NT), while a negative value indicates an easier item. From a measurement perspective, an important decision to make is whether Q3 should be dropped due to evidence of DIF. However, we ought to recall that Q3 was not only the most difficult item (see Fig. 9.1, Wright map), but the option probability curve (Fig. 9.2c) also supports the monotonicity assumption of the Rasch model, in which the probability of a correct response increases an ability goes up. Together,

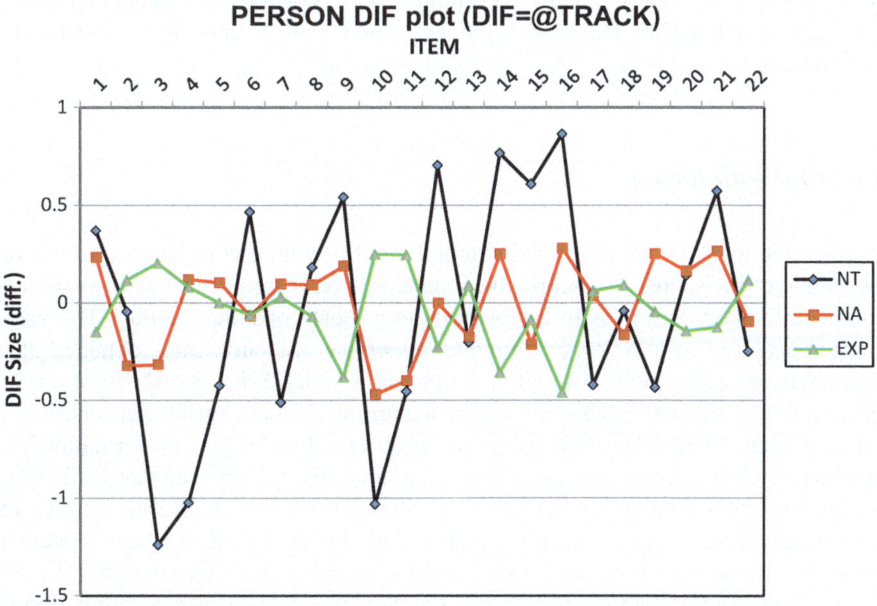

Fig. 9.3 Person DIF plot for academic track

this suggests that Q3 does provide useful information that can differentiate higher ability from lower ability students. With respect to consequential validity, the DIF results for Q3 highlight a disadvantage for NT students. It is possible that the content focus of Q3—*classify parts of cells between plant and animal*—may be outside the NT curriculum (in which case the item should be revised in future iterations of this instrument). If this is not the case, improvements in instruction and learning should be considered to bridge the educational disadvantage for students in the NT track, specifically for this and related items assessing similar content foci.

Interestingly, while there were visibly large distances among the three tracks, for example, Q4 (all subgroups), Q10 (NT, EXP), Q14 (NT, EXP), and Q16 (NT, EXP), none of the comparisons were statistically significant ($p < 0.001$). For instance, the largest DIF of -1.28 for Q10 between NT and EXP had a p-value of 0.58. Nonetheless, recall that this item was also flagged for item misfit. This possibly indicates that the item's unreliability may have been influenced by DIF (Salzberger, Newton, & Ewing, 2014). One item that exhibited an inconsistent DIF was Q5. While a significant DIF was found between NT and NA (-0.53, $p = 0.001$), it was not significant between NT and EXP, as well as NA and EXP. Examination of DIF among the remaining item-pairs did not reveal any that were significant at $p < 0.001$.

An important question when DIF is found is whether the removal of misfit items can improve the fit of the model. To examine this issue, we reanalyzed the data without the items that did not exhibit DIF (i.e., Q3, Q10 and Q11). Our results showed negligible differences in model fit (e.g., personal reliability remained at 0.73) and a marginal improvement in explained variance (from 25 to 27%). More practically, however, the removal of Q3 will leave a larger "bare" portion at the upper end of our item representativeness. Therefore, there is a case for all 22 items in the instrument to be retained.

External Validation

In our final analysis, we examined external validity with a correlation analysis of the Science test scores (transformed to standardized Rasch scaled scores) with a number of survey variables to establish its empirical construct validity. The variables considered were *Science prior attainment* (i.e., Science grade obtained at a national examination administered in the previous year), *Science task-specific self-efficacy* (e.g., "classify objects or events according to their attributes/properties", "draw evidence-based conclusions based on observations or given information"; 8 items; $\alpha = 0.91$), *Science self-concept* (e.g., "I have always believed that SCIENCE is one of my best subjects"; 4 items; $\alpha = 0.90$) and classroom attentiveness (e.g., In my Science class, I keep my attention on the work during the entire lesson"; 3 items; $\alpha = 0.89$). In line with theoretical expectations, our analysis showed that the 22-item Science test exhibited good external validity. Science test was most strongly correlated with prior Science achievement ($r = 0.516$), Science self-concept ($r = 0.219$), self-efficacy ($r = 0.155$) and attentiveness ($r = 0.161$). All correlation coefficients are significant at $p < 0.001$.

Discussion

A concept inventory on the topic of cells, pitched at the grade 7 level, was developed and validated in this study using the Rasch model. To the best of our knowledge, an inventory of this nature has not been reported, and so it reflects a useful contribution to the literature.

Overall, the instrument exhibits reasonably good psychometric properties. In relation to validity, the key issue is whether it purports to measure what it is supposed to measure. This is supported by face validity of the items, which was done by a team of educators who are conversant with the topic of cell systems at the lower secondary level. It has to be noted that face validity relates to the content in the instrument, and can only be done by experts—the Rasch model or, for that matter, any other statistical model, is not the platform to do this. The original 33-item instrument was reduced to a 22-item instrument through a process of iteration. The reliability of this version of the instrument is good and is supported by two numerical measures: person reliability (0.73) and item reliability (1.00).

The item-person map reflects reasonably good targeting though it also indicates the need to include more difficult items to better cater to students of higher ability levels. While the span of the test items is about 3 logits, that for the distribution of persons is about 5 logits—of interest to note is that in the range between -1.5 logit and $+1.5$ logit, where all the items are located, about 80% of all persons are also found herein. When the data for the sample was partitioned on the basis of gender and subjected to Rasch analysis, no differential item functioning was detected. That is, item measures were invariant with respect to gender. However, DIF was noted when the sample was partitioned on the basis of academic track—we attribute this to the asymmetry of the sub-sample sizes, and it has been noted in the literature. Infit and Outfit statistics for all the test items were within the acceptable range. Person separation was slightly lower than the recommended range but still acceptable. Consistent with observations from the item map, this result further suggests that the range of test items may not totally match the range of ability levels that exist in the data. Again, this supports the call for more difficult items to be included in order to improve test validity as well as its ability to consistently differentiate between persons. External validity, based on correlation analysis of the Rasch-modelled science test scores with a number of survey variables, also establishes the construct validity of the instrument.

As regards uni-dimensionality of the instrument, the Rasch dimension emerging from PCA of the residuals accounted for 25.1% of the variance, that is, it is below the common 50% threshold. Here, we have to note that it is quite common in studies using Rash-modelling for the Rasch dimension to be less than 50% (Fischer, 2006; Linacre, 2006; Cervellione, Lee, & Bonanno, 2008). Thus, the 25.1% variance for the Rasch dimension in our study is not unreasonable as content examination of the test items did not reveal a meaningful secondary dimension—these fulfill the criterion of face validity with respect to the topic of study. More importantly, it has to be noted that a test which is totally unidimensional is almost impossible to come up with (Planinic, et al., 2010).

Though the items in the instrument were selected from a diversity of sources, rather than developed from scratch, this does not diminish the utility of the instrument for such studies. It is a common practice in the literature to develop concept inventories from scratch. The present study shows that it is also possible to survey sources such as textbooks, test papers and assessment books to come up with suitable items for such an inventory, with considerable savings in time and resources. This can represent another approach to develop concept inventories. Online item banks can also be consulted in this regard, though it was not done so for this study.

Implications

The topic of cells in the lower secondary science syllabus is basic in the study of biology. However, it is also a topic that is fraught with a number of misconceptions and learning difficulties (Vlaardingerbroek, Taylor, & Bale, 2014; Williams, DeBarger, Montgomery, Zhou, & Tateet, 2012; Flores, Tovar, & Gallegos, 2003). This is also reflected in the present study, where a good number of distracters in all questions have at least 10% selection—a common threshold to categorize a distracter as a misconception. The instrument developed for this study can thus be used by teachers as a tool to probe students' understanding of cells as well as identify their misconceptions on this topic. It can be completed by students in 30 min, and thus it is easy to administer as well as extract data for use by teachers. The instrument can be obtained from the authors on request.

Limitations

The concept inventory developed for this study, though reasonably comprehensive (22 items), surveyed only limited aspects of the topic of cell systems in the syllabus. Thus, the findings from this study are constrained by this limitation. It is also assumed that students diligently answered the questions, based on their understanding, and that no guesswork was involved. Further, given the lack of items targeted at high ability students (above 2 logits), more difficult items could be included in future iterations of the test.

Conclusion

A 22-item concept inventory on the Biology topic of cells has been compiled from various sources and validated in this study using the Rasch model. Overall, the instrument demonstrates reasonably good psychometric properties and can be used by teachers to assess students' understanding of the topic as well as the presence of misconceptions on the topic.

References

Anderson, D. L., Fisher, K. M., & Norman, G. J. (2002). Development and evaluation of the conceptual inventory of natural selection. *Journal of Research in Science Teaching, 39*(10), 952–978.

Behizadeh, N., & Engelhard, G. (2015). Valid writing instrument from the perspectives of the writing and measurement communities. *Pensamiento Educativo. Revista de Investigación Educacional Latinoamericana, 52*(2), 34–54.

Bond, T. G., & Fox, C. M. (2007). *Applying the Rasch model: Fundamental measurement in the human sciences* (2nd ed.). Mahwah, NJ: Lawrence Erlbaum Associates.

Bond, T. G., & Fox, C. M. (2015). *Applying the Rasch model: Fundamental measurement in the human sciences* (3rd ed.). Mahwah, NJ: Lawrence Erlbaum Associates.

Bowling, B. V., Acra, E. E., Wang, L., Myers, M. F., Dean, G. E., Markle, G. C., et al. (2008). Development and evaluation of a genetics literacy assessment instrument for undergraduates. *Genetics, 178*(1), 15–22.

Bretz, S. L., & Linenberger, K. J. (2012). Development of the enzyme–substrate interactions concept inventory. *Biochemistry and Molecular Biology Education, 40*(4), 229–233.

Caleon, I. S., & Subramaniam, R. (2010a). Development and application of a three-tier diagnostic test to assess secondary students' understanding of waves. *International Journal of Science Education, 32*(7), 939–961.

Caleon, I. S., & Subramaniam, R. (2010b). Do students know what they know and what they don't know? Using a four-tier diagnostic test to assess the nature of students' alternative conceptions. *Research in Science Education, 40*(3), 313–337.

Cervellione, K., Lee, Y. S., & Bonanno, G. R. (2008). Rasch modeling of the self deception scale of the balanced inventory of desirable responding. *Educational and Psychological Measurment, 69*(3), 438–458.

Dick-Perez, M., Luxford, C. J., Windus, T. L., & Holme, T. (2016). A quantum chemistry concept inventory for physical chemistry classes. *Journal of Chemical Education, 93*(4), 605–612.

Engelhard, G. (2009). Using IRT and model-data fit to conceptualize differential item and person functioning for students with disabilities. *Educational and Psychological Measurement, 69*(4), 585–602.

EPH. (2015). *PSLE topical examination questions: Science (2013–2015)*. Educational Publishing House.

Fischer, G. H. (2006). Rasch models. In C. Rao & S. Sinharay (Eds.), *Handbook of statistics* (Vol. 26, pp. 979–1027)., Psychometrics Amsterdam, The Netherlands: Elsevier.

Flores, F., Tovar, M. E., & Gallegos, L. (2003). Representation of the cell and its processes in high school students: an integrated view. *International Journal of Science Education, 25*(2), 269–286.

Frisbie, D. A., & Ebel, R. L. (1991). *Essentials of educational measurement*. Englewood Cliffs, NJ: Prentice-Hall Inc.

Fulmer, G. W. (2015). Validating proposed learning progressions on force and motion using the force concept inventory: Findings from Singapore secondary schools. *International Journal of Science and Mathematics Education, 13*(6), 1235–1254.
Fulmer, G. W., Chu, H. E., Treagust, D. F., & Neumann, K. (2015). Is it harder to know or to reason? Analyzing two-tier science assessment items using the Rasch measurement model. *Asia-Pacific Science Education, 1*(1), 1.
Haladyna, T. M., & Downing, S. M. (1989). Validity of a taxonomy of multiple-choice item-writing rules. *Applied Measurement in Education, 2*(1), 51–78.
Hestenes, D., Wells, M., & Swackhamer, G. (1992). Force concept inventory. *The Physics Teacher, 30*(3), 141–158.
Hestenes, D., & Wells, M. (1992). A mechanics baseline test. *The Physics Teacher, 30*(3), 159–166.
Kane, M. T. (2013). Validating the interpretations and uses of test scores. *Journal of Educational Measurement, 50*(1), 1–73.
Linacre, J. M. (2006). *A user's guide to WINSTEPS: Rasch model computer program*. Chicago: Winsteps.com.
Linacre, J. M. (2018). *A user's guide to WINSTEPS MINISTEP Rasch-model computer programs*. Chicago: Winsteps.com.
Lindell, R. S., Peak, E., & Foster, T. M. (2007, January). Are they all created equal? A comparison of different concept inventory development methodologies. *AIP Conference Proceedings, 883*(1), 14–17.
Messick, S. (1989). Validity. In R. L. Linn (Ed.), *Educational measurement* (3rd ed., pp. 13–104). New York, NY: Macmillan.
Messick, S. (1995). Validity of psychological assessment: Validation of inferences from persons' responses and performances as scientific inquiry into score meaning. *American Psychologist, 50*(9), 741–749.
Ministry of Education. (2013). *Science syllabus primary*. Curriculum Planning and Development Division, Ministry of Education, Singapore. Retrieved from https://www.moe.gov.sg/docs/default-source/document/education/syllabuses/sciences/files/science-primary-2014.pdf.
Morris, G. A., Harshman, N., Branum-Martin, L., Mazur, E., Mzoughi, T., & Baker, S. D. (2012). An item response curves analysis of the force concept inventory. *American Journal of Physics, 80*(9), 825–831.
Planinic, M. (2006). Assessment of difficulties of some conceptual areas from electricity and magnetism using the conceptual survey of electricity and magnetism. *American Journal of Physics, 74*(12), 1143–1148.
Planinic, M., Ivanjek, L., & Susac, A. (2010). Rasch model based analysis of the force concept inventory. *Physical Review Special Topics-Physics Education Research, 6*(1), 010103.
Sadler, P. M. (1998). Psychometric models of student conceptions in science: Reconciling qualitative studies and distractor-driven assessment instruments. *Journal of Research in Science Teaching, 35*(3), 265–296.
Salzberger, T., Newton, F. J., & Ewing, M. T. (2014). Detecting gender item bias and differential manifest response behavior: A Rasch-based solution. *Journal of Business Research, 67*(4), 598–607.
Sreenivasulu, B., & Subramaniam, R. (2013). University students' understanding of chemical thermodynamics. *International Journal of Science Education, 35*(4), 601–635.
Treagust, D. F. (1988). Development and use of diagnostic tests to evaluate students' misconceptions in science. *International Journal of Science Education, 10*(2), 159–169.
Vlaardingerbroek, B., Taylor, N., & Bale, C. (2014). The problem of scale in the interpretation of pictorial representations of cell structure. *Journal of Biological Education, 48*(3), 154–162.
Williams, M., DeBarger, A. H., Montgomery, B. L., Zhou, X., & Tate, E. (2012). Exploring middle school students' conceptions of the relationship between genetic inheritance and cell division. *Science Education, 96*(1), 78–103.

Chapter 10
Big Changes in Achievement Between Cohorts: A True Reflection of Educational Improvement or Is the Test to Blame?

Celeste Combrinck

Abstract Large-scale assessments aim to monitor changes in educational sectors by testing students at set intervals. When significant changes in achievement occur between cycles of participation, questions arise as to whether the changes indicate true improvement or can be attributed to aspects of the study, such as the instrument properties. The assessment instruments rely on the assumption of measurement invariance. This chapter demonstrates the application of Rasch theory to investigate measurement invariance and the degree thereof. The participation of South Africa in *The Progress in International Reading Literacy Study* (PIRLS) is used as an exemplar. Between the 2006 and 2016 cycles of testing, an upward shift of one standard deviation was found for reading literacy achievement of students who wrote the test in isiZulu in the fifth grade. Evidence from Rasch applications for assessing measurement invariance in the cross-national achievement survey with regard to South African participants is examined and the implications for future assessments and educational monitoring are discussed. The contribution of Rasch theory was to provide evidence of internal measurement invariance in large-scale assessments between cohorts and the degree of invariance achieved. The article concludes that Rasch models offer sufficient evidence of internal measurement invariance.

Keywords Educational achievement · Large-scale assessment · Differential item and bundle functioning · Measurement invariance · Rasch models · Reading literacy performance

Introduction and Context

Measurement Invariance

In developing countries with multi-cultural contexts, the quality of education remains immensely challenging to measure over time and between groups. When significant

C. Combrinck (✉)
University of Pretoria, Groenkloof, South Africa
e-mail: celeste.combrinck@up.ac.za

M. S. Khine (ed.), *Rasch Measurement*,
https://doi.org/10.1007/978-981-15-1800-3_10

changes are observed between cohorts, it is natural to question the reason for the change. Questions arise as to whether the changes are true educational improvements, or can be attributed to other factors, such as psychometric properties of the test. The purpose of large-scale assessments is to provide rigorous data that offers evidence of true change and makes comparability between groups and countries possible (Desa, Van de Vijver, Carstens, & Schulz, 2019; Huff, Steinberg, & Matts, 2010; Nortvedt & Buchholtz, 2018). Large-scale assessments are designed by subject matter experts to be scientifically sound, undergo extensive field testing and refinement to produce instruments that offer accurate reflections of the latent trait. Measurement invariance is the assumption that the same underlying construct is measured consistently across groups or over time (Bialosiewicz, Murphy, & Berry, 2013; Rutkowski & Svetina, 2014). Crucial for comparisons within a population, measurement invariance can be investigated at the person, item or time level (Bond & Fox, 2015; Boone, Staver, & Yale, 2014; Linacre, 2019). Specific objectivity, measurement invariance of item difficulty and person achievement, is established when items are compared independently of persons as is done when applying Rasch models (Andrich & Marais, 2019). When measurement invariance is questionable, no other conclusions can be confidently drawn regarding the results (Rutkowski & Svetina, 2014).

Investigating measurement invariance is most often approached with the application of structural equation modelling (SEM), and confirmatory factor analysis (CFA) is a preferred method (Bashkov & Finney, 2017; Maydeu-Olivares, Cai, & Hernandez, 2011; Millsap, 2011). While the limitations of SEM for examining measurement invariance has been acknowledged, this mostly lead to studies of how to deal with the limitations within an SEM framework (Bofah & Hannula, 2014; Desa et al., 2019; Rutkowski & Svetina, 2014). Multigroup models aimed at investigating factorial invariance are highly sensitive to assumptions being met, including invariant reference group results, large samples, uniform item functioning and interval level data (Distefano, Mindrila, & Monrad, 2013; Fukuhara & Kamata, 2011; Meade, 2013; Millsap, 2011). Factor analysis approaches could be viewed as complimentary when applied in conjunction with Rasch models to negate limitations (Boone et al., 2014; Randall & Engelhard, 2010) or Rasch analysis can be used independently to investigate measurement invariance (Engelhard, 2013; Finch, French, & Hernandez Finch, 2019). The current study focuses on the advantages of applying Rasch models for purposes of assessing internal measurement invariance to the exclusion of factorial models.

The theoretical point of departure is that Rasch measurement theory provides the required evidence of internal measurement invariance to judge the validity of inferences (Andrich, 2011; Fisher, 2001; Long, Craig & Dunne; 2012; Thomas, 2011). Internal indications of item and bundle functioning form the basis for assessing measurement invariance and are directly linked to selecting least biased assessments (Asún, Rdz-Navarro & Alvarado, 2017; Engelhard, 2008; Finch et al., 2019). Measurement invariance that would be acceptable to draw inferences is viewed as being a matter of degree (Desa et al., 2019) and the combination of Differential Item Functioning (DIF) and Differential Bundle Functioning (DBF) are used to draw conclusions from the exemplar and make recommendations for future research.

The Reading Literacy Study

The *Progress in International Reading Literacy Study* (PIRLS) is a global assessment of reading literacy in more than 50 countries, comparing cohorts once every five years (Howie et al., 2017a; Mullis, Martin, Foy & Hooper, 2017). South Africa participated in the 2006, 2011 and 2016 cycles at both fourth grade and fifth grade levels. A rotated-test design with 12 passages, two per booklet was used to assess reading literacy comprehension. In the South African context, the English versions of the passages are adapted and then translated into the other 10 official spoken languages. The nine African languages perform significantly below the other two languages in the PIRLS reading achievement assessment and the results have been a cause for concern (Howie et al., 2017b; Howie, van Staden, Tshele, Dowse & Zimmerman, 2012). Results from the 2006 cycle for the nine African languages at fourth grade were psychometrically unstable and could not be used due to particularly low achievement. Therefore the easier version of the PIRLS test was administered to all fourth grade students, and at the fifth grade the more difficult passages were used to asses only one of the African languages in 2016 to evaluate whether educational changes had taken place in the ten year period. Two of the easier passages were included in the fifth grade testing for conjoint scaling purposes and to measure a wider range of abilities (Howie et al., 2017a).

The teaching and learning of African languages is problematic for many reasons. Some of the challenges include dialects not being acknowledged, historical disadvantage, current poverty, rurality, lack of policy implementation and a dearth of resources within the languages (Beukes, 2009; Mohangi, Nel, Stephens, & Krog, 2016; Mtsatse & Combrinck, 2018; Wildsmith-Cromarty, 2012). The long-lasting influence of colonisation on the written format and classification of the African languages also remains an obstacle (Mtsatse & Combrinck, 2018). Reading literacy improvements were detected for some of the African languages, and an especially big improvement for isiZulu at Grade 5 was found. But good news is often and understandably met with scepticism, especially a large and significant increase.

Rasch theory can make a contribution to questions of true improvement by investigating the stability of items and assessments between cycles of participation. The current study examines measurement invariance between two cohorts by applying Rasch models to assess item functioning between rounds of participation as well as various combinations of items in the form of test bundles.

Methods

This chapter investigates internal measurement invariance by applying the Rasch partial credit model. The comparisons include both common items as well as equivalence comparisons of different tests when difficulty of items and groups of items are compared. The 2006 cohort are treated as the reference group and the 2016 cohort as the focal group.

Research Questions

The aim of the study is to investigate internal measurement invariance by applying Rasch models and discussing the degree that invariance was achieved. Related research questions are:

(1) Is there significant Differential Item Functioning (DIF) of the common items between cycles of participation for the isiZulu group?
(2) Is there significant Differential Bundle Functioning (DBF) between cycles of participation, especially for the common linking items?
(3) How much internal measurement invariance is sufficient for valid inferences to be drawn?

Sample

A two-stage stratified cluster sampling design was used wherein schools were sampled in proportion to size. Thereafter classes were randomly sampled within to represent languages and provinces respectively for the fifth grade South African student population (LaRoche, Joncas, & Foy, 2017). The grade 5 sample was stratified for three languages, one of which was an African language, is iZulu. In the 2006 PIRLS cycle, 1733 students wrote the isiZulu test and in the 2016 cycle there were 2015 isiZulu students who participated. Demographic variables showed that the 2006 and 2016 cohorts were similar in age, gender, home language and socio-economic status. However, the 2016 cohort were significantly more likely to be from suburban areas (31%) when compared to the original 2006 cohort (15%). A greater percentage (72%) of the 2016 cohort also came from the Kwa-Zulu Natal province whereas the 2006 cohort had a lower percentage from the province (60%). The cohorts have similar backgrounds as expected, though the migration to more suburban areas may indicate changes taking place within the population.

Instruments and Administration

The study used a rotated-test design, in which 12 reading literacy passages were arranged in a matrix of 16 booklets (Howie et al., 2017b). Trend passages in the rounds of the PIRLS cycles link assessments, creating the opportunity for monitoring changes. Each booklet has a fiction and non-fictional passage followed by approximately 13–15 questions per passage. Assessment questions per passage have a balance of multiple choice type items and constructed response items. Students read and answered the questions independently. Between the 2006 and 2016 assessments, there were four common passages with 51 items in total. The assessments were originally in English, and were translated into isiZulu through translation and back translation processes which included an international verification. South Africa follows the standard PIRLS study design as prescribed by the International Association for Educational Achievement (IEA). The tests were administered by trained and independent assessors adhering to the standardised procedures.

Data Analysis

The Rasch partial credit model was used to analyse the item responses and overall assessment functioning for the 2006 and 2016 cohorts together as well as independently. Items had maximum scores of up to four categories, but the majority of the items (77%) were dichotomous. Winsteps Version 3.93.10 was utilised to conduct the analysis (Linacre, 2017b). There were 255 unweighted items from 18 passages, of which 51 items (20%) were common items (four trend passages). The 2006 and 2016 cohorts were analysed together via stacking ($n = 3838$) as well as separately per cycle.

Differential Item Functioning (DIF) analyses were conducted in Winsteps to assess significant differences between the 2006 and 2016 cohorts for children who wrote the assessment in isiZulu. DIF contrasts above 0.50 logits indicate differences of half a standard deviation, and larger than 0.64 can be classified as moderate to large effect sizes (Bond & Fox, 2015; Linacre, 2017a). A significant probability of observing difference is shown as $p < 0.05$. Differential Test Functioning (DTF) was conducted to compare item locations in the two separate cohorts as an additional gauge of anchor item functioning (Linacre, 2017a; Zenisky, Hambleton & Robin, 2003).

Differential Bundle Functioning (DBF) was conducted by applying non-parametric statistics as the item measures were not normally distributed (Shapiro-Wilk > 0.05). DIF analysis of the anchor items was conducted first to identify potential bias in items between cycles of participation, and DBF was conducted secondly to analyse item groupings and their functioning for the two cohorts and overall. Using a multi-stage method for examining potential differences between cycles of testing produces more trustworthy results (Zenisky et al., 2003). Differential booklet functioning was not examined as trend passages were spread across booklets and the consistency of the passages between rounds was the focus of the current study (Beretvas & Walker, 2012). DBF could have been conducted after removing items which contain DIF, but the current analysis includes items with DIF in the DBF analysis to assess whether the large sample of items could compensate for anchor items with DIF (Sandilands, Oliveri, Zumbo & Ercikan, 2013).

Results

Differential Item Functioning (DIF)

Table 10.1 shows the summary statistics for all items per cycle, combined as well as the statistics for the common (linking) items only. In each cycle at least half of the sample (randomly assigned) answered the anchor (common) items. Most notable in Table 10.1 is the very low person separation index, which indicates low discrimination

Table 10.1 Rasch summary statistics all items and anchor items per cycle and stacked

		2006 all items	2016 all items	2006 and 2016 all items	2006 common items	2016 common items	2006 and 2016 common items
Person	Sample *N*	1733	2105	3838	1108	1169	2029
	Mean	0.65	−0.97	−1.45	−1.66	−1.60	−1.48
	Standard deviation	0.20	0.37	0.89	0.86	1.07	0.90
	Min	1.57	0.51	1.47	−3.70	−4.77	−3.95
	Max	0.34	−2.94	−5.19	1.49	1.84	1.62
	Separation index	0.73	0.95	1.12	0.00	0.68	0.42
	Reliability (model)	0.35	0.47	0.56	0.00	0.31	0.15
Item	Item *N*	255	255	255	51	51	51
	Mean	0.00	0.00	0.00	0.00	0.00	0.00
	Standard deviation	1.24	1.33	1.43	1.04	0.07	1.10
	Min	4.04	4.28	4.20	−2.29	0.08	−2.65
	Max	−2.56	−3.32	−3.99	2.39	0.42	2.58
	Separation index	4.71	7.88	6.56	4.66	6.68	8.43
	Reliability (model)	0.96	0.98	0.98	0.96	0.98	0.99

Table 10.2 Anchor items significantly more difficult between 2006 and 2016 cycles of participation

Item	Measure 2006	S.E. 2006	Measure 2016	S.E. 2016	DIF contrast	d.f.	Prob.	Interpretation
Flowers10	−0.54	0.20	0.34	0.16	−0.88	321	0.001	Difficulty > 2016
Flowers12	0.96	0.27	1.74	0.28	−0.79	360	0.046	Difficulty > 2016
Leonardo8	0.72	0.23	2.46	0.46	−1.74	440	0.001	Difficulty > 2016
Sharks2	−0.05	0.16	−0.57	0.12	0.52	476	0.010	Difficulty > 2006
Sharks3	−0.32	0.15	0.44	0.15	−0.76	537	0.000	Difficulty > 2016
Sharks6	−0.28	0.16	0.53	0.16	−0.82	512	0.000	Difficulty > 2016
Sharks7	0.38	0.15	1.04	0.15	−0.66	447	0.002	Difficulty > 2016
Shiny Straw11	−0.78	0.16	−1.28	0.12	0.50	415	0.013	Difficulty > 2006
Shiny Straw9	0.44	0.16	−0.36	0.09	0.80	347	0.000	Difficulty > 2006

power (Linacre, 2017a). The low person reliability is primarily a consequence of poor achievement, the person mean is between half and one and half standard deviations below the item mean per bundle. As the test was far too difficult for the sample, they cluster at the lower end of the scale leaving very little opportunity to discriminate between different ability levels.

The lack of sample-item targeting may be due to problems with teaching and learning African languages as well as the challenges of translation (Essien, 2018; Mtsatse & Combrinck, 2018; van der Berg, Spaull, Wills, Gustafsson, & Kotzé, 2016). Low achievement in the African languages has made comparisons within the languages as well as with other language groups particularly difficult. PIRLS is the only nationally representative study which assesses African languages presently available and therefore the only gauge of teaching and learning taking place (Howie et al., 2017a). Table 10.2 shows items which exhibited significant differential item functioning (DIF) between the two rounds of participation.

In total, nine out of the 51 anchor items (18%) displayed significant DIF between cycles of participation for children who wrote the assessment in isiZulu. Four of the items came from one passage, an informational passage with complex terminology referring to biological aspects of sharks. It should be noted that translating such a passage into an African language is especially challenging as many of the terms may not be available. All of the items exhibited non-uniform DIF, indicating that items may be too unbalanced to assess underlying abilities consistently. DIF contrasts do show more than half a standard deviation in difference for most items, the largest of which was more than 1.5 logits of contrast. Most of the items were more difficult for the 2016 cohort when compared to the 2006 cohort, despite the 2016 group having overall higher achievement. While person reliability ranges for the different passages per language group, the reliability of the *Sharks* passage was especially low at 0.367 for the isiZulu group overall (both cycles), whereas those who wrote the test in English had an acceptable reliability for the *Sharks* passage at 0.783. Item and

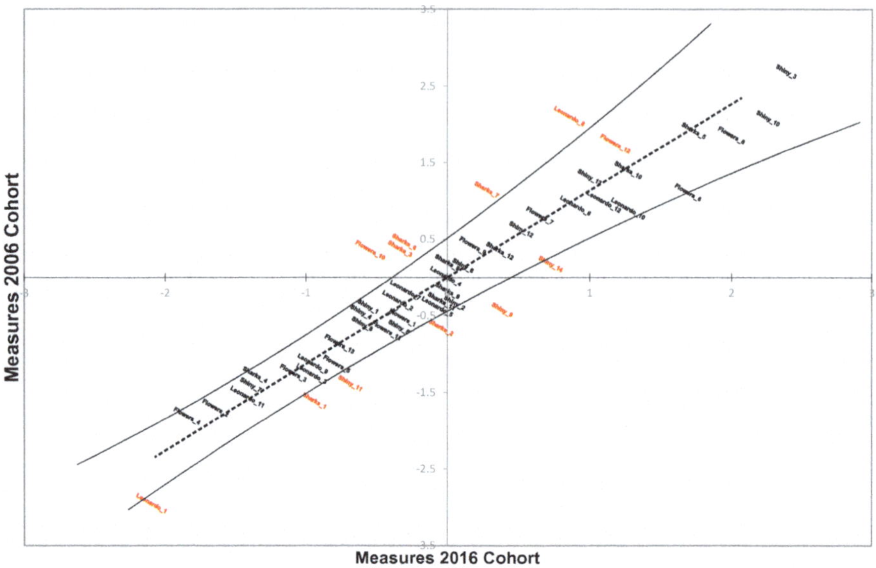

Fig. 10.1 Scatterplot of measures 2006 and 2016 per anchor item

test functioning become challenging to interpret when the majority of the sample performed at the lower end of the scale, an aspect of this case in particular.

To assess anchor item functioning between rounds with another method, the 2006 measures of persons for the anchor items were plotted against the 2016 person measures in Fig. 10.1.

Most of the items identified in the original DIF (see Table 10.2) were also found in the Differential Test Functioning (DTF) analysis shown in Fig. 10.1, but an additional three items were significant in the DTF showing the importance of investigating items using a combination of methods. The majority of the anchor items are within the 95% confidence interval bands. The disattenuated correlation is very high at 0.96 and meets the expected requirements for the same items administered to separate but similar cohorts (Bond & Fox, 2015). Rasch results of Principle Component Analysis (PCA) showed that the passages had one strong, underlying construct and the unexplained variance in contrasts were below 1.4 which provided evidence of unidimensionality.

Differential Bundle Functioning (DBF)

The possibility that the 2016 passages in their entirety (excluding anchor passages) were easier was assessed. Item difficulty for each item was exported from Winsteps using the IFILE option, and the difficulties were imported into IBM SPSS version

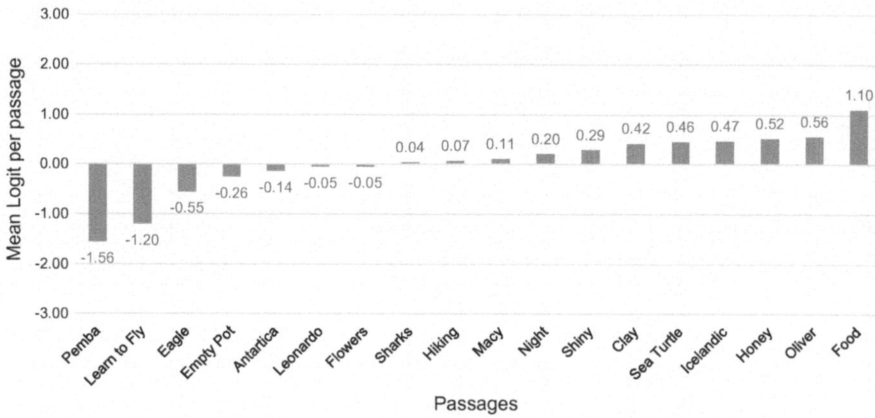

Fig. 10.2 Mean difficulty in logits per passage based on item difficulties

25 (IBM Corp., 2017). In Fig. 10.2, the mean logits of passage difficulty is shown, based on the item logits per passage.

Passages were compared by applying the Kruskal–Wallis test and conducting Bonferroni post hoc tests (Field, 2018). There were only two passages in the 2016 collection which were significantly easier than other passages, namely *Pemba the Sherpa* and *Learn to Fly* ($p < 0.05$). Both of these passages were specifically designed to measure at the lower end of the scale, especially in developing contexts. The easier passages measure a wider range of abilities, and though they are significantly easier, this did not affect the overall difficulty for the 2016 round where they were included. In terms of bundle comparisons, the anchor passages had the least number of total items ($n = 51$), whereas the 2016 passages has the largest number of items ($n = 130$) due to more passages being utilised and the 2006 bundle had a moderate number of items ($n = 74$). Figure 10.3 shows the mean logits per bundle and their spread.

Mean item bundle difficulties were comparable for anchor items ($M = -0.03$, $SD = 1.02$) and the 2006 passages ($M = -0.05$, $SD = 1.38$). The 2016 items had a lower mean indicating they were easier overall ($M = -0.28$, $SD = 1.51$). The easier nature of the 2016 passages were due to the two passages measuring at the lower end of the scale, but did not result in a significantly lower mean as shown in Table 10.3.

Finch et al. (2019) report that when assessments are approximately equal in length, using any of the available effect size formulas yield useful comparisons. A calculation of the effect size between 2016 and 2006 DBF resulted in $r_{\text{bundle}} = -0.116$ which is classified as a small effect and an effect size of $r_{\text{bundle}} = -0.091$ between the 2016 bundle and the anchor item bundle, a negligible difference (Cohen, 1988; Finch et al., 2019).

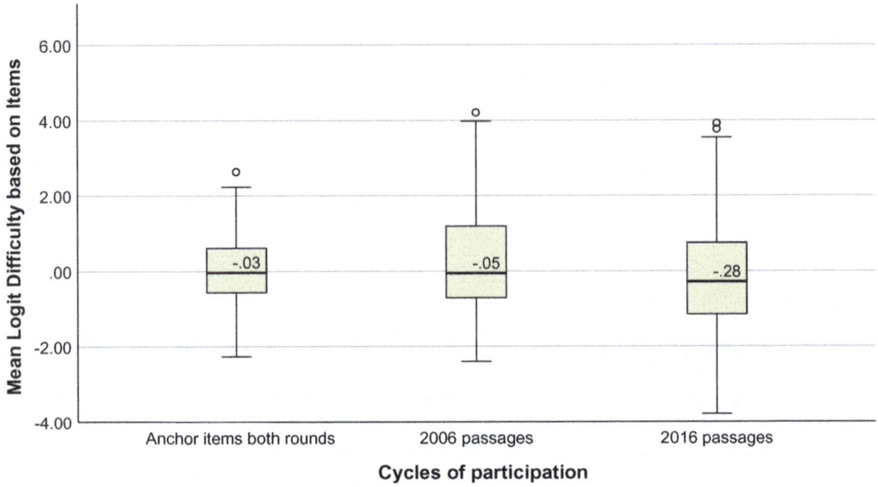

Fig. 10.3 Mean in logits per bundle and spread

Table 10.3 Bonferroni comparisons item bundles

(I) Item bundles		Mean difference (*I-J*)	Std. error	Sig.	95% confidence interval	
					Lower bound	Upper bound
Anchor items both rounds	2006 passages	−0.16	0.25	1.00	−0.77	0.44
	2016 passages	0.22	0.23	1.00	−0.33	0.77
2006 passages	Anchor items both rounds	0.16	0.25	1.00	−0.44	0.77
	2016 passages	0.38	0.20	0.17	−0.10	0.87
2016 passages	Anchor items both rounds	−0.22	0.23	1.00	−0.77	0.33
	2006 passages	−0.38	0.20	0.17	−0.87	0.10

Discussion and Implications

The results showed significant DIF between 2006 and 2016 rounds of participation for approximately 18–23% of the common items. More than half of the items displaying significant DIF came from one particular passage. The discovery of significant DIF between similar cohorts answering the assessment in the same language indicates a need for further examination of the items. While having no DIF is desirable, the identification is also useful to future design of assessments and understanding the complexity of measuring language ability. The presence of DIF was also be assessed for the potential impact it would have on DBF.

Investigation of passage difficulties indicated two passages in the 2016 round which were significantly easier, but both passages were specifically designed to measure at the lower end of the scale (easier by design). When the overall difficulty of all the 2006 passages was compared to that of the 2016 passages, no statistically significant differences were found between the two rounds of assessments (lack of DBF). There were also no significant differences between overall difficulties of the anchor items over rounds. Lack of DBF may indicate that the large number of items (255 items) as a whole compensated for the problematic anchor items. In general, the Rasch model supports equivalence of the assessment instrument between the two rounds of testing, while also highlighting specific items and passages where the substance of the items require attention. The improvement from 2006 to 2016 in isiZulu was not due to passage items difficulty drift and Rasch models offered evidence for internal measurement invariance.

The sufficiency of measurement invariance is a matter of degree. While completely invariant measures would be ideal, they may not always be present in practice (Koller, Maier, & Hatzinger, 2015). Instead, assessments showing tolerable levels of measurement invariance are sought (Finch et al., 2019). In the case of translated items, measurement invariance will be violated at times due to the inherently dissimilar natures of languages and complexity of translation for meaning (Medvedev, Titkova, Siegert, Hwang &Krägeloh, 2018). A balanced approach is sought, so that items displaying DIF can be reasonably absorbed across groups and not significantly impact total test results (Hope, Adamson, McManus, Chis & Elder, 2018). Based on the review and analysis conducted in the current study, guidelines emerged in terms of applying Rasch models to assess measurement invariance and are discussed below.

Guidelines for applying Rasch models to assess measurement invariance:

(1) ***A minimal number of items displaying DIF***: Differential Item Functioning (DIF) should be minimal, preferably absent. However, measurement invariance as discussed in this chapter is a matter of degree. The degree is linked to the overall functioning of the assessment and potential implications of biased items. If some items display DIF, the global test functioning should be examined in conjunction with the potentially threatening items to determine if the assessment can yield valid and reliable inferences for groups. If items displaying potential bias impacts results, especially in high stakes scenarios, caution is advised and the exclusion of common items with significant DIF may be required. However, a certain degree of DIF could be tolerable if overall scores are not significantly impacted.

(2) ***Measurement invariance of test or item groupings***: Differential Bundle Functioning (DBF) depends on collections of items coherently assessing the underlying construct across groups with common items. When there is a lack of DBF,

evidence for the global functioning of the assessment is present and a stronger case can be made for valid and reliable inferences being drawn from the results.

(3) ***Setting criteria for measurement invariance***: The degree of measurement invariance adequate for comparisons depends on the study and the criteria selected by the researchers. As with program evaluation, criteria should be devised a priori and evaluated in terms of predictive or concurrent validity. Rasch applications can provide evidence for internal item and instrument measurement invariance as well as violations, but the decision of adequacy for comparisons requires further investigation. Large-scale assessments are designed to facilitate comparability, but inherent differences between groups and assessment versions may result in limitations that should be acknowledged. Practical implications of threats to measurement invariance should assessed, for example does DIF influence DBF? What effect sizes are shown in DIF and DBF and can the effect sizes be classified as moderate or large? When effect sizes become large, the internal measurement invariance may be threatened to a degree which requires rescaling of results without problematic items.

(4) ***Suitability of Rasch models to evaluate internal measurement invariance***: The application of Rasch models is sufficient for investigating internal measurement invariance. Other methods may have constricting assumptions wherein the model is manipulated to fit the data, unidimensionality is not investigated but forced with loadings and distributions are fixed. Factor analysis and other forms of structural equation modelling (SEM) were designed for interval data, and analysts do not necessarily deal with the categorical nature of assessment items when applying SEM models. Furthermore, models such as CFA require large sample sizes which may result in significant misfit. Rasch addresses these limitations by converting ordinal data to a true interval, logit scale and benchmarking item and person performance against the principles of measurement. Rasch analysis also tolerates large amounts of missing data well, useful in the analysis of planned missing data as found in large-scale assessments with rotated matrix designs. Rasch models provide statistical indications of whether invariant assessment was implemented across groups (Differential Item Functioning) and between groups of items (Differential Bundle Functioning). The focus when applying Rasch models is on item functioning and whether meaningful inferences can be derived from the instrument. Construct relevance and meaningfulness rather than statistical fit are evaluated by Rasch models.

(5) ***Contribution of Rasch models to measurement invariance***: By providing evidence for internal measurement invariance, Rasch frees the researcher and audience to interpret the results beyond the trustworthiness of the assessment. Once satisfactory measurement invariance has been established, the focus can shift towards the practical implications of educational improvement. Most notably, the clinical or practical significance of progress in achievements and the broader implications of interventions take centre stage.

Conclusion and Limitations

Rasch models offer sufficient evidence of internal measurement invariance with the advantage of items, persons and global test functioning examined in terms of the gold standard, the principles of measurement. Statistics derived from Rasch analysis is also identifies potential threats to invariance and unidimensionality. Measurement invariance requires a hierarchy of item difficulty that remains stable over time and within populations regardless of ability per group. By applying Rasch models the stability of item ordering and functioning over time are assessed.

The current study demonstrated an evaluation of internal measurement invariance by applying the Rasch partial credit model. The study was limited to one language group, where the common items were completed at two different time points by two distinct cohorts. Despite the cohorts being separated by ten years, they had similar demographic characteristics and answered the same common items. Future research could apply the same techniques to longitudinal studies or examine item and bundle functioning across a wider variety of groups and subject domains.

Acknowledgements The Department of Research and Innovation at the University of Pretoria are acknowledged for funding a writing retreat and providing feedback and support.

References

Andrich, D., & Marais, I. (2019). *A course in Rasch measurement theory: Measuring in the educational, social and health sciences*. Singapore: Springer.

Andrich, D. (2011). *Rasch models for measurement*. United States of America: Sage.

Asún, R. A., Rdz-Navarro, K., & Alvarado, J. M. (2017). The sirens' call in psychometrics: The invariance of IRT models. *Theory & Psychology, 27*(3), 389–406.

Bashkov, B., & Finney, S. (2017). *Apples to apples: How to investigate whether you are measuring the same construct over time*. SAGE Research Methods Cases.

Beretvas, S., & Walker, C. (2012). Distinguishing differential testlet functioning from differential bundle functioning using the multilevel measurement model. *Educational and Psychological Measurement, 72*(2), 200–223.

Beukes, A. (2009). Language policy incongruity and African languages in post apartheid South Africa. *Language Matters, 40*(1), 35–55.

Bialosiewicz, S., Murphy, K., & Berry, T. (2013). *Do our Measures Measure up? The Critical Role of Measurement Invariance* [Demonstration Session at the American Evaluation Association, Washington, DC]. Retrieved from http://comm.eval.org/HigherLogic/System/DownloadDocumentFile.ashx?DocumentFileKey=63758fed-a490-43f2-8862-2de0217a08b8.

Bofah, E., &Hannula, M. (2014). *Structural equation modelling: Testing for the factorial validity, replication and measurement invariance of students' views on mathematics*. SAGE Research Methods Cases.

Bond, T. G., & Fox, C. M. (2015). *Applying the Rasch model: Fundamental measurement in the human sciences* (3rd ed.). New York: Routledge.

Boone, W. J., Staver, J. R., & Yale, M. S. (2014). *Rasch analysis in the human sciences*. London: Springer.

Cohen, J. (1988). *Statistical power analysis for the behavioral sciences* (2nd ed.). New York: Academic Press.

Desa, D., Van de Vijver, F. J. R., Carstens, R., & Schulz, W. (2019). Measurement invariance in international large-scale assessments: Integrating theory and method. In T. P. Johnson, B.-E. Pennell, I. Stoop, & B. Dorer (Eds.), *Advances in comparative survey methodology* (pp. 881–910). New York, NY: Wiley.

Distefano, C., Mindrila, D., &Monrad, D. M. (2013). Investigating factorial Invariance of teacher climate factors across school organizational levels. In M. Khine (Ed.), *Application of structural equation modeling in educational research and practice* (pp. 257–275). Rotterdam: Sense.

Engelhard, G. (2008). Historical perspectives on invariant measurement: Guttman, Rasch, and Mokken. *Measurement: Interdisciplinary Research & Perspective, 6*(3), 155–189.

Engelhard, G. (2013). *Invariant measurement: Using Rasch models in the social, behavioral, and health sciences*. New York: Routledge.

Essien, A. (2018). The role of language in the teaching and learning of early grade mathematics: An 11-year account of research in Kenya, Malawi and South Africa. *African Journal of Research in Mathematics, Science and Technology Education, 22*(1), 48–59.

Field, A. (2018). *Discovering statistics using IBM SPSS statistics* (5th ed.). London, UK: Sage Edge.

Finch, W. H., French, B. F., & Hernandez Finch, M. E. (2019). Quantifying item invariance for the selection of the least biased assessment. *Journal of Applied Measurement, 20*(1), 13–26.

Fisher, W. P., Jr. (2001). Invariant thinking vs. invariant measurement. *Rasch Measurement Transactions, 14*(4), 778–781. Downloaded from https://www.rasch.org/rmt/rmt144e.htm.

Fukuhara, H., & Kamata, A. (2011). A bifactor multidimensional item response theory model for differential item functioning analysis on testlet-based items. *Applied Psychological Measurement, 35*(8), 604–622.

Hope, D., Adamson, K., McManus, I., Chis, L., & Elder, A. (2018). Using differential item functioning to evaluate potential bias in a high stakes postgraduate knowledge based assessment. *BMC Medical Education, 18*(1), 64–64.

Howie, S. J., Combrinck, C., Roux, K., Tshele, M., Mokoena, G. M., & McLeod Palane, N. (2017a). *PIRLS literacy 2016 progress in international reading literacy study 2016: South African children's reading literacy achievement*. Pretoria: Centre for Evaluation and Assessment. Downloaded from https://repository.up.ac.za/handle/2263/65780.

Howie, S. J., Combrinck, C., Tshele, M., Roux, K., McLeod Palane, N., & Mokoena, G. M. (2017b). *PIRLS 2016 progress in international reading literacy study 2016 grade 5 benchmark participation: South African children's reading literacy achievement*. Pretoria: Centre for Evaluation and Assessment. Downloaded from https://repository.up.ac.za/handle/2263/65221.

Howie, S. J., van Staden, S., Tshele, M., Dowse, C., & Zimmerman, L. (2012). *South African children's reading literacy achievement summary report*. Pretoria: Centre for Evaluation and Assessment. Downloaded from https://repository.up.ac.za/handle/2263/65996.

Huff, K., Steinberg, L., & Matts, T. (2010). The promises and challenges of implementing evidence-centered design in large-scale assessment. *Applied Measurement in Education, 23*(4), 310–324.

IBM Corp. Released. (2017). *IBM SPSS statistics for windows, version 25.0*. Armonk, NY: IBM Corp.

Koller, I., Maier, M., & Hatzinger, R. (2015). An empirical power analysis of quasi-exact tests for the Rasch model: Measurement invariance in small samples. *Methodology, 11*(2), 45–54.

LaRoche, S., Joncas, M., & Foy, P. (2017). *Sample design in PIRLS 2016*. In I. V. S. Mullis, M. O. Martin, P. Foy, & M. Hooper (Eds.), *PIRLS 2016: Methods and procedures in PIRLS 2016*. Boston College: TIMSS & PIRLS International Study Center.

Linacre, J. M. (2017a). *Winsteps® Rasch measurement computer program User's Guide*. Beaverton, Oregon: Winsteps.com.

Linacre, J. M. (2017b). *Winsteps® computer software version 3.93.10*. Beaverton, OR: Winsteps.

Linacre, J. M. (2019, March 8). *Re: Can lack of invariance be a good thing?* [Online discussion group: Rasch Measurement Forum]. Retrieved from http://raschforum.boards.net/thread/1064/lack-invariance-good-thing?page=1&scrollTo=5106.

Long, C., Craig, T., & Dunne, T. (2012). Meeting the requirements of both classroom-based and systemic assessment of mathematics proficiency: The potential of Rasch measurement theory: Original research. *Pythagoras, 33*(3), 1–16.

Maydeu-Olivares, A., Cai, L., & Hernandez, A. (2011). Comparing the fit of item response theory and factor analysis models. *Structural Equation Modeling: A Multidisciplinary Journal, 18*(3), 333–356.

Meade, A. (2013). Statistical approaches to measurement invariance. *Structural Equation Modeling: A Multidisciplinary Journal, 20*(1), 168–174.

Medvedev, O., Titkova, E., Siegert, R., Hwang, Y., & Krägeloh, C. (2018). Evaluating short versions of the five facet mindfulness questionnaire using Rasch analysis. *Mindfulness, 9*(5), 1411–1422.

Millsap, R. (2011). *Statistical approaches to measurement invariance*. New York: Routledge.

Mohangi, K., Nel, N., Stephens, O., & Krog, S. (2016). An overview of grade R literacy teaching and learning in inclusive classrooms in South Africa. *Per Linguam: A Journal of Language Learning, 32*(2), 47–65.

Mtsatse, N., & Combrinck, C. (2018). Dialects matter: The impact of dialects and code-switching on the literacy and numeracy achievement of isiXhosa Grade 1 learners in the Western Cape. *Journal of Education, 72*, 19–36.

Mullis, I. V. S., Martin, M. O., Foy, P., & Hooper, M. (2017). *PIRLS 2016 international results in reading*. Boston College: TIMSS & PIRLS International Study Center.

Nortvedt, G., & Buchholtz, N. (2018). Assessment in mathematics education: Responding to issues regarding methodology, policy, and equity. *Mathematics Education, 50*(4), 555–570.

Randall, J., & Engelhard, G. (2010). Using confirmatory factor analysis and the Rasch model to assess measurement invariance in a high stakes reading assessment. *Applied Measurement in Education, 23*(3), 286–306.

Rutkowski, L., & Svetina, D. (2014). Assessing the hypothesis of measurement invariance in the context of large-scale international surveys. *Educational and Psychological Measurement, 74*(1), 31–57.

Sandilands, D., Oliveri, M., Zumbo, B., & Ercikan, K. (2013). Investigating sources of differential item functioning in international large-scale assessments using a confirmatory approach. *International Journal of Testing, 13*(2), 152–174.

Thomas, M. (2011). The value of item response theory in clinical assessment: A review. *Assessment, 18*(3), 291–307.

van der Berg, S., Spaull, N., Wills, G., Gustafsson, M., & Kotzé, J. (2016). *Identifying binding constraints in education: synthesis report for the programme pro-poor policy development (PSPPD). Research on socio-economic policy (RESEP).* Stellenbosch: Department of Economics at the University of Stellenbosch.

Wildsmith-Cromarty, R. (2012). Reflections on a research initiative aimed at enhancing the role of African languages in education in South Africa. *Journal for Language Teaching, 46*(2), 157–170.

Zenisky, A. L., Hambleton, R. K., & Robin, F. (2003). Detection of differential item functioning in large-scale state assessments: A study evaluating a two-stage approach. *Educational and Psychological Measurement, 63*, 51–64.

Part III
Validation Studies with Rasch Analysis

Chapter 11
A Rasch Analysis Approach to the Development and Validation of a Social Presence Measure

Karel Kreijns, Monique Bijker and Joshua Weidlich

Abstract Social presence theory was developed by Short et al. (The social psychology of telecommunications. Wiley, London, 1976) to explain the impact of different media such as text, audio, or video on interpersonal communication. They defined social presence as "the salience of the other person in the interaction," which was interpreted as the degree to which the other person is perceived as physical "real" in the communication. Social presence theory was first applied by Gunawardena (Int J Educ Telecommun 1:147–166, 1995) for online educational contexts. Since then it has become an important construct for summarizing the effects of mediated communication on the social interaction and the group dynamics that happen in distributed collaborative learning groups. However, a robust scale for measuring perceptions of social presence is still lacking. Although Short, Williams, and Christie did measure social presence by using four semantic differential scales, they never validated this scale. Indeed, other social presence instruments have come to existence but none of these instruments tapped physical realness of others as the single trait of interest. Furthermore, questions may arise about the psychometric qualities of these instruments as they, at best, used exploratory and confirmatory factor analyses but did not account for the nonlinearity of rating scale steps and other issues. To fill this gap, the current research aimed at developing a robust social presence measure by using the Rasch measurement model as a rigid construct validation method. The findings of the Rasch analyses (fit of items and persons, unidimensionality, category probability curves) in Winsteps version 4.4.1 revealed two dimensions of social presence: Awareness of others and Proximity with others. The first was measured with 15 items while the latter was measured with 12 items. The psychometric quality of the Awareness 15-item set was good to excellent whereas the quality of the Proximity 12-item set was moderate to good. Future research is aimed to improve the psychometric qualities even more and also to determine whether the two dimensions are actually inconsequential (Linacre in *Detecting multidimensionality in Rasch data using Winsteps Table 23*, 2018b).

K. Kreijns (✉) · M. Bijker
Open University of the Netherlands, Heerlen, The Netherlands
e-mail: karel.kreijns@ou.nl

J. Weidlich
Heidelberg University of Education, Heidelberg, Germany

M. S. Khine (ed.), *Rasch Measurement*,
https://doi.org/10.1007/978-981-15-1800-3_11

Keywords Rasch measurement model · Social presence · Awareness of others · Proximity with others

Introduction

Through the rise of internet and accessible and affordable information and communication technology, educational settings today routinely make use of technology to deliver instruction and mediate communication. For example, online (collaborative) learning relies in large part on computer-mediated communication (CMC) for social-interaction among students as well as between students and instructors. Even today, with increasingly sophisticated technology, this educational landscape is still dominated by text-based asynchronous communication (e.g., message boards), in learning management systems (Legon & Garrett, 2018). Unlike face-to-face communication, CMC usually conveys little socio-emotional cues. Psychologically, this can impact not only how this type of communication is perceived but also how the communication partner is perceived (Walther, 1992, 1996). In learning settings where almost everything is technologically mediated, this may have a profound impact on the experience. Thus, researchers have turned to the concept of social presence to understand the mechanisms governing beneficial learning climates and interpersonal connections among students in these settings. A large corpus of research has since emerged, showing that the degree of social presence directly and indirectly influences the online learning experience in many different ways, for example by being related to satisfaction, perceived learning, and group climate (Gunawardena & Zittle, 1997; Richardson, Maeda, LV, & Caskurlu, 2017; Richardson & Swan, 2003; Weidlich & Bastiaens, 2017).

Unfortunately, the concept of social presence is also contested; a plethora of different definitions of social presence can be found in the literature (Lowenthal & Snelson, 2017). Moreover, they are often convoluted. For example, Lowenthal (2010) observed that the continuum of definitions ranges from social presence as the salience of the other person in the interaction to the degree of an interpersonal emotional connection. For example, Gunawardena and Zittle (1997) define it as "the degree to which a person is perceived as a 'real person' in mediated communication" (p. 9). On the other hand, Tu and McIsaac (2002) interpret it as a "measure of the feeling of community that a learner experiences in an online learning environment" (p. 131). Some of them may fall somewhere in the middle of the continuum, as is the case with Rourke, Anderson, Garrison, and Archer (2001) when they define it as "the ability of learners to project themselves socially and affectively into a community of inquiry" (p. 50). When considering the research, these heterogeneous and often convoluted definitions makes differentiating social presence from other related—but not synonymous—variables difficult. For a more in-depth review of how scholars have defined social presence in the past and which variables are often entangled with social presence, refer to Lowenthal and Snelson (2017) and Weidlich, Kreijns, Rajagopal, and Bastiaens (2018), respectively.

Unsurprisingly, the lack of consistency is also reflected in attempts to measure social presence. Rourke et al. (2001) established twelve indicators of social presence along the dimensions affective, interactive, and cohesive responses. However, this behavioral approach to measuring social presence does not have the individual student as unit-of-analysis, but instead the overall Community of Inquiry (CoI). Focusing more on individual students' perceptions, a CoI survey instrument was also developed (Arbaugh et al., 2008). Outside of the CoI framework, there are many more social presence measures (e.g., Gunawardena 1995; Gunawardena & Zittle, 1997; Tu, 2002). Because these measures are based on convoluted definitions of social presence, they too may be convoluted. Indeed, Kreijns, Kirschner, Jochems, and van Buuren (2011) and Kreijns et al. (2014) showed that many of these measures do not exclusively measure social presence, but are 'contaminated' with "varying aspects of an amorphous set of variables [...] to varying degrees" (p. 371).

It is a problem for a science aiming to be cumulative if basic cornerstones are undermined and reinterpreted in every other new study. If we want to stop the invalid approach of treating social presence as a shapeshifter, it is necessary to adopt a clear and precise definition of the phenomenon. We aim to do this by taking the original Short, Williams, and Christie (1976) definition as a starting point: social presence as "the degree of salience of the other person in the communication and the consequent salience of the interpersonal relationships". In line with recent arguments by Öztok and Kehrwald (2017) and Lowenthal and Snelson (2017), we restrict our definition to one idea, namely the first part, the salience of the communication partner. In other words, social presence is the psychological phenomenon that the other is perceived as "real" in the communication; the subjective feeling of being with other salient social actors in a mediated space.

Through this clarification, a measure tapping this and only this phenomenon can be constructed. Only then can social presence be disentangled from its correlates, allowing us to gradually learn from our empirical study of the phenomenon. In the following sections, we will shortly review some previous attempts to measure social presence and how these have fallen short in different ways. Then, we outline our approach of constructing a social presence measure with the Rasch measurement model, based on the precise and narrow definition of the phenomenon.

Theoretical Framework

As early scholarship in social presence focused on the intrinsic qualities of the communication medium to convey socio-emotional cues, measures of social presence were accordingly concerned with these fixed properties. Short et al. (1976) used a semantic differential approach with four-word pairs: personal-impersonal, sensitive-insensitive, warm-cold, and sociable-unsociable. However, they did not provide any information about validation processes accompanying this measure.

Gunawardena (1995) developed a measure for social presence by extending this approach to 17 bipolar items aimed at soliciting "student reactions on a range of feeling towards the medium of CMC" (p. 150). These items included for example stimulating-dull, personal-impersonal, warm-cold, and helpful-hindering. Although this research is framed in terms of social presence, these items do not exclusively focus on one construct but on many different things. Just like Short et al. (1976), Gunawardena did not report information about validity and reliability of her measure.

Shortly thereafter, Gunawardena and Zittle (1997) developed a 14-item social presence scale. They constructed items around the concept of immediacy (Wiener & Mehrabian, 1968), a notion integral to but not identical with social presence. Example items of this scale are "CMC is an excellent medium for social interaction", "I felt comfortable interacting with other participants in the conference", and "The moderators created a feeling of an online community". Although some items may be closely related to or identical to perceptions of social presence, there are also items that certainly are not. The authors report a Cronbach's α of 0.88, which is misleading, taking into account that the measure is unlikely to be unidimensional as per face validity. Even today, this scale remains a popular way of measuring social presence in online learning contexts (Richardson et al., 2017).

Another well-cited early measure of social presence was presented by Tu (2002) and used by Tu and McIsaac (2002). Here, social presence consists of three dimensions: Social context, online communication, and interactivity. Additionally, privacy was found to be a major factor related to these dimensions. Here, too, social presence is understood as a quality that students ascribe to the communication medium, not a phenomenological experience that may vary independently of the medium used for CMC. From a measurement point of view, it is problematic that these dimensions focus on variables that are peripheral, but not exclusive to the phenomenological experience of the realness of the other.

More recently, a Community of Inquiry (CoI) survey instrument of social presence was developed (Arbaugh et al., 2008; Carlon et al., 2012; Diaz, Swan, Ice, & Kupczynski, 2010). Here, social presence is operationalized among the three dimensions of open communication, group cohesion, and personal/affective projection. Again, variables that are peripheral to the phenomenological experience of social presence are used as the basis of measurement. In addition, Lowenthal and Dunlap (2014) found that, in itself, this measure does not align well with the CoI indicators it purports to represent.

Kreijns et al. (2011) first presented a measure that was based on the "realness" dimension, i.e. the narrow definition of social presence. Yet, it has three drawbacks. First, it made an explicit distinction between synchronous and asynchronous communication settings. A possible difference in the degree to which Social Presence is perceived in both environments should be irrelevant because, according to the Rasch measurement model, a social presence measurement instrument is expected to measure invariantly in both settings. However, the instrument will probably show that each setting produces different perceptions of social presence. This is comparable with a thermometer meant to measure temperatures in the desert as well as on the north or south pole. Second, with only five items it may not fully represent the breadth and depth of the experience of social presence (Messick, 1996). Third, it was validated through exploratory factor analyses, which assumes that the measures that are used are interval measures, whereas only Rasch modeling can produce more robust measures by transforming qualitatively ordered data into interval measures if the data fit the Rasch measurement model (see for other issues related to factor analysis and Rasch modeling: Sick, 2011).

Recently, Öztok and Kehrwald (2017) wondered if it may be time to kill social presence. That is, should we skip this shapeshifting concept and find a more refined alternative to provide the necessary vocabulary for understanding mediated learning experiences? We suggest that with a (1) precise definition and (2) a psychometrically robust approach to developing a measure, it is, in fact, possible to restore and purify social presence. Now that we have done the first step (i.e. precise definition), we move on to the second step and propose the Rasch measurement model (Bond & Fox, 2015; Rasch, 1960) as the process for developing and improving a social presence measure. Our approach will be outlined in the following chapters.

Construction of the Social Presence Measure

The construction of the set of items that measure social presence followed the guidelines outlined by the construct-modeling framework of Wilson (2005; see also: Duckor, Draney, & Wilson, 2009). The framework represents a development cycle in which four building blocks are central, namely: (1) construct maps, (2) items design, (3) outcome space, and 4) measurement model. It was anticipated that the Rasch measurement model (Bond & Fox, 2015; Rasch, 1960; Wright & Masters, 1982) would be applied. Therefore, the goal is the construction of a variable map or Wright map, which is a visual representation of the latent variable. This visual representation is a line on which the item step-calibrations are placed in an ordered way from low to high (Engelhard, 2013; Chap. 4). At the same time, the Rasch measurement model depicts the person capabilities (endorse-abilities) similarly on the same line. The calibrations are the difficulty levels of the item step categories and the person positions on the line are the degrees to which the persons endorse the measured phenomenon. As a consequence, the Wright map, thus, can be regarded as a yardstick, very similar to a ruler where centimeters are shown by small strokes at precise, equal distances from each other.

Construct Maps

In this building block, the latent variable is determined. In the current study, the latent variable is social presence, which is defined as the degree of perceived physical realness of the other persons when communicating through telecommunication media.

Items Design

The Rasch measurement model prescribes that scale items must vary in their degree of difficulty so to be able to differentiate respondents of different ability. To be precise: the Rasch measurement model requires items that are easy, moderate and hard to endorse by respondents in order to differentiate respondents who have low, average and high perceptions of the physical realness of the other persons in mediated communication. How easy, moderate and hard items are endorsed is expressed in the calibrations of these items. The Rasch analyses will reveal those calibrations by producing the Wright map.

Kreijns, Weidlich, and Rajagopal (2018) made the first attempt to construct such a set of items. The Rasch analyses in this first attempt revealed that 10 out of 16 items could form a unidimensional scale with satisfying psychometric properties. This preliminary social presence measure was excellent in differentiating respondents who had high perceptions of the realness of the other persons but felt short in the differentiation of respondents with low perceptions due to a lack of easy items. The current research was a follow-up of that research and enlarged the set of 10 items with 20 new items that aimed to fill the gap between items that are easy and difficult to endorse. In addition, though the preliminary social presence measure was found to be unidimensional, the Rasch analyses signaled a potential issue regarding its dimensionality caused by two or three items. The current administration of the 30-item social presence measure further investigated this issue. Figure 11.1 depicts all the items used for analyzing the enlarged social presence measure. Each item used the preamble "In this learning environment …." To save space, Fig. 11.1 is ahead of the Rasch analyses and also shows the results these analyses reported in the Results section. As already can be seen, two dimensions emerged from the Rasch analyses: *Awareness of the others* and *Proximity with the others*.

Outcome Space

The previous research of Kreijns et al. (2018) regarding the preliminary social presence measure made clear that the use of Likert scales with seven rating scale steps (1 = totally disagree, 2 = disagree, 3 = somewhat disagree, 4 neither disagree or agree, 5 = somewhat agree, 6 = agree, 7 = totally agree) was problematic. The use of seven rating scale steps confused respondents and categories had to be collapsed (2 and 3, and 4 and 5). Therefore, the current research used Likert scales with five rating scale steps (1 = totally disagree; 2 = disagree; 3 = neither disagree or agree; 4 = agree; 5 = totally agree), see also Fig. 11.1.

Nr Item	Item	*M*	*SD*	item calibration	SE	infit MNSQ	infit ZSTD	outfit MNSQ	outfit ZSTD	n
Preambule: In this learning environment …										
Awareness of the others (Cronbach's α = .92)[3]										
A01[1]	… I only can get a glimpse of my fellow students	2.73	1.13	.91	.15	1.22	1.39	1.22	1.42	80
A02[2]	… I can form distinct impressions of some of my fellow students	2.72	.92	.89	.15	.93	-.39	.94	-.36	79
A03[1]	… I know my fellows students are here too but I do not 'see' them	2.82	1.17	.71	.15	1.12	.79	1.13	.85	79
A04	… my fellow students are not abstract at all, which was what I first expected	2.82	.89	.69	.15	.66	-2.44	.66	-2.47	78
A05[1]	… I feel my fellow students are far away	2.90	1.13	.57	.15	.86	-.88	.86	-.96	79
A06[1]	… I do not know who my fellow students are	3.00	1.14	.44	.15	.95	-.25	.95	-.20	80
A07[2]	… it feels as if I deal with 'real' persons and not with abstract anonymous persons	3.04	1.01	.41	.15	.81	-1.30	.81	-1.03	79
A08[1]	… nothing more than that I am aware of my fellow students	3.27	.84	.13	.15	1.14	.91	1.14	1.26	75
A09[2]	… it feels as if all my fellow students are 'real' physical persons	3.33	1.00	-.16	.15	.85	-.99	.85	-.65	79
A10[1]	… nothing more than that I feel distant from my fellow students	3.39	1.09	-.24	.15	1.06	.45	1.06	.32	80
A11[1]	… it feels like none of my fellow students are here	3.36	1.21	-.25	.15	1.25	1.56	1.25	1.36	76
A12	… I am aware of my fellow students	3.45	.92	-.38	.15	1.15	.98	1.15	.93	76
A13[1]	… my fellow students do not really live for me	3.70	1.08	-.81	.15	.90	-.61	.90	-.94	79
A14[1]	… I am the only one present	3.80	1.06	-.87	.16	1.17	1.06	1.17	.59	74
A15[1]	… I feel none of my fellow students wants to communicate with me	4.33	.82	-2.05	.18	.92	-.41	.92	-1.03	78
Proximity with the others (Cronbach's α = .94)[3]										
P01	… I feel that I can see my fellow students right in the eyes	1.38	.63	2.72	.27	1.22	1.12	.89	-.07	76
P02	… my fellow students are very near to me	1.81	.89	.85	.21	1.18	1.10	1.12	.63	79
P03	… I constantly feel that my fellow students are around	1.87	.84	.63	.21	.97	-.14	.88	-.58	79
P04[2]	… it feels as if all my fellow students and I are in the same room	1.91	.85	.50	.21	.93	-.39	.89	-.52	79
P05[2]	… it feels as if we are a face to face group	1.97	.77	.32	.21	.92	-.41	.89	-.56	75
P06[2]	… it feels as if all my fellow students and I are in close proximity	2.10	.96	-.12	.20	.88	-.68	.88	-.67	79
P07	… I am sure my fellow students are here too	2.16	.99	-.31	.20	.74	-1.67	.71	-1.89	79
P08[2]	… I can really see my fellow students as if they were in front of me	2.18	.92	-.35	.20	1.08	.54	1.11	.69	79
P09	… I can make a clear picture of all of my fellow students	2.27	.85	-.56	.20	1.13	79	1.27	1.51	74
P10	… I feel a sense of my fellow students' presence	2.25	.97	-.59	.20	.79	-1.31	.76	-1.55	79
P11[2]	… I strongly feel the presence of my fellow students	2.34	1.05	-.85	.19	1.04	.32	1.02	.15	79
P12[2]	… all of my fellow students feel that I am a 'real' physical person	2.82	.99	-2.21	.20	1.22	1.24	1.20	1.18	71
Removed items										
	… it feels like my fellow students are just passers-by									
	… I imagine I can feel my fellow students									
	… I only get a vague notion of my fellow students									

[1] These items were reversed coded

[2] These items were reused from the preliminary social presence measure (Kreijns, Weidlich, & Rajagopal, 2018)

[3] See about the use of Cronbach's α: Linacre (1997)

All items used a 5-point Likert scale (1 = *totally disagree*, 5 = *totally agree*).

Fig. 11.1 The two dimensions of the social presence measure: awareness of others and proximity with others

Measurement Model

As already mentioned above, the Rasch measurement model was applied because the model, and its types of analyses, are superior to measurement models based on classical test theory (CTT; see: Crocker & Algina, 1986) for construct validation of measures. Rasch analyses take many issues into account that CTT does not, which results in the development of measures that are as robust as those found in the physical domain. According to Boone (2016; see also: Pallant & Tennant, 2007; Tennant & Conaghan, 2007; Wright, 1992) these issues pertain, amongst others, to the non-linearity of the rating scale steps, the dependency on the sample of respondents, and the imputation of missing values.

Method

Respondents

Respondents were 82 students of the largest distance university in Germany, Fern Universität in Hagen. This convenience sample consisted of students enrolled in B.A. Educational Science. Seventy-three students were female and nine male. Mean age was 36 years. Data collection was conducted over the summer semester of 2018.

Procedure

Students were recruited through the learning management system Moodle, in which most course activities take place. On the central message board of the course, students were notified of the survey and asked to participate, with no course credit or reward attached to participation. The provided link directed them from the learning environment directly to Limesurvey, where they were informed about the upcoming survey, e.g., guarantee of anonymity, right to withdraw their data, and estimated duration. The raw set of 30 items was only a part of the survey, with other scales and measures also pertaining to student's perceptions and experiences in the learning environment. The survey took a total of about 20 min to complete.

Analysis

Rasch analyses were conducted on the 30 items that form the social presence measure. These items were designed to provide qualitatively ordered measures of physical realness of the other persons in the communication. All items used Likert scales with five rating scale steps to get an item score. The Winsteps software version 4.4.1 was used for conducting the analyses (Linacre, 2018a). For simple descriptive analyses, SPSS version 24 was used.

Conducting the Rasch analyses was an iterative process. The first step was detecting and removing persons who for obvious reasons would not contribute to scale construction or would not fit the Rasch measurement model beforehand. These persons included those respondents who did not give any response on all items or from whom the person profile was unexpected; for instance when the person profile showed responses from which it is suspected that they were deliberately given out of convenience or out of carelessness. In general, when the person's responses on all items of a measure are all 3's (i.e., the "neutral" choice), this may count as an unexpected profile given the fact that items differ in their level of difficulty and, thus, responses above or below 2 are expected. Of course, those latter persons would have been identified in the next steps and then removed but the a priori removal of them saves time. Extreme persons, however, were not removed; extreme persons are those respondents whose person profile shows responses on all 30 items either as all 1's (these persons are minimum extremes) or as all 5's (these persons are maximum extremes). In general, if the person profile shows responses that are all 1's, it means that a measure is not able to differentiate between persons with (very) low ability, and when the profile shows responses that are all 5's, it means that the measure is incapable to differentiate between persons with (very) high ability.

The second step was detecting persons and items that misfit the Rasch model but that can be "repaired." In general, repairing means that some responses in the person profile on particular items are marked as missing if these responses are unexpected; that is, when they bring about the person and item infit and outfit MNSQ and ZSTD values to fall outside the safe zone. The safe zone is for MNSQ those values between 0.5 and 1.5 and for ZSTD values between −1.9 and +1.9 (Linacre, 2002). Indeed, such practice is advocated by Linacre: "[t]o evaluate the impact of any misfit, replace suspect responses with missing values and examine the resultant changes to the measures" (2002, p. 878). Thus, repairing the person's profile affects person and item infit and outfit MNSQ and ZSTD values; the goal is that these person and item infit and outfit values will eventually fall within the safe zone; Repairing and checking person and item infit and outfit values is also an iterative process; the procedure is fully described in Boone, Staver, and Yale (2014, Chap. 8). Hereby, they stated that for repairing the person profile, person outfit values should be inspected as the outfit statistic is more sensitive to outliers and easier to manage (see also Linacre, 2002). Boone et al. (2014) recommends that for items, the item outfit MNSQ values should be inspected and for persons, the person outfit ZSTD values. With regard to person outfit ZSTD values, they found out from experience that the safe zone could be relaxed somewhat; that is, the safe zone for person outfit ZSTD values is between −3 and +3. Nevertheless, not only the person and item outfit values are inspected, infit should be inspected as well. Infit statistics are more sensitive to inliers, that is, to the patterns of responses to items targeted on the person. Though, they are hard to repair (Linacre, 2002). If, however, for some persons, the person and item infit and outfit values remain outside the safe zone, whatever reparation is applied to the person profile, it may be decided to remove these persons with the consequence to completely rerun the second step (Curtis, 2004; Pallant & Tennant, 2007). Such complete rerun of the second step is also necessary in case for items, the item infit and outfit MSNQ and ZSTD values will still not fall in the safe zone regardless of how many person profiles are repaired or persons removed and, thus, the item have to be removed. A complete rerun means that all person profiles reparations are undone before the re-rerun with the removed persons or items is performed.

The third step was inspecting whether the social presence measure emerges as a unidimensional or multidimensional Rasch model. This inspecting is done by performing a principal component analyses (PCA) on the residuals to detect potential off-dimensional item-correlated activity (Linacre, 2018b; Smith, 2002). The reported PCA results include values for the raw unexplained variances in the first contrast; these values are expressed in Eigenvalue units that correspond to the number of items that potentially measure something different than the other items. Linacre (2018b) pointed out that accidental correlations—up to two or three items—are not uncommon. Thus, when the raw unexplained variances in the first contrast exceed more than two items, decisions on whether there are items measuring something else should take these accidental correlations into account; that is, only the non-accidental correlations should be considered. To determine the accidental correlations, Linacre (2018b) advised analyzing simulated data produced by the Winsteps program while assuming a unidimensional Rasch model with item calibrations and person measures derived from the observed data. Furthermore, Pearson correlations and, more important, the disattenuated correlations between item cluster 1 and 2 should be inspected. According to Linacre (2018b), correlations > 0.70 indicate items probably measuring the same thing, and correlations < 0.30 indicate items measuring different things. Correlations between 0.30 and 0.70, however, mean that multidimensionality may potentially exist.

The fourth step was inspecting the ordering functioning of the rating scale steps. Linacre (2004) has drawn up six criteria: The first is a minimum of 10 persons for each step category. The second is that the average step category calibrations must increase monotonically when the rating scale step number is also increasing. The third is that the step calibrations (or thresholds) must increase monotonically when the rating scale step number is also increasing. The fourth criterion requires the outfit MNSQ statistics to be < 2.00. The fifth is that the threshold distance between the step thresholds should be greater than 1.4 but no more than 5.0 logits. The sixth criterion holds that the category probability curves should show a distinct peak for each rating scale step category.

The fifth step was inspecting the Wright-maps. For that purpose, two different Wright-maps were drawn in the same figure, one at the left side and one at the right side of that figure. The left Wright map is showing the distribution of the item rating scale step numbers (right of the left *Y*-axis) and, at the same time, the distribution of the person measures (left of the left *Y*-axis). The position of the item rating scale step number on the *Y*-axis indicates that the probability of an endorsement by a person, whose measure is at the same position on the vertical axis, is 50% to be in that rating scale step or those above, and 50% to be in the adjacent lower rating scale step or those below. Thus, when the item rating scale step number, for example, is 2, it refers to the 50% threshold between the rating scale steps 1 and 2. The Wright map only shows the rating scale step numbers 2, 3, 4, and 5, which stands for the 50% thresholds between the rating scale steps 1 and 2, 2 and 3, 3 and 4, and 4 and 5 respectively. Minimum extreme persons (if any) are depicted at the lowest position on the vertical axis whereas maximum extreme persons (if any) are depicted at the highest positions. The right Wright map is showing the distribution of the item calibrations along the right Y-axes. The item calibration is the position on the vertical axis at which the probability of an endorsement by a person, whose measure is at the same position on the vertical axis, is 50% to be in the higher rating scale steps and 50% to be in the lower rating scale steps. Both Wright-maps give insight into some psychometric properties. First, the distribution of the item calibrations on the Y-axis may indicate gaps in which the measurement of persons is less accurate than other areas on the Y-axis. Also, items may be too easy or too difficult to endorse by respondents; the first will cause many maximum extreme persons, the latter will cause many minimum extreme persons. Then, some items may have almost the same positions on the Y-axis and, thus, their item calibrations are almost the same. In future administrations of the social presence measure, only one of these items would be sufficient. Second, the ordering of the rating scale steps (see the fourth step) is made visible, which makes it easy to see any irregularities.

Results

The first series of Rasch analyses on the complete set of 30 items revealed in the first and second step severe infit and outfit problems with two items of this set, namely the item "... it feels like my fellow students are just passers-by" and the item "... I imagine I can feel my fellow students' breath." These problems could not be removed even when quite a number of person profiles were repaired on these items or persons removed. It was decided to remove these two items. A complete rerun of the second step was performed with the remaining set of 28 items. In this step 33 person profiles were repaired and 19 persons removed before persons and items were all in the safe zone. Furthermore, the analyses showed that for the item "...I only get a vague notion of my fellow students" category 4 was easier to endorse than category 3; these categories were endorsed by 13 and 18 persons of the remaining 63 respectively. These numbers were substantial and, therefore, the item was removed. A similar problem was identified with the item "...I constantly feel that my fellow students are around;" category 5 was easier to endorse than category 4. But here these categories were endorsed by only 2 and 1 person of the 63 respectively. Therefore, this item was not removed but kept under watch in the next analyses. Because four person profiles belonged to the removed persons and three repairs pertained to the newly removed item, the analyses effectively continued with 29 repaired person profiles: 18 profiles had 1 repair, 3 had 2 repairs, 4 had 3 repairs, 2 had 4 repairs, 1 had 9 repairs and 1 had 11 repairs. The persons with the latter two profiles were also kept under watch in the next analyses because of the high number of repairs.

The third step revealed that the scale had at least two dimensions: the unexplained variance in the first contrast was 4.94 Eigenvalue units (see Fig. 11.2, which is showing a part of the Winsteps Table 23.0), which corresponds to about five items. Furthermore, Pearson correlation and disattenuated correlation of the first and third item clusters were 0.53 and 0.62 respectively. These findings suggested that while some items are measuring something else, there is still a moderate correlation between these items and the other items. As already mentioned before, according to Linacre (2018b), correlations below 0.70 indicate that multidimensionality potentially may exist and, thus, need to be investigated.

To determine the accidental correlations simulated data were used (Linacre, 2018b). These data showed an unexplained variance in the first contrast of 2.39 Eigenvalue units. Thus, two to three items were accidentally correlated. Given the unexplained variance in the first contrast of the observed data, it meant that at least

```
Table of STANDARDIZED RESIDUAL variance in Eigenvalue units = ITEM information units
                                          Eigenvalue   Observed   Expected
Total raw variance in observations     =    72.7785 100.0%         100.0%
  Raw variance explained by measures   =    45.7785  62.9%          62.8%
    Raw variance explained by persons  =    16.3004  22.4%          22.4%
    Raw Variance explained by items    =    29.4781  40.5%          40.5%
  Raw unexplained variance (total)     =    27.0000  37.1% 100.0%   37.2%
    Unexplned variance in 1st contrast =     4.9411   6.8%  18.3%
    Unexplned variance in 2nd contrast =     3.0343   4.2%  11.2%
    Unexplned variance in 3rd contrast =     2.1838   3.0%   8.1%
    Unexplned variance in 4th contrast =     2.1174   2.9%   7.8%
    Unexplned variance in 5th contrast =     1.6104   2.2%   6.0%
```

Fig. 11.2 Reported explained and unexplained variances

two to three items were indeed measuring something else. Winsteps Table 23.2 suggested two sets of items that potentially could form a dimension. It was decided to continue with separate analyses with these two sets of items; the first set contained 15 items whereas the second set contained 12 items. Because the two items sets were derived from the 27 remaining items, the three removed items were not included in the separated analyses. As the items of the first set referred to the awareness of others in mediated communication, this item set was designated as Awareness of others, or for short, the Awareness 15-item set. In contrast, the items of the second set referred to the proximity with others in mediated communication. Therefore, this item set was designated as Proximity with others, and the item set as the Proximity 12-item set.

Before continuing with the separated analyses, we performed ancillary analyses and cross-plotted all 82 person measures as measured by the first Awareness 15-item set against the person measures as measured by the second Proximity 12-item set; see Fig. 11.3. Hereby, item calibrations and item structure-thresholds were anchored in so far that anchoring did not cause displacements in the item calibrations to exceed 0.50 logits (O'Neill, Peabody, Tan & Du, 2013). Because all displacements were between −0.17 and 0.19, all items could be anchored and none had to be freely estimated. Anchoring was accomplished by using the IFILE and SFILE options of Winsteps and was based on 63 persons (19 persons were removed). The plot also shows the 95% confidence band. The plot revealed that 39% of the person measures were beyond the 95% confidence band, which is significantly more than the 5% that can be expected at random. In addition, the analysis indicated that the person measures as measured by the two item sets correlated with 0.63, whereas the disattenuated correlation was 0.71, which is substantial, but not redundant. In sum, these findings underlined the conclusion that indeed there are two distinct dimensions.

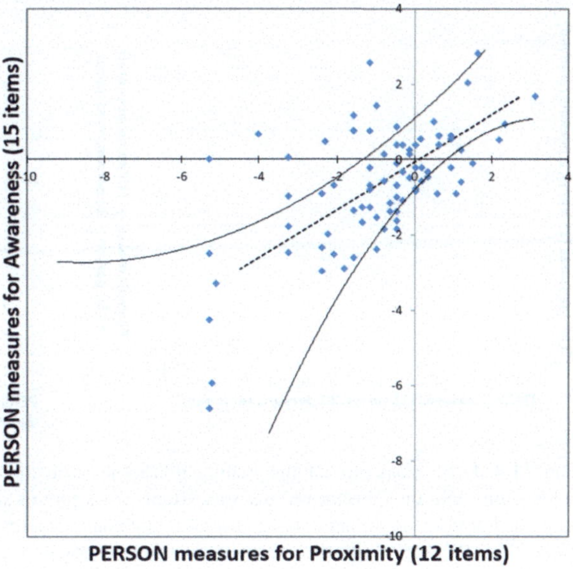

Fig. 11.3 Cross-plot of all 82 person measures as measured by the awareness 15-item set against the measures as measured by the proximity 12-item set. Items were anchored on 63 persons

First Item Set: Awareness of the Others

Separated series of Rasch analyses were performed on the Awareness 15-item set. Before these analyses were performed, all removed persons were reentered and person profiles restored in the original state; that is, all reparations were undone.

During the performance of the first and second step, two persons had to be removed; these persons were identified as the persons who had the most reparations in the person profiles in the previous analyses,. A complete rerun of the second step turned out in minor reparations of some person profiles (14 profiles had 1 repairs, 6 had 2 repairs, and 1 had 4 repairs) to get all items within the safe zone. This was not true for the persons but it could only be achieved by the removal of yet another 21 persons. Cross-plotting the items calibrations with the two removed persons against the calibrations with the 23 removed persons only resulted in small shifts of the calibrations (see Fig. 11.4 left pane). The Pearson correlation between the two sets of item calibrations was 0.998 and the disattenuated correlation 1.0. Cross-plotting all 82 person measures where the items were anchored using 80 persons (two persons were removed) against all 82 measures where the items were anchored using 59 persons (23 persons were removed) resulted also in small shifts of the measures (see Fig. 11.4 right pane). The Pearson correlation between the two sets of person measures was 0.999 and the disattenuated correlation 1.0. Therefore, it was decided to keep the 21 persons in the analyses and ignore the fact that not all persons were in the safe zone.

Inspection onto potential dimensionality in the third step revealed an unexplained variance in the first contrast of 2.86 Eigenvalue units and for the simulated data the unexplained variance in the first contrast was 2.02 Eigenvalue units. This means that

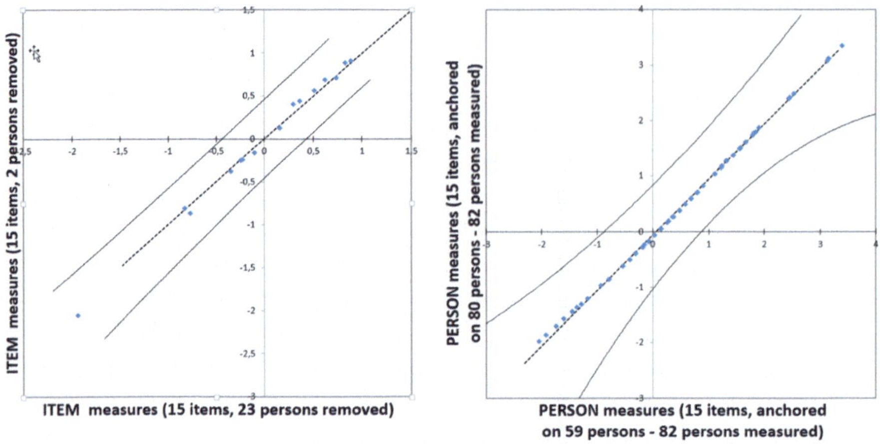

Fig. 11.4 Left: cross-plot of the items calibrations with the two removed persons against the calibrations with the 23 removed persons. Right: cross-plot of all 82 person measures where items were anchored using 80 persons against all 82 person measures where items were anchored using 59 persons; the one minimum extreme person is not shown

only one item could be held accountable for measuring something different, which is the usual case in Rasch measurement. Pearson correlation and disattenuated correlation of the first and third item clusters were 0.53 and 0.65 respectively, indicating a moderate correlation between the first and third item cluster but this was less of an issue given the fact that inspection of the unexplained variance in the first contrast did not signal multidimensionality. Consequently, the conclusion was that the Awareness 15-item set is a unidimensional Rasch measurement model.

In the fourth step, an inspection of the ordering functioning of the rating scale step categories. Each step category (see Table 11.1) contained more observed persons than the minimum of 10 persons. The average step category calibrations were ordered and increased monotonically as did the step thresholds. Outfit MNSQ were all < 2.00. However, in regard to the threshold distances, the distance between rating scale step 4 and 5 was 1.29 and, thus, did not meet the requirement that the distance should be at least 1.4. Distance peaks were detectable in the category probability curves (see

Table 11.1 Summary of the ordering functioning of the awareness rating scale step categories

Rating scale step number	Observed persons	Average calibration	Outfit MNSQ	Step threshold	Threshold distance
1	73 (6%)	−1.59	0.88	None	None
2	229 (20%)	−0.62	1.04	−2.38	None
3	391 (33%)	0.23	1.05	−0.77	1.61
4	302 (26%)	1.07	1.00	0.93	1.70
5	176 (15%)	2.32	0.94	2.22	1.29

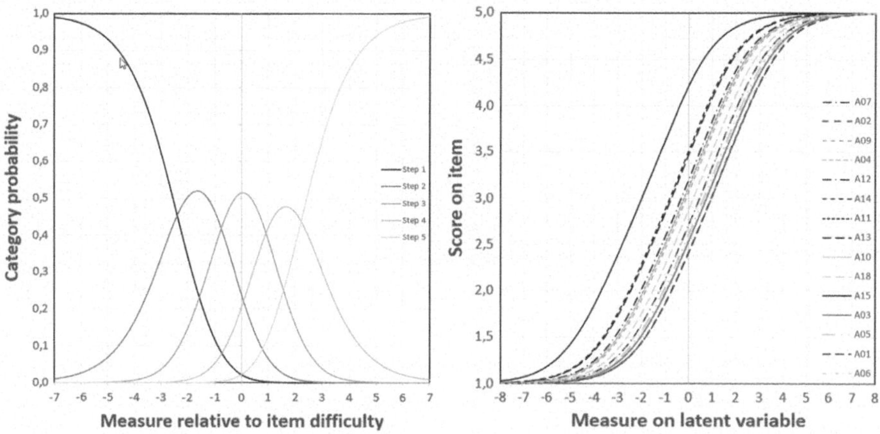

Fig. 11.5 Left: category probability curves for the awareness 15-items set. Right: item characteristic curves for the awareness 15-items set

Fig. 11.5 left pane). In additions, the item category curves were also inspected (see Fig. 11.5 right pane) but no irregularities were observed.

Finally, the Wright map was also inspected; Fig. 11.6 shows two Wright-maps of the Awareness 15-item set. Both Wright-maps show four psychometric properties of this set. First, the mean person measure (including the one minimum extreme person) is 0.44 and the mean item calibration is 0.00 (by definition), a difference of 0.44 logits. Because the mean person measure is a bit more than the mean item calibration, it means that the items were slightly easy to endorse by the respondents. Thus, respondents had no real difficulty in perceiving the awareness of others. Ideally, the mean item measure should be about 1 logit lower than the mean person measure (Linacre, 2000, p. 27); it is now < 1 logit lower than the mean person measure. Second, in the left Wright map, the item rating scale step numbers are all in an ascending order (i.e., rating scale step 2, at the bottom, followed by rating scale step 3 and then rating scale step 4, and rating scale step 5 at the top), which positively adds to the construct validity of the measure (Baghaei, 2008). Third, the left Wright map shows that the higher end of the person measure distribution along the Y-axis is well covered by the highest item rating scale step (i.e., item rating scale step number 5). Nevertheless, the Wright map indicates that the measure would benefit from items with calibrations that are higher than item A01's calibration, which currently represents the highest calibration of 0.91. Consequently, the current item set was moderate in differentiating persons with (very) high perceptions of the awareness of the others whereas it could excellently differentiate persons with low and average perceptions of awareness of the others. This indicates that there was some underrepresentation of the awareness dimension of social presence (Messick, 1996) which might slightly undermine the statistical validity (i.e., the reliability). Fourth, the items A01 and A02 were almost of the same difficulty level, as were the items A03 and A04, the items A05 and A06, the items A09, A10, and A11, and the items A13 and A14. This suggests that these

```
TABLE 12.6                                                                                    TABLE 12.2
INPUT: 82 PERSON  30 ITEM  REPORTED: 80 PERSON  15 ITEM  5 CATS   WINSTEPS 4.4.1
-----------------------------------------------------------------------------------------------------------------------------------------

MEASURE  PERSON - MAP - ITEM - 50% Cumulative probabilities (Rasch-Thurstone thresholds)     MEASURE PERSON - MAP - ITEM
           <more>|<rare>    2           3           4            5                                        <more>|<rare>
    4            +                                                                                              +
                 |                                                                                              |
                 |                                                                                              |
                 |                                                                                              |
              X  |                                            A01.5                                             |
                                                              A02.5
              X  |                                            A03.5                                             |
                                                              A04.5
    3         X T+                                            A05.5                                            T+
                 |                                            A06.5                                             |
                                                              A07.5
                 |                                                                                              |
              X  |                                            A08.5                                             |
           XXXX  |                                            A09.5                                             |
                 |                                            A10.5                                             |
                                                              A11.5
    2            +                                            A12.5                                             +
            XXX  |                                A01.4                                                         |
                                                  A02.4
            XXX S|                                A03.4       A13.5                                            S|
           XXXX  |T                               A04.4       A14.5                                             |T
                                                  A05.4
        XXXXXXX  |                                A06.4                                                         |
                                                  A07.4
            XXX  |                                                                                              |
    1       XXX  +                                A08.4                                                         +
              X  |S---------------------------------------------------------------------------------------------|S A01       A02
         XXXXXX  |--------------------------------A09.4---------------------------------------------------------|  A03       A04
                                                  A10.4
                                                  A11.4
              X M|--------------------------------A12.4--------------------------------------------------------M|  A05       A06
       XXXXXXXX  |--------------------------------------------A15.5---------------------------------------------|  A07
             XX  |-------------------A01.3----------------------------------------------------------------------|  A08
                                     A02.3
    0      XXXX  +M                  A03.3        A13.4                                                         +M
                                     A04.3        A14.4
           XXXX  |-------------------A05.3----------------------------------------------------------------------|  A09       A10       A11
       XXXXXXXX  |-------------------A06.3----------------------------------------------------------------------|  A12
                                     A07.3
              X  |                                                                                              |
              X S|                   A08.3                                                                     S|
             XX  |S---------------------------------------------------------------------------------------------|S A13       A14
   -1         X  +                   A09.3                                                                      +
                                     A10.3
                                     A11.3
              X  |                   A12.3        A15.4                                                         |
             XX  |                                                                                              |
            XXX  |T                  A13.3                                                                      |T
              X  |       A01.2       A14.3                                                                      |
                         A02.2
              X T|       A03.2                                                                                 T|
                         A04.2
   -2         X  +-------A05.2----------------------------------------------------------------------------------+  A15
                 |       A06.2                                                                                  |
                         A07.2
                 |       A08.2                                                                                  |
                 |                                                                                              |
                 |       A09.2                                                                                  |
                 |       A10.2       A15.3                                                                      |
                         A11.2
   -3            +       A12.2                                                                                  +
                 |                                                                                              |
                 |       A13.2                                                                                  |
                         A14.2
                 |                                                                                              |
                 |                                                                                              |
                 |                                                                                              |
   -4            +                                                                                              +
                 |                                                                                              |
                 |                                                                                              |
                 |                                                                                              |
                 |       A15.2                                                                                  |
                 |                                                                                              |
   -5         X  +                                                                                              +
           <less>|<freq>    1           2           3            4                                        <less>|<freq>
EACH "X" IS 1 PERSON
```

Fig. 11.6 Left: Wright map for the Awareness 15-item set showing the distribution of the item rating scale step numbers (right of the left axis) and at the same time showing the distribution of the person measures (left of the left vertical axis). Right: Wright map showing the distribution of the item calibrations (right of the right axis) similar difficulty level items are exchangeable and do not need all to be included in future administrations of the social presence measure.

Second Item Set: Proximity with the Other

Separated series of Rasch analyses were performed on the Proximity 12-item set. And here too, before these analyses were performed, all removed persons were reentered and person profiles restored in the original state; that is, all reparations were undone.

During the performance of the second step, three persons had to be removed and minor reparations of some person profile had to be done after a complete rerun (1 profile had 3 repairs, 1 had 4 repairs, 1 had 5 repairs, and 1 had 9 repairs) before all items were in the safe zone. This was not true for persons and even after the removal of yet another 19 persons did not bring all persons within the safe zone. Cross-plotting the items calibrations with the three removed persons against the calibrations with the 22 removed persons, however, only resulted in small shifts of the calibrations (see Fig. 11.7 left pane) except for one item but the shift was still acceptable as the item was still in within the 95% confidential band. The Pearson correlation between the two sets of item calibrations was 0.986 and the disattenuated correlation 1.0. Cross-plotting all 82 person measures where the items were anchored using 79 persons (three persons were removed) against all 82 measures where the items were anchored using 60 persons (22 persons were removed) resulted also in acceptable shifts of the measures (see Fig. 11.7 right pane). The Pearson correlation between the two sets of person measurements was 0.997 and the disattenuated correlation 1.0.

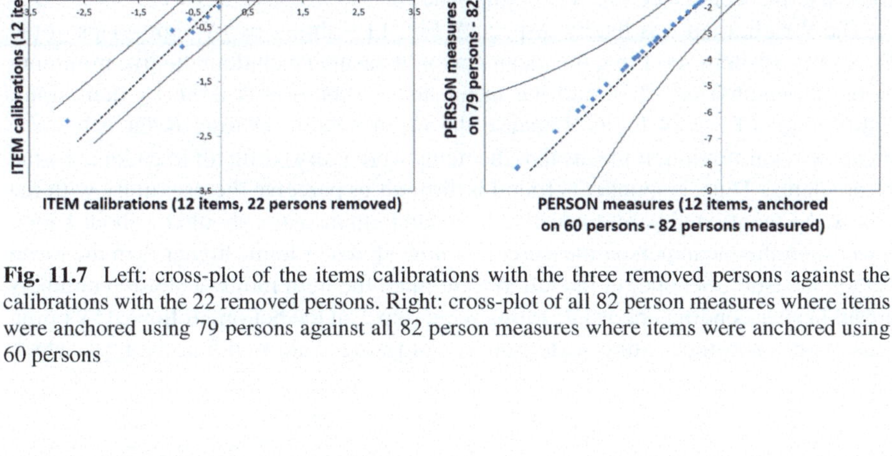

Fig. 11.7 Left: cross-plot of the items calibrations with the three removed persons against the calibrations with the 22 removed persons. Right: cross-plot of all 82 person measures where items were anchored using 79 persons against all 82 person measures where items were anchored using 60 persons

Table 11.2 Summary of the ordering functioning of the proximity rating scale step categories

Rating scale step number	Observed persons	Average calibration	Outfit MNSQ	Step threshold	Threshold distance
1	294 (32%)	−4.68	0.91	None	None
2	343 (37%)	−2.50	0.89	−3.92	None
3	217 (23%)	−0.89	1.05	−1.24	2.68
4	66 (7%)	1.12	0.88	1.22	2.46
5	8 (1%)	1.63	2.09	3.94	2.72

Therefore, it was decided to keep the 19 persons in the analyses and ignore the fact that not all persons were in the safe zone.

However, for four items, endorsing category 5 was easier to endorse than category 4. But category 5 was endorsed by only 1 person. Therefore, these four items were not removed but kept under watch in the next analyses.

Inspection onto potential dimensionality in the third step revealed an unexplained variance in the first contrast of 2.73 Eigenvalue units and for the simulated data the unexplained variance in the first contrast was 1.91 Eigenvalue units. This means that only one item can be held accountable for measuring something different, which is—as pointed out previously—usually the case in Rasch measurement. Pearson correlations and disattenuated correlation of the first and third item clusters were 0.64 and 0.82 indicating a high correlation between the first and third item cluster. The conclusion is therefore that this Proximity 12-item set is a unidimensional Rasch measurement model.

The fourth step entailed the inspection of the ordering functioning of the rating scale step categories. Each step category (see Table 11.2) contained more observed persons than the minimum of 10 persons except for step category 5, which had eight observed persons. Nevertheless, the average step category calibrations were ordered and increased monotonically as did the step thresholds. Outfit MNSQ were all < 2.00 except for category 5, which was a little higher than 2.00. Furthermore, all threshold distances were at least 1.4 and no more than 5.0. Distance peaks were detectable in the category probability curves (see Fig. 11.8 left pane); the item category curves were also inspected (see Fig. 11.8 right pane) but no irregularities were observed.

The Wright map was finally inspected; Fig. 11.9 shows two Wright-maps of the Proximity 12-item set. First, the mean person measure (including the five minimum extreme persons) is −2.74 and the mean item calibration is 0.00 (by definition), a difference of −2.74 logits. Because the mean person measure is far below the mean item calibration, it means that the items were (very) difficult to endorse by the respondents. Thus, respondents found it difficult to perceive the proximity with the others. As mentioned before, ideally, the mean item measure should be about 1 logit lower than the mean person measure; it is now almost 3 logits higher than the mean person measure. Second, in the left Wright map, the item rating scale step numbers are all in an ascending order (i.e., rating scale step 2, at the bottom, followed by rating scale step 3 and then rating scale step 4, and rating scale step 5 at the top), which

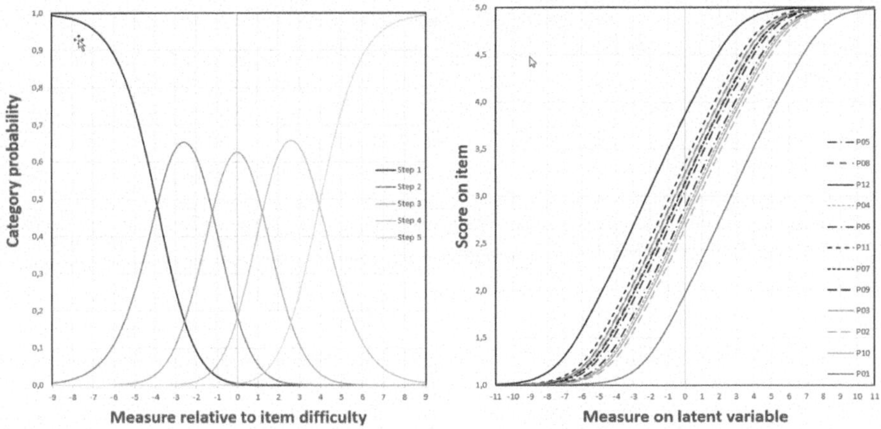

Fig. 11.8 Left: category probability curves for the Proximity 12-items set. Right: item characteristic curves for the Proximity 12-items set

positively adds to the construct validity of the measure (Baghaei, 2008). Third, the left Wright map shows that the higher end of the person measure distribution along the *Y*-axis is excellently covered by the highest item rating scale step (i.e., item rating scale step number 5) but this was not the case when looking the lower end. The right Wright map shows that it would be better also to have items whose calibrations are lower than that of item P12, the item with the lowest calibration of −2.21. Therefore, this proximity 12-item set insufficiently measured persons with (very) low to average perceptions of proximity with the others whereas it could excellently differentiate persons with (very) high perceptions of it. This explains the presence of five minimum extreme persons. It further indicates that there is underrepresentation of the proximity dimension of social presence (Messick, 1996) which could undermine the statistical validity (i.e., the reliability) of the Proximity 12-item set. Fourth, some items were almost of the same difficulty level; these were the items P02 and P03, the items P07 and P08, and the items P09 and P10. Future administrations of the social presence measure may take advantage out of this.

Summary Statistics

The summary statistics for both items' sets are shown in Table 11.3. This table show parts of the Winsteps Table 3.1. As can be seen, these statistics are all excellent.

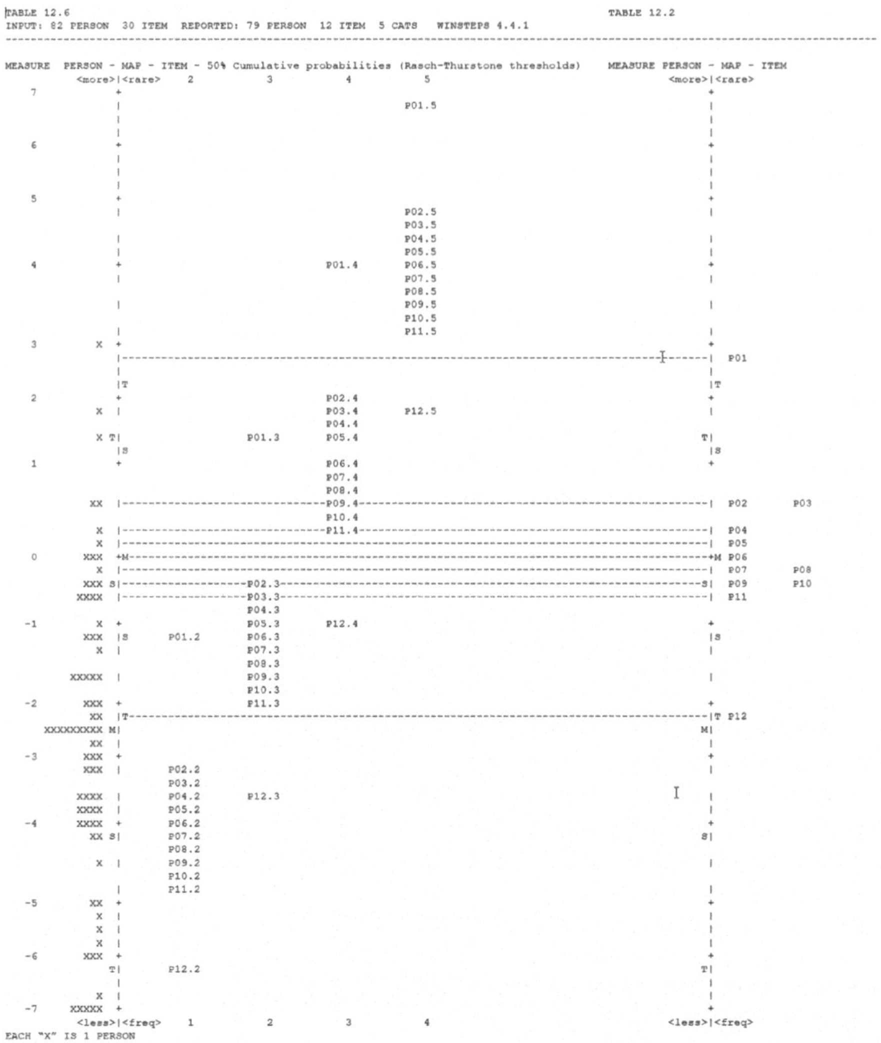

Fig. 11.9 Left: Wright map for the Proximity 12-item set showing the distribution of the item rating scale step numbers (right of the left axis) and at the same time showing the distribution of the person measures (left of the left vertical axis). Right: Wright map showing the distribution of the item calibrations (right of the right axis)

Discussion

Although currently quite a number of social presence measures exist, they rarely address the underlying latent variable, namely perceived physical realness of the other persons when communicating through telecommunication media. This is because many different definitions of social presence exist, which was the very reason for

Table 11.3 Summary statistics

	Awareness of others	Proximity with others	Criterion
Summary of measured (non-extreme) persons	*79*	*74*	
Person separation	2.94	3.10	If > 3.0 excellent If > 2.0 good If > 1.5 acceptable[a]
Person reliability	0.90	0.91	
Number maximum extreme score	0	0 (0%)	
Number minimum extreme score	1 (1.3%)	5 (6.3%)	
Deleted persons	2 (2.6%)	3 (4.1%)	
Summary of measured (extreme and non-extreme) persons	*80*	*79*	
Person separation	3.03	2.98	If > 3.0 excellent If > 2.0 good If > 1.5 acceptable[a]
Person reliability	0.90	0.90	
Person raw score-to-measure correlation	0.96	0.96	
Cronbach's α	0.92	0.94	
Summary of measured (non-extreme) item	*16*	*12*	
Item separation	4.86	5.13	If > 0.1.5 suitable for analyzing at the individual level If > 2.5 suitable for analyzing groups[b]
Item reliability	0.96	0.96	
Item raw score-to-calibration correlation	−0.99	−0.98	

[a]Duncan, Bode, Lai, and Perera (2013; p. 953)
[b]Tennant and Conaghan (2007)

us to get back to the original definition of Short et al. (1976). This definition is "the degree of salience of the other person in the communication and the consequent salience of the interpersonal relationships" (p. 65). The first part of this definition was identified as "social presence" and is referring to the degree of the realness of the others in the communication. Furthermore, all these social presence measures were either not validated (e.g., the four bipolar scales of Short et al., 1976), or based their validation on those not validated scales (see Tu, 2002, who remarked that the scale of Gunawardena & Zittle, 1997, basically was validated by the strong and positive correlations with bipolar scales derived from the Short, Williams, and Christie's instrument of five bipolar scales), or—at best—validated by using classical test theory (CTT) exploratory factor analyses but not always in combination with confirmatory factor analyses. Whenever they were tested in CFA, the measures were not tested for their invariance across samples. As pointed out, CCT has been criticized to have a number of problematic issues including assuming rating scale steps to be linear while it is not. Therefore, CTT total scores (the sum of the scores of the individual items) are also not linear and differences between two consecutive CTT total scores cannot be assumed to be of equal intervals (Wright, 1992). It is for all these reasons that the Rasch measurement model was used as a rigid construct validation method.

The Rasch analyses revealed that measuring realness of the others in a mediated environment implied that two distinct dimensions have to be addressed, namely Awareness of the others and Proximity with the others. Awareness of others was assessed by a 15-items set. The psychometric quality of the Awareness 15-item set was good to excellent, though this set could be improved in differentiating persons with (very) high perceptions of the awareness of the others but is excellent in differentiating persons with low and average perceptions of awareness of the others. Proximity with others was assessed by a 12-items set. The psychometric quality of the Awareness 15-item was moderate to good given the fact that it insufficiently measured persons with (very) low to average perceptions of proximity with the others whereas it could excellently differentiate persons with (very) high perceptions of it. Our future research may look at these issues and test newly created items that will fill the current gaps. The two dimensions may explain why definitions emphasizing awareness of the others or proximity with others (or co-presence) exist in the social presence literature. For example, Tu (2002) defined social presence as "the degree of person-to-person awareness, which occurs in the computer environment" (p. 34). Biocca and Nowak (2001) defined it as "level of awareness of the co-presence of another human, being or intelligence", and Kim (2011) as "the specific awareness of relations among the members in a mediated communication environment and the degree of proximity and affiliation formed through it" (p. 766). Finally, Sung and Mayer (2012) defined online social presence "as the subjective feeling of being connected and together with others during computer mediated communication" (p. 1739). Our future study will also include more respondents in the Rasch analyzes than the 82 people used in the current analyzes, although Linacre (1994) found that only 30 items administered to 30 respondents can produce useful measures. These respondents will be taken from different online settings (e.g., MOOCs, virtual classes, online collaborative learning) to test the measurement instrument's invariance across these settings.

Our findings, however, differ from Short et al. (1976) conviction that social presence should be regarded as a single dimension. Our future research should investigate this issue. One direction is pointed out by Linacre (2018b): perhaps the two dimensions represent the same strand—which is social presence as realness of the other—in a similar manner as "addition" and "subtraction" within "arithmetic," causing inconsequential dimensions. Furthermore, Linacre (2018a): stated that in some cases an instrument may be declared as unidimensional for the purpose of the measurement (see also, https://tinyurl.com/yxflh64z).

Once a reliable measurement instrument is available for social presence as the realness of the others in the communication, attention can be put on the antecedents and consequences of social presence. In particular, with respect to the latter, we will focus on the second part of the Short, Williams, and Christie's definition of social presence (i.e., "the consequent salience of the interpersonal relationships"), which we have identified as social space. Social space is the network of interpersonal relationships that exists among communicating persons, which is embedded in group structures of norms and values, rules and roles, beliefs and ideals (Kreijns, Van Acker, Vermeulen, & van Buuren, 2014, p. 11). A sound social space is manifest when it is characterized by a sense of belonging, feeling of connectedness, mutual trust, open atmosphere, shared social identity, and sense of community (Kreijns et al., 2018). With respect to the antecedents of social presence, the social presence literature has listed numerous potential antecedents. Amongst them are immediacy and intimacy behaviors (Short et al., 1976; Wei, Chen, & Kinshuk, 2012), and social respect, social sharing, open mind, social identity, and intimacy. (Sung & Mayer, 2012).

References

Arbaugh, J. B., Cleveland-Innes, M., Diaz, S. R., Garrison, R., Ice, P., Richardson, J., et al. (2008). Developing a community of inquiry instrument: Testing a measure of the community of inquiry framework using a multi-institutional sample. *Internet and Higher Education, 11*(13), 133–136.

Baghaei, P. (2008). The Rasch model as a construct validation tool. *Rasch Measurement Transactions, 22*(1), 1145–1146.

Biocca, F., & Nowak, K. (2001). Plugging your body into the telecommunication system: Mediated embodiment, media interfaces, and social virtual environments. In C. Lin & D. Atkin (Eds.), *Communication technology and society: Audience adoption and uses* (pp. 407–447). Waverly Hill, VI: Hampton Press.

Bond, T., & Fox, C. M. (2015). *Applying the Rasch model: Fundamental measurement in the human sciences* (3rd ed.). New York, London: Routledge.

Boone, W. J., Staver, J. S., & Yale, M. S. (2014). *Rasch analysis in the human sciences*. Dordrecht, The Netherlands: Springer.

Boone, W. J. (2016). Rasch analysis for instrument development: Why, when, and how? *CBE-Life Sciences Education, 15*(4). https://doi.org/10.1187/cbe.16-04-0148.

Crocker, L., & Algina, J. (1986). *Introduction to classical and modern test theory*. New York: Holt, Rinehart and Winton.

Carlon, S., Bennett-Woods, D., Berg, B., Claywell, L., LeDuc, K., Marcisz, N. … Zenoni, L. (2012). The community of inquiry instrument: Validation and results in online health care disciplines. *Computers & Education, 59*(2), 215–221.

Curtis, D. D. (2004). Person misfit in attitude surveys: Influences, impacts and implications. *International Education Journal, 5*(2), 125–144.

Diaz, S. R., Swan, K., Ice, P., & Kupczynski, L. (2010). Student ratings of the importance of survey items, multiplicative factor analysis, and the validity of the community of inquiry survey. *Internet and Higher Education, 13*(1), 22–30.

Duckor, B., Draney, K., & Wilson, M. (2009). Measuring measuring: Toward a theory of proficiency with the constructing measures framework. *Journal of Applied Measurement, 10*(3), 296–319.

Duncan, P. W., Bode, R. K., Lai, S. M., & Perera, S. (2013). Rasch analysis of a new stroke-specific outcome scale: the stroke impact scale. *Archives of Physical Medicine and Rehabilitation, 84*(7), 950–963.

Engelhard, G., Jr. (2013). *Invariant measurement: Using Rasch models in the social, behavioral, and health sciences*. New York and London: Routledge.

Gunawardena, C. N. (1995). Social presence theory and implications for interaction and collaborative learning in computer conferences. *International Journal of Educational Telecommunications, 1*(2&3), 147–166.

Gunawardena, C. N., & Zittle, F. J. (1997). Social presence as a predictor of satisfaction within a computer-mediated conferencing environment. *American Journal of Distance Education, 11*(3), 8–26.

Kim, J. (2011). Developing an instrument to measure social presence in distance higher education. *British Journal of Education Technology, 42*(5), 763–777.

Kreijns, K., Kirschner, P. A., Jochems, W., & van Buuren, H. (2011). Measuring perceived social presence in distributed learning groups. *Education and Information Technologies, 16*(4), 365–381.

Kreijns, K., Van Acker, F., Vermeulen, M., & van Buuren, H. (2014). Community of inquiry: Social presence revisited [Special Issue: Inquiry into "communities of inquiry:" Knowledge, communication, presence, community]. *E-Learning and Digital Media, 11*(1), 5–18. https://doi.org/10.2304/elea.2014.11.1.5.

Kreijns, K., Weidlich, J., & Rajagopal (2018). *The psychometric properties of a preliminary social presence measure using Rasch analysis*. In V. Pammer-Schindler, et al. (Eds.), *Proceedings of the thirteenth European conference on technology enhanced learning (EC–TEL 2018)* (pp. 31–44) (LNCS 11082). Springer, AG. https://doi.org/10.1007/978-3-319-98572-5_3.

Legon, R., & Garrett, R. (2018). The changing landscape of online learning. *A deeper dive CHLOE*. Retrieved from https://www.qualitymatters.org/sites/default/files/research-docs-pdfs/2018-QM-Eduventures-CHLOE-2-Report.pdf.

Linacre, J. M. (1994). *Sample size and item calibration [or person measure] stability*. Retrieved from www.rasch.org/rmt/rmt74m.htm.

Linacre, J. M. (1997). KR-20/Cronbach alpha or Rasch person reliability: Which tells the "truth"? *Rasch Measurement Transactions, 11*(3), 580–581.

Linacre, J. M. (2000) Computer adaptive testing: A methodology whose time has come. *MESA Memorandum No. 69*. Available from https://www.rasch.org/memo69.pdf.

Linacre, J. M. (2002). What do infit, outfit, mean-square and standardize mean? *Rasch Measurement Transactions, 16*(2), 878.

Linacre, J. M. (2004). Optimising rating scale category effectiveness. In E. V. Smith Jr. & R. M. Smith (Eds.), *Introduction to Rasch measurement: Theory, models, and applications* (pp. 258–278). Maple Grove, MN: JAM Press.

Linacre, J. M. (2018a). *A user's guide to Winsteps/Ministeps Rasch-model computer programs: Program manual 4.3.1*. Available at winsteps.com.

Linacre, J. M. (2018b). *Detecting multidimensionality in Rasch data using Winsteps Table 23*. Available from http://tinyurl.com/yxzomgwy.

Lowenthal, P. R. (2010). The evolution and influence of social presence theory on online learning. In *Online education and adult learning: New frontiers for teaching practices* (pp. 124–139). IGI Global.

Lowenthal, P. R., & Dunlap, J. C. (2014). Problems measuring social presence in a community of inquiry. *E-Learning and Digital Media, 11*(1), 19–30.

Lowenthal, P. R., & Snelson, C. (2017). In search of a better understanding of social presence: An investigation into how researchers define social presence. *Distance Education, 38*(2), 141–159.

Messick, S. (1996). Validity and washback in language testing. *Language Testing, 13*(3), 241–256.

O'Neill, T., Peabody, M., Tan, R. J. B., & Du, Y. (2013). How much item drift is too much? *Rasch Measurement Transactions, 27*(3), 1423–1424.

Öztok, M., & Kehrwald, B. A. (2017). Social presence reconsidered: Moving beyond, going back, or killing social presence. *Distance Education, 38*(2), 259–266.
Pallant, J. F., & Tennant, A. (2007). An introduction to the Rasch measurement model: An example using the Hospital Anxiety and Depression Scale (HADS). *British Journal of Clinical Psychology, 46*(1), 1–18.
Rasch, G. (1960). *Probabilistic models for some intelligence and attainment tests*. Kopenhagen: Danmark Paedagogiske Institut.
Richardson, J., & Swan, K. (2003). Examining social presence in online courses in relation to students' perceived learning and satisfaction. *Journal of Asynchronous Learning Network, 7*(1), 68–88.
Richardson, J. C., Maeda, Y., Lv, J., & Caskurlu, S. (2017). Social presence in relation to students' satisfaction and learning in the online environment: A meta-analysis. *Computers in Human Behavior, 71,* 402–417.
Rourke, L., Anderson, T., Garrison, D. R., & Archer, W. (2001). Assessing social presence in asynchronous text-based computer conferencing. *Journal of Distance Education, 14*(2), 51–70.
Short, J., Williams, E., & Christie, B. (1976). *The social psychology of telecommunications*. London: Wiley.
Sick, J. (2011). Rasch measurement and factor analysis. *SHIKEN: JALT Testing & Evaluation SIG Newsletter, 15*(1), 15–17.
Sung, E., & Mayer, R. E. (2012). Five facets of social presence in online distance education. *Computers in Human Behavior, 28*(5), 1738–1747.
Smith, E. V., Jr. (2002). Understanding Rasch measurement: Detecting and evaluating the impact of multidimensionality using item fit statistics and principal component analysis of residuals. *Journal of Applied Measurement, 3*(2), 205–231.
Tennant, A., & Conaghan, P. G. (2007). The Rasch measurement model in rheumatology: What is it and why use it? When should it be applied and what should one look for in a Rasch paper? *Arthritis and Rheumatism, 57*(8), 1358–1362.
Tu, C.-H. (2002). The measurement of social presence in an online learning environment. *International Journal on E-Learning, 1*(2), 34–45. Norfolk, VA: Association for the Advancement of Computing in Education (AACE).
Tu, C. H., & McIsaac, M. (2002). The relationship of social presence and interaction in online classes. *The American Journal of Distance Education, 16*(3), 131–150.
Walther, J. B. (1992). Interpersonal effects in computer-mediated interaction: A relational perspective. *Communication Research, 19*(1), 52–90.
Walther, J. B. (1996). Computer-mediated communication: Impersonal, interpersonal, and hyperpersonal interaction. *Communication Research, 23*(1), 3–43.
Wei, C.-W., Chen, N.-S., & Kinshuk (2012). A model for social presence in online classrooms. *Educational Technology Research and Development, 60*(3), 529–545.
Weidlich, J., & Bastiaens, T. J. (2017). Explaining social presence and the quality of online learning with the SIPS model. *Computers in Human Behavior, 72,* 479–487.
Weidlich, J., Kreijns, K., Rajagopal, K., & Bastiaens, T. (2018, June). What social presence is, what it isn't, and how to measure it: A work in progress. In *EdMedia + Innovate Learning* (pp. 2142–2150). Association for the Advancement of Computing in Education (AACE).
Wiener, M., & Mehrabian, A. (1968). *Language within language: Immediacy, a channel in verbal communication*. New York: Apple-Century-Crofts.
Wilson, M. (2005). *Constructing measures: An item response modeling approach* (2nd ed.). Mahwah, NJ: Lawrence Erlbaum Associates.
Wright, B. D. (1992). Raw scores are not linear measures: Rasch vs. classical test theory CTT comparison. *Rasch Measurement Transactions, 6*(1), 208.
Wright, B. D., & Masters, G. N. (1982). *Rating scale analysis*. Chicago, IL: MESA Press.

Chapter 12
Construct Validity of Computer Scored Constructed Response Items in Undergraduate Introductory Biology Courses

Hye Sun You, Kevin Haudek, John Merrill and Mark Urban-Lurain

Abstract "Psychometrically sound" assessments possess the ability to make valid inferences of students' conceptual understanding. However, there is a lack of validated assessments in college biology education. This study assesses the psychometric properties of the constructed response (CR) biology questions to establish construct validity and reliability. We used a polytomous Rasch Partial Credit Model to validate the eight CR items. Responses from 437 students were scored by automated scoring models that were trained on data scored by experts. All items reflected unidimensional construct of biology and local independency. The findings suggest that the instrument is a promising and valid tool to assess undergraduates' biology concepts from introductory biology courses, but needs further revision to strengthen the psychometric properties, adding more items for low performing students and improving person reliability. The significance of this study lies in its potential to contribute to creating more valid and reliable CR assessments through Rasch calibration.

Keywords Rasch validation · Partial credit model · Constructed response items · Computer scoring · College biology

Introduction

Assessments have the potential not only to demonstrate students' understanding but also to inform instructional decisions to enhance their learning. Ideas about assessment have changed over the last several decades, expanding the variety of possible assessment formats in education (Bell & Cowie, 2001). Selected response exams are a preferred and common assessment format to assess students' scientific knowledge and skills due to the advantages of ease of administration and high-speed, reliable

H. S. You (✉)
Arkansas Tech University, Russellville, AR, USA
e-mail: hyou@atu.edu

K. Haudek · J. Merrill · M. Urban-Lurain
Michigan State University, East Lansing, MI, USA

M. S. Khine (ed.), *Rasch Measurement*,
https://doi.org/10.1007/978-981-15-1800-3_12

scoring. This is true in many large, enrollment, college science courses. Multiple-choice (MC) tests are especially common in introductory college science classes due to class size and grading support issues (Stanger-Hall, 2012). Most concept inventories for college biology consist mainly of MC items with typical incorrect ideas or misconceptions as distractors (e.g., Biology Concept Inventory (BCI); Conceptual Assessment of Natural Selection (CANS). Despite the popularity of MC tests, these questions provide limited opportunity for students to construct explanations and elaborate on their scientific understanding, often assessing fragmented bits of knowledge and basic skills. Heyborne, Clarke, and Perrett (2011) emphasized that MC items and open-ended questions were not a similar tool to evaluate student achievement and thus MC tests are not a suitable substitute for free response items revealing scientific evidence. Moreover, the MC exam format hinders the development of college students' critical thinking (Stanger-Hall, 2012).

Due to the disadvantages of the MC items, a growing body of evidence indicates the value of assessments based on constructed response (CR) items (e.g., Nehm & Schonfeld, 2008). CR items allow students to express their knowledge in their own language and inform teachers of students' views of the nature of science, level of scientific literacy, and ability to interpret scientific evidence. The NRC Framework (2012) encourages building and restructuring explanatory models, problem-solving, and argumentation via writing in response to CR items, as an authentic scientific practice (Rivard & Straw, 2000). Furthermore, students learning science often have a mixture of "scientific" and "non-scientific" ideas. Such cognitive structures may be difficult to uncover using closed-form assessments alone (Hubbard, Potts, & Couch, 2017). In order to uncover these scientific, naïve and mixed models of student thinking, our research team collects student explanatory writing about scientific phenomena using CR items. Our research team (www.msu.edu/~aacr) also develops and applies computer scoring models to predict expert ratings of student responses, which can overcome the difficulty of scoring a large set of responses.

A critical component in test development is ensuring that the assessment measures are validated. Validation is the process of evidence-based judgment that supports the appropriateness of the inferences that are made from student responses for specific assessment uses (Messick, 1989b). The purpose of this study is to provide evidence for the construct validity of CR items developed by our research group using the Partial Credit Rasch Model. Rasch models are useful in the development of a new scale or revision of an existing scale for the validation purpose because the models test whether the observed data fit the model. In other words, the Rasch models assess whether the response pattern observed in the data matches the theoretical pattern expected by the model (Embretson & Reise, 2000). This allows us to examine person- and item-fit statistics and determine the reasons for any misfit and what corrections can be made. Furthermore, Rasch models provide evidence for different aspects of construct validity such as a person-item map and invariance of person or item (Boone, 2016: Smith, 2001; You, 2016). Among diverse Rasch models, the Partial Credit Model (PCM) is appropriate for our CR items in which each item has a unique rating scale structure (i.e., different score ranges) and unequal thresholds across items, while the rating scale model (RSM) can be used when all items share the same rating scale structure (e.g., Likert-scale).

Literature Review and Theoretical Framework

Assessments in College Biology

There are numerous assessments and tests related to college biology but only a handful of research studies has clearly evaluated the assessment practices and their validation through psychometric models for college biology learning and teaching (Goubeaud, 2010). Couch, Wood, and Knight (2015) developed the Molecular Biology Capstone Assessment (MBCA) which aims at assessing understanding of core concepts in molecular and cell biology and the ability to apply these concepts in novel scenarios. The assessment consists of 18 multiple-true/false questions. These items were administered to 504 students in upper-division courses such as molecular biology, cell biology, and genetics. In statistical analyses, the MBCA has an acceptable level of internal reliability (Cronbach's alpha = 0.80) and test-retest reliability (r = 0.93). The students had a wide range of scores with only a 67% overall average. This assessment was ultimately intended to provide faculty with guidance for improving undergraduate biology curriculum and instructional practices by pinpointing conceptually difficult areas.

Goldey and his colleagues (2012) added new assessment items for a guided-inquiry biology course to the traditional assessment format of MC and essay. The new items require higher-order thinking skills to explain what happens in a real-world problem (e.g., malaria) while the traditional questions assess a more basic understanding of course content. Specifically, the purpose of the new items is to evaluate students' core biological practices including testing a hypothesis, obtaining information from the primary literature, analyzing data, interpreting results and writing in a disciplinary style in inquiry-based learning. For instance, students were given a figure and caption from a recent research article regarding the investigation of a real-world problem and asked to identify the dependent and independent variables, interpret the pattern of the graph, and/or propose a follow-up experiment to address questions that emerge from the findings. They developed and implemented the new assessment with the inquiry-based approach but have not shown psychometric evidence for the validation of the tool.

Alonso, Stella, and Galagovsky (2008) created an assessment called "Understand Before Choosing" (UBC), targeting massive enrollment freshman biology courses, in which they combined the benefits of the traditional multiple-choice test with those of the open-ended question test as a quick and objective way of evaluating knowledge, comprehension, and ability to apply the material taught. Each UBC test provides short paragraphs that describe a concrete example of the topic being evaluated and is accompanied by a set of MC questions. The UBC assessment requires students to relate their knowledge to the information provided in the text and with the question posed; thus, it enables assessment of not only recalling facts but also other levels of cognitive skills such as comprehension and application of concepts. In order to evaluate the quality of the UBS, only discrimination and difficulty ratios have been reported. Other measures of the validity and reliability of the tool have not yet been reported.

Todd and Romine (2016) adapted and validated the Learning Progression-based Assessment of Modern Genetics (LPA-MG) for college students. To evaluate the construct validity of ordered multiple-choice (OMC) items, they used two Rasch models of partial credit (Masters, 1982) and rating scale (Andrich, 1978). They indicated that overall, the instrument provides valid and reliable measures for introductory college students even though there are slight deflation of the reliability and three misfit items. Also, the data suggested that the average student has a good understanding of the molecular and genetic models but a poor understanding of the meiotic model and the relationship between the three models.

Recently, Couch and his colleagues (2019) developed the General Biology-Measuring Achievement and Progression in Science (GenBio-MAPS) assessment to evaluate student understanding of the core concepts contained in a biology degree program. The instrument consists of 39 question stems and 175 accompanying true-false items in a multiple-true-false format in which each stem question introduces a biological scenario followed by a series of independent true-false items. They administered the final version of the instrument to more than 5000 students in 152 courses at 20 institutions with general biology programs. Each student answered a random subset of 15 question stems including a total of 60–75 true-false items. They employed both classical test theory (e.g., overall student scores, traditional item difficulty: percentage of students answering each item correctly and confirmatory factor analysis (CFA), etc.) and Rasch modeling approaches to generate estimates of psychometric properties (e.g., item difficulties and differential item functioning (DIF), person reliabilities and so on). The measure revealed the unidimensionality through the different fit indexes of the CFA. The Rasch analysis displayed the acceptable person reliability of 0.82 and item fit statistics between 0.5 and 1.5 values. The DIF test showed significant differences in individual items based on ethnicity and gender.

In sum, previous literature has mainly focused on developing and validating closed-ended questions such as MC and true-false for in-class assessments in college biology courses and there is little research about the validation of the CR test format using psychometric methods (especially, Rasch models). This study contributes to the existing literature on validation of college science tests.

Assessment Triangle

Assessment, as defined in the National Science Education Standards (NRC, 1996), is "a systematic, multi-step process involving the collection and interpretation of educational data" (p. 76). Assessment specialists believe assessment is a process of

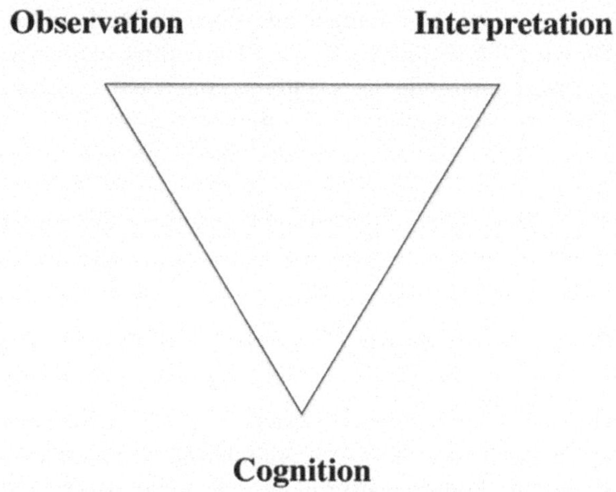

Fig. 12.1 Assessment triangle (NRC, 2001)

reasoning from evidence—"of using a representative performance or set of performances to make inferences about a wider set of skills or knowledge" (NRC, 2014, p. 48). The National Research Council (NRC, 2001) portrayed this process of reasoning from evidence as a triangle with three corners—cognition, observation, and interpretation to emphasize their connected relationships (see Fig. 12.1). Cognition, in assessment design, is "a theory or set of beliefs about how students represent knowledge and develop competence in a subject domain" (NRC, 2001, p. 44), which are important to measure. In measurement terminology, the assessed knowledge and skills are referred to as "constructs". An assessment should start from an explicit and clearly well-defined construct because the design and selection of the tasks need to be tightly linked to the specific inferences about student learning. If the intended constructs are clearly specified, the design of specific items or tasks and their scoring rubric could provide clear inferences about the students' capabilities. A second corner of the triangle is the observation of the students' capabilities in a set of assessment tasks designed to show what they know and can do. The assessments are based on theories and beliefs concerning knowledge and cognitive processes to acquire valid and rich responses. Thus, observations support the inferences that will be made based on the assessment results. The Interpretation vertex includes all the methods and tools to infer the results of observations that have been collected. Statistical or qualitative models can be used for methods or tools to identify and interpret the patterns of the data collected through assessment tasks. The interpretation model needs to fit the type of data collected through observation. Through interpretation, the observations of students' performances are synthesised into inferences about their knowledge, skills and other attributes being assessed. The method used for a large-scale standardized test might involve a statistical model. For a classroom assessment, it could be a less formal method of drawing conclusions about a student's understanding on the basis of the teacher's experiences with the student, or it could provide an interpretive framework to help make sense of different patterns in a student's contributions to practicing and responding to questions. Pellegrino (2012) asserted in the NRC report *Knowing What Students Know*: "These three elements—cognition, observation, and interpretation—must be explicitly connected and designed as a coordinated whole. If not, the meaningfulness of inferences drawn from the assessment will be compromised" (p. 2). It is recommended that assessments should be equipped with a design process that coordinates the three elements of the triangle, instead of focusing on a single vertex (e.g., observations), to support the intended inferences.

Rasch Analysis for Construct Validation: Partial Credit Model

Messick (1989a) defined construct validity as: "the evidence and rationales supporting the trustworthiness of score interpretation in terms of explanatory concepts that account for both test performance and relationships with other variables" (p. 34). The Rasch model is the simplest model in item response theory (IRT) developed by Rasch (1960) and is regarded as a powerful psychometric technique that is used in education and psychological testing to develop and validate assessment data on both the item and test level (Lord, 1980). This study employs a Rasch model to provide the evidence and rationale in obtaining a valid and reliable assessment tool. Rasch models (1960, 1980) are based on the probability of each response as a function of the latent traits (i.e., examinees' ability (θ)) and the item difficulty parameters that characterize the items (Embretson & Reise, 2000). The Rasch models describe psychometric properties using item fit as well as separation-reliability statistics. When the fits are appropriate and the estimates of the item parameters are reasonably acceptable, the Rasch model suggests that the measure has adequate construct validity (Hinkin, Tracey, & Enz, 1997).

Rasch models are based on a set of fairly strong assumptions, unlike classical test theory (CTT). If the assumptions are not met, the validity of the psychometric estimates is severely compromised. The Rasch model requires that the construct being measured in the assessment is unidimensional. Another important assumption is local independence. The local independence assumes that an item response to one question is not contingent on a response to another question (Embretson & Reise, 2000), which provides us with statistically independent probabilities for item responses. When the Rasch model satisfies the assumption of unidimensionality and local independence, the latent trait estimates are not test-dependent, and item parameters are not sample-dependent (Yang & Kao, 2014).

Among a variety of the Rasch models, CR items can be analyzed with the Partial Credit Model (PCM) developed by Masters (1982). This model analyzes items with multiple response categories ordered by the levels of proficiency they represent, and partial credit is assigned for completing several steps in the problem-solving process (Embretson & Reise, 2000). The PCM is appropriate for analyzing items with more than two levels of response (Embretson & Reise, 2000). Unlike the Rasch rating scale model, the PCM allows items to have different numbers of response categories and does not assume the distance between response thresholds is uniform for all items.

The PCM can be expressed mathematically with the following formula:

$$P_{ix}(\theta) = \frac{\exp[\sum_{x=0}^{m}(\theta - b_{ik})]}{\sum_{x=0}^{m}\exp[\sum_{k=0}^{x}(\theta - b_{ik})]}$$

where θ is the level in the latent construct of person, b_{ik} is the item step difficulty parameter with the transition from category $k - 1$ to category k, and m is the number of steps in an item (maximum score of the item).

The PCM requires that the steps within an item should be completed in order. One credit is given to each step completed. A response in category k is awarded a partial credit of k out of possible full credit m. However, thresholds need not be ordered. In other words, harder steps could be followed by easier steps or vice versa.

Methods

Participants and Instrument

A total of 437 undergraduate students from three introductory biology courses at two public universities in the United States participated in this study during the 2016–2017 academic year. All responses on the eight CR items were collected via a web-based learning management system (i.e., D2L) and scored by a computerized ensemble scoring method. Briefly, a set of classification algorithms is "trained" on a set of responses coded by experts using an evaluation rubric. This generates a computer scoring model, which can be applied to predict scores of a new set of data (for example see: Haudek, Prevost, Moscarella, Merrill, & Urban-Lurain, 2012; Moharreri, Ha, & Nehm, 2014).

The Scientific Literacy in Introductory Biology (SLIB) assessment set consists of eight constructed response items designed for use in college-level introductory biology courses. The items *Energy from grape, Photosynthesis, Root cells and, Weight loss* are adapted from previous work creating diagnostic question clusters and focus on tracing matter and energy through chemical transformations (Parker et al., 2012; Weston, 2015; Wilson et al., 2006). The *Cell type* item is designed to assess students' knowledge of how information is stored and regulated in cells (Smith, Wood, & Knight, 2008). These items were scored using dichotomous analytic rubrics which are scored either as 0 for the absence of a construct or 1 for the presence of the construct. For example, the rubric of the *Weight loss* item (*"Your friend loses 15 lb on a diet, where does the mass go?"*) has a total of seven conceptual themes built via literature review, qualitative and computerized lexical analyses. Among seven bins, a rubric bin regarding *physiological process—exhalation* captures responses that indicate mass has been released into the air. The central dogma items, *Replication, Transcription*, and *Translation* were developed to assess how students trace effects of a point mutation where a single nucleotide base is changed from a sequence of DNA on the downstream mRNA and protein product. The scoring models for these items are based on a three-level holistic rubric where responses are scored as correct (2), incomplete/irrelevant (1) or incorrect (0) (Prevost, Smith, & Knight, 2016). We used the summed score of the rubric bins for each question with dichotomous analytic rubrics. The incorrect/non-normative bins were reverse-scored to 0. Table 12.1 shows the items and the range of points.

Data Analyses

The purpose of this study is to evaluate the psychometric properties of the polytomous CR items using the Rasch model, Partial Credit Model (PCM), and to make improvements based on these results. Specific aims of the study were to (a) assess unidimensionality, or whether the set of items represented a single construct; (b) examine local independence; (c) assess item fit and person fit; (d) assess item separation index and reliability; (e) examine person separation index and reliability; and (f) compare item difficulty and biology literacy level using an item-person map. Winsteps Version 4.40 (Linacre, 2019a) was used to perform the Rasch analysis.

(1) Assumptions of Rasch analysis: There are two critical assumptions for Rasch models: unidimensionality and local independence (Embretson & Reise, 2000). With the essential unidimensionality assumption, only one dominant latent ability is needed to model item responses, even though minor dimensions are present in the data. Local independence indicates that a response to one question is not contingent on a response to another question (Embretson & Reise, 2000).

(a) **Unidimensionality**. Unidimensionality is a basic and foundational assumption in both CTT and IRT; "a single latent variable is sufficient to explain the common variance among item responses" (Embretson & Reise, 2000, p. 226). The construct being measured in the assessment should be unidimensional (Hattie, 1985). A threat to unidimensionality could severely compromise estimates of reliability and construct validity.

In this study, principal component analysis of the standardized residuals was used to examine whether a substantial factor existed in the residuals after the primary measurement dimension has been estimated. If the items measure a single latent dimension, then the remaining residual variance reflects random variation. The Winsteps program provides the percent of total variance explained by each of the principal components and the number of residual variance units explained. Each item included in the analysis accounts for one unit of residual variance. The Scientific Literacy in Introductory Biology (SLIB) consists of eight items, thus, the maximum number of residual variance units is 8. If the percent of the variance explained by the eigenvalue of the first contrast in the correlation matrix of the residuals is less than 2.0, then the contrast is at the noise level, which means the assumption of unidimensionality is satisfied (Linacre, 2019a, b). Additional criteria were considered for unidimensionality using item fit statistics, as discussed below.

Table 12.1 Calibration summary of eight SLIB items

Item	Item difficulty (logit)	SE (logit)	Infit	Outfit
1. ***Energy from grape*** (0–6 points): *You eat a sweet and juicy grape. Explain how a molecule of glucose from that grape can be used to move your little finger.*	0.05	0.05	0.66	0.67
2. ***Photosynthesis*** (0–6 points): *A mature maple tree can have a mass of 1 ton or more (dry biomass, after removing the water), yet it starts from a seed that weighs less than 1 g. Explain this huge increase in biomass; where did the biomass come from and by what process?*	−1.24	0.05	1.34	1.34
3. ***Root cells*** (0–5 points): *Not all cells in plants (e.g., root cells) contain chlorophyll required for photosynthesis. How do these cells get energy?*	−0.84	0.05	0.92	0.93
4. ***Weight loss*** (0–5 points): *You have a friend that lost 15 lbs on a diet. Where did the mass go?*	−0.04	0.05	1.27	1.31
5. ***Cell type*** (0–5 points): *Using your knowledge of genetics, explain how human brain cells and heart cells are different*	−0.42	0.05	1.03	1.03
6. ***Replication*** (0–2 points): *The following DNA sequence occurs near the middle of the coding region of a gene DNA 5' A A T G A A T G G* G A G C C T G A A G G A 3' There is a G to A base change at the position marked with an asterisk. Consequently, a codon normally encoding an amino acid becomes a stop codon. How will this alteration influence DNA replication?*	0.63	0.05	0.86	0.89
7. ***Transcription*** (0–2 points): *How will this alteration influence transcription?*	0.66	0.05	0.95	0.96
8. ***Translation*** (0–2 points): *How will this alteration influence translation?*	1.21	0.06	0.68	0.73

(b) **Local independence**. When the Rasch model satisfies the assumption of local independence, the latent trait estimates are not test-dependent, and item parameters are not sample-dependent, which allows statistically independent probabilities for item responses (Yang & Kao, 2014). A violation of the local independence assumption leads to overestimation of the reliability and test information function, and inappropriate standard error estimates of items (Sireci, Thissen, & Wainer, 1991). We used Yen's (1993) Q_3 statistic to assess local independence. There are $n(n-1)/2$ correlation pairs, where is the number of items. The mean value of the Q_3 statistic should be close to $-1/(n-1)$ (Yen, 1993).

(2) **Item fit**: Item fit indicates the extent to which the response to a particular item is consistent with the way the sample respondents have responded to the other items. The Rasch model provides two indicators of misfit, information-weighted (infit) and outlier sensitive (outfit) statistics. The Information-weighted (Infit) mean-square (MNSQ) is sensitive to unexpected response patterns to items close to the person's ability level and the *outfit* mean-square is more sensitive to unexpected response on items far from the person's level (i.e., outlier) (Linacre, 2019b). The Rasch model predicts that both the infit and outfit will be close to 1.0. Statistics greater than 2.0 can indicate significant differences from the model expectations where statistics less than 0.5 denote that less information is being provided by the respondents due to less variation. (Linacre, 2019b). For example, when the infit for an item is close to 1.0 the outfit is greater than 2.0, low performers chose the correct answer to very difficult items. There are several acceptable fit ranges from which researchers can adopt based on the type of tests such as MC test (0.7–1.3), clinical observation (0.5–1.7), or rating scale (0.6–1.4) (Bond & Fox, 2007) but we employed the range of the MNSQ value suggested by Linacre (2002), 0.5–1.5. An item is thus considered misfit if both infit MNSQ and outfit MNSQ > 1.5 or < 0.5. The item fit indices support unidimensionality. A misfit situation may indicate the item measures a different underlying construct.

(3) Person fit: Person-fit indices [reported in mean-square (MNSQ) values] examine the pattern of actual scores versus the pattern of expected scores, which allows assessing the meaningfulness of a score at the individual level (Boone, Staver, & Yale, 2014). The fit indices are based on the consistency of an individual's item response pattern with some proposed model of valid item responses. If we have abnormal response patterns (e.g., a high performing student unexpectedly answers an easy item incorrectly and vice versa), further examinations into the responses would be necessary. A general rule of thumb for the mean-square statistic of Infit and Outfit of a person is less than 0.5 or greater than 1.5, it shows a poor person fit (Linacre, 2002).

(4) Item reliability and separation: Item separation describes how much differentiation there is among items (Wright & Masters, 1982). Item separation is useful to distinguish items that are easier to answer from items that are more difficult to answer. The separation coefficient can be defined as "the square root value of the ratio between the true person variance and the error variance" (Boone et al., 2014, p. 222). Low item separation (<3, with item reliability <0.9) suggests the sample is not large enough to establish the item separation (Linacre, 2019b). Adding a wider range of people helps differentiate the items successfully.

(5) Person reliability and separation: The person separation statistic expresses how well person ability is spread to show individual differences. Person separation is thus helpful to sort people into different groups. The person separation is similar to Cronbach's alpha, but it is often a lower value because it does not include perfect scores in the computation (Wright & Mok, 2000). An instrument with a low person separation (<2, with person reliability of <0.8) suggests that the assessment is not sensitive enough to distinguish between high and low performers.

(6) Item difficulty and person ability: In IRT, person ability (i.e., θ) is estimated relating to item difficulty, so each item and person ability are indicated on a common logit scale (Bond & Fox, 2007). When a person's ability is equal to the item difficulty in the logit scale, the probability of succeeding on the item is 50%. The person-item map provides visual information regarding bandwidth of person ability and hierarchy of the items on the same scale of logits (Boone et al., 2014). The graphical nature of the map allows immediate understanding of the relative location of the ability of examinees and item difficulties. The average of the item difficulty has been set as a logit value of 0. Difficult items have large, positive logit scores, whereas easy items have large, negative scores (Reise & Waller, 2002). On the person side of the vertical line in the map, M indicates mean of the persons and S and T represents one standard deviation from the mean and two standard deviations from the mean, respectively. Similarly, on the item side of the vertical line, M is mean of the item difficulties and S and T are one standard deviation from the mean of item difficulties and two standard deviation from the mean, respectively (Boone et al., 2014).

Results

(1) Assumptions for the Rasch model

(a) Unidimensionality. The PCA of the standardized residuals revealed that 44% (overall) of the total variances were explained by the measure and the first contrast of residual had an eigenvalue of 1.87 (cutoff value: less than 2.0; Linacre, 2019b) as well as the percent of the variance explained by the first contrast was 13.1%, indicating that the eight items can be treated as a unidimensional measure. The SLIB's latent trait can be defined as conceptual biology knowledge. An evaluation of the SLIB's unidimensionality involves the investigation of trends in the data that do not fall under the umbrella of this latent trait.

(b) Local Independence. For the eight items, there was a total of 28 Q_3 correlations. The mean of Q_3 correlations across eight items was −0.139 with a standard deviation of 0.073. This value is very close to the target value of −0.143 for an 8-item test. This result suggests that the items were sufficiently locally independent to carry out Rasch analysis.

(2) Item fit: The Rasch model predicts that both the Infit and Outfit are close to 1.0, indicating the observed response pattern fits the model. As shown in Table 12.1, the analysis revealed Infit statistics ranging from 0.66 to 1.34; all eight items were within the acceptable range of 0.5–1.5 (Linacre, 2002). The Outfit statistics of all items ranged from 0.67 to 1.34, also indicating an appropriate fit. These also support the unidimensional structure of the SLIB.

(3) Person fit: Examination of person fit revealed 18 (4.1%) persons with an infit or output value above 2.00, and 60 (13.7%) of the sample to have an infit or outfit statistic above 1.5. 49 (11.2%) of the total sample to have infit or outfit below 0.5. This pattern may suggest that 25% of the student population in this study display unexpected student response behaviors.

(4) Item reliability and separation: The item separation is 14.45 (>3), which indicates that the assessment has very good variability. In addition, the item separation-reliability is 1.00, which indicates an excellent internally consistent measure.

(5) Person reliability and separation: The items show low person separation (0.56) and reliability (0.24). Low person separation (<2, person reliability <0.8) implies that the instrument may not be not sensitive enough to differentiate between high and low performers (Bond & Fox, 2007). The low person separation-reliability of 0.24 is not acceptable internal consistency. For sound person reliability, additional items that are well aimed at the targeted latent trait may be needed or having a wide range of distribution of ability across the sample is another way of increasing person reliability (Bond & Fox, 2007).

(6) Item difficulty and individual SLIB level: The item difficulties and associated standard errors are reported in Table 12.1. The higher the logit scores, the greater the item difficulty. The item difficulty ranges from −1.24 to 1.21 logits. The easiest item is *Photosynthesis* (−1.24; SE = 0.05). The most difficult item is *Translation* (1.21; SE = 0.06). The students' SLIB levels range from a low of −2.19 to a high of 0.71. The average level of student ability was −0.44 (SD = 0.47). The students' ability level and item difficulty measures were moderately distributed along the same continuum on the item-person map (see Fig. 12.2). A large proportion of students fall between 0 and −1 logits which suggests that the items were too difficult for the majority of the sample and/or that sample is performing below their predicted ability. Also, a comparison of the mean location score for people with the zero score for item sets enables us to evaluate how well items measure students' abilities. A mean person ability close to zero represents the ideal difficulty level of items (Bond & Fox, 2007). The map indicates that the mean for students (M = −0.44, SD = 0.47) is lower than the mean for item difficulties (M = 0.00, SD = 0.77). The map reveals there are no items for a person with the lowest levels of achievement (i.e., located at logits −1.5 to −2.5).

Fig. 12.2 Item-person map of the SLIB items

```
MEASURE      PERSON - MAP - ITEM
          <higher ability>|<more difficult>
    2                     +
                          |
                          |T
                          |
                          |  Translation
    1                     +
                        . |S
                        . T|  Replication    Transcription
                       ## |
                      .## |
    0           .####### S+M Energyfromgrape Weightloss
                     #### |
         .############ M|  Celltype
               .###### |
               .###### |S Rootcells
   -1                ### S+
                      .# |  Photosynthesis
                      .# T|
                        . |T
                        . |
   -2                   . +
                        . |
                          |
           <lower ability>|<less difficult>
  EACH "#" IS 9: EACH "." IS 1 TO 8
```

Discussion

Many national reports for college biology education articulate pedagogical recommendations to enhance scientific literacy (e.g., Bio2010, Vision and Change). Especially, the 2011 Vision and Change emphasized focusing on helping students construct critical core biology knowledge. This shift is reflected in efforts to develop concept inventories and other assessments for undergraduate biology education (e.g., the molecular biology capstone assessment (Couch et al., 2015) and the BioMaPS project (McCarthy & Fister, 2010)). College instructors and students devote a large proportion of their class time to assessment activities where the assessments are used as a means for understanding and improving student learning, and for revising, curricular and instructional practices. However, there has been a lack of psychometrically validated assessments for college biology education. Even within those efforts noted above, there is very little research focusing on the psychometric validity of the CR items for gaining college students' conceptual understanding and proficiency through scientific practices (e.g., constructing explanation). This study fills this void, providing the psychometric properties of a set of CR questions targeted for introductory college biology.

The Rasch model provides the psychometric properties through an estimation in the relationship between the ability of a particular examinee and the characteristics of a particular item. Especially, reliability, item difficulties, and fit statistics are helpful in evaluating the validity and reliability of measures. The results of the study established the unidimensionality of the SLIB measure and the appropriateness of the item and person fits, and excellent item separation and reliability. However, the person separation and reliability were particularly low, which indicates the current SLIB is not differentiating students' abilities well. For improvement of the person separation and reliability index, more items to elicit a wide range of students' conceptual understanding could be added. Also, some previous studies showed that as the number of scoring categories increased, item and person separation statistics increased (e.g., Zhu, Updyke, & Lewandowski, 1997); thus, if the range of the item scores expands, the person separation and reliability could be improved. Our population in introductory biology courses, on average, are performing at a lower level than the items. The mean of our population is aligned with *cell type* item (*Using your knowledge of genetics, explain how human brain cells and heart cells are different*). This means that the level of the item difficulty is situated to measure the group's knowledge. The comparison of the location of the mean of item difficulty (0.00) and the mean of respondents (-0.44) provides more guidance on the difficulty level of items that can be added to help shift the means closer together. The measurement precision of the SLIB could be improved by including additional easier items to capture the lower performing students. The additional easy items help instructors to decide the minimum level of teaching and provide the information of fundamental concepts which the low performers should first master to progress toward the next level of desirable scientific literacy. The results of the improved assessment could enable instructors to incorporate additional instructional supports for low performing students. Also, our data showed that 25% of the students have less predictable responses (i.e., a high performing student unexpectedly answers an easy item incorrectly and vice versa). This could be due to the time in the semester when data was collected. The data was collected in the middle of the semester before the students had mastered the relevant scientific concepts and principles needed to explain the phenomena in the eight questions. Future studies that investigate the relative performance difference between pre- and post-test may provide evidence about why the items were not perfectly matched with the student population.

On the item-person map, we see great overlap between the person measure and item measure but there is a slight mismatch between the most difficult item, *Translation* (1.21) and the highest person ability (0.71). The majority of students in this study are below the three genetics items regarding central dogma and a nonsense mutation, indicating that many students did not understand the details of how a point mutation in DNA affects the production of a protein. Among the three questions related to the central dogma, *Translation* was the most difficult items on the SLIB, which means that the majority of students did not grasp the scientific fact; a stop codon (i.e., TGA in DNA) prematurely terminates the amino acid sequence and prevents the correct protein from being produced.

One of the criticisms of undergraduate biology is the lack of psychometrically-informed assessments actually used in undergraduate biology courses (Momsen, Long, Wyse, & Ebert-May, 2010). Among a wide variety of assessment forms, CR assessments afford students meaningful opportunities to construct an explanation based on their scientific ideas and principles. Especially, the CR items developed and revised in the study with thorough qualitative review aid instructional decisions by providing class-wide information about how a range of students' ideas align with normative and/or non-normative scientific explanations. As such, many biology instructors can benefit from the SLIB by recognizing where students are struggling and addressing the problems as a part of formative assessment and instructional scaffolding.

Ensuring that the qualitatively validated SLIB assessment is also psychometrically sound is a critical component for the use of the formative assessment. The significance of this study lies in its potential to contribute valid and reliable information about the SLIB using the Rasch model and serves as a baseline for future CR items that will be developed and calibrated in our research group with stronger psychometric properties. In order to further examine the SLIB's validity including generalizability, future research is needed to replicate and extend the findings with a wide variety of college students from diverse school settings. By having a more diverse sample, future studies would be better positioned to discern if person and item performance is influenced by contextual differences between learning contexts.

Conclusion

Assessments, understood as scaffolding tools, should be critical supports for instruction. National documents for science education such as the *Framework* (NRC, 2012), *Next Generation Science Standards* (NGSS Lead States, 2013), and, *Vision and Change* (AAAS, 2011), encourage students to engage in multiple scientific practices in the context of core disciplinary ideas. The development of CR items and automatic scoring models of those items will allow faculty to have students construct explanations and form arguments rather than placing emphasis on memorizing facts. Such instructional environments could broaden the opportunities for students to learn and apply science in real-life contexts and eventually lead to improved biology literacy. This study contributes to the body of knowledge related to validation of classroom-based CR assessments in college biology but these principles can be applied to CR items across a range of STEM disciplines.

Acknowledgements This material is based upon work supported by the National Science Foundation (DUE 1561159, DUE 1323162 and DUE 1660643). Any opinions, findings and conclusions or recommendations expressed in this material are those of the author(s) and do not necessarily reflect the views of the NSF.

References

Alonso, M., Stella, C., & Galagovsky, L. (2008). Student assessment in large-enrollment biology classes. *Biochemistry and Molecular Biology Education, 36*(1), 16–21.

American Association for the Advancement of Science. (2011). *Vision and change in undergraduate biology education: A call to action.* Washington, DC.

Andrich, D. (1978). A rating formulation for ordered response categories. *Psychometrika, 43*(4), 561–573.

Bell, B., & Cowie, B. (2001). The characteristics of formative assessment in science education. *Science Education, 85*(5), 536–553.

Bond, T. G., & Fox, C. M. (2007). *Applying the Rasch model: Fundamental measurement in the human sciences* (2nd ed.). Mahwah, NJ: L. Erlbaum.

Boone, W. J., Staver, J. R., & Yale, M. S. (2014). *Rasch analysis in the human sciences*. Dordrecht: Springer, Netherlands.

Boone, W. J. (2016). Rasch analysis for instrument development: Why, when, and how? *CBE—Life Sciences Education, 15*(4), rm4.

Couch, B. A., Wood, W. B., & Knight, J. K. (2015). The molecular biology capstone assessment: A concept assessment for upper-division molecular biology students. *CBE—Life Sciences Education, 14*(1), ar10.

Couch, B. A., Wright, C. D., Freeman, S., Knight, J. K., Semsar, K., Smith, M. K., … & Brownell, S. E. (2019). GenBio-MAPS: A programmatic assessment to measure student understanding of vision and change core concepts across general biology programs. *CBE—Life Sciences Education, 18*(1), ar1.

Embretson, S. E., & Reise, S. P. (2000). *Item response theory for psychologists*. New York: Formats. *CBE-Life Sciences Education, 16*(2), ar26.

Goldey, E. S., Abercrombie, C. L., Ivy, T. M., Kusher, D. I., Moeller, J. F., Rayner, D. A., … & Spivey, N. W. (2012). Biological inquiry: A new course and assessment plan in response to the call to transform undergraduate biology. *CBE—Life Sciences Education, 11*(4), 353–363.

Goubeaud, K. (2010). How is science learning assessed at the postsecondary level? Assessment and grading practices in college biology, chemistry and physics. *Journal of Science Education and Technology, 19*(3), 237–245.

Hattie, J. (1985). Methodology review: Assessing unidimensionality of tests and ltenls. *Applied Psychological Measurement, 9*(2), 139–164.

Haudek, K. C., Prevost, L. B., Moscarella, R. A., Merrill, J., & Urban-Lurain, M. (2012). What are they thinking? Automated analysis of student writing about acid–base chemistry in introductory biology. *CBE—Life Sciences Education, 11*(3), 283–293.

Heyborne, W. H., Clarke, J. A., & Perrett, J. J. (2011). A comparison of two forms of assessment in an introductory biology laboratory course. *Journal of College Science Teaching, 40*(5), 28–31.

Hinkin, T. R., Tracey, J. B., & Enz, C. A. (1997). Scale construction: Developing reliable and valid measurement instruments. *Journal of Hospitality & Tourism Research, 21*(1), 100–120.

Hubbard, J. K., Potts, M. A., & Couch, B. A. (2017). How question types reveal student thinking: An experimental comparison of multiple-true-false and free-response formats. *CBE-Life Sciences Education, 16*(2), ar26.

Linacre, J. M. (2002). What do infit and outfit, mean-square and standardized mean? *Rasch Measurement Transactions, 16*(2), 871–882.

Linacre, J. M. (2019a). Winsteps® (Version 4.4.1) [Computer Software]. Beaverton, Oregon: Winsteps.com. Retrieved January 1, 2019, from https://www.winsteps.com/.

Linacre, J. M. (2019b). *Winsteps® Rasch measurement computer program User's Guide*. Beaverton, Oregon: Winsteps.com.

Lord, F. M. (1980). *Applications of item response theory to practical testing problems*. Hillsdale, NJ: Lawrence Erlbaum Associates.

Masters, G. N. (1982). A Rasch model for partial credit scoring. *Psychometrika, 47*(2), 149–174.

McCarthy, M. L., & Fister, K. R. (2010). Biomaps: A roadmap for success. *CBE—Life Sciences Education*, *9*(3), 175–180.

Messick, S. (1989a). Validity. In R. L. Linn (Ed.), *Educational measurement* (3rd ed., pp. 13–103). New York: Macmillan.

Messick, S. (1989b). Meaning and values in test validation: The science and ethics of assessment. *Educational Researcher, 18*(2), 5–11.

Moharreri, K., Ha, M., & Nehm, R. H. (2014). EvoGrader: An online formative assessment tool for automatically evaluating written evolutionary explanations. *Evolution: Education and Outreach, 7*(1), 15.

Momsen, J. L., Long, T. M., Wyse, S. A., & Ebert-May, D. (2010). Just the facts? Introductory undergraduate biology courses focus on low-level cognitive skills. *CBE—Life Sciences Education*, *9*(4), 435–440.

National Research Council. (1996). *National science education standards*. Washington, DC: National Academy Press.

National Research Council. (2001). *Knowing what students know: The science and design of educational assessment*. Washington, DC: The National Academies Press.

National Research Council. (2003). *BIO2010: Transforming undergraduate education for future research biologists*. Washington, DC: The National Academies Press.

National Research Council. (2012). *A framework for K-12 science education: Practices, crosscutting concepts, and core ideas*. Washington, DC: The National Academies Press.

National Research Council. (2014). *Developing assessments for the next generation science standards*. Washington, DC: The National Academies Press. https://doi.org/10.17226/18409.

Nehm, R. H., & Schonfeld, I. S. (2008). Measuring knowledge of natural selection: A comparison of the CINS, an open-response instrument, and an oral interview. *Journal of Research in Science Teaching, 45*(10), 1131–1160.

NGSS Lead States. (2013). *Next generation science standards: For states, by states*. Washington, DC: National Academies Press.

Parker, J. M., Anderson, C. W., Heidemann, M., Merrill, J., Merritt, B., Richmond, G., et al. (2012). Exploring undergraduates' understanding of photosynthesis using diagnostic question clusters. *CBE—Life Sciences Education, 11*(1), 47–57.

Pellegrino, J. W. (2012). Assessment of science learning: Living in interesting times. *Journal of Research in Science Teaching, 49*(6), 831–841.

Prevost, L. B., Smith, M. K., & Knight, J. K. (2016). Using student writing and lexical analysis to reveal student thinking about the role of stop codons in the central dogma. *CBE—Life Sciences Education, 15*(4), ar65.

Rasch, G. (1960/1980). *Probabilistic models for some intelligence and attainment tests*. (Copenhagen, Danish Institute for Educational Research), expanded edition (1980) with foreword and afterword by B.D. Wright. Chicago: The University of Chicago Press.

Reise, S. P., & Waller, N. G. (2002). Item response theory for dichotomous assessment data. In F. Drasgow & N. Schmitt (Eds.), *The Jossey-Bass business & management series. Measuring and analyzing behavior in organizations: Advances in measurement and data analysis* (pp. 88–122). San Francisco, CA, US: Jossey-Bass.

Rivard, L. P., & Straw, S. B. (2000). The effect of talk and writing on learning science: An exploratory study. *Science Education, 84*(5), 566–593.

Sireci, S. G., Thissen, D., & Wainer, H. (1991). On the reliability of testlet-based tests. *Journal of Educational Measurement, 28*(3), 237–247.

Smith, E. V. (2001). Evidence for the reliability of measures and validity of measure interpretation: A Rasch measurement perspective. *Journal of Applied Measurement, 2*(3), 281–311.

Smith, M. K., Wood, W. B., & Knight, J. K. (2008). The genetics concept assessment: A new concept inventory for gauging student understanding of genetics. *CBE—Life Sciences Education*, *7*(4), 422–430.

Stanger-Hall, K. F. (2012). Multiple-choice exams: An obstacle for higher-level thinking in introductory science classes. *CBE—Life Sciences Education, 11*(3), 294–306.

Todd, A., & Romine, W. L. (2016). Validation of the learning progression-based assessment of modern genetics in a college context. *International Journal of Science Education, 38*(10), 1673–1698.

Weston, M., Haudek, K. C., Prevost, L., Urban-Lurain, M., & Merrill, J. (2015). Examining the impact of question surface features on students' answers to constructed-response questions on photosynthesis. *CBE—Life Sciences Education, 14*(2), ar19.

Wilson, C. D., Anderson, C. W., Heidemann, M., Merrill, J. E., Merritt, B. W., Richmond, G., et al. (2006). Assessing students' ability to trace matter in dynamic systems in cell biology. *CBE—Life Sciences Education, 5*(4), 323–331.

Wright, B. D., & Masters, G. N. (1982). *Rating scale analysis: Rasch measurement*. Chicago: Mesa Press.

Wright, B. D., & Mok, M. (2000). Understanding Rasch measurement: Rasch model overview. *Journal of Applied Measurement, 1*(1), 83–106.

Yang, F. M., & Kao, S. T. (2014). Item response theory for measurement validity. *Shanghai Archives of Psychiatry, 26*(3), 171–177.

Yen, W. M. (1993). Scaling performance assessments: Strategies for managing local item dependence. *Journal of Educational Measurement, 30*(3), 187–213.

You, H. S. (2016). Rasch validation of a measure of reform-oriented science teaching practices. *Journal of Science Teacher Education, 27*(4), 373–392.

Zhu, W., Updyke, W. F., & Lewandowski, C. (1997). Post-hoc Rasch analysis of optimal categorization of an ordered-response scale. *Journal of Outcome Measurement, 1*(4), 286–304.

Chapter 13
An Analysis of the Psychometric Properties of the Social Responsibility Goal Orientation Scale Using Adolescent Data from Sweden

Daniel Bergh

Abstract In the Achievement Goal Theory, different reasons for learning are contrasted. Mastery and Performance are most commonly used while less attention is paid to Social Responsibility goal orientations, despite that this is an integral part of many curricula. The purpose of this chapter is to examine the psychometric properties of a scale of Social Responsibility goal orientation by means of the polytomous Rasch model. The analysis is based on longitudinal data among Swedish students. One cohort (born 1992) of students in school year 9 (15–16 years old) were subjected to analysis. In total, 6,010 students responded to a paper-and-pencil questionnaire. A scale consisting of six polytomous items is analysed. General-fit statistics as well as their graphical representations (ICC) are used to evaluate the fit to the Rasch model. The social responsibility scale seems to fit the Rasch model fairly well, with good separation of individuals, and showing no reversed item thresholds, i.e., the response categories work as intended. However, there are indications of Differential Item Functioning (DIF) by gender and local dependency.

Keywords Student motivation · Student goal orientation · Psychometric analysis · Modern test theory · Rasch model

Introduction

Motivation is considered one of the key determinants of educational outcomes in school, relevant for student grades and academic success. Students may differ in their motivation for school work, both in forms and degrees. Related to motivation, in the Achievement Goal Theory, different reasons for learning are contrasted. Thus, originally the mastery-goal orientation was contrasted to the performance goal orientation. Students adopting a mastery orientation have a desire to develop their competence by improving learning as much as possible. Mastery oriented students can thus be focused on learning a content or in order to develop specific skills. In

D. Bergh (✉)
Karlstad University, Centre for Research on Child and Adolescent Mental Health, Karlstad, Sweden
e-mail: daniel.bergh@kau.se

M. S. Khine (ed.), *Rasch Measurement*,
https://doi.org/10.1007/978-981-15-1800-3_13

contrast, performance oriented students focus on demonstrating their competence by outperforming other students, to show teachers that they are better than other students, or at least not worse than others (Senko, 2016).

Much of the research on goal orientations has been focused on academic goals while less attention has been paid to Social Responsibility as a goal orientation, despite the fact that competences related to these goals are integral parts of many curricula. However, Wentzel was early in her studies on social responsibility (Wentzel, 1991, 1993). Social goals and responsibility have been suggested to influence academic achievement directly, but also indirectly. By the improvement of social interactions with teachers and peers, prosocial and compliant behaviors may facilitate classroom learning by promoting achievement-oriented behaviors (Wentzel, 1993).

Psychometric analyses of Social Responsibility goal orientation scales have dominantly been conducted using factor analytical approaches (see for instance Giota (2010), Rawlings, Tapola, and Niemivirta (2017)). Adopting a Rasch measurement perspective (Rasch, 1960/1980), it may be possible clarify the characteristics of common measures of the Social Responsibility goal orientation. Thus, it would be possible to rule out how a proposed composite measure works as a whole, but also whether it is possible to invariantly compare groups based on the individual items.

Aims

At a general level of analysis, the purpose of this study is to analyse a scale of Social Responsibility Goal Orientation by means of the Polytomous Rasch Model. As there may be reasons to believe that aspects connected to the student role and achievement goals are interpreted differently by boys and girls, a specific aim is to investigate potential Differential Item Functioning (DIF) by gender, at a finer level of analysis.

An initial stage of the analysis has also been presented at the Seventh International Conference on Probabilistic Models for Measurement Developments with Rasch Models, held in Perth in 2018 (Bergh & Giota, 2018). However, the analysis has been refined since the conference presentation. Therefore, even though the title of the conference presentation and the chapter presented here are similar, the analysis, results and conclusions are similar only in parts.

Methods

Participants and Data Collection

The data subjected to analysis in this study is based on one cohort from the ongoing Swedish longitudinal Evaluation Through Follow-up (ETF) project (Svensson, 2011). These ETF-data include one cohort of students, those born in 1992, collected in 2008, at the end of the Swedish compulsory school, when the students attend school year 9 and are 15–16 years old. In collaboration with Statistics Sweden, ETF has since its start in 1961 collected data in Swedish comprehensive School (in year 6 and for some cohorts in year 3 and 9) and upper-secondary school. All students were sampled by Statistics Sweden when they attend school year 3. Thereafter, the students are followed-up in school year 6, 9 and 12. At an initial stage, a stratified sample of municipalities was drawn, and thereafter, a sample of school classes within the selected municipalities. The oldest cohort was born in 1948 and the youngest in 2004.

Each ETF-cohort represents about 10% of the total student population. The data collection include questionnaire data, administrative and register data that is collected and added throughout the lifespan.

The 1992 cohort comprised 9,890 students, out of which 6,010 responded to the postal paper-and-pencil survey administered in school year 9. This corresponds to a response rate of 61%.

Instrument

In this study 6 items intended to measure the student Social responsibility goal orientation, were used. Based on previous research (Giota, 2001), the items were developed as a part of the School Motivation Items (SMI) battery using confirmatory factor analysis (Giota, 2010). Social responsibility was then defined as achievement in order to maintain interpersonal commitments, to meet social role obligations, and to adhere to social and moral norms. The items that apply is provided in Table 13.1, using the response format (0) "Never/almost never", (1) "Rarely", (2) "Sometimes", (3) "Often", and (4) "Always/almost always".

Table 13.1 Items

How often are you trying to do the following in school:
Item 1: *Get things done in time*
Item 2: *Be a responsible student*
Item 3: *Be a student who does well in school*
Item 4: *Work hard even if it is difficult*
Item 5: *Do my very best*
Item 6: *Be helpful*

Measurement Model

In this study the concordance between observed data and the expected Rasch model (Rasch, 1960/1980) is analysed by means of the Rasch model for ordered response categories, also called the Polytomous Rasch Model, which is an extension of the Simple Logistic Model:

$$\Pr\{X_{ni} = x\} = \frac{e^{x\beta_n - \delta_i)}}{1 + e^{\beta_n - \delta_i}}. \quad (13.1)$$

Thus, in the dichotomous case, item locations are denoted by δ and person locations denoted by β. The relationship between items and persons is central; the probability of a specific response is a function of the relationship between person parameter estimates and item parameter estimates, consequently β-δ. A positive value from the subtraction implies probabilities greater than 0.5. Commonly, social scientific data are not restricted to dichotomous response formats. Instead, the polytomous response format may be more applicable in many situations. The Polytomous Rasch Model, or the Rasch model for ordered response categories (Andrich, 1978; Wright & Masters, 1982) takes the general form

$$\Pr\{x_{ni} = x\} = \frac{e^{-\tau_{1i} - \tau_{2i} \ldots - \tau_{xi} + x(\beta_n - \delta_i)}}{\sum_{x'=0}^{m_i} e^{-\tau_{1i} - \tau_{2i} \ldots - \tau_{x'i} + x'(\beta_n - \delta_i)}} \quad (13.2)$$

Thus, in the polytomous case a central concept is threshold. Given a situation with five response categories (0, 1, 2, 3, 4), a threshold specifies the point at which the probability for choosing one out of two answers is equal, for instance an answer of 0 or 1. The concept of threshold is also important since this is the point where most information is found. In the equation above the threshold parameter is denoted by τ and the item score by x in the numerator. Given that there is concordance between the expected Rasch model and the data, the item discriminations are the same, as is illustrated in Fig. 13.1.

Analysis of Fit

General fit statistics (Chi-Squared) as well as their graphical representations (ICC) are used in order to evaluate the fit to the Polytomous Rasch Model. The Chi-Squared statistic for analysis of fit is conducted by comparing the total score of persons in approximately equally sized class intervals with the sum of expected values. Thus, this is resulting in an approximate Chi-Squared statistic with C-1 degrees of freedom. The fit statistics are based on comparisons between observed and expected values. The summation of Chi-Square values for individual items forms a total Chi-Square value describing a global overall test of fit of the model.

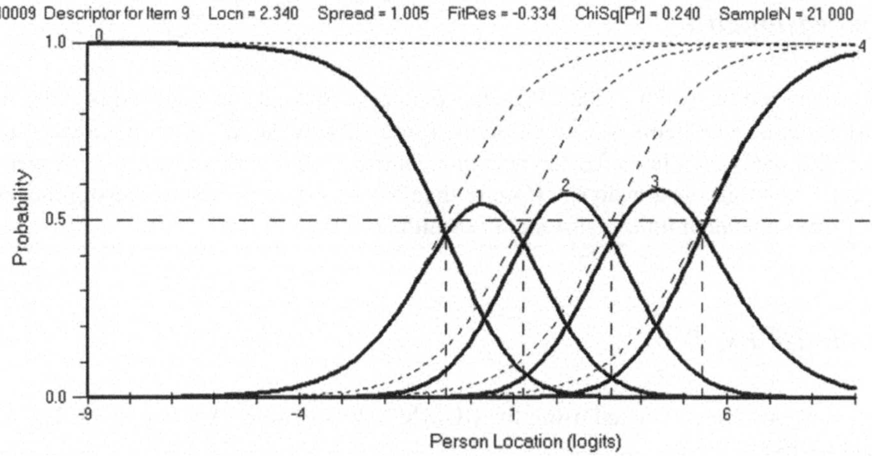

Fig. 13.1 An example of a category probability curve showing the latent dichotomous threshold characteristic curves with equal slopes

Given this setup of the Chi-Squared statistic, it is sensitive to sample size, as has been concluded by many scholars. When using relatively large samples, as in this study, strategies to handle large samples in statistical test of fit may be considered. Based on previous experiences (See Bergh, 2015a, b), in this study an approach comparing the original sample with a random sample of 1,000 individuals is applied when using the Chi-Squared statistical test of fit. However, it is important to recognize the potential influence of random error in this situation. Nevertheless, the random sample approach is considered to serve as a good approximation of the test of fit statistic given a specific sample size. The comparison between the Chi-Square values based on original sample and those base on a random sample therefore tells us whether it is likely that sample size has been influential on the statistical test of fit. It is important that the efforts and discussions about fit statistics and sample size continue, even though it may be difficult to find one single solution to the issue.

In addition to the Chi-Squared statistic, two-way analysis of variance of residuals (ANOVA) was used in order to find out whether the items work invariantly across sub-groups of individuals, i.e. to study Differential Item Functioning (DIF).

Local Dependency

Within modern test theory a presumption is that items should be locally independent from each other. When the response to one item governs the response to another item, this requirement has been violated. The occurrence of local dependency is analysed by using residual correlation analysis. Thus, strong residual correlations may indicate local dependency (Andrich, Humphry, & Marais, 2012).

Dimensionality

As suggested by Smith (2002), Principal Component Analysis was used in order to group items. The items were then divided into subsets based on the findings from the PCA analysis. Thereafter the person locations within each subset of items were compared using *t*-test analysis. If more than 5% of the comparisons are significant this may indicate multidimensionality (Smith, 2002).

Software Used

All analyses are conducted using the RUMM2030 software (Andrich, Sheridan, & Luo, 2013).

Results

Frequencies

In Table 13.2, the distribution of responses in each of the response categories for the six items are presented. Thus, a general pattern shown implies larger proportions into the often or always/almost always categories, as compared to into the never/almost never or rarely categories. For instance, in the item 'Get things done in time' about 9% of the students respond to one of the first two response categories while about 72% score in one of the last two categories (Often or always/almost always). This pattern largely applies to all items. The largest proportion in the Always/almost

Table 13.2 Distribution of responses into the response categories of the six items. Percent (*n*)

Item	Never/almost never	Rarely	Sometimes	Often	Always/almost always
Get things done in time	2.4 (145)	6.2 (369)	19.1 (1134)	39.3 (2333)	32.9 (1950)
Be responsible	2.8 (165)	8.3 (494)	23.1 (1372)	35.7 (2115)	30.1 (1785)
Be a student who does well in school	3.5 (210)	8.9 (528)	24.6 (1459)	34.3 (2030)	28.7 (1700)
Work hard even if it is difficult	1.9 (115)	7.1 (419)	28.6 (1696)	38.0 (2254)	24.4 (1446)
Do my very best	0.8 (49)	3.4 (199)	16.2 (960)	39.3 (2329)	40.3 (2390)
Be helpful	1.5 (89)	5.5 (324)	25.6 (1519)	42.4 (2514)	25.0 (1485)

always category is found in the "Do my very best" item where 40% respond to this category. This is also the item with the smallest proportion responses into the never/almost never category.

Targeting

Given this response format, in a composite measure of the social responsibility goal orientation constituted by the above six items, a low score implies weak orientation whereas a high score translate to strong social responsibility goal orientation. In Fig. 13.2, information about the distribution of persons and item thresholds is presented in simultaneously.

Thus, Fig. 13.2 reflects the response format also observed also in Table 13.2, showing that a small proportion of the participants responding into one of the two first response categories (Never/almost never, or Rarely), while a larger proportion respond into the two last categories (Always/almost always or Often). As a consequence, the overall mean location of persons is positive (1.31), and with a negatively skewed distribution. From Fig. 13.2 it can also be seen that the item-threshold distribution implies that there are item thresholds along the latent trait. This is important as the locations where most information is located is where the item thresholds are located. Unfortunately, there are also locations where item thresholds are missing. For instance, at locations of 3–4 logits, persons with strong social responsibility orientation, there are no item threshold close. This implies that the measurement would be improved by including additional items with higher difficulty. It can further be observed that there is one more location (between 1 and 2 logits) where item thresholds are missing. Unfortunately, this is the location where most persons are located. In addition, there are locations in the beginning of the continuum (−2 to −1 logits) with many item thresholds, but few persons.

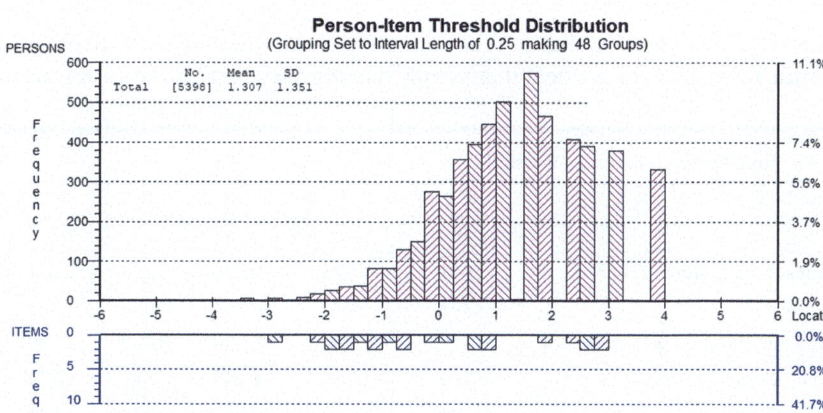

Fig. 13.2 Person-item distribution

It is should also be noted that there are differences in mean location, based on the social background of the participants. For instance, boys are on average located (1.02) further to the left (reflecting weaker social responsibility orientation) compared to the mean location of girls (1.58). Similarly, students from families with compulsory school as the highest attained educational level are located (1.21) further to the left (weaker orientation), compared to those from families with upper-secondary school as highest parental educational level (1.24), while the mean location of students from families with higher education (1.37) reflect stronger social responsibility goal orientation (not shown in figure).

Reliability Indices

Reliability indices provide important information on how well an instrument separates the persons that are to be measured (Traub & Rowley, 1991). In this study, the Person Separation Index (PSI) (Andrich, 1982), equivalent to the test reliability of person separation, sometimes also called the reliability of case estimates (Wright & Masters, 1982), is used. This reliability indicium is analogous to the traditional Cronbach's α (Cronbach, 1951) coefficient. A high value implies high reliability (consistency). However, reliability coefficients are influenced by the number of items included in the composite measure. Thus, longer tests (including many items) generally have higher reliability coefficients than shorter tests (with few items) (Traub & Rowley, 1991). Based on the 6 items included in the proposed social responsibility goal orientation measure, the PSI is 0.81, reflecting relatively high reliability consistency, given the number of items.

Item Locations and Thresholds

In Table 13.3, the item locations and the centralized item thresholds are displayed. Thus, from Table 13.3 it is evident that item 5 "Do my very best" is the easiest one,

Table 13.3 Item locations and item thresholds

Thresholds					
Item	Location	1	2	3	4
Get things done in time	0.011	−1.673	−0.836	0.238	2.271
Be responsible	0.143	−2.024	−0.864	0.505	2.383
Be a student who does well in school	0.318	−1.788	−0.950	0.499	2.238
Work hard even if it is difficult	0.169	−2.268	−1.245	0.688	2.824
Do my very best	−0.686	−2.180	−0.913	0.548	2.545
Be helpful	0.044	−2.030	−1.235	0.543	2.722

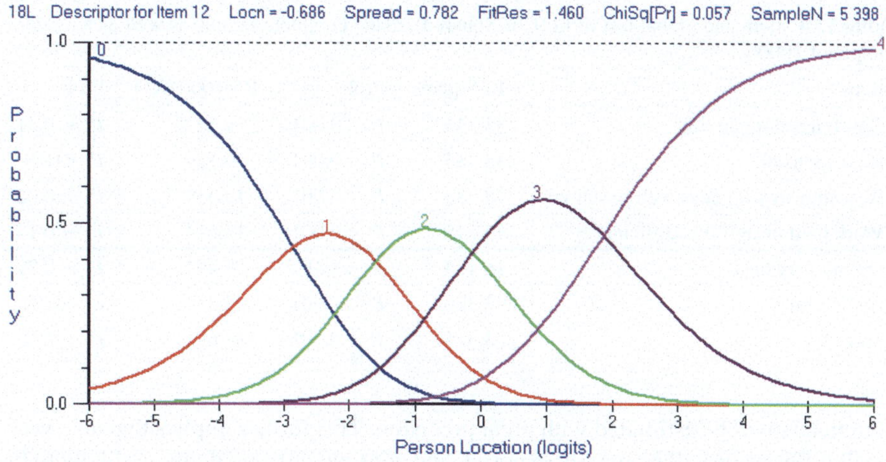

Fig. 13.3 An example of a category probability curve (using item 5: "Do my very best")

followed by item 1 "Get things done in time", with respect to their mean locations along the latent trait. They are thus reflecting lower degrees of social responsibility goal orientations. On the contrary, item 3 "Be a student who does well in school" and item 4 "work hard even if it is difficult" are the two hardest items reflecting students with strong social responsibility goal orientations. From Table 13.3 it can also be observed that there are no reversed item thresholds, i.e., the empirical ordering of thresholds are the same as the expected, and the response categories are working in the same way as intended.

Figure 13.3 shows an example of a Category Probability Curve (CPC) illustrating how the response categories work for a specific item (Do my very best). Thus, there should be a location a long the latent trait where each response category is the most likely. Thus, given locations at the beginning of the latent trait (e.g. at −5 logits, reflecting weak orientations) the most likely response would be in the "Never/almost never" category. For a person located at −2 logits, the most likely response is into the "Rarely" category, while a person located at 1 logit, or 4 logit the most likely responses would into the "Often" or "Always/almost always" categories, respectively. In a situation with reversed item thresholds, this empirical ordering does not apply. An example of this may be in a situation when the response category "Rarely" empirically would be located before the "Never/almost never" category.

Item Fit

In Table 13.4, the Chi-Squared item fit using 10 class interval is displayed, using the complete sample as well as a random sample of 1000 persons. Chi-Squared statistics is very sensitive to sample size. Thus, when using a large sample size, the

Table 13.4 Item and global test of fit (Chi-Squared), using complete sample as well as a random sample of 1000

Item	Chi-Square	Prob.	RS 1000 (X^2)	Prob.
Get things done in time	33.333	$P < 0.001$	9.352	$P = 0.41$
Be responsible	233.785	$P < 0.001$	39.184	$P < 0.01$
Be a student who does well in school	98.739	$P < 0.001$	19.559	$P = 0.02$
Work hard even if it is difficult	47.645	$P < 0.001$	13.614	$P = 0.14$
Do my very best	16.483	$P = 0.057$	5.491	$P = 0.79$
Be helpful	293.326	$P < 0.001$	45.431	$P < 0.01$
Total X^2	723.311	$P < 0.001$	132.60	$P < 0.01$

parameters will be estimated with great precision. This further implies that also very small differences will be readily exposed, and consequently, no items are likely to fit the model (Andrich, 1988). Therefore, it is conceivable that when using the complete sample containing more than 5,000 persons, the large sample size may influence the statistical test of fit results. As can be seen in Table 13.4, using the complete sample all items but one (Do my very best) show substantial misfit to the Polytomous Rasch Model. In particular item 6 (be helpful) and item 2 (be responsible) show severe misfit to the model. Using a random sample of 1,000 persons degreases the size of the Chi-Square values substantially. Using this approach, the worst and best fitting items are the same. Further, the two worst fitting items both still show *p*-values far below 0.01, which is also true for the global (total X^2) test of fit. Thus, it is not likely that the misfit shown to be due to sample size, regarding these two items.

In Fig. 13.4a–f, the Item Characteristic Curves (ICC) for the six items are shown. The ICCs show the expected response to a specific item given the respondents location along the latent trait. Therefore, the ICCs are useful in order to observe response patterns on individual items on a common latent trait. Thus, in item 2 (be responsible), the ICC reveals that this item discriminate more than expected according to the model. Thus, students located in the lower end of the latent trait are scoring lower than expected, whereas students located in the higher end of the same latent trait score higher than expected. The opposite pattern is true for item 6 (Be helpful). On other items the observations are close to the expected curve.

Thus, on empirical grounds it is reasonable to exclude item 2 and item 6 from the model, due to the fact that they show substantial misfit according to the model. However, this may also be justified from a conceptual point of view. All other items regards the actual learning process and the student role whereas item 2 and item 6 are more general and less specific. For instance, it may be difficult to interpret what is meant by being a responsible student or being helpful, in what situations and to which person. Therefore, it is not very clear how these two items may be connected to the actual learning process or the student role.

Therefore, item 2 and item 6 was removed from the model based on the empirical and conceptual arguments, thus retaining only the four items listed in Table 13.5.

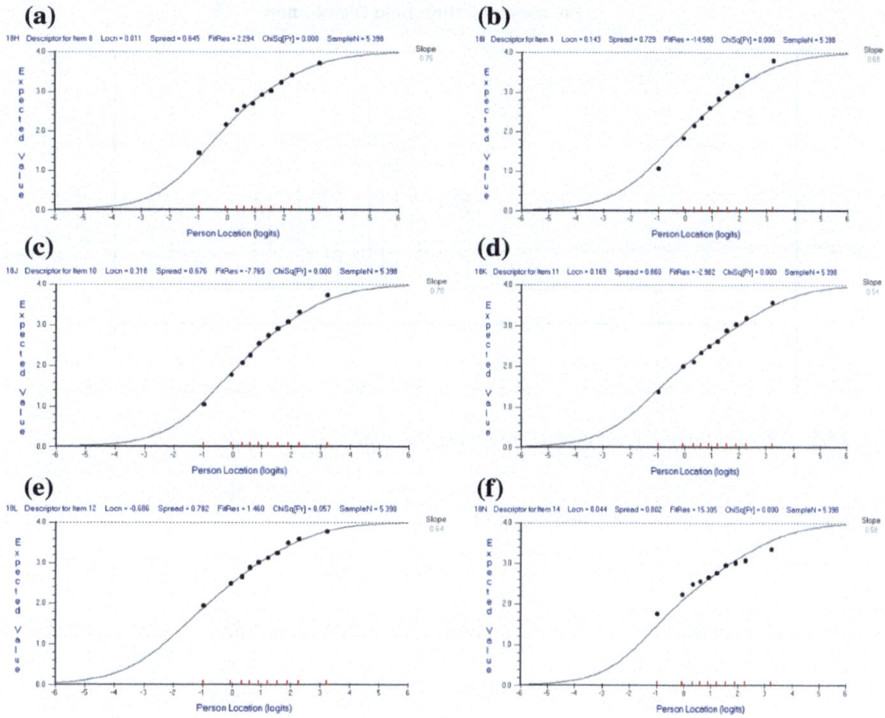

Fig. 13.4 **a** Get things done in time (Item 1). **b** Be responsible (Item 2). **c** Be a student who does well in school (Item 3). **d** Work hard even if it is difficult (Item 4). **e** Do my very best (Item 5). **f** Be helpful (Item 6)

Table 13.5 Remaining items

Items
How often are you trying to do the following in school:
Item 1: *Get things done in time*
Item 3: *Be a student who does well in school*
Item 4: *Work hard even if it is difficult*
Item 5: *Do my very best*

The remaining items may be considered to measure adherence to expectations of being a good student, thus conforming to the student role.

Figure 13.5 shows the person-item threshold distribution after removing item 2 (Be responsible) and item 6 (Be helpful). Thus, from Fig. 13.5 it is clear that the distribution using the retained four items is similar as to the original person-item distribution (mean location of persons 1.2). However, the item reduction also reduces the PSI-value somewhat, from 0.81 to 0.74 based on only four items.

Table 13.6 shows the item locations and item thresholds in the new situation using only four items. Thus, in this model item 5 (Do my very best) is still the easiest item,

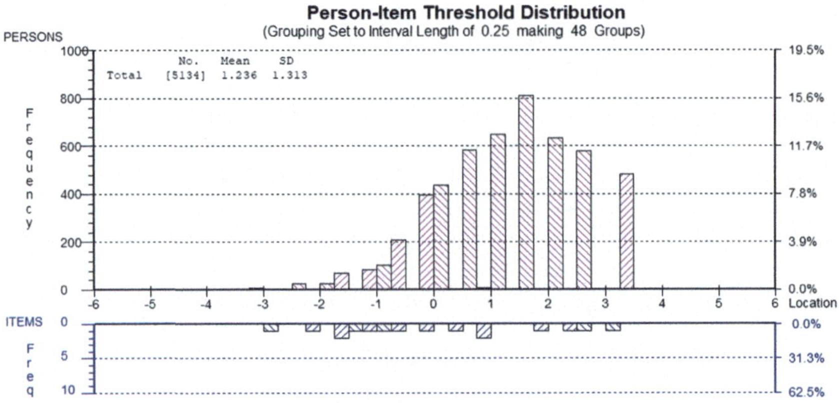

Fig. 13.5 Person item distribution after removing two items

Table 13.6 Item locations and item thresholds

Thresholds					
Item	Location	1	2	3	4
Get things done in time	0.060	−1.720	−0.856	0.242	2.334
Be a student who does well in school	0.391	−1.771	−0.988	0.473	2.285
Work hard even if it is difficult	0.227	−2.351	−1.294	0.685	2.959
Do my very best	−0.678	−2.301)	−0.924	0.584	2.641

and item 3 (Be a student who does well in school) is the hardest item. This means that the item location order is the same as in the original model. In this new situation, also, no reversed item thresholds can be observed, implying that the empirical ordering of the response categories are the same as intended, thus the response categories work as intended.

Table 13.7 shows the Chi-Squared statistical test of fit revisited. The test of global (total) fit is improved substantially compared to in the original model. It is also notable that Item 1 (Get things done in time) and Item 3 (Be a student who does well

Table 13.7 Item and global test of fit (Chi-Squared), using complete sample as well as a random sample of 1000

Item	Chi-Square	Prob.	RS 1000 (X^2)	Prob.
Get things done in time	28.905	$P = 0.0003$	8.142	$P = 0.32$
Be a student who does well in school	51.811	$P < 0.001$	14.031	$P = 0.06$
Work hard even if it is difficult	59.794	$P < 0.001$	10.107	$P = 0.18$
Do my very best	24.211	$P = 0.002$	8.968	$P = 0.25$
Total X^2	164.721	$P < 0.001$	41.249	$P = 0.051$

in school) shows improvement in this reduced model. However, Item 4 (Work hard even if it is difficult) and item 5 (Do my very best) are misfitting a bit more in this new situation. Thus, despite that the new model shows improved fit, overall, two items show increased misfit, while two items show improvements due to the exclusion of the two worst fitting items from the original model. Thus, in this new situation all items are misfitting, using the complete sample of about 5,000 individuals. However, using a random sample of 1000 individuals all items show Chi-Square values corresponding to *P*-values greater than 0.01. From Table 13.7 it is also clear that the overall (total) test of fit is non-significant using a random sample of 1000 individuals. It can also be seen that the two best and worst fitting items are the same in the analysis as when using the complete sample.

However, one should always be cautious using single random samples, due to the uncertainties connected to random variation. In the examples here, random samples are merely used in order to understand the influence that large samples may have on statistical test of fit analysis.

In Fig. 13.6a–d, the ICC curves for the remaining four items is Shown. Thus, the overall pattern is that the observed values in the 10 class intervals are very close to what is expected by the Rasch model. However, regarding Item 1 (Get things done in time), the response pattern reveals that students located in the beginning of the latent trait are prone to respond with a higher value than expected. Thus, in class interval 1–4 the observed mean value is located slightly above the expected curve. Therefore, this item is discriminating a bit less than expected, and consequently it also show a positive fit residual. Regarding item 4 (work hard even if it is difficult), there is an opposite pattern. This item discriminates a bit more than expected, which is also confirmed by its negative fit residual. Thus, students located in the beginning (class

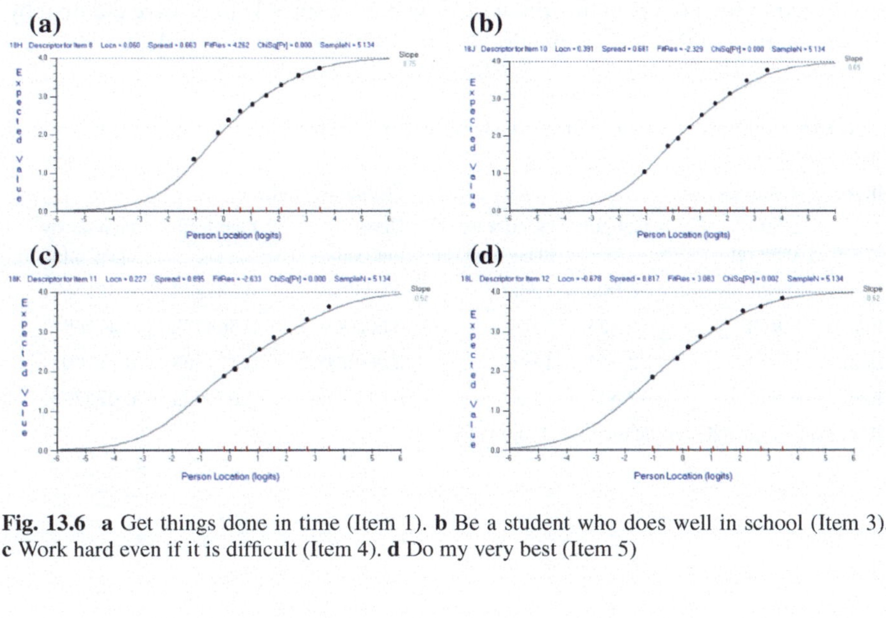

Fig. 13.6 **a** Get things done in time (Item 1). **b** Be a student who does well in school (Item 3). **c** Work hard even if it is difficult (Item 4). **d** Do my very best (Item 5)

interval 1–4) of the latent trait (weak social responsibility goal orientation), score a lower value than expected on this specific item. The overall pattern also reveals that Item 1 and Item 5 have a similar pattern in that they both discriminates less than expected whereas Item 4 and Item 3 discriminates at bit more than expected.

Differential Item Functioning (DIF)

Differential Item Functioning can be analysed both graphically and statistically, and so has been done in this study. Statistically, Two-Way Analysis of Variance of residual (ANOVA) has ben used in order to find out whether the items work invariantly across subgroups of individuals. In particular one item showed a significant DIF effect by sex, using the statistical approach. In Table 13.8, the interpretation of the F-values shown in the column labeled Class Interval, should be equivalent to those of the Chi-Squared statistical test reported earlier. Thus, it can be seen that Item 5 and Item 1 is the best fitting items whereas Item 3 and Item 4 show worse fit. It is also possible to confirm from the ANOVA-table that the item order with respect to probability values are the same in the Chi-Squared test of fit as in the ANOVA version of the test fit.

In Table 13.8 it can also be seen that Item 5 (Do my very best) is the only item showing a significant DIF effect. It can further be seen that there were no gender by class interval interaction regarding DIF. In Fig. 13.7 the analysis of DIF is depicted graphically. Thus, from Fig. 13.8, it can be seen that girls score higher than boys on this particular item.

It is also found in other studies that girls generally adhere to social expectations as reflected in Item 6. From that point of view it is reasonable to resolve the item by gender, i.e. to split the item by gender. In Fig. 13.8 this operation is depicted.

Table 13.8 Analysis of variance of residuals for test of DIF between genders as well as test of class interval fit

Item	*F*-values			Probability values		
	Class interval	Gender	Gender by class interval	Class interval	Gender	Gender by class interval
Item 1	2.687	0.006	1.569	0.005942	0.937823	0.321367
Item 3	6.910	0.325	1.021	0.000000	0.568726	0.417691
Item 4	9.469	2.536	1.608	0.000000	0.111268	0.117003
Item 5	2.462	17.543	1.781	0.011620	0.000025	0.075796

Bonferony adjusted significance level: 0.004167

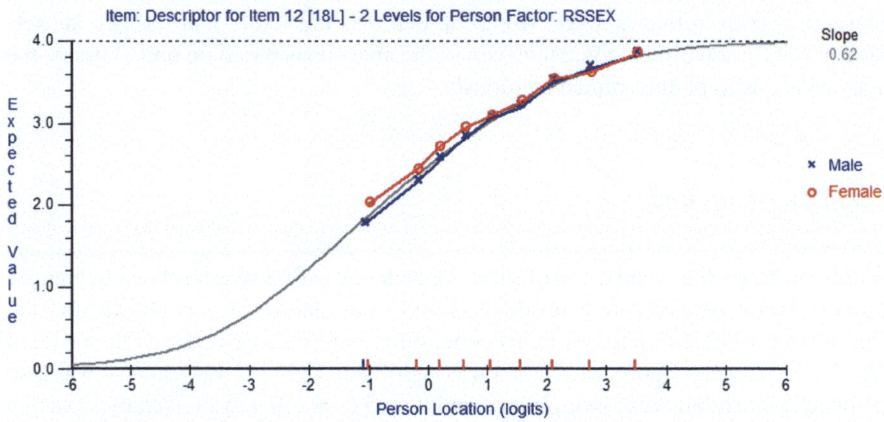

Fig. 13.7 ICC showing differential item functioning on item "Do my very best"

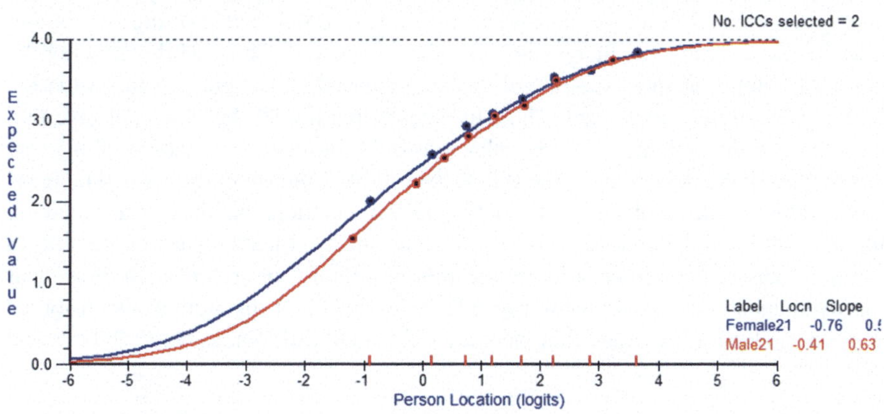

Fig. 13.8 ICC showing differential item functioning on item "Do my very best", resolved by splitting the item by gender

Dimensionality

Principal component analyses were undertaken in order to study the dimensionality of the analysed latent trait. The PCA-analysis was undertaken in order to group the items according to their PC-loadings. Thus, Item 1 (Get things done in time) and Item 5 (Do my very best) were grouped together whereas Item 3 (Be a student who does well in school) and Item 4 (Work hard even if it is difficult) were formed an another group, based on the PCA analysis. The person locations in each of these item subsets of items were where compared using *t*-tests. However, the proportions of significant *t*-tests did not exceed the critical value of 5%. This means that the person locations in the two supsets of items are not significantly different from each other. Thus, the interpretation from that analysis would be that it is not likely that the two subsets belong to different dimension. However, as the analysis is based on only 4 items, the analysis needs to be interpreted cautiously.

Local Dependency

In order to study the occurrence of local dependency, a first step has been to analyse the correlation between item residuals. From that analysis it was shown that the four items formed two pairs of items containing two items each. Thus, the residual correlation between Item 1 and Item 4 was significant ($r = -0.451$), and so was also the residual correlation between Item 3 and Item 5 ($r = -0.425$). Given these strong correlations, it is likely that the items within each item pair to be locally dependent.

In order to distinguish trait dependency and response dependency, a strategy is to combine dependent items into higher order items (Marais & Andrich, 2008). In the analysis conducted here, the dependent items were combined forming two higher order items. In doing so changes in PSI-values appeared. Thus, while reducing the number of items in most cases will cause decreased PSI-values, in this situation the PSI-was slightly increased. Thus, in the original model that does not take into account local dependency, the PSI-value was 0.74. In this new situation taking into account also local dependency, the PSI-value is 0.78. Consequently, a small increase in PSI-values could be observed. From Fig. 13.9 it is evident that the operation taking into account local dependency have made clear improvements regarding item fit. In a similar manner the higher order item combining Item 3 and Item 5 also show clear improvements, which is shown in Fig. 13.10. In Fig. 13.11 this item is also resolved by gender. Thus, it is evident that there are only small differences between boys and girls.

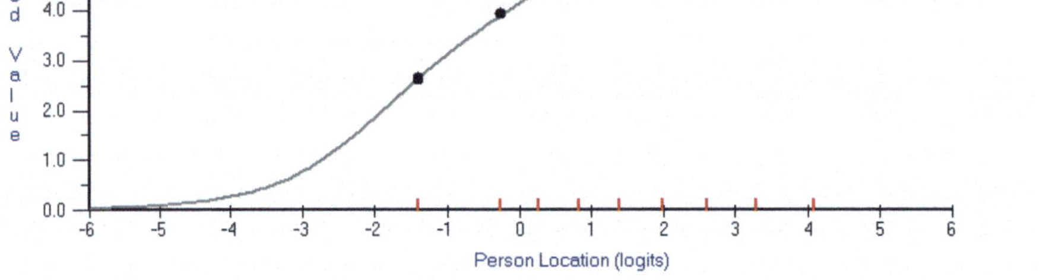

Fig. 13.9 ICC showing the combined item including Item 1 (Get things done in time) and Item 4 (Work hard even if it is difficult)

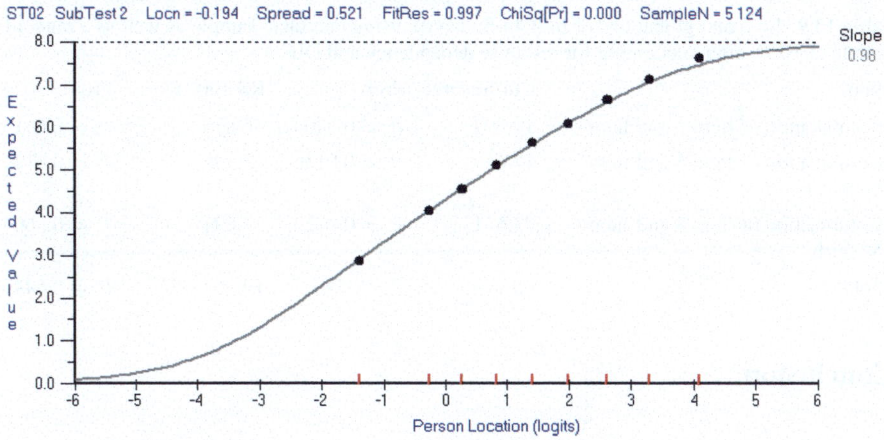

Fig. 13.10 ICC showing the combined item including Item 3 (Be a student who does well in school) and Item 5 (Do my very best)

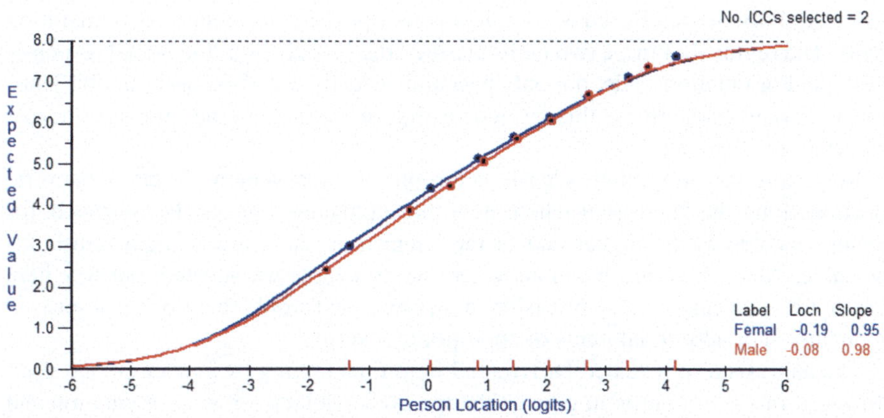

Fig. 13.11 ICC showing the combined item including Item 1 (Get things done in time) and Item 4 (Work hard even if it is difficult), resolved by gender

Global and Item Test of Fit Revisited

In Table 13.9, test of fit is analysed again, after accounting for local dependency and Differential Item Functioning (DIF). From this analysis, it is clear that taking into account the local dependency as well as the Differential Item Functioning, was very beneficial from a statistical point of view. However, using the complete sample the combination of item 3 and 5 still show a significant P-value below the critical level of 0.00333 using the Bonferroni correction. Using a random sample of 1000 all items fit the model, and also the global fit show a non-significant result.

Table 13.9 Item and global test of fit (Chi-Squared), using complete sample as well as a random sample of 1000, after accounting for response dependency and DIF

Item	Chi-Square	Prob.	RS 1000 (X^2)	Prob.
Combination of Item 1 and Item 4	19.607	$P = 0.0204$	6.875	$P = 0.651$
Combination of Item 3 and Item 5—boys	17.661	$P = 0.0136$	5.395	$P = 0.612$
Combination of Item 3 and Item 5—girls	23.511	$P = 0.0013$	7.694	$P = 0.360$
Total X^2	60.779	$P < 0.001$	19.964	$P = 0.644$

Conclusion

The analysis presented in this chapter was based on items developed within a confirmatory factor analysis framework in a different context, and by using a different age and student cohort than the one subjected to analysis here. At first glance the original model seemed to work fairly well. However, after been subjected to analysis under the Polytomous Rasch Model, it was first possible to identify two misfitting items. The removal of these two items clarified the properties of the Social responsibility goal orientation scale, not only psychometrically but also conceptually. Thus, it is more reasonable to use this revised version of the scale to measure student role expectation adherence.

Regarding targeting, there clearly is a room of improvement. There are several location along the latent trait where item thresholds are missing. For instance, for persons located in the higher end of the latent trait, there are no item thresholds available. Also, there are locations where many people are located, but few item thresholds are available. The precision of measurement would therefore be improved by inclusion of additional items of appropriate severity.

The analysis also revealed Differential Item Functioning by gender on one item. However, this is not surprising given the research available on goal orientation and gender, showing that girls commonly score higher than boys in items connected to aspects of student role adherence. It therefore be important to realize that the student role of boys and girls may be interpreted differently.

Finally, the analysis also showed that items within two pairs of items where locally dependent on each other. Thus, the response to one item may be governed by the response to the other item. This problem was handled by the creation of two "super items" where the two dependent items were combined. After taking these actions, the now revised Social responsibility scale works better according to the polytomous Rasch Model.

References

Andrich, D. (1978). A rating formulation for ordered response categories. *Psychometrika, 43*(4), 561–573.

Andrich, D. (1982). An index of person separation in latent trait theory, the traditional KR-20 index, and the Guttman scale response pattern. *Educational Research and Perspectives, 1982*(9:1), 95–104.

Andrich, D. (1988). *Rasch models for measurement*. Newbury Park: Sage Publications.

Andrich, D., Humphry, S., & Marais, I. (2012). Quantifying local, response dependence between two polytomous items using the Rasch model. *Applied Psychological Measurement, 36*(4), 309–324.

Andrich, D., Sheridan, B., & Luo, G. (2013). *RUMM2030: A windows program for the Rasch unidimensional measurement model*. Perth, Western Australia: RUMM Laboratory.

Bergh, D. (2015a). Chi-Squared test of fit and sample size—A comparison between a random sample approach and a Chi-square value adjustment method. *Journal of Applied Measurement, 16*(2), 204–217.

Bergh, D. (2015b). Sample size and Chi-Squared test of fit—A comparison between a random sample approach and a chi-square value adjustment method using Swedish adolescent data. In Q. Zhang & H. Yang (Eds.), *Pacific Rim Objective Measurement Symposium (PROMS) 2014 Conference Proceedings: Rasch and the Future* (pp. 197–211). Berlin, Heidelberg: Springer, Berlin Heidelberg.

Bergh, D., & Giota, J. (2018). *The social responsibility goal orientation—An analysis of the psychometric properties of a scale using adolescent data from Sweden*. Paper presented at the Seventh International Conference on Probabilistic Models of Measurement Developments with Rasch Models, Perth, Australia.

Cronbach, L. (1951). Coefficient alpha and the internal structure of tests. *Psychometrica,* (16), 297–334.

Giota, J. (2001). *Adolescents' perceptions of school and reasons for learning*. Göteborg: Acta Universitatis Gothoburgensis.

Giota, J. (2010). Multidimensional and hierarchical assessment of adolescent' motivation in school. *Scandinavian Journal of Educational Research, 54*(1), 83–97.

Marais, I., & Andrich, D. (2008). Formalizing dimension and response violations of local independence in the unidimensional Rasch model. *Journal of Applied Measurement, 9*(3), 200–2015.

Rasch, G. (1960/1980). *Probabilistic models fore some intelligence and attainment tests* (Copenhagen, Danish Institute for Educational Research). Expanded edition (1980) with foreword and afterword by Benjamin D. Wright. Chicago: The University of Chicago Press.

Rawlings, A. M., Tapola, A., & Niemivirta, M. (2017). Predictive effects of temperament on motivation. *Efectos Predictivos del Temperamento en la Motivación, 6*(2), 148.

Senko, C. (2016). Achievement goal theory. A story of early promises, eventual discords, and future possibilities. In K. R. Wentzel & D. B. Miele (Eds.), *Handbook of motivation at school*. New York: Routledge.

Smith, E. V. J. (2002). Detectinng and evaluating the impact of multidimensionality using item fit statistics and principal component analysis of residuals. *Journal of Applied Measurement, 3*(2), 205–231.

Svensson, A. (2011). Utvärdering genom uppföljning. Longitudinell individforskning under ett halvsekel [Evaluation through follow up. Longitudinal individual research during half a century]. *Acta Universitatis Gotoburgensis,* (305).

Traub, R. E., & Rowley, G. L. (1991). Understanding reliability. *Educational Measurement: Issues and Practice.*

Wentzel, K. R. (1991). Relations between social competence and academic achievement in early adolescence. *Child Development,* (5), 1066. https://doi.org/10.2307/1131152.

Wentzel, K. R. (1993). Does being good make the grade? Social behavior and academic competence in middle school. *Journal of Educational Psychology, 85*(2), 357–364.

Wright, B. D., & Masters, G. N. (1982). *Rating scale analysis*. Chicago: MESA Press.

Chapter 14
Using Graphical Loglinear Rasch Models to Investigate the Construct Validity of the Perceived Stress Scale

Tine Nielsen and Pedro Henrique Ribeiro Santiago

Abstract The Rasch model has been generalized and extended into what is now known as the class of Rasch models. In this chapter, we will explain in nontechnical terms the extension known as graphical loglinear Rasch models (GLLRM), which can be used to test model with departures from the pure Rasch model in terms of uniform local dependence (LD) or uniform differential item functioning (DIF). To demonstrate the utility of these models, we display the psychometric properties of the perceived stress scale (PSS) in two studies conducted in Australia and Denmark. Although the studies differed in cultural context, nature of the sample (nationally representative n = 3,857 and higher education students n = 1,552), and version of the PSS used (PSS-14 and PSS-10), consistent results were found. The analysis showed that the PSS consists of two subscales (Perceived Stress and Perceived Lack of Control), which is congruent with previous CFA literature. In addition, in both countries Items 7 and 10 were locally dependent and Items 1 and 3 displayed DIF by gender. For the Australian nationally representative sample, targeting was poor for both subscales, while for the Danish sample of higher education students targeting was excellent. Implications regarding the application of the PSS are discussed.

Keywords Perceived stress scale · Rasch model · Graphical loglinear Rasch model · Construct validity · Differential item functioning

Introduction

The Rasch model (RM; Rasch, 1960) is by some regarded as a statistical model with a latent variable, by some as a unique measurement model, and by some as a special case of the class of item response theory models (Christensen, Kreiner, & Mesbah, 2013). The authors of this chapter adhere to the broad view combining the three, as we regard the RM as the most parsimonious statistical measurement model

T. Nielsen (✉)
University of Copenhagen, Copenhagen, Denmark
e-mail: tine.nielsen@psy.ku.dk

P. H. R. Santiago
University of Adelaide, Adelaide, SA, Australia

M. S. Khine (ed.), *Rasch Measurement*,
https://doi.org/10.1007/978-981-15-1800-3_14

with a latent variable in the class of item response theory (IRT) models (Fischer & Molenaar, 1994; van der Linden & Hambleton, 1997). The Rasch model was originally developed for use with dichotomous (i.e., binary) items and for analyzing responses to ability tests (Kreiner, 2013; Olsen, 2001; Rasch, 1960). Some of the earliest work of Rasch, which led to what we now know as the Rasch model was concerned with measurement of abilities in educational and other ability testing settings, e.g., reading ability of children, which were slow readers, and cognitive abilities and intelligence of young men at the time of conscription for the Danish army (Kreiner, 2013; Olsen, 2001; Teasdale, 2009). The Rasch model is employed as a confirmatory measurement model, where the objective is to test whether data complies with the Rasch model and its assumptions, so that we can know whether the measurement scale under investigation has the gold standard properties following from fit to the Rasch model or not. How many of the assumptions of the Rasch model are formally tested, and the statistics used for this purpose, depends on the software implementation used in specific analysis, and thus also how many of the assumptions are inferred from the fit to the model rather than tested directly. This has shifted over time, so that it is now possible to test all assumptions in newer implementations (and these are still developing), whereas assumptions were more likely inferred from fit to the model in older software implementations.

The assumptions of the Rasch model for dichotomous items are (Kreiner, 2013): (a) unidimensionality, in the sense that the set of items measure a single latent construct. (b) Monotonicity, meaning that the probability of a correct or positive response to an item will increase as the score of the person parameter increases. (c) Consistency, such that all items in a scale are positively correlated. (d) Local independence, in the sense that all items are conditionally independent given the score on the latent variable. (e) No differential item functioning (DIF), meaning that items are conditionally independent of any (relevant) background variable given the score on the latent variable, or put differently that responses to an item should not differ systematically for subgroups of respondents if these are at the same level on the latent construct being measured. (f) Homogeneity, in the sense that the rank order of the item difficulties should be the same for all respondents.

The consequences of fit of a set of item responses to the Rasch model are that (1) the summed raw score is a sufficient statistics for the estimated person parameter (the Rasch score, if you will), and (2) the measurement scale is specifically objectivity (Rasch, 1961). Both of these properties are exclusively the result of fit to the Rasch model, not any other IRT model (Kreiner, 2007; Mesbah & Kreiner, 2013; Tennant & Conaghan, 2007), and we consider them highly desirable properties, because of what they entail for the measurement scale in question. Statistical sufficiency of the raw sum score means that all information on the person parameter is contained in the sum score, so that the conditional distribution of item responses given the total score does not depend on the estimated person parameter (Nielsen, Nyholm Kyvsgaard, Møller Sildorf, Kreiner, & Svensson, 2017—technical supplement). This is a desirable property for some users and in some applications where the sum scores are preferred for ease of interpretation or other reasons. Fit to the Rasch model means that there is a one-to-one relationship between the raw scores and the so-called Rasch scores. The one-to-one relationship between the scores is what is used to convert the raw scores to the Rasch scores, which are typically on a logit scale and thus usually construed as an interval scale. The logit scale is often preferred for its interval scale properties. However, if the scale in question is a very short one with few items and thus a narrow range, it might also be argued that the actual scale, even though it is a logit scale, is somewhat less than an interval scale and somewhat more than an ordinal scale. Furthermore, meaningful interpretation of differences is usually difficult as the unit of measurement no longer relates to the instrument. Second, the relationship between raw sum score and person parameters is mostly linear. This means that in many samples the raw scores can provide a reasonable approximation of the person parameters for most of the distribution. Beyond the debate, the property of the raw sum score as a sufficient statistic for the person parameter provides theoretical justification and creates more flexibility for practitioners to choose raw scores over person parameters in their own research—compared to other IRT or psychometric models. We thus leave this discussion here, and leave it up to the individual researcher or practitioner to make up her mind in each case of application. Specific objectivity means that within the *specific* frame of reference of the study conducted (not the entire population) the scale provides objective measurement. Objective in the sense that the comparisons of persons are unbiased by the choice of items, and comparisons of items are unbiased by the choice of persons (Kreiner, 2013; Rasch, 1961). One might phrase it more simply: with a self-efficacy scale the result of comparing persons' level of self-efficacy should not depend on the choice of self-efficacy items, and the result of comparing the difficulty level of the items should not depend on the sampling of persons. This is possible, because the Rasch model analysis is conducted within a conditional frame of inference, which makes it possible to separate item parameters from person parameters (Kreiner, 2013).

Some Generalizations of the Rasch Model to Polytomous Items

The Rasch model for polytomous items (PRM) was first introduced by Rasch himself at a symposium in Berkely in 1960 (Andersen, 1994) and then formally proposed by Andersen, one of Rasch's students (Mesbah & Kreiner, 2013). The PRM was later proposed in a different parameterization by Masters (1982) as the so-called partial credit model (PCM). Furthermore, a slightly different version of the PRM/PCM—slightly since it only differs in the notion that the item thresholds should be equal rather than free to differ—was proposed with the so-called rating scale model (RSM; Andrich, 1978). As there is no reason why item thresholds should be the same in many of the nonability scales used in psychology, social science, or epidemiology, referring to our later example, there is no reason that the point on the latent scale where the probability of choosing on response is equal to the probability of choosing the next response category (i.e., an item threshold) should be the same for all items. The PRM and the PCM are based on the same assumptions as the RM for dichotomous items; therefore, a scale fitting the PCM retains the same properties as a scale fitting the dichotomous RM (Kreiner, 2013; Mesbah & Kreiner, 2013). In the analysis part of this chapter, we simply use the term RM for Rasch model, when employing a polytomous Rasch model.

Some Extensions of the Rasch Model

In addition, the Rasch model has been extended to multivariate, and mixture Rasch models to deal with more than one scale, where each scale is a Rasch scale and the correlation between subscales are included in the model (von Davier & Carstensen, 2007). These models can both serve as multidimensional Rasch models and as longitudinal Rasch models depending on how they are used (von Davier & Carstensen, 2007). The Rasch model for a scale and time point has also been extended. The specific extension which we are concerned within this chapter is that of the graphical loglinear Rasch models (Kreiner & Christensen, 2002, 2004, 2007), which combines loglinear Rasch models (e.g., Kelderman, 1984) with graphical Rasch models (Kreiner, 1993).

Graphical Loglinear Rasch Model

The development of the graphical loglinear Rasch model was a result of combining the loglinear Rasch model (Keldermann, 1984, 1997) with the graphical Rasch model (Kreiner, 1993).

With the graphical Rasch model Kreiner (1993) extended instrument validation by the Rasch model (i.e., measurement model) to include the associations of the instrument with exogenous variables (i.e., criterion validity or simple association) (Fig. 14.1, left panel). In the example of perceived stress, this allows for both a validation analysis of a set of items assumed to make up a perceived stress scale by the Rasch model, including analysis of conditional independence of items, and items and exogenous variables (i.e. LD and DIF), and at the same time investigating how this measure is associated with, for example, gender, age, workplace, etc. For further details, we refer to Kreiner (1993).

The loglinear Rasch model (Keldermann, 1984), later extended for polytomous items (Keldermann, 1997), allowed to incorporate two specific departures from the Rasch model; uniform local dependence and uniform DIF, as interaction terms in the Rasch model. Thus, it was possible to test the fit of a set of item responses to a loglinear Rasch model rather than just a Rasch model. With the same example of perceived stress, this allows not only to test whether items function differentially with regard to gender but also to include gender-DIF terms in the model, if this is indeed the case, and thus testing whether the perceived stress items fit a Rasch model for females and another Rasch model for males. In the same manner, the loglinear Rasch model allows both to test whether items are locally dependent, and if not to include

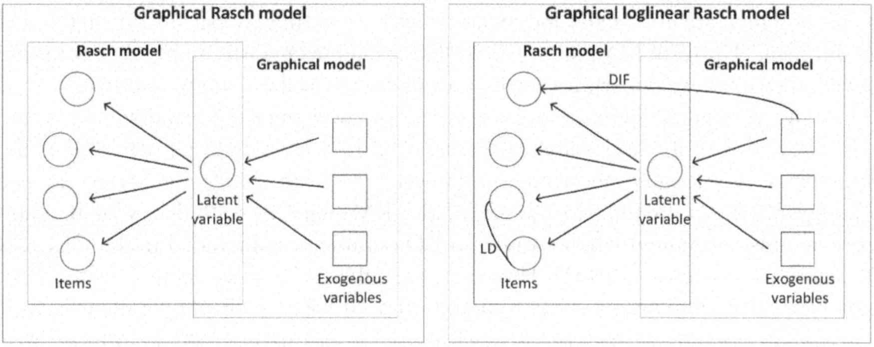

Fig. 14.1 Illustrations of the graphical Rasch model (left) assuming conditional independence (i.e., no LD and no DIF), and the graphical loglinear Rasch model (right) allowing local dependence and/or DIF

a LD-term in the model for which fit of the perceived stress items are tested. This parametrization of uniform DIF and/or LD thus provides important benefits when doing item analyses, namely, formal statistical testing of both DIF and LD on the entire study sample as well fit to the entire loglinear Rasch model with the interaction terms included, as neither splitting items (for DIF) nor creating composite items (of LD items) are necessary during analysis.

The graphical loglinear Rasch model combined these models, as described by Kreiner and Christensen (2002) and illustrated in the right-hand panel of Fig. 14.1:

> *Rasch models describing the dependence of item responses on the latent variable. There are no exogenous variables* [background variables defining subgroups for DIF-analysis, ed.] *in this family of models. Items are assumed to be locally dependent.*
>
> *Graphical Rasch models are models with both items and exogenous variables. Items are assumed to be unbiased and locally independent. The model decomposes into a measurement component—a Rasch model—and a graphical model describing associations between the latent variable and the exogenous variables.*
>
> *Loglinear and graphical Rasch models* [what we now term graphical loglinear Rasch models, ed.] *are models permitting uniform local dependence and uniform item bias* [DIF, ed.]. *That is, association among items and exogenous variables that do not depend on the latent variable.* (Kreiner & Christensen, 2002, pp. 195, original underlining).

In this way, the GLLRM integrates the Rasch model (relationship between items and latent trait), the graphical Rasch model (relationship between items, latent trait, and exogenous variables) and loglinear Rasch model (parametrization of uniform LD and uniform DIF) into a single set of statistical tools for item analysis (Fig. 14.1).

In short, the graphical loglinear Rasch model extends the RM with additional interaction parameters to incorporate uniform LD and uniform DIF into the model. In our work with instruments that do not measure abilities, but rather psychological traits, states, conditions, and symptom collections, measured with relatively short scales, we consider the GLLRM an extremely useful alternative to simply discard items that do not fit the Rasch model. The GLLRM allows us to retain items involved in DIF or which are not locally independent, as long as these departures from the RM are uniform.[1] Uniform LD and uniform DF does not necessarily imply that items are flawed, though these departures have consequences for the scale in question.

Locally dependent items convey less information than independent items and thus will result in a lower reliability compared to what would be achieved if the same items were locally independent (Hamon & Mesbah, 2002). Local dependence does not affect the distinctive feature of the RM, namely, sufficiency of the sum score, as this is retained when a uniform LD parameter is included in the GLLRM (Kreiner & Christensen, 2002). However, the other distinctive feature of the RM, namely specific objectivity, is not retained for a GLLRM with LD parameters, as it is no longer possible to select items (within the scale) in a complete arbitrary way (Kreiner & Christensen, 2007). Exclusion of just one locally dependent item, rather than both, will mean that the remaining items no longer fit the Rasch model (Kreiner & Christensen, 2007).

The consequences of DIF are (potentially) more severe. In the GLLRM itself, sufficiency of the sum score is retained within the subgroups, when a uniform DIF parameter is included (Kreiner & Christensen, 2002). In the case of DIF, specific objectivity is no longer retained in the strict sense, as again it is not possible to select items arbitrarily, as DIF would be present (or disappear) dependent on the selection of items (Kreiner & Christensen, 2007). However, for subsequent comparison of scores between subgroups, the scores of some subgroups will be biased and this might lead to wrong conclusions on group differences, depending on the severity of the DIF. Thus to extend the use of scores beyond the measurement model, a conversion table showing how the person parameters in each of the subgroups involved in DIF are related to the sum score should be provided. For the same purpose, the sum score should, in all DIF-subgroups except a reference group, be equated for DIF. The latter can be done via the person parameter values in the subgroups (Kreiner & Christensen, 2002, 2007, Kreiner & Nielsen, 2013).

Thus, both in the case of uniform DIF and in the case of uniform LD, the items still serve the purpose of measuring the latent construct and could be retained. Whether the described consequences of retaining items in a GLLRM with LD and/or DIF rather than throwing them away is considered a small or expensive price to pay for, we leave it up to the individual researchers. Here, we suffice to say that we in many cases, including the example analyses in this chapter, have considered the price low. Thus, we have followed the suggestion of Kreiner and Christensen (2007) to term this essential validity and essential objectivity, as we think in these cases measurement is not invalid or afflicted by systematic error due to arbitrary decisions in scale construction, as long as the appropriate adjustments are made.

Another advantage of using the GLLRM is that the uniform LD and DIF discovered with analysis by GLLRM can contribute valuable information as how to modify items toward achieving a scale with improved psychometric properties (i.e., Rasch

[1] *"Uniform DIF exists when the statistical relationship between the item response and group is constant for all levels of a matching variable"* (Hanson, 1998, pp. 244.).

model properties or less complex GLLRM), as a strategy for this purpose, and based on GLLRM results, has been proposed by Nielsen and Kreiner (2013).

Strategy of Analysis

The overall strategy of analysis that we apply when conducting item analysis by Rasch and graphical loglinear Rasch models follows these steps. Initially, we test the fit of the set of item responses to the Rasch model (dichotomous or polytomous). This is not a single test of fit, but rather it consists of overall test of homogeneity and DIF, tests of item fit, tests for local independence between items and item-wise tests of DIF (see the next section for details). If fit to the Rasch model is rejected, we then proceeded to catalogue the departures from the RM. If the departures are only in the form of uniform LD and/or DIF, we proceed to test the fit of the item responses to the GLLRM adjusting for these departures, using the same set of "diagnostics" as previously. If fit to the GLLRM is rejected, we either proceed to search for more LD and/or DIF to define another and more complex GLLRM, as we might have missed something, or we eliminate the most problematic item and then run the entire cycle of analysis again.

Statistical Methods

To test the overall homogeneity (i.e., comparison of item parameters in low and high scoring groups) and for a global test of DIF (i.e., comparison of item parameters in subgroups) we use Andersen's (1973) conditional likelihood ratio test (CLR). The fit of individual items is tested by comparing the observed item-rest-score correlations with the expected item-rest-score correlations under the model (Kreiner, 2011), as well as by conditional infit and outfit statistics (Christensen & Kreiner, 2012).

The presence of LD and DIF was tested with conditional tests of independence between item pairs (presence of LD) and between items and exogenous variables (presence of DIF) given the rest-scores (Kreiner & Christensen, 2004). We also used confirmatory tests of no DIF or LD to determine whether all interaction terms were needed. For this purpose we used Keldermann's (1984) likelihood ratio test for each of the included interaction terms, using the GLLRM without a certain term as the null hypothesis and the GLLRM with the term included as the alternative (Kreiner & Nielsen, 2013). With regard to the magnitude of LD and DIF, partial gamma coefficients (Goodman-Kruskal rank correlation, 1954) are used. In the particular software implementation used, these can be reported in two forms; the gamma coefficients resulting from the item screening (Kreiner & Christensen, 2011), which do not take into account any other instances of DIF or LD, as gamma coefficient under the GLLRM (i.e., taking into account the other instances of LD and/or DIF in the model) (Kreiner & Nielsen, 2013). In this chapter, we show the first type, as this allows for better comparison across studies with differing exogenous variables and instances of LD and DIF, and refer the reader to Nielsen and Dammeyer (2019) and Santiago, Nielsen, Smithers, Roberts, and Jamieson (submitted), where the second type is reported.

The Benjamini–Hochberg procedure is used to adjust for false discovery rate (FDR) due to multiple testing, whenever appropriate (Benjamini & Hochberg, 1995).

In GLLRMs reliability is estimated using Hamon and Mesbah's (2002) Monte Carlo approach for reliability taking into account any local response dependence between items to avoid inflation. Targeting is assessed graphically as well as numerically. Numerically, the item target values (i.e., where an item holds most information for the study population or a subgroup, if the item functions differentially) can be compared—these should preferably be spread out along the latent scale. One might also compare the test target values to the mean scores (sum score or person parameter) in the study population or subgroup—these should be close. Finally, two targeting indices can be calculated (Kreiner & Christensen, 2013): The test information target index is the mean test information divided by the maximum test information for theta, and the root mean squared error (RMSE) target index is the minimum standard error of measurement divided by the mean standard error of measurement for theta. Both indices should have a value close to one. Graphical evaluations of targeting are facilitated by item maps plotting the distribution of person parameters against the distribution of the item thresholds onto the latent scale, and the test information function.

We used the DIGRAM software package for all item analyses by Rasch and graphical loglinear Rasch models and the model graphs (Kreiner, 2003; Kreiner & Nielsen, 2013), and we used R for the remaining graphs, while drawing on output from DIGRAM (R Core Team, 2013). The R-code for these graphs was developed by the second author.

The Perceived Stress Scale

In research, the most widely used psychological instrument to measure stress is the perceived stress scale (PSS; Cohen, Kamarck, & Mermelstein, 1983). The PSS was developed aiming to provide a measure of *perceived stress* and as an alternative to the life-event scales which were commonly used at that time, such as the Holmes–Rahe Stress Inventory (Holmes & Rahe, 1967). The Holmes–Rahe Stress Inventory measures the *number of stressful events* experienced by an individual over the last year by applying a predetermined score to items such as "Death of spouse" or "Gain of new family member" based on how stressful these events supposedly are. For example, the event "Death of Spouse" was assigned the score of 100, the item "Death of a close friend" was assigned the score of 37 and the item "Mortgage over $10,000" would correspond to a score of 10. The respondent would then endorse the items that indicate the stressful events he/she experienced last year and stress was measured by summing the scores from each individual event.

The development of the PSS by Cohen, Kamarck, and Mermelstein (1983) was based on a seminal theory by Lazarus' (1966) which emphasized that instead of the number and nature of events experienced, what was important was the individual *perception* of whether the events were stressful or not. Folkman, Lazarus, Dunkel-Schetter, DeLongis, and Gruen (1986) proposed that the stress reaction to an event was not objectively determined by the type of event (e.g., death of a partner, being fired, and among others), but was rather a cognitively mediated process. The rationale was that no event was stressful in itself. Instead for an event to generate a stress reaction, it needed to be *appraised as threatening* and there should be a perception of insufficient *coping resources*. For example, the event "Mortgage over $10.000" might generate different stress reactions according to the respondent's personal income. For a multimillionaire respondent, a mortgage over $10.000 might not necessarily represent a financial burden; hence, the event will not be appraised as threatening and produce a stress reaction. The PSS was initially developed as a 14-item instrument (1983); however, following a validity study in a representative US sample, four items were deleted and the PSS-10 and PSS-4 were created. All the items of the PSS-10 and PSS-4 are items present in the original PSS-14 (Cohen & Williamson, 1988).

Over the past decades, the psychometric properties of the PSS have been extensively studied, mostly by factor analytical studies in many cultures and countries. The majority of studies indicate that the PSS, in all its versions, is composed of two distinct dimensions, the Perceived Stress and Perceived Lack of Control subscales (Lee, 2012). The two dimensions are conceptually consistent with Lazarus' theories about stress (Folkman et al., 1986; Lazarus, 1966). For example, the item "How often during the last month have you felt troubles were piling up so high you could not deal with them?" from the Perceived Stress subscale evaluates events *appraised as threatening*, while the item "How often during the last month have you felt able to handle your personal problems?" evaluates the respondent's *coping resources*. However, despite the reproducibility of the PSS dimensionality across studies, a main concern is that the two-factor solution consistently accounted for less than 50% of the total variance (Lee, 2012). These results suggested that besides the latent traits (i.e., "Perceived Stress" and "Perceived Lack of Control"), there are additional sources influencing the PSS item responses. Since the majority of previous studies focused on dimensionality and reliability, the application of modern item-response theory methods such as the GLLRM to the PSS can easily disclose whether these influences could in fact be something we can adjust for (i.e., uniform LD and/or DIF) or not. In the PSS literature, item-response theory models have only recently been applied (Taylor, 2015) and a few studies have evaluated DIF (Cole, 1999; Dougherty, Cooley, & Davidorf, 2017; Gitchel, Roessler, & Turner, 2011; Lavoie & Douglas, 2012; Taylor, 2015).

To provide an in-depth investigation of the psychometric properties of the PSS, two recent studies using GLLRMs were conducted in two distinct cultures, Australia and Denmark. The GLLRM was chosen to evaluate the psychometric properties of the PSS since the loglinear parameters can precisely indicate other sources of influence on item responses (i.e., DIF and LD interaction parameters) beyond what can be explained by the latent variables (i.e., "Perceived Stress" and "Perceived Lack of

Control"). The full results of the individual studies in Australian and Denmark were reported elsewhere (Nielsen & Dammeyer, 2019; Santiago et al., submitted). In this chapter, we discuss the major similarities across the two studies, their contribution to the PSS literature and the implication of the GLLRMs use for future psychometric research.

Communalities Between Studies

The first study, in Australia, evaluated the psychometric properties of the PSS-14 in a representative sample of the Australian population (n = 3,857). The PSS-14 was applied in the population-based cross-sectional study Australia's National Survey of Adult Oral Health 2004–2006 (Slade, Spencer, & Roberts-Thomson, 2007). The sample was mostly composed of females (62%), participants with tertiary education (67%), employed (59%) and with a mean age of 50.3 years (SD = 14.8).

The second study, in Denmark, evaluated the psychometric properties of the PSS-10, in the Danish consensus translation (Eskildsen et al., 2015), with a sample of 1.552 Danish university students. The sample comprised technical students (n = 935) enrolled at the Danish Technical University (DTU), and who completed the PSS-10 as part of a "big data" social science project (Stopczynski et al. 2014); and psychology students (n = 617) enrolled at the University of Copenhagen (UCPH), who completed the PSS-10 as part of a large student survey in the course Personality Psychology. The sample was equally composed of male and female students (46% female), while the majority of students (80%) were between 20 and 25 years old. In both countries, all participants provided informed consent.

Dimensionality and items: The first commonality between the two studies was dimensionality. In both studies the two dimensions of Perceived Stress (PS) and Perceived Lack of Control (PLC) subscales, which is a general consensus and have been widely reported in psychometric research (Lee, 2012), were confirmed (see Nielsen & Dammeyer, 2019; Santiago et al., submitted, for tests of dimensionality). However, the similarities across Australia and Denmark were not restricted to the number of dimensions, but comprised also the items retained in each subscale (that is, the items which were not excluded due to misfit). In the Australian study, the four items of the PSS-14 removed by Cohen and Williamson (1988) in the development of PSS-10 (PSS14: item 4[2]—*"... dealt successfully with irritating life hassles?"*, item 5—*"...effectively coped with important changes in your life?"*, item 12—*"...found yourself thinking about all the things you have to accomplish?"* and item 13—*"... felt able to control the way you spend your time?"*) performed poorly and were also excluded. Therefore, although the PSS-14 was originally applied in Australia, the items that were retained closely resembled the PSS-10 structure and the Danish

[2]As all items start with the identical text: *"How often during the last month have you...."*, we leave this out when showing items texts.

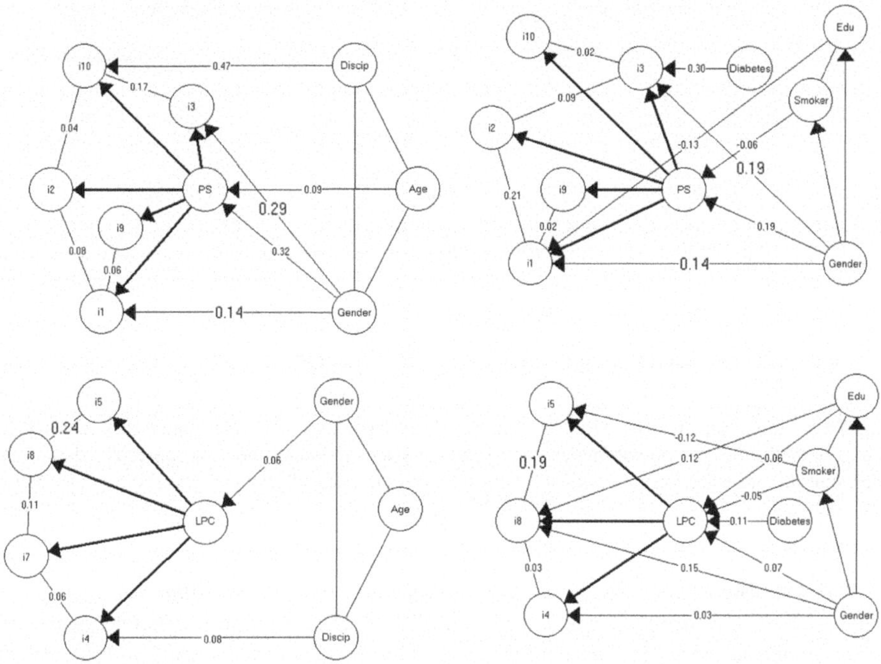

Fig. 14.2 GLLRMs of the Perceived Stress and Perceived Lack of Control subscales in Denmark (left) and Australia (right). *Notes* The Markov graph nodes represent the item numbers, the exogenous variables and the latent trait. Disconnected nodes indicate that variables are conditionally independent and partial γ informs the magnitude of the LD and DIF. Selected γ coefficients are graphically displayed larger to indicate the similarities across studies (e.g., Item 1 DIF by gender in Denmark ($\gamma = 0.14$) and Australia ($\gamma = 0.14$))

study.[3] In both countries, with the expection of item 7, the same items were present in the final GLLRMs for the Perceived Stress and Perceived Lack of Control subscales (Fig. 14.2).

Additionally, Item 6 (*"…found that you could not cope with all the things that you had to do?"*) misfitted in both countries, even when adjusting for false discovery rate due to multiple testing: Denmark (Infit = 1.220, SE = 0.023, p < 0.00001; Outfit = 1.228, SE = 0.036, p < 0.00001; observed item-restscore correlation = 0.526, expected item-restscore correlation = 0.604, SE = 0.017, p < 0.00001; FDR 5% limit = 0.03158, FDR 1% limit = 0.00316); and Australia (Infit = 1.145, SE = 0.023, p < 0.001; Outfit = 1.155, SE = 0.023, p < 0.001; observed item-restscore correlation = 0.555, expected item-restscore correlation = 0.579, SE = 0.010, p = 0.013); FDR 5% limit = , FDR 1% limit =). The Item Characteristic Curves (ICCs) for Item 6 are displayed in Fig. 14.3.

[3]From this point, although the numeration of the items of the PSS-14 and PSS-10 differ (e.g., item 5 of the PSS-10 *"…felt that things were going your way?"* is item 7 of the PSS-14), the numeration of the PSS-10 is adopted to make comparisons clearer across studies.

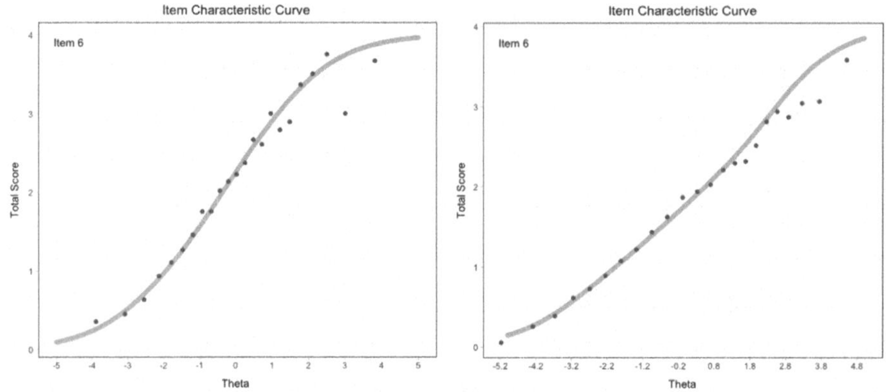

Fig. 14.3 Item characteristic curve of item 6 in Denmark (left) and Australia (right). *Notes* The x-axis indicates the person parameter (theta) and the y-axis indicates the item score. The dark dots represent the observed item responses for each total score and the grey curve is the expected item responses

It is possible to see that, in both countries, Item 6 (*"…found that you could not cope with all the things that you had to do?"*) displayed a similar pattern of misfit for respondents with high-perceived stress. That is, participants with high levels of perceived stress *on average* endorsed lower categories (e.g., "fairly often" rather than "very often") than expected under the Rasch model. The misfit of Item 6 has been previously reported (Yokokura et al., 2017).

Overall homogeneity: In the Danish and the Australian study, we found strong evidence against homogeneity for both subscales (all $p < 0.001$), when assuming the pure RM. Assuming the final GLLRMs with uniform local dependence and uniform DIF shown in Fig. 14.2, no evidence was found against overall homogeneity in either study (all p > above 0.10) (Nielsen & Dammeyer, 2019; Santiago et al., submitted).

DIF: First, with the test of global DIF, differing degrees of evidence of DIF were found across the two studies. In Denmark (Nielsen & Dammeyer, 2019), strong evidence of DIF relative to academic discipline was found for both subscale (both $p < 0.001$), while moderate evidence was found for DIF relative to gender and age in the perceived stress subscale (both $p < 0.01$). In Australia (Santiago et al., submitted), strong evidence of DIF was found relative to three different background variables for the PLC scale and two background variables for the perceived stress subscale (all $p < 0.001$), while only weak or no evidence of DIF were found with the remaining background variables. Second, several iterations of analysis using the two item level tests for no DIF and the presence of DIF, respectively, were conducted in both studies, until no more DIF could be detected, while the presence of DIF already included in the models were confirmed. Third and last, the global test of DIF were conducted for each of the GLLRMs resulting from the step-wise analyses for DIF (and LD) and used to report that no further evidence of DIF could be found after correcting the critical level for false discovery rate due to multiple testing (Australia: all but one $p > 0.05$ with the last $p > 0.01$. Denmark: all $p > 0.05$.).

The second similarity across countries was that the DIF pattern of specific items. For example, in the Perceived Stress subscale, Item 1 (*"…felt upset because of something that happened unexpectedly?"*) ($\gamma_{DEN} = 0.14$; $\gamma_{AUS} = 0.14$) and Item 3 (*"…felt either nervous or stressed?"*) ($\gamma_{DEN} = 0.29$; $\gamma_{AUS} = 0.19$) displayed DIF by gender (Fig. 14.4).

The ICCs in Fig. 14.3 indicate that given the same level of the latent trait (i.e., "Perceived Stress"), women systematically endorsed higher categories of items 1 and 3. Or, in other words, item 3 was more *easily* endorsed by women than by men independently of their stress level. The DIF of item 1 and/or item 3 due to gender has been previously reported by other studies (Cole, 1999; Gitchel, Roessler, & Turner, 2011).

The implication of the DIF is that, since women more readily endorsed items 1 and 3 than did males at the same level of perceived stress, the female total scores will be higher than the total scores of men even though they are actually equally stressed. Therefore, the total scores no longer represent a valid measure of perceived stress in the population. In this case, it is necessary to adjust the score to account for the influence of DIF according to gender, which can easily be done within the GLLRM framework. As an example, we show part of the conversion and DIF-adjustment table the PS subscale for the Danish study in Table 14.1.

It is possible to see in Table 14.1 that the DIF-adjusted scores are different from the observed scores. When items are affected by DIF, the use of observed scores can lead to wrongful conclusions when comparing subgroups. For example, in the Danish study, the mean PS observed score of female students was 12.86 ($SE = 0.14$), while the observed score of male students was 10.95 ($SE = 0.12$) ($M_{diffobs} = 1.91$, $p < 0.001$). The DIF-adjusted mean PS score for female students was 12.12 ($SE = 0.14$), while the DIF-adjusted mean PS score for male students was 10.57 ($SE = 0.11$) ($M_{diffadj} = 1.55$, $p < 0.001$). Although it is clear that female students were more stressed than male students, the true difference in score was 1.55, while the observed difference in score of 1.91 was inflated 0.36 due to systematic error as a result of DIF.

LD: The fourth similarity was the amount of LD found in the subscales across the two studies. Particularly similar was the LD between item 5 *"… felt things were going your way?"* and item 8 *"… felt you were on top of things?"* ($\gamma_{DEN} = 0.24$; $\gamma_{AUS} = 0.19$). The LD between these two items is a case of *response dependence*. This means that, given the same level of Perceived Lack of Control, respondents who endorsed that *"…. things were going their way"* were more likely to endorse that they *"…. feel they were on top of things"* (item 8) (and vice versa) compared to other items such as *"…. been able to control irritations in your life"* (item 7). Thus, the responses to one item depends not only on the latent trait measured (as required) but also on responses to one or more other items.

One consequences of lack of conditional independence of the items in a scale (i.e., LD between items) concerns reliability. For example, a reliability index such as the Cronbach's α is derived under the assumption that items are conditionally independent, and the calculation is based on the correlation between items. The problem is that the positive correlation between items 5 and 8 is not caused only

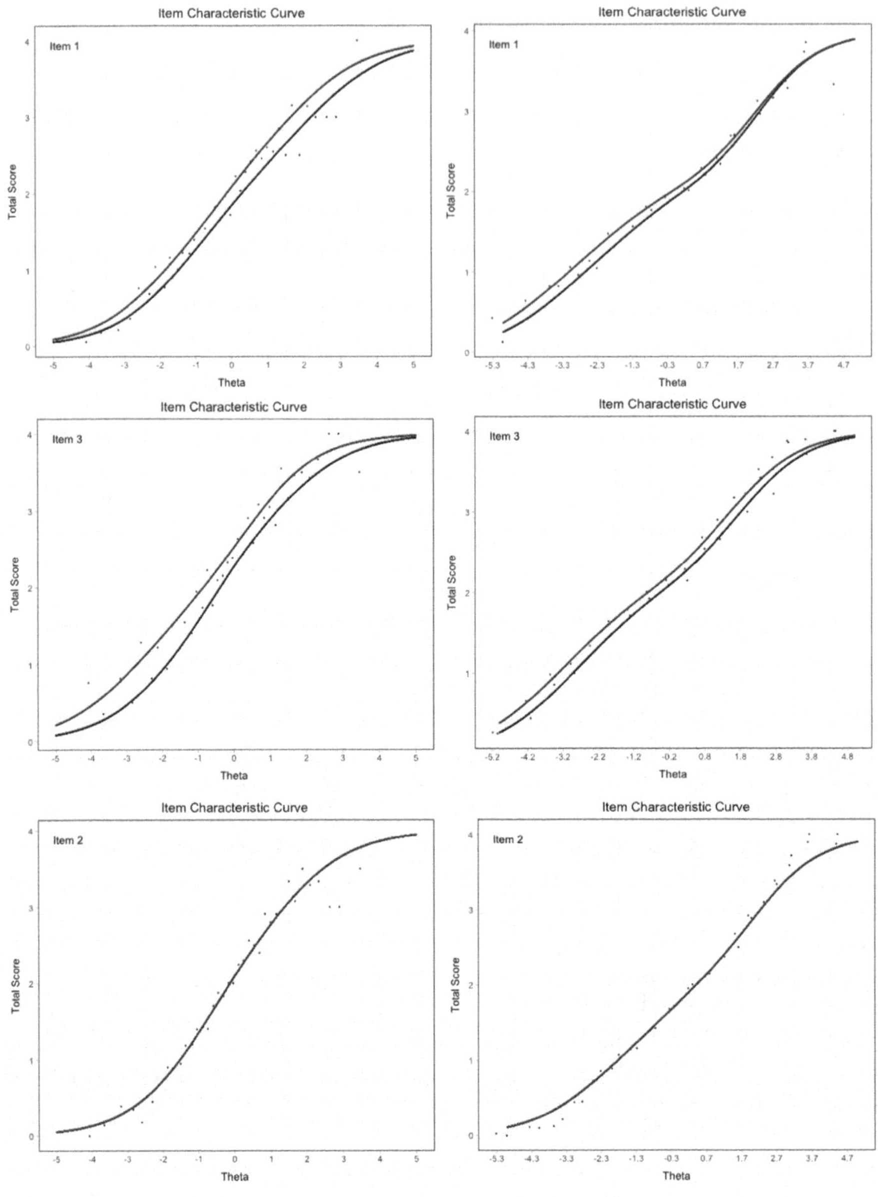

Fig. 14.4 Differential item functioning of items 1 and 3 in Denmark (left) and Australia (right). *Notes* The x-axis indicates the latent trait and the y-axis indicates the item score. The expected item response curves and observed item responses are displayed for women (top) and men (middle) in the same plot, to illustrate the DIF of Items 1 and 3. The ICCs for Item 9 is displayed (bottom) to exemplify absence of DIF

Table 14.1 Conversion of raw scores to weighted maximum likelihood estimates of person parameters and adjustment of the raw score for DIF relative to gender and academic discipline in the Danish study

Reference group: male psychology students		Female technical students	
Observed raw score	Person parameter	DIF-adjusted raw score	Person parameter
5.00	−3.451	5.00	−4.073
6.00	−2.424	5.68	−2.837
7.00	−1.939	6.49	−2.292
8.00	−1.585	7.38	−1.923
9.00	−1.282	8.34	−1.620
10.00	−1.004	9.34	−1.342
11.00	−0.742	10.37	−1.075
12.00	−0.495	11.41	−0.814
13.00	−0.260	12.44	−0.559
14.00	−0.034	13.47	−0.309
15.00	0.190	14.47	10.05
16.00	0.414	15.45	0.173
17.00	0.637	16.40	0.402
18.00	0.859	17.34	0.623
19.00	1.082	18.28	0.842
20.00	1.310	19.24	1.066
21.00	1.551	20.24	1.308
22.00	1.821	21.30	1.580
23.00	2.145	22.42	1.899
24.00	2.582	23.63	2.313
25.00	3.404	25.00	3.062

Notes We only show the conversion between raw scores and person parameters from the reference group to another subgroup, and likewise for the DIF-adjustment of the raw score (this column is replicated from Table S2 in Nielsen and Dammeyer (2019))

by the latent variable (i.e., Perceived Lack of Control), but also due to increased probability of endorsing item 5 following the endosement of item 10 and vice versa. The consequence of this is that increased correlation between two items will lead to an inflation of Cronbach's α, if the LD is not accounted for in the calculation. For example, the PLC subscale Cronbach's α was 0.81(Australia) and 0.75 (Denmark), while the Monte Carlo procedure taking LD into account provided overall reliabilities of 0.74 (Australia) and 0.68 (Denmark). Thus, had we not accounted for LD in the reliability estimates, we would have reported inflated levels of reliability for the two samples.

In psychometric research, an influential paper by MacCallum, Roznowski, and Necowitz (1992) on factor analysis recommended caution regarding the inclusion of model parameters beyond the latent trait, in which *"a common example is the covariances among error terms"* (p. 491), based on the notion that the inclusion of such parameters *"may merely fit chance characteristics of the original sample, rather than representing aspects of the model that generalize to other samples and to the population"* (p. 492). Given the lack of empirical evidence about local independence in the PSS literature, these recommendations seem to be interpreted by researchers as an indication that local dependence between items should not be investigated at all. The results from Australia and Denmark indicate that the LD between item 5 and 8 is not an "idiosyncratic characteristic of the sample," but rather a characteristic of the instrument. LD between these two items has also recently been reported in an indigenous Australian population, though with no indication of the strength (Santiago, Roberts, Smithers, & Jamieson, 2019).

Targeting: The comparison of the targeting across studies also provides insight into the functioning of the PSS. In Australia, the overall Test Information Target Index of the PS scale was 0.60, indicating that the PS subscale provided only 60% of the total information available. The examination of the Item Maps (Fig. 14.5) shows that the majority of respondents in Australia were less stressed than the stress levels the PS subscale is designed to evaluate.

On the other hand, in Denmark, the overall Test Information Target Index of the PS scale was 0.82, indicating that more than 80% of the total information available regarding perceived stress was captured by the items. Once again, it is possible to see the good targeting for the Danish students by the examination of the information function (i.e., how much information is available at each trait level) in Fig. 14.4. In Fig. 14.4 (top left graph), the information function is high across the majority of the theoretical population distribution relative to its peak. That is, for the majority of Danish students, the PS subscale provides almost as much information as the information available for a perfectly targeted instrument. The divergence between Australian population and Danish students is even higher regarding the PLC subscale (Fig. 14.4).

The interpretation of these results is clear. The PS and PLC subscales are well-targeted to the Danish university students (technical and psychology), a population which has been consistently reported as being at risk for stress (Storrie, Ahern, & Tuckett, 2010); while the PS targeting was moderate and PLC targeting was poor for the Australian general population.

What Can We Conclude on the PSS So Far Using the GLLRM

The analysis with GLLRM and the similarities across both countries provides new in-depth knowledge on the psychometric properties of the PSS. The combined results from both studies suggest that

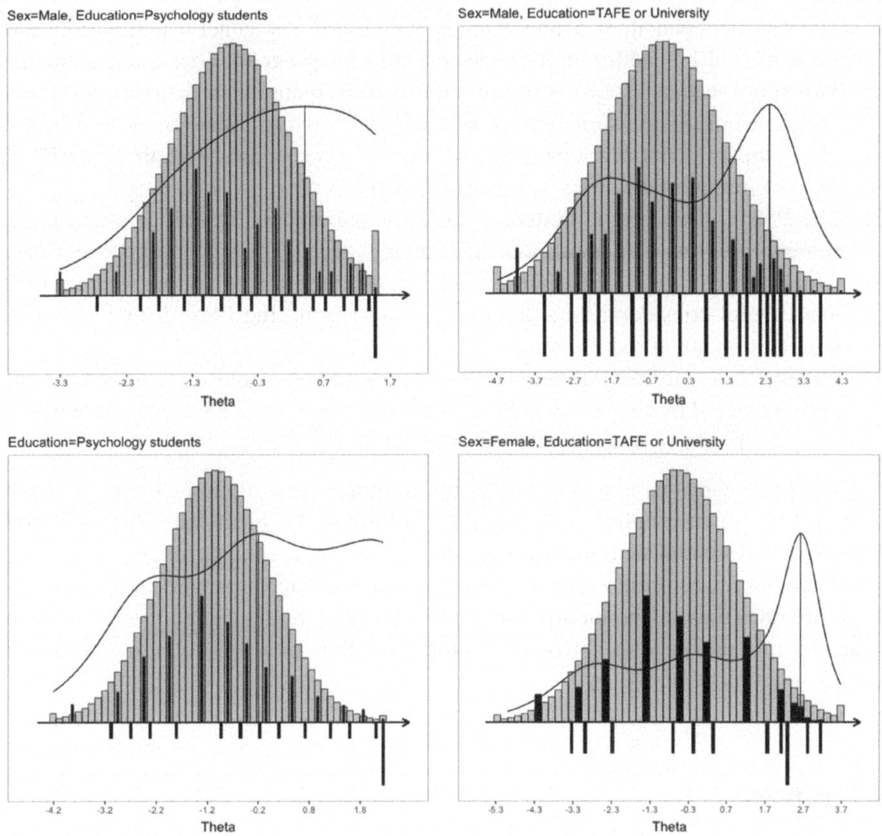

Fig. 14.5 Selected item maps of the Perceived Stress scale in Denmark (top left) and Australia (top right) and Perceived Lack of Control subscale in Denmark (bottom left) and Australia (bottom right). *Notes* The black bars above the line display the person parameters (WML estimates). The grey bars display the theoretical population distribution under the assumption of normality. The fluctuating line is the information function, with a vertical line denoting the point of maximum information. The black bars below the line display the item thresholds. The two Danish item maps shown here are extracts from Fig. 14.2 in Nielsen and Dammeyer (2019)

(1) Item 1 and 3 of the PSS have DIF by gender, a result also reported with US Multiple Sclerosis patients (Gitchel et al., 2011). We thus find it more than likely that gender-DIF is an inherent issue in the instrument likely to be present in other (all?) populations and with diverse language versions. We thus recommend that DIF-analysis is conducted in future applications of the PSS-10 and PSS-14, and that scores are adjusted accordingly to achieve unconfounded comparison of perceived stress between men and women.

(2) The LD between item 5 and item 8, was found for general population and students and has additionally been reported for pregnant aboriginal women.[4] This suggests that it is also a property of the instrument rather than the individual samples. For this reason, and because LD is known to inflate the lower bound of reliability if not accounted for, we urge further studies with the PSS-10 or PSS-14 to undertake analysis of local dependence.
(3) The PSS is found to be better targeted for populations at risk of stress (e.g., students and pregnant aboriginal Australian women[5]) than general populations, which makes sense. This finding has yet to be replicated further, but suggest that careful consideration should be given to using the PSS-10 or PSS-14 in populations not at risk for stress.
(4) Finally, the many deviations of the resulting models from ideal measurement as represented by the "pure" RM indicate a threat to the PSS construct validity, again particularly so in populations not at risk for stress.

The RM provides valid and objective measurement encompassed by the requirements of unidimensionality, monotonicity, homogeneity, local independence, and absence of differential item functioning. When measurement instruments in the real world fail these requirements, GLLRM can be used to determine whether these deviations are ones that can be incorporated into a testable model and adjusted for when using the instrument with different populations, thus possibly retaining essential validity and objective.

References

Andersen, E. B. (1973). A goodness of fit test for the Rasch model. *Psychometrika, 38*(1), 123–140.

Andersen, E. B. (1994). Polytomous Rasch models and their estimation. In G. H. Fischer & I. W. Molenaar (Eds.), *Rasch models. Foundations, recent developments, and applications* (pp. 271–292). New York, Springer.

Andrich, D. (1978). Rating formulation for ordered response categories. *Psychometrika, 43,* 561–573. https://doi.org/10.1007/BF02293814.

Benjamini, Y., & Hochberg, Y. (1995). Controlling the false discovery rate: A practical and powerful approach to multiple testing. *Journal of the Royal Statistical Society. Series B (Methodological),* 289–300.

Christensen, K. B., & Kreiner, S. (2012). Item fit statistics. *Rasch models in health* (pp. 83–104). London: Wiley.

Christensen, K. B., Kreiner, S., & Mesbah, M. (2013). *Rasch models in health.* London: Wiley.

Cohen, S., Kamarck, T., & Mermelstein, R. (1983). A global measure of perceived stress. *Journal of Health and Social Behavior, 24*(4), 385. https://doi.org/10.2307/2136404.

Cohen, S., & Williamson, G. (1988). Psychological stress in a probability sample of the United States. In S. Spacapan & S. Oskamp (Eds.), *The social psychology of health: Claremont symposium on applied social psychology* (pp. 31–37). Newbury Park, CA: Sage Publications.

[4]Santiago et al. (2019) used a modified version of the PSS14, where the first part of the items had been changed to refer to the last year rather than the last month.

[5]See note 4.

Cole, S. R. (1999). Assessment of differential item functioning in the perceived stress scale-10. *Journal of Epidemiology and Community Health, 53*(5), 319.

Dougherty, B. E., Cooley, S.-S. L., & Davidorf, F. H. (2017). Measurement of perceived stress in age related macular degeneration. *Optometry and vision science: Official publication of the American Academy of Optometry, 94*(3), 290.

Eskildsen, A., Dalgaard, V. L., Nielsen, K. J., Andersen, J. H., Zachariae, R., Olsen, L. R., et al. (2015). Cross-cultural adaptation and validation of the Danish consensus version of the 10-item perceived stress scale. *Scandinavian Journal of Work, Environment & Health, 41*(5), 486–490. https://doi.org/10.5271/sjweh.3510.

Fischer, G. E. & Molenaar, I. W. (Eds). (1994). *Rasch models. Foundations, recent developments, and applications.* New York, Springer.

Folkman, S., Lazarus, R. S., Dunkel-Schetter, C., DeLongis, A., & Gruen, R. J. (1986). Dynamics of a stressful encounter: Cognitive appraisal, coping, and encounter outcomes. *Journal of Personality and Social Psychology, 50*(5), 992.

Gitchel, W. D., Roessler, R. T., & Turner, R. C. (2011). Gender effect according to item directionality on the perceived stress scale for adults with multiple sclerosis. *Rehabilitation Counseling Bulletin, 55*(1), 20–28.

Goodman, L. A., & Kruskal, W. H. (1954). Measures of association for cross classifications. *Journal of the American statistical association, 49*(268), 732–764.

Hamon, A., & Mesbah, M. (2002). Questionnaire reliability under the Rasch model. In *Statistical methods for quality of life studies* (pp. 155–168). Springer.

Hanson, B. (1998). Uniform DIF and DIF defined by differences in item response functions. *Journal of Educational and Behavioral Statistics, 23*(3), 244–253.

Holmes, T. H., & Rahe, R. H. (1967). The social readjustment rating scale. *Journal of Psychosomatic Research, 11*(2), 213–218.

Kelderman, H. (1984). Loglinear Rasch model tests. *Psychometrika, 49*(2), 223–245.

Kelderman, H. (1997). Loglinear multidimensional item response models for polytomously scored items. In W. van der Linden & R. Hambleton (Eds.), *Handbook of modern item response theory* (pp. 287–304). New York: Springer.

Kreiner, S. (1993). Validation of index scales for analysis of survey data: The symptom index. In Kathryn Dean (Ed.), *Population health research: Linking theory and methods* (pp. 116–144). London: Sage Publications.

Kreiner, S. (2003). *Introduction to DIGRAM*, Department of Biostatistics, University of Copenhagen, Copenhagen, Denmark.

Kreiner, S. (2007). Validity and objectivity. Reflections on the role and nature of Rasch Models. *Nordic Psychology, 59,* 268–298. https://doi.org/10.1027/1901-2276.59.3.268.

Kreiner, S. (2011). A note on item-restscore association in Rasch models. *Applied Psychological Measurement, 35*(7), 557–561. https://doi.org/10.1177/0146621611141022.

Kreiner, S. (2013). The Rasch model for dichotomous items. In K. B. Christensen, S. Kreiner, & M. Mesbah (Eds.), *Rasch models in health.* London: Wiley.

Kreiner, S. & Christensen, K. B. (2002). Graphical Rasch models. In M. Mesbah, B. F. Cole, & M.-L. Ting Lee (Eds.), *Statistical methods for quality of life studies* (pp. 187–203). Bosten, Kluwer Academic Publishers.

Kreiner, S., & Christensen, K. B. (2004). Analysis of local dependence and multidimensionality in graphical loglinear Rasch models. *Communications in Statistics-Theory and Methods, 33*(6), 1239–1276.

Kreiner, S., & Christensen, K. B. (2007). Validity and objectivity in health-related scales: Analysis by graphical loglinear Rasch models. In *Multivariate and mixture distribution Rasch models* (pp. 329–346). Springer.

Kreiner, S., & Christensen, K. B. (2011). Item screening in graphical loglinear Rasch models. *Psychometrika, 76*(2), 228–256.

Kreiner, S., & Christensen, K. B. (2013). Person parameter estimation and measurement in Rasch models. *Rasch models in health* (pp. 63–78). London: Wiley.

Kreiner, S., & Nielsen, T. (2013). *Item analysis in DIGRAM 3.04. Part I: Guided tours. Research report 2013/06*. University of Copenhagen, Department of Public Health.

Lavoie, J. A., & Douglas, K. S. (2012). The perceived stress scale: Evaluating configural, metric and scalar invariance across mental health status and gender. *Journal of Psychopathology and Behavioral Assessment, 34*(1), 48–57.

Lazarus, R. S. (1966). *Psychological stress and the coping process*. New York, NY: McGraw-Hill.

Lee, E.-H. (2012). Review of the psychometric evidence of the perceived stress scale. *Asian Nursing Research, 6*(4), 121–127.

MacCallum, R. C., Roznowski, M., & Necowitz, L. B. (1992). Model modifications in covariance structure analysis: The problem of capitalization on chance. *Psychological Bulletin, 111*(3), 490.

Masters, G. N. (1982). A Rasch model for partial credit scoring. *Psychometrika, 47*(2), 149–174.

Mesbah, M. & Kreiner, S. (2013). The Rasch model for ordered polytomous items. In K. B. Christensen, S. Kreiner, & M. Mesbah (Eds.), *Rasch models in health* (pp. 27–42). London: ISTE Ltd, Wiley. https://doi.org/10.1002/9781118574454.ch2.

Nielsen, T., & Dammeyer, J. (2019). Measuring higher education students' perceived stress: An IRT-based construct validity study of the PSS-10. *Journal of Studies in Educational Evaluation, 63,* 17–25. https://doi.org/10.1016/j.stueduc.2019.06.007.

Nielsen, T. & Kreiner S. (2013). Improving items that do not fit the Rasch model: Exemplified with the physical functioning scale of the SF-36. *Annales de L'I.S.U.P. Publications de L'Institut de Statistique de L'Université de Paris, Numero Special, 57*(1–2), 91–108.

Nielsen, J. B., Nyholm Kyvsgaard, J., Møller Sildorf, S., Kreiner, S., Svensson, J. (2017). Item analysis using Rasch models confirms that the Danish versions of the DISABKIDS® chronic-generic and diabetes-specific modules are valid and reliable. *Health and Quality of Life Outcomes, 15*(44), with technical supplement.

Olsen, L. W. (2001). *Essays on George Rasch and his contributions to statistics*. PhD Dissertation, Department of Economics, University of Copenhagen, Copenhagen, Denmark.

R Core Team. (2013). R: A language and environment for statistical computing.

Rasch, G. (1960). *Probabilistic models for some intelligence and attainment tests*. Copenhagen: Danish Institute for Educational Research.

Rasch, G. (1961). On general laws and the meaning of measurement in psychology. The Regents of the University of California. Retrieved from http://projecteuclid.org/euclid.bsmsp/1200512895.

Santiago, P. H. R., Roberts, R., Smithers, L. G., & Jamieson, L. (2019). Stress beyond coping? A Rasch analysis of the Perceived Stress Scale (PSS-14) in an Aboriginal population. *PLoS ONE, 14*(5), e0216333.

Santiago, P. H. R., Nielsen, T., Smithers, L. G., Roberts, R., & Jamieson, L. (submitted). Measuring stress in Australia: Validation of the Perceived Stress Scale (PSS-14) in a Nationally Representative Sample.

Slade, G. D., Spencer, A. J., & Roberts-Thomson, K. F. (Eds.). (2007). *Australia's dental generations: The national survey of adult oral health, 2004–06.* Australian Institute of Health and Welfare.

Stopczynski, A., Sekara, V., Sapiezynski, P., Cuttone, A., Madsen, M. M., & Larsen, J. E. (2014). Measuring large-scale social networks with high resolution. *Public Library of Science ONE, 9*(4), e95978. https://doi.org/10.1371/journal.pone.0095978.

Storrie, K., Ahern, K., & Tuckett, A. (2010). A systematic review: Students with mental health problems—a growing problem. *International Journal of Nursing Practice, 16*(1), 1–6.

Taylor, J. M. (2015). Psychometric analysis of the ten-item perceived stress scale. *Psychological Assessment, 27*(1), 90.

Teasdale, T. W. (2009). The Danish draft board's intelligence test, Borge Priens Prove: Psychometric properties and research applications through 50 years. *Scandinavian Journal of Psychology, 50,* 633–638.

Tennant, A., & Conaghan, P. G. (2007). The Rasch measurement model in rheumatology: What is it and why use It? When should it be applied and what should one look for in a Rasch paper? *Arthritis and Rheumatism, 57,* 1358–1362. https://doi.org/10.1002/art.23108.

van der Linden, W. J., & Hambleton, R. K. (1997). *Handbook of item response theory*. New York: Springer.

von Davier, M., & Carstensen, C. H. (Eds.). (2007). *Multivariate and mixture distribution Rasch models. Extensions and applications*. Springer: New York.

Yokokura, A. V. C. P., Silva, A. A. M. d., Fernandes, J. d. K. B., Del-Ben, C. M., Figueiredo, F. P. d., Barbieri, M. A., & Bettiol, H. (2017). Perceived Stress Scale: Confirmatory factor analysis of the PSS14 and PSS10 versions in two samples of pregnant women from the BRISA cohort. *Cadernos de Saúde Publica, 33*, e00184615.

The manufacturer's authorised representative in the EU is Springer Nature Customer Service Centre GmbH, Europaplatz 3, 69115 Heidelberg, Germany. If you have any concerns regarding our products, please contact ProductSafety@springernature.com

Printed and bound by CPI Group (UK) Ltd, Croydon, CR0 4YY
30/09/2026
02225556-0003